The Visual J++ Handbook

About the Author

Brian Maso is a Windows/Internet contractor with 5 years experience. Working for Intel corporation, he is the chief Java expert for the NetMM group. Maso has also worked with a division of the Hearst Corporation, figuring out how to bring their medical and pharmaceutical information database applications onto the World Wide Web. He has also been involved with designing school administrative systems using WWW interfaces in Java. Brian graduated in 1991 from The Johns Hopkins University in Baltimore with a degree in Electrical Engineering.

The Visual J++ Handbook

Brian Maso

Osborne McGraw-Hill
Berkeley New York St. Louis San Francisco
Auckland Bogotá Hamburg London Madrid
Mexico City Milan Montreal New Delhi Panama City
Paris São Paulo Singapore Sydney
Tokyo Toronto

Osborne **McGraw-Hill**
2600 Tenth Street
Berkeley, California 94710
U.S.A.

For information on translations or book distributors outside the U.S.A., or to arrange bulk purchase discounts for sales promotions, premiums, or fundraisers, please contact Osborne/**McGraw-Hill** at the above address.

The Visual J++ Handbook

Copyright © 1997 by The McGraw-Hill Companies. All rights reserved. Printed in the United States of America. Except as permitted under the Copyright Act of 1976, no part of this publication may be reproduced or distributed in any form or by any means, or stored in a database or retrieval system, without the prior written permission of the publisher, with the exception that the program listings may be entered, stored, and executed in a computer system, but they may not be reproduced for publication.

1234567890 DOC 9987

ISBN 0-07-882266-1

Publisher
Brandon A. Nordin

Acquisitions Editor
Wendy Rinaldi

Project Editor
Mark Karmendy

Editorial Assistant
Ann Sellers

Associate Editors
Cynthia Douglas, Heidi Poulin

Technical Editor
Michael Connell

Copy Editor
Dennis Weaver

Proofreader
Pat Mannion

Indexer
Matthew Spence

Computer Designer
P. J. Beckwith

Illustrator
Richard Whitaker
Leslee Bassin
Lance Ravella

Quality Control Specialist
Joe Scuderi

Information has been obtained by Osborne/**McGraw-Hill** from sources believed to be reliable. However, because of the possibility of human or mechanical error by our sources, Osborne/**McGraw-Hill**, or others, Osborne/**McGraw-Hill** does not guarantee the accuracy, adequacy, or completeness of any information and is not responsible for any errors or omissions or the results obtained from use of such information.

This book is dedicated to my uncritical critic and lovable late-night working session companion, Ciaran Blumenfeld.

Contents at a Glance

1. **The Java Language** 1
2. **The Visual J++ Environment** 39
3. **GUI Basics** 73
4. **AWT Controls and Menus** 105
5. **Graphics** 145
6. **Applets** 181
7. **Java and COM in Visual J++** 219
8. **File I/O and Streams** 251
9. **Networking in Java** 281
10. **Database Programming in Java** 309
11. **Utility and Language Class Reference** 345
12. **Other Java APIs** 397

Index 423

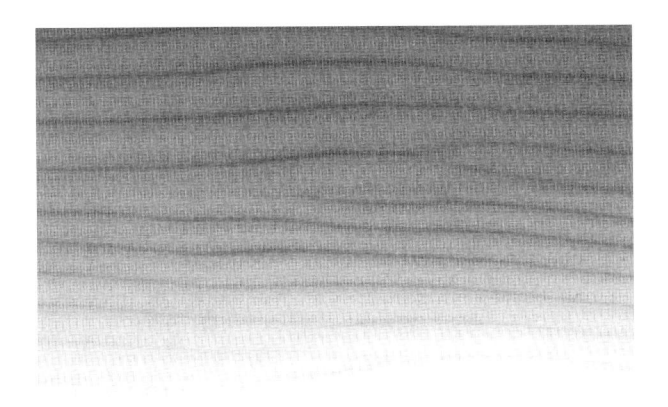

Table of Contents

Acknowledgments .... *xvii*
Introduction .... *xix*

1 ▬ The Java Language 1
    Java Basics 3
        Bytecode and .CLASS Files 3
        Classes 3
        Class Inheritance 4
    Variables 7
        Instance and Class Data 9
        Member Data Protection and Access
            Specifiers 9
    Methods 12
        Some Notes on the Java Syntax 13
        Java Method Access Specifiers 13
        Class Constructors 14
        Creating and Destroying Objects 17
        The Destructor Method 19
        Calling Object Methods 19
        The Static Initializer Method 20

The this Variable	21
Strings	22
Arrays	23
Arrays of Objects	24
Initializing Arrays	25
Multidimensional Arrays	25
Alternative Declarative Syntax for Arrays	25
Method Overloading	26
Method Overriding	28
Abstract Methods	29
Casting Variables	30
Casting Between Built-In Types	31
Run-Time Type Identification	32
Interfaces	33
Packages	35
.CLASS File Locations	36
Copackage Access Privileges	37
The Form of Java Programs	37

2 ■ The Visual J++ Environment — 39

Exploring the Visual J++ CD	41
Installing Visual J++	41
Other CD Options	45
Introduction to the Visual J++ Interface	45
Project Toolbar	46
Using Toolbars	46
The Rest of the Visual J++ Toolbars	47
Customizing and Creating Toolbars	49
The InfoViewer Window	49
InfoViewer Navigation	51
Projects	52
ClassView	55
FileView	58
Building Projects	59
Debugging	60
Starting a Debugging Session	62
Stopping a Debugging Session	62
Stepping Through a Program	63
Breakpoints	66
Performing a QuickWatch	67
The Watch Window	69

	The Variables Window	70
	The Call Stack Window	71
3	**GUI Basics**	**73**
	GUI Example: HelloX	74
	Building HelloX in Visual J++	75
	Components	76
	Custom Components	85
	Containers and LayoutManagers	87
	LayoutManagers: Placing Components Within Containers	88
	The Various LayoutManagers	90
	Designing Custom LayoutManagers	94
	Using null for the LayoutManager	97
	A Comprehensive Example: TabbedPanels	98
	Parts Is Parts	103
4	**AWT Controls and Menus**	**105**
	The Built-in AWT Controls	106
	The Label Class	107
	The Button Class	109
	The Checkbox Class	111
	The Scrollbar Class	113
	The TextField and TextArea Classes	116
	The List Class	120
	The Choice Class	124
	Creating GUIs with the ResourceWizard	126
	Menus	135
	Menus, MenuItems, and Menu Bars	135
	MenuItems	138
	Menus	140
	Using ResourceWizard to Make Menu Classes	141
	Summary	144
5	**Graphics**	**145**
	Graphics and Display Surfaces	146
	Getting a Surface's Graphics Object	147
	Graphics Objects	149
	The Current Color	150
	The Clipping Rectangle	152
	The Current Font	155

Painting Mode	162
Drawing Graphics	165
Drawing Lines	165
Drawing Rectangles	166
Drawing Polygons	166
Drawing Ovals	169
Drawing Arcs	169
Drawing Images	170
Animation	171
Animation Frame Time-Sequencing: The Animator Applet	173
Double Buffering	176

6 ■ Applets ... 181

The Anatomy of Applets	183
Applet-Aware Browsers	184
Embedding Applets in Web Pages	185
Applet Parameters	191
The Four Applet Lifetime Methods	192
Using the Applet Wizard	196
The Applet Class	203
Applet Information Methods	203
Browser/Applet Communication Methods	205
Special Security Restrictions on Applets	208
What's Not Allowed	209
COM Restrictions	217

7 ■ Java and COM in Visual J++ ... 219

The Java and COM Models	221
In COM Terms	223
Typelibs and Java/COM Shim Classes	223
Generating Java/COM Shim Classes	224
Taking a Look at COM Interfaces	226
Using COM Objects in Java	228
COM Object Properties	230
COM Enumeration Types in Java	232
COM Using Java Objects	233
Defining Java Interfaces So COM Understands Them	235
The Object Description Language	239
Writing the Java Class	245

        Registering the Java Class as a COM Object 248
        Registering the Java Class as a DCOM Object 249

8 ■ File I/O and Streams 251
    The InputStream and OutputStream Classes 252
        Physical InputStream Classes 253
        The InputStream Class Methods 254
        Filter Input Stream Classes 260
        Chaining FilteredInputStreams 267
        Custom FilterInputStreams 267
        OutputStreams 270
    Parsing an InputStream 272
        A StreamTokenizer Example 277
    Summary 280

9 ■ Networking in Java 281
    The Internet Language: TCP/IP 282
        IP Addresses 283
        Ports in Cyberspace 287
        Creating Socket Connections 288
        Sending and Receiving Nonguaranteed Data 293
    Creating Internet Servers 294
        The ServerSocket Class 294
    URLs and Protocols 298
        URLs 300
    Summary 307

10 ■ Database Programming in Java 309
    Data Access Objects 311
        Redistribution of the Jet Engine 311
        Creating the DAO Java/COM Classes 312
        The DBEngine Object 313
        Workspaces 316
        Databases and TableDefs 320
        Record Sets: Looking at a Table's Records 325
        Executable Queries 333
        DAO Summary 334
    Remote Data Objects 334
        Building the RDO Java/COM Shim Classes 335
        The rdoEngine Object 336
        RDO Environments 336

Database Connections	338
RDO Result Sets	340
Quick JDBC Description	343
Summary	343

11 Utility and Language Class Reference ... 345

The java.util Storage Classes	348
The Enumeration Interface	348
The Stack Class	350
The Vector Class	351
The Hashtable Class	356
The Properties Class	358
The BitSet Class	360
The Observer/Observable Framework	361
Observable Objects	361
The Observer Interface	365
An Observable/Observer Applet Example	365
The Date Class	372
The Random Class	373
The java.lang Numeric Classes	373
Class Objects and Class Loaders	379
The Class Class	380
Class Loaders	385
The Math Class	388
The Run-Time System Classes	389
The Runtime and System Classes	390
Spawning External Processes	390
The System Class	392
The SecurityManager	394

12 Other Java APIs ... 397

Remote Technologies APIs	398
Media APIs	399
Object Serialization	400
Adding Serialization to Visual J++	400
Object Serialization in Java 1.1	409
Remote Method Invocation	410
Getting RMI Libraries	411
Stubs and Skeletons	412
Remoting an Object	414
Remote Interfaces	415

RMI Summary	418
Java Beans	418
Other New APIs	419
2D Animation	419
3D Graphics	420
Multimedia Framework	420
Summary	421

Index **423**

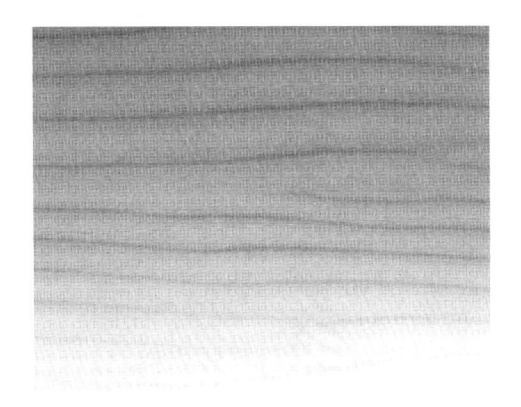

Acknowledgments

I would like to thank the helpful people at Microsoft, and also Michael C. for his great eyes and capable technical expertise. But mostly I would like to thank my editors at Osborne. They have been very professional and fun to work with.

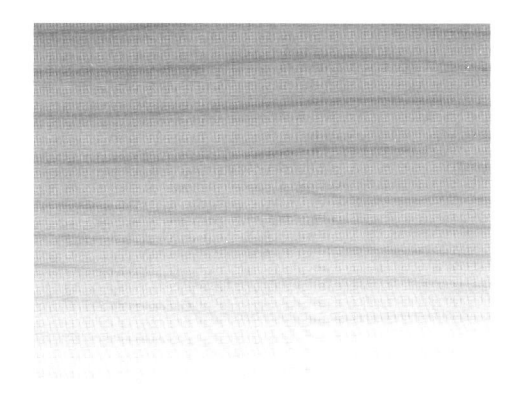

Introduction

Java: Hope vs. Hype

No doubt you have heard a lot of hype about the Java language recently. It has been called a network standard for executable modules, a multimedia delivery system, the "next wave" for the World Wide Web, and even "Visual Basic killer" and "C++ killer". It does seem strange that all this attention has been focused on what is, after all, just another programming language, doesn't it? Actually, Java has so many nice programming features that most of the hype is deserved, or at least not completely undeserved. Since you have bought (or are thinking about buying) this book, you must have suspected that this is the case.

You are in good company. Microsoft Corp. also believes Java has a bright future as a programming language. Not only have they created an entire visual IDE (Integrated Development Environment) for developing in Java, but they have also bought licenses to include Java as part of all its future operating systems. That is quite a vote of confidence from the industry giant, who usually engineers desktop PC revolutions instead of licensing them from other companies.

The purpose of this book is to show you the ins and outs of Visual J++, Microsoft's visual development environment for Java. Whether you are already using Visual J++, or you are just thinking about getting it, this book will give you valuable and timesaving insights into the premier Java development environment for the Windows PC.

Java Features

There are three features built into the Java language that make it worth learning and using. Several other features also make it attractive, but the three elements that are making programmers around the world turn their heads are architecture independence, Internet support, and security.

Java was designed from the beginning to be architecture independent. That is, you can take programs written and compiled in Java using, say, a Unix platform, and run the executable files on a completely different platform such as Windows 95. Java abstracts the details of the operating system and hardware away from the programmer so that all platforms appear to be the same. You can also develop programs in Java that are very system-dependent: programs that require certain system resources that are only available on a particular platform. Architecture-independent programming is good, however, because it makes the task of programming more efficient. You no longer have to create a different version of an application for every platform you want to support. Instead, you write your program once and it runs the same on every Java-capable platform.

Since the incredible growth of the Internet as a prospective arena for distribution of information and software, a lot of interest in programming for the Internet has been generated. Given that the Internet is comprised of millions of machines with different operating systems and different hardware platforms, the architecture-neutral Java language couldn't have appeared on the scene at a better time. Being architecturally neutral, Java is perfect for the Internet. The designers of Java saw this obvious applicability and built a rich set of Internet support into Java. Using the Java language, you can "do" HTTP (the WWW protocol) and FTP almost as easily as file I/O. You can also send executable Java "applets," or mini-applications, across the network to run remotely within WWW pages.

Other people have developed ways of sending executable content over the Internet. Unfortunately, these methods have proven to be the perfect computer virus delivery mechanism. Worms, devastating programs that brought the Internet to its knees at least once in the recent past, are programs that exploit the Internet's openness to attack. Java, on the other hand, has built-in security measures that make it almost impossible to attack machines across the Internet using Java applets. While some concerned voices have been raised complaining about the programming restriction placed on Java applets so that security can be assured, I personally prefer Java's restrictive barriers to, say, ActiveX's "trust" mechanisms. "Electronic trust" is as oxymoronic as "electronic love" or "electronic fealty." Java takes a much more proactive approach to the security problem, providing the programmer and user with a very high level of security for the Internet.

Visual J++

So, once you've committed yourself to programming in Java, you want the very best development platform for that language, right? That's Visual J++ by Microsoft. Visual J++ is a full-featured integrated development environment for Java that runs on Win32 platforms (Windows 95 and Windows NT).

Visual J++ is a personality module of the popular Developer's Studio by Microsoft. If you've used Developer's Studio before (for example, if you are a Visual C++ programmer), then you will find yourself programming in Java very quickly using Visual J++.

Visual J++ has added some great tools that make developing for Java extremely easy and fast. The Applet Wizard tool helps you generate WWW applets quickly using almost no programming whatsoever. The various options, bells, and whistles that the Applet Wizard can build into your applets are presented to you using the popular Wizard dialog format, which is so easy to use that you practically need no documentation whatsoever.

There are many features that Visual J++ brings to Java that, while being extremely powerful, are not quite so facile as the Applet Wizard. And that's why we wrote this book. In order for you to get the very most out of Visual J++, to get your programming done even faster and to use all of the 20th century features of Visual J++, you need a guide book from knowledgeable experts.

The Java/COM bridge that is built right into the Java Virtual Machine for Windows, as well as the COM-based database APIs DAO and RDO, need detailed explanation and sample programs that will make it all easy for you. Chapter 7, which details how to use COM objects from within Java as well as how to make your Java objects into COM objects, holds a lot of information that would take you weeks, if not months, of exploration to figure out. Chapter 10, which details the DAO and RDO APIs includes information that is just not available in Visual J++'s vast amount of online help.

How This Book Is Organized

In short, *The Visual J++ Handbook* gives you complete mastery over both the Java language and this exciting new Java development environment by Microsoft. Here is a short summary of what you can expect from the chapters found in this book.

Chapter 1, "The Java Language," is a detailing of this new language from the perspective of a C++ programmer. All you need to know to get your object-oriented programming skills working in Java is included in this chapter. This chapter explains the Java form of object-oriented classes and objects, creating and destroying Java objects, and the Java syntax.

Chapter 2, "The Visual J++ Environment," details all you need to know about Visual J++, from how to install the system, through a tour of its most impressive features. Debugging, development, project management, how to get the many sample applications and applets included with Visual J++ working—all of these topics are covered in detail, without any need for guesswork or danger of falling into any beginner pitfalls.

Chapter 3, "GUI Basics," explains how to do generic windows programming in Java. The classes and APIs you learn about in this chapter are usable not only in Windows but in any windows-capable operating system. From Macintosh to X-Windows and O/S2, Java provides a completely system-independent windowing model.

Chapter 4, "AWT Controls and Menus," details various built-in GUI controls of Java. Scrollbars, listboxes, pushbuttons, etc., are all fully covered. You'll know how to make great user interfaces quickly in Java after studying this chapter.

The Graphics class in Java is the single API you use to do all graphics and text rendering in Java. Chapter 5, "Graphics," details the use of this class to make fantastic displays in your Java programs, as well as how to do animation.

Chapter 6, "Applets," explains one of the very best features of Java: WWW-distributable applets. Applets are a simple extension of the GUI model in Java, but they add an incredible amount of flexibility to your HTML pages. This chapter shows you all the important features and capabilities, as well as the security restrictions, of applets.

Chapter 7, "Java and COM in Visual J++," walks you through the Java Virtual Machine for Windows using Java and COM together on Win32 machines. Microsoft has added a Java/COM bridge to Java, and this chapter explains in detail how to use it. After reading this chapter, you will be able to create and use both Java objects from external COM code, as well as COM objects from within your Java code.

Chapter 8, "File I/O and Streams," explains the Java streaming model. This is a very important model in Java because it is used universally in File I/O and in Internet communications. You will want to become familiar with this model in order to be a real Java guru.

Chapter 9, "Networking in Java," shows you how to communicate across the Internet in Java. Since Java was built with the Internet in mind, you may

Introduction

find this one of the easiest chapters in the book. No kidding! Using Java and Visual J++, the Internet is easy.

Chapter 10 is called "Database Programming in Java." There are no less than three separate but equally usable APIs for relational database programming in Java. The DAO and RDO APIs are included in Visual J++, and you can use them through the Java/COM bridge in the Java Virtual Machine for Windows. The JDBC API was created by the JavaSoft (the current owners of the Java language) to do completely system-independent database development in Java.

Chapter 11, "Utility and Language Class Reference," details the storage and system classes of the Java language.

Chapter 12, "Other Java APIs," lists the up-and-coming Java APIs that have not yet been either released by JavaSoft or widely distributed on the Internet. While most of these APIs are not available with your Visual J++ development environment, you get an introduction to them in this chapter so that you may be aware of them, and may choose to download and start using their SDKs right away.

CHAPTER 1

The Java Language

Java is a new, object-oriented language created to make programming for the Internet faster and easier. Before buying this book, no doubt at least once the thought crossed your mind, "Do I really need to learn (yet another) new programming language?!" Developers with gray around the temples remember when desktop development involved Pascal. Then C took over. More recently, you have had to learn C++. In between, you might have had to use one or more of a dozen interpreted or special-use languages: Perl, Shell scripts, Smalltalk, etc.

All of these languages have pros and cons for use in different environments. Each of them has been assessed for use on the new programming frontier: the Internet. For one reason or another, each of them has been found wanting. One of the biggest concerns of the Internet is security: security of client systems against viruses and other attacking processes, and security of information servers against attack from the very client systems they're trying to serve.

Consider the C language for a moment. C is an extremely powerful language, providing direct access to extremely low-level operating system calls. Many desktop C compilers have facilities to allow you to include assembly language code in your C files. Unfortunately for C, all this power is way too much for general Internet programming. It is just far too easy using C to attack a client of a server system: no resources on a system that allows a program written in C to run is safe. Also, programs written in C must be recompiled, and possibly rewritten for every different platform it is to run on. But the very essence of the Internet is that of disparate platforms. It would be next to impossible to write a program in C that, after compilation, runs equally well on a Macintosh, a Unix system, and a Windows system.

Borrowing features and syntax from several different languages, the Java language is designed to be the best of both worlds. While powerful, it is also designed to be very secure. While a very extensible and elegant language, it is designed to be platform-independent.

Java borrows most of its basic syntax from C/C++ (by far the most popular languages for designing applications on personal computers). This makes it very easy for C/C++ programmers to learn Java, and the learning curve will be that much more flat. From Smalltalk, Java borrows concepts like garbage collection and a solid object model. From Objective-C, Java gets the "interface" concept, which is very important for making the Java/COM bridge. In Java, you get a secure, powerful, easy-to-learn, platform-independent object-oriented language that's the best thing going for Internet programming.

Because this book is written with an assumption that you are familiar with the object-oriented programming basics in C++, this chapter (that describes the Java language) includes a description of how object-oriented programming is done in Java. A detailed description of the complete Java syntax is outside the scope of this book. For such a detailed explanation, you should consult the book *Learn Java Now*, included with your Visual J++ package. That book describes the Java syntax fully. This chapter, on the other hand, describes how Java is different from and similar to C++ and other object-oriented programming languages.

The Java Language

Java Basics

When you talk about *Java*, you are really talking about two different things. There's the Java language, which is what you write your classes in and compile. The other part of Java is the *Java virtual machine*. In order to make sure your Java programs are indeed platform-independent, there is a single architecture that all Java programs are compiled to. That is, when you compile a Java program on a Windows/Intel x86 platform, you get the same compiled output that you do on a Macintosh or a Unix system. The compiler compiles not to the native platform, but to an abstract platform called the Java virtual machine, or JVM (or sometimes just VM). When you run a Java program, it is really run within an instance of a JVM, often implemented in software as an interpreter. Microsoft and Apple have both created software versions of the Java virtual machine that will be bundled with those companies' respective operating systems in the future.

So you see, you can run any compiled Java program on any Windows platform that includes the Microsoft JVM. Microsoft has made arrangements to include a JVM in every Windows operating system in the near future. That means Java will not only be the best language for Internet programming, but it will also become a good language for general desktop development in Windows.

Bytecode and .CLASS Files

A single file of Java source code defines one or more Java classes, including definition and implementation within the same file. This is different than C++, in which you declare a class in a .H header file, and implement that class in a .C or .CPP implementation file. The file extension used for Java source files is .JAVA

A single Java source file is compiled by a Java compiler, such as the JV Ccompiler included with Visual J++, or Sun's *javac* compiler included with Sun's Java Developers Kit. For each class defined in the Java source file, the compiler creates a class file with a .CLASS extension. This class file contains *bytecodes* for the Java virtual machine. Bytecodes are the binary instruction set of the Java virtual machine. These class files can be transferred from system to system and used on any system that has a JVM instance present.

Classes

In any object-oriented language a class is a description of a type of object. It describes three things that are common to all objects of that class:

- **Member data** Sometimes also called the object's state. A class declares zero or more member variables that *belong* to objects of that class. For example, a Point class, designed to represent a point on the 2D plane, may declare that Point objects have two pieces of members data: an *x* value and a *y* value.
- **Class methods** Functions or operations each object of the class can perform. Usually, these methods operate by telling something about the object's data or by modifying the object's data. For example, a Point class designed to represent a point on the 2D plane may declare a method called magnitude( ) that calculates the distance of the point from (0, 0).
- **Base class** Classes may be *extended from* other classes. In C++, as in Java, this is called inheritance. You should understand inheritance first, and how to declare class inheritance in Java, before understanding other Java class concepts.

Class Inheritance

As stated previously, a Java class can be declared as extended from another Java class, as in this example:

```
class Bar {
    // Member data and class method definitions
}

class Foo extends Bar {
    // Member data and class method definitions
}
```

This is essentially stating that Foo has all the member data and class methods defined in the Bar class, plus some additional declarations of its own. For a more concrete example, you could define a Door class, used to describe doors. A door can be open or closed, so you might define the Door class with a boolean member variable describing whether or not the door is opened, along with methods for opening or closing the door:

```
class Door {
    boolean isOpen;

    void open( ) { isOpen = true; }
    void close( ) { isOpen = false; }
}
```

This is a great class. You could make an instance of this class to define your front door, your back door, your garage door, etc. But, what if your front door has a lock on it? I'm sure this isn't too much of a stretch, as your front door probably does have a lock on it. You need more state data for your class indicating whether or not the door is locked. In this case, you might define a LockingDoor class to describe your front door. Since the LockingDoor class does everything that a Door class does, plus a little bit more, you would find it easiest to define your LockingDoor class as *extending from* your Door class:

```
class LockingDoor extends Door {
    // You automatically get the isOpen member variable,
    // and the open( ) and close( ) methods from the
    // Door base class.

    boolean isLocked;

    void lock( )   { isLocked = true; }
    void unlock( ) { isLocked = false; }
}
```

You could continue a chain of extended classes by declaring LockingAlarmedDoor class, which is a LockingDoor class with an additional alarm. You could extend the chain by declaring a LockingAlarmedSecretDoor class, which is a LockingAlarmedDoor class that can hide or unhide itself (i.e., it would have hide( ) and unhide( ) member methods).

At least one value of deriving classes from each other should be obvious from this example: code reuse. The code written from the original Door class (the open( ) and close( ) methods) never needs to be written again from the derived classes LockingDoor, LockingAlarmedDoor, LockingAlarmedSecretDoor, etc. Not having to rewrite means you save time. There are other uses for extending classes that will be explained in subsequent sections of this chapter for those readers who are not familiar with object-oriented programming.

Unlike C++, Java only supports single inheritance. That is, in C++ you may declare a class as deriving from multiple parent classes, and your class would inherit all of the capabilities and member data from each of the base classes. This can be quite nice and make for elegant programming, but it also often makes for a very confusing source code. The designers of Java decided that multiple inheritance, such as is available in C++, leads to source code that is just too confusing (which it can be, as you might know from experience with C++). Therefore, when declaring your Java class, you may only specify a single base class using the *extends* keyword, as in the previous LockingDoor example. The Java *interface* is used to approximate multiple inheritance, as explained in a following section of this chapter.

The Object Class

In fact, all classes in Java except one ultimately extend from a single class: the Object class. By default, when you declare a class that does not extend from any other class, the phrase "extends Object" is implicit. These two declarations of the Point class are equivalent. They compile to virtually the same bytecode:

```
class Point {
    int x;
    int y;
}

class Point extends Object {
    int x;
    int y;
}
```

So, what are the member data and methods of the Object class? Since all classes ultimately are derived from it, then its members are always inherited members of any Java class. In fact, the Object class has no member data variables. It does have member methods, though. The following table lists those methods and describes them. Each of these methods will be explained in more depth in the other chapters of this book, as each of them is integrally involved with the Java programming language.

Object Class Method	Description
getClass( )	The basis of run-time type identification. You can identify the class of any arbitrary object using this method.
hashCode( )	Used in Hashtables, returns a pseudo-unique value for any object. (The Hashtable class is a storage class described in Chapter 11.)

Object Class Method	Description
equals( )	Tells whether or not an object equals another object. The meaning of this method is changed for various classes. In general, this returns true if two object references refer to the exact same object. The String class, on the other hand, returns true if two strings have the same characters in them.
clone( )	Creates a new object that is an exact copy of the original object.
toString( )	Returns a string appropriate for displaying to a user. The string describes the type and state of the object.
notify( ), notifyAll( ), and wait( )	Used in thread synchronization.
finalize( )	A place holder for the destructor method.

Variables

Member data is stored in variables, also known as *fields*. Variables, a concept common to all programming languages, represent specific types of information within a space in the computer's memory. The use and type of the information are implicit in the variable's *type*. For example, a number variable represents a whole number, and it can be added, subtracted, multiplied, or divided with another number.

In Java classes, you declare member variables within the class definition. Here's an example:

```
class Point {
    int x;
    int y;
}
```

This example defines a class, named Point, with just two member variables, *x* and *y*. These two variables are both of type *int*, which means a 32-bit (4-byte) integer value. That's pretty simple.

Java has several "built-in" variable types, such as *int*. The following table lists each of these types and describes them. Those of you who know C/C++ will recognize these built-in data types. These basic types allow you to do most necessary mathematical operations.

Built-In Type	Description
char	A 16-bit Unicode character. (Unicode is a new, universal character set theoretically capable of describing characters in *any* existing language. Unicode is the internal representation of character data in 32-bit Windows.)
byte	An 8-bit signed integer value. Possible values range from -128 to 127.
short	A 16-bit signed integer value. Possible values range from -32,768 to 32,767.
int	A 32-bit signed integer value. Possible values range from -2,147,483,648 to 2,147,483,647.
long	A 64-bit signed integer value. Possible values range between two numbers of much higher magnitude than a pocket calculator can figure out exactly. That is, from -2 raised to the 63, up to 2 raised to the 63 (minus 1).
boolean	A Boolean value. The special Java keywords *true* and *false* describe the two possible values.
float	Single-precision IEEE 754 floating point number.
double	A Double-precision IEEE 754 floating point number.

While these built-in types bear a great deal of resemblance to C/C++ numerical data types, there are a few distinctions you should be aware of. First, note that the char, short, int, and long data types have a defined bit width that does not change. ANSI C numerical types, on the other hand, may change based on the platform you compile your code on. For example, 16-bit Windows (Windows 3.x) defines the int type as a 16-bit integer, while 32-bit Windows operating systems (Windows 95 and Windows NT) define ints as 32-bit integers. That means that the exact same C code compiled for these two different Windows platforms will actually compile differently. What a pain it is to keep track of these differences and try to account for them in your code! Java obviates the need for this extra maintenance overhead by defining the built-in types to always have the same meaning for any JVM implementation.

Also, you can see that there are no pointers in Java. This is probably the most significant difference between Java and C/C++. Java uses only *references*, a concept also contained in C++ (though not C). The use of references, and how they make Java more secure and easier to program in than C/C++, is explained in another section of this chapter.

Instance and Class Data

Objects of the Point class from the preceding example will each have two 32-bit integer values stored within them: *x* and *y*. These values are unique to each instance of the Point class. That is, given two different Point objects, each will have two 32-bit spaces reserved in memory. This is called *instance data*.

You can also declare class variables that are shared between all objects of that class. Use the *static* keyword when declaring the variable, like this:

```
class Point2 {
    int x;
    int y;

    static int x_origin = 0;
    static int y_origin = 0;
}
```

All objects of the Point2 class, in addition to the two 32-bit *x* and *y* integers unique to each instance, now share two 32-bit integer values called *x_origin* and *y_origin*. Saying they are shared means that if one Point2 object changes the value of *x_origin*, then all Point2 objects will see the value of *x_origin* change. On the other hand, if another Point2 object changes its *x* value, no other Point2 object's *x* value will be altered. The value *x* is instance data, and *x_origin* is *static class data*.

Member Data Protection and Access Specifiers

If you look at an object as a black box, some of the object's data may be publicly available for other objects to examine and change. You may not want your object's member data to be changeable in this way, however. For example, consider the LockingDoor class from the previous example. All LockingDoor class objects have a boolean *isLocked* member variable. You wouldn't want external class code to be able to change this value arbitrarily. That would be like taping a key outside your front door! Instead, you want to force external objects to use your lock( ) and unlock( ) methods only. Your

LockingDoor objects control the value of the *isLocking* variable completely within the open( ) and close( ) method code. As a black box, you don't want your *isLocking* variable to be exposed outside the object; you want it to be encapsulated within your object.

There are three different access specifiers in Java used to control access to member variables. The *public* keyword specifies that a member variable is completely exposed to all external code, and thus can be freely examined or modified by anyone. The previous Point class had x and y member variables that you can make available in this way using the *public* keyword, like this:

```
class Point {
    public int x;
    public int y;
}
```

The opposite of public is *private*. The private keyword indicates that no code external to the object's member methods may examine or modify a member variable. Use this access specifier to control all access to a member variable. The *isLocked* member variable of the LockingDoor class from the preceding example is a good example of a private member variable. Instead of making the member available to any other code, you would want to control access to this member as a private member, like this:

```
class LockingDoor extends Door {
    private boolean isLocked;

    void lock( ) { isLocked = true; }
    void unlock( ) { isLocked = false; }
}
```

Note that the lock( ) and unlock( ) methods of the LockingDoor class may access the *isLocked* variable, but no other Java objects can access this member. The only way external code could modify the value of this variable is by using the LockingDoor method lock( ) or unlock( ). This sample code, which does not compile, demonstrates how private variable members cannot be accessed directly, even in derived classes.

```
class PasswordLockingDoor extends LockingDoor {
    private String m_strPassword;

    void unlockWithPassword(String strPossiblePassword) {

        if(m_strPassword == strPossiblePassword)
            isLocked = false;
        // Illegal!! Can't access private isLocked
```

        }
}

Even though PasswordLockingDoor is derived from LockingDoor, it cannot access the inherited *isLocked* member variable, because it is private to the LockingDoor class.

Public and private are two extremes. Public allows anyone to examine or modify a member variable. The private access modifier allows no code other than the class' member methods to examine or modify this value. In fact, a reference to this member variable by any other class, including a class derived from LockingDoor, will result in a compilation error (as demonstrated by the PasswordLockingDoor class). Consider the *isOpen* boolean member variable of the Door class, the class upon which the LockingDoor class is derived. This is a member you want LockingDoors to have access to, but not any other classes. That is, you would not want to allow someone to open a locked door without unlocking it first, which could be accomplished if *isOpen* were a public member of the Door class: you would simply set the LockingDoor object's *isOpen* member to true. Use the *protected* access specifier to allow only derived classes to have access to a member variable, as in this example:

```java
public class Door {
    protected boolean isOpen;
            // only this and derived classes can use

    void open( ) {
        isOpen = true;
    }

    void close( ) {
        isOpen = false;
    }
}

public class LockingDoor extends Door {
    private isLocked;

    void lock( ) {
        // Can only lock closed doors...
        if( !isOpen ) { return; }

        // OK. access to isOpen allowed
        isLocked = true;
    }

    void unlock( ) {
```

```
        // Can only unlock locked doors...
        isLocked = false;
    }
}
```

See that the LockingDoor's lock( ) method can access its inherited *isOpen* member variable, since that member was declared as *protected* in the parent class (Door). An external class, which does not inherit from Door, would not be able to access this member. The default access protection, the one used when no access specifier is used, is termed *private to package*. The later section of this chapter that explains Java packages will explain this type of access in detail. The following table summarizes the access specifiers and their meaning.

Variable Access Specifier	Description
private	Only methods of the class in which the variable is a member may access the variable directly.
protected	Only methods of the package in which the variable is a member or classes derived from the class in which the variable is declared may access the variable directly.
public	Any method of any class may access the variable directly.
<default>	Termed *private to package*, this means only classes that belong to the same package as the class in which the variable is a member may access the variable directly. Class packages are explained in detail later in this chapter.

Note that in alpha and beta versions of Java, there was an additional access specifier called *private protected*. Perhaps because of the confusion created by this ambiguous name, use of this type of access specifier has been discontinued in Java. You may run across legacy code that includes this specifier. Be aware that its use is no longer considered legal syntax.

Methods

All Java executable code lives within Java class methods. There is no such thing as executable Java code that is not within a Java class method. This differs from C/C++, where functions may be declared within the global scope, meaning they do not belong to any class. In Java, there is no such thing as a function or any type of executable code that is not declared as a member of a class.

Some Notes on the Java Syntax

Java code looks a whole lot like C/C++ functions. That's not just a happy coincidence. You'll find that your knowledge of C and C++ will make it very easy for you to program in Java. The actual code looks very similar. For example, this dense line of C++ code:

```
for( int ii=0 ; (anVals[++ii] << (ii & 0xF0)) > anThreshholds[ii] ; ii++)
```

Looks like this in Java:

```
for( int ii=0 ; (anVals[++ii] << (ii & 0xF0)) > anThreshholds[ii] ; ii++)
```

That is, they are exactly the same. Almost all the same precedence rules, syntax, etc. that define C++ are also used to define the Java language syntax. It would be far beyond the scope of this book to review the C++ syntax, so if you are completely unfamiliar with that language you should grab a C++ or Java language primer.

It would be easier to describe where Java differs from C++, rather than list all the ways the two languages are similar. First, you have already seen how to declare classes in Java and how Java only supports single inheritance. How you declare Java classes is probably the largest syntactic difference between the two languages. Instead of using the C++ ":" operator, in Java you use the *extends* keyword:

```
class LockingDoor extends Door {
    ...
}
```

Java Method Access Specifiers

The next big difference is how you declare and implement class methods in Java. While in C++ you may use the *private*, *protected*, or *public* access specifiers like labels to include several different method and member variables within a single access specifier, in Java you must explicitly indicate the access assigned to each method or member variable. Also, Java does not permit methods with optional or a variable number of parameters. When declaring Java methods, you use the same access specifiers you use with Java member variables: specifically, *private*, *protected*, or *public*. They mean the same thing when applied to methods as they do when applied to variables. That is, a private method may only be called by that class' code. Protected methods may only be called by that class' or any derived class' code or code in the package in which it is declared. Public methods may be called by any other class' code.

For example, the Door class defined previously has two methods: open( ) and close( ). You should declare these methods as *public*, meaning code from any class may call them:

```
class Door {
    protected boolean isOpen;

    public void open( ) {
        isOpen = true;
    }

    public void close( ) {
        isOpen = false;
    }
}
```

Class Constructors

As in C++, there is a special method called the *class constructor*. The constructor is run whenever an object of the class is created. The constructor acts as an object initializer. It is the appropriate place to initialize member variables, create other objects—anything you need to do to make sure the object is ready to be used. For example, the Door and LockingDoor classes have member variables that should be initialized before a Door or LockingDoor object is used. For any door that is created, you would want to have *isOpen* be false, and any locking door should have *isLocked* also be false:

```
class Door {
    protected boolean isOpen;

    public Door( ) {
        isOpen = false;
    }

    ...
}

class LockingDoor extends Door {
    private boolean isLocked;

    public LockingDoor( ) {
        isLocked = false;
    }

    ...
}
```

The Java Language

As you can see, a class' constructor is a function that always has the same name as the class itself. In addition, the constructor method has no return type. This is unlike any other class method. All other class methods must be declared with a return type. The class constructor, on the other hand, can never be declared with a return type.

So, what happens when you don't declare a constructor? Java creates an implicit one for you. The implicit one that is created has *public* access and doesn't really do anything. Thus, these two pieces of code do the same thing:

```
class Point {
    int x;
    int y;
}
```

and

```
class Point {
    int x;
    int y;

    public Point( ) {
    }
}
```

You can also have parameters passes to your class' constructors. Just declare the parameters in the parameter list of the constructor like you would for any other function, which is just like you would in C/C++:

```
class Point {
    int m_x;
    int m_y;

    public Point(int x, int y) {
        m_x = x;
        m_y = y;
    }
}
```

The previous example demonstrates how you can pass initializer values to a class constructor. Those values are used to initialize the values of the internal member variables *m_x* and *m_y* of the Point class.

Constructor methods are chained together up the class hierarchy. That is, whenever a derived class' constructor is called, the base class constructor is called. To illustrate this point, this code

```
class Door {
    public Door( ) {
        System.out.println("Door being created!");
    }
}

class LockingDoor {
    public LockingDoor( ) {
        System.out.println("LockingDoor being created!");
    }
}
```

will produce this output whenever a new LockingDoor object is created:

```
Door being created!
LockingDoor being created!
```

See? As part of the LockingDoor constructor method, the base class (Door) constructor method is called. In fact, it is called before any of the LockingDoor constructor method code is run, which is why the line "Door being created!" was printed first.

You may explicitly call an alternate constructor using the special *this* keyword. Just like in C++, the *this* keyword refers to the instance of the object whose code is being run. Within a constructor, you may also use *this* to call an alternate constructor, as in the following example:

```
class Point {
    private int m_x;
    private int m_y;

    public Point( ) {
        this(0, 0);
    }

    public Point(int x, int y) {
        m_x = x;
        m_y = y;
    }
}
```

The no-parameter constructor automatically calls the two-parameter constructor with the *x* and *y* parameters each set to zero.

Use the *super* keyword to call an alternate version of the base class' constructor. By default, the no-parameter constructor of the base class is called as part of a derived class constructor. But, as the following example demonstrates, you may use an alternative version of the base class constructor:

```java
class Door {
    private boolean isOpen;

    public Door( ) {
        this(true);
    }

    public Door(boolean isInitiallyOpen) {
        isOpen = isInitiallyOpen;
    }
}

class LockingDoor extends Door{
    private boolean isLocked;

    public LockingDoor( ) {
        // Use Door constructor with door initially closed.
        super(false);
        isLocked = false;
    }
}
```

Note that if you are going to use the *super* keyword to specify an alternate base class constructor to use, you must use it before doing anything else in the constructor. The following code will not compile because it tries to call an alternative base class constructor after performing some other operations.

```java
class LockingDoor extends Door {
    private boolean isLocked;

    public LockingDoor( ) {
        isLocked = false;
        super(false);       // Illegal! Must call base class constructor first
    }
}
```

Creating and Destroying Objects

In Java, there is no such thing as objects being declared on the stack. All objects are explicitly created using the *new* operator, as in this example, which declares a Door variable and assigns a new Door object to it:

```java
Door d = new Door( );
```

All Java objects must be created explicitly using the *new* operator. You assign the created Java objects to object variables of the same type. See in the previous line of code how a Door variable *d* is declared, and then is assigned a new Door object created by the *new* operator. The variable is then said to hold a *reference* to the object. When no references to an object are held (i.e., when all variables holding reference to an object are either assigned different values or fall out of scope), then the object is marked internally by the JVM. The Java system asynchronously deallocates any such marked objects. This is called *garbage collection*, and it is one of nicest features of Java for programming.

In this way, you never actually need to destroy or deallocate objects in Java. The JVM does it for you when all references to the object are lost. This example illustrates how references control a Java object's life in memory:

```
public void MyMethod( ) {
    Door d = new Door( );       // First Door created.
    d = new Door( );            /* Second Door created. Ref to first door is
                                 * lost, since variable reassigned with a
                                 * different Door object's ref. First Door
                                 * will be deallocated asynchronously. */
}                               /* Ref to second Door lost, since variable
                                 * d went out of scope. Second Door will
                                 * now be deallocated asynchronously. */
```

Notice that at no time do you use C/C++ pointers. There is no such thing as pointers in Java. All objects are controlled solely through references. At first, this may seem like a serious loss of power compared with C/C++. Maybe in some circumstances it is. But, by using references and allowing the JVM to destroy your objects for you when all references to them are dropped, you will save yourself countless hours diagnosing memory leaks and other associated problems. You will never need to write another piece of memory management code in Java, since the JVM controls all memory management for you.

The parameters passed as part of using the new operator determine which class constructor is used to initialize a new object, as in this example:

```
class Point {
    int m_x;
    int m_y;

    public Point( ) {
        this(0, 0);
    }

    public Point(int x, int y) {
```

```
            m_x = x;
            m_y = y;
        }
    }

    class MyProgram {
        public void static main(String astrArgs[]) {
            Point origin = new Point( );  // Point (0, 0) created.
            Point p = new Point(5, 5);    /* Second Point constructor used.
                                           * Point (5, 5) is created. */
        }
    }
```

The part of the JVM responsible for destroying objects with no references to them is called the *garbage collector*. The garbage collector is actually a separate thread that runs within the JVM, constantly looking for objects marked for destruction. Since the garbage collector is a separate thread, then garbage collection is obviously an asynchronous operation. That is, an object is not necessarily destroyed the instant its last reference is lost. And in fact, there is no guarantee as to when the garbage collector will eventually get around to destroying such objects. If your program is hot and heavy into calculating, then the garbage collector thread may not be allocated any processor time-slices to run until your calculations are completed. Rest assured, though, that the garbage collector will eventually get around to destroying your objects marked for deletion. To force a synchronous round of garbage collection, you can do so using the *System.gc( )* method.

The Destructor Method

As in C++, Java classes can have a destructor method. The Java object destructor method will be called when the garbage collector finally gets around to destroying your object. Since there is no such thing as allocated memory in Java, you will probably find you have much less need for a destructor method than you would in C++.

All Java destructors have the same name: *finalize( )*. You may remember that finalize( ) is a method inherited from the Object class, which is the ultimate base class of all other Java classes. When you implement a finalize( ) method, you are declaring code that will be run immediately prior to the object being removed from memory altogether.

Calling Object Methods

The *dot* operator is used to call an object method. This example demonstrates calling an object's methods:

```
class Point {
    public int m_x;
    public int m_y;

    public String toString( ) {
        return "Point (" + m_x + ", " + m_y + ")";
    }
}

class MyProgram {
    public static void main(String astrArgs[]) {
        Point p = new Point( );
        p.m_x = 5;
        p.m_y = 6;
        System.out.println(p.toString());
    }
}
```

which would produce this output if compiled and ran:

`Point (5, 6)`

You can see that the same dot operator is used both to access the object's member variables and to call the object's methods. That is, the line referring to *p.m_x* assigns a value to the *p* object's *m_x* member variable. The line referring to *p.toString( )* calls the *p* object's toString( ) method.

The Static Initializer Method

To initialize static member variables, you can create one or more static member initializer pieces of code. These pieces of code are all appended together into a single *class initializer* method. The class initializer method is run immediately when the class is loaded into the JVM, before any object of that type is created. Simply use the *static* keyword to denote chunks of static initializer code, as in this example:

```
class School {
    private static String m_strPrincipal;
    private static string m_strSecretary;

    static {
        m_strPrincipal = "Ms. Doherty";
        m_strSecretary = "Mr. Svenson";
    }

    private static String m_strFirstGradeTeacher1;
```

The Java Language

```
    private static String m_strFirstGradeTeacher2;

    static {
        m_strFirstGradeTeacher1 = "Mrs. Danielson";
        m_strFirstGradeTeacher2 = "Mr. York";
    }
}
```

This code will create a single class initializer method, which will assign values to the four static member Strings *m_strPrincipal*, *m_strSecretary*, *m_strFirstGradeTeacher1*, and *m_strFirstGradeTeacher2*. Only a single static initializer method is created, built from the various blocks of static initializer code declared in the class.

Obviously, code within blocks of static initializer code cannot refer to nonstatic member variables. That should be pretty obvious, since when the static initializer code is run, there is no extant object of the class. The static initializer is run immediately when the class is loaded into the JVM, before any object of the class is created.

The this Variable

Within a Java method, there is always a variable named *this* that is in scope. The *this* variable is a reference to the object whose method is being called. The *this* variable is very similar to C++'s *this* pointer, the difference being that in Java *this* is a reference, since there are no pointers in Java. The following example demonstrates how *this* refers to the object whose method is being called. The isOrigin( ) method of this Point class implementation demonstrates the use of the *this* reference:

```
class Point {
    private int m_x;
    private int m_y;
    private static Point m_origin;

    static {
        m_origin = new Point(0, 0);
    }

    public Point(int x, int y) {
        m_x = x; m_y = y; //
    }

    public Point getOrigin( ) {
        return m_origin;
    {
```

```
    public boolean isOrigin( ) {
        return (this == m_origin);
    }
}
```

You see the isOrigin( ) method of the previous example tests to see if the object whose method is being called (the object referred to by the *this* variable) is the same as a previously allocated static Point object.

Strings

It was stated previously that all Java objects must be explicitly allocated using the *new* operator. Actually, that's not true. There are two types of objects that have special syntactic ways of being allocated in Java: Strings and arrays. This section talks about String objects.

First, objects of the String class are automatically created whenever a reference to a line of characters in quotes occurs in Java code. That is, the following lines of code are completely legal in Java, since quoted characters are in fact String objects:

```
String s = "This is a string object.";

int len = "You can call my methods!".length();
```

Next, two operators have special meaning when used with String objects. The "+" operator acts as a concatenator when either of its right or left operators are in fact strings. This makes it very easy to create and work with strings in Java:

```
String strConcat = "The time" + " is now!";
```

If only one of the "+" operator's operands is a string, then the other is automatically converted into its string form and concatenated. This makes it very easy to generate human-readable strings, much more so than in C/C++:

```
int nHours = 5;
int nMinutes = 22;
int nSeconds = 45;

...
String strMessage = "The time is " + nHours + ":" + nMinutes + ":" + nSeconds;
The previous code will generate a String strMessage equal to

"The time is 5:22:45"
```

The built-in Java types (boolean, char, int, etc.) all have automatic, obvious translations into strings. Java objects, however, don't. Therefore, every class implements a toString( ) method that is used by Java to convert an object to a string whenever it is necessary, as in the case of concatenation of the object with a string.

The equals( ) method, which all String objects inherit from the Object class, is reimplemented in the String class. Normally, the equals( ) method returns true if two object references refer to the exact same object. The String class implementation of equals( ) returns true if two different String objects have the exact same string of characters. That is, while this code segment would set *fEqual* to false:

```
Point p1 = new Point(1, 1);
Point p2 = new Point(1, 1);
boolean fEquals = p1.equals(p2);
```

this code segment would set *fEquals* to true, since the two strings are equivalent:

```
String str1 = "Marvy!";
String str2 = "Mar" + "vy!"; // == "Marvy!"
boolean fEquals = str1.equals(str2);
```

Arrays

Arrays are handled quite a bit differently in Java than in C++. In Java, an array is actually a type of object. That is, all arrays are derived from the Object class, and thus can be cast as type Object, and do everything that you could do with an object. That's actually quite interesting, and gives you some impressive capabilities you cannot achieve easily in C++.

First things first. To declare an array, you do it pretty much the same way you would do it in C++. This example piece of code declares an array of five integers:

```
int aArray[5];
```

Like the String class, there are syntactic methods for implicitly allocating arrays, as the previous line of code demonstrates. That means you don't always have to use the new operator to create arrays, even though arrays are objects. Of course, you can use the new operator; you just don't have to:

```
int aArray[] = new int[5];
```

Actually, there are several different ways of declaring or creating arrays in Java. The first, most basic, most C-like, looks like this:

```
<type> <var-name>[<length>];
```

This allocates an array of known size, and puts a reference to that Array object into the *<var-name>* variable. Got that? *<var-name>* is a variable with a reference to an object. The type of *<var-name>* is *<type>*[]. For example, the variable *aArray* in this example:

```
int aArray[10];
```

has type *int[]*. And this variable *aObjects*:

```
Object aObjects[15];
```

has type *Object[]*.

You could reassign either of these variables to alternative Array objects, allocated either implicitly or explicitly, as this example demonstrates:

```
int aArray[5];         // First array of integers allocated.
...
aArray = new int[15];  // Reference to first array dropped, will be garbage
                       // collected. Second array allocated, ref assigned to
                       // aArray.
```

This is quite a bit different than C++, where arrays declared with a size cannot be resized or anything. It's just important to remember that your array variables, just like any other object variables, are actually holding a reference to an object. That object is of type *<type>*[].

Arrays of Objects

When you allocate an array of objects, you should be aware that you are not allocating the actual objects yet, only an array of references to objects. What does that mean? Well, it means this code is illegal:

```
Point aPoints[5];      // Array of Point references allocated

aPoints[0].m_x = 10;   /* Illegal! Point object for aPoints[0] has not
                        * yet been allocated!
```

Instead, you must write code like this to allocate actual objects for your arrays:

The Java Language

```
Point aPoints[5];        // Array of Point references allocated

                         // Create Points for array to refer to
for(int ii=0 ; ii<5 ; ii++)
    aPoint[ii] = new Point( );

aPoints[0].m_x = 10;     // OK. Point object for aPoints[0] was allocated
```

In fact, only arrays of built-in types can be used without doing this kind of *for-loop*. For example, an int array does not require this kind of for-loop, since the elements of the array are actual ints, not references to anything that needs to be initialized.

Initializing Arrays

When you create arrays of built-in types, you may specify a list of initializing values, much the same as you may do in C++. An example looks like this:

```
int an[] = {5, 7, 9, 10, 5, 2, 7, 8, 13};
```

which would allocate a new array of integers with nine int elements, much the same as the same code would do in C++.

Multidimensional Arrays

It's easy to declare and work with multidimensional arrays in Java. This is how you allocate a two dimensional array of integers:

```
int aan[10][10];
```

When allocating multidimensional arrays of objects, remember that the same rule about allocating the actual objects after the array is created is still in effect. This sample code demonstrates the correct way to initialize such arrays of objects:

```
Point aap[10][10];

for(int ii=0 ; ii<10 ; ii++)
   for(int jj=0 ; jj<10 ; jj++)
       aap[ii][jj] = new Point( );
```

Alternative Declarative Syntax for Arrays

There's another, non-C++ syntax for declaring arrays in Java. Instead of placing the [] subscription operator after the variable name, you may also place it after the array type indicator. These two declarations of the main( ) method of a class are equivalent. The only difference is the location of the [] subscript operator in the parameter list. They both compile to the same bytecode:

```
public static void main(String astrArgs[]) {
    ...
}
```

is the same as

```
public static void main(String[] astrArgs) {
    ...
}
```

Similarly, these two declarations of the *an* array are also equivalent.

```
int an[10];
```

is the same as

```
int[10] an;
```

Method Overloading

To overload a method means to provide alternate implementations that use different numbers or types of parameters. You have already seen a little bit of overloading if you consider the constructor method. In previous examples explaining the constructor method, you have seen that you may provide more than one implementation of a class' constructor, as long as each unique implementation takes a different number or type of parameters. This example reemphasizes the point:

```
class Point {
    private int m_x;
    private int m_y;

    public Point( ) {
        this(0, 0);
    }

    // Overloaded constructor: takes different number and type of
    // parameters than previously declared constructors.
    public Point(int x, int y) {
```

```
            m_x = x;
            m_y = y;
        }
    }
```

Similarly, you may provide overloaded implementations of any class method, as long as each unique implementation requires a different number or type of parameter. This is pretty much the same as the same concept in C++: method overloading means reusing the same method name, but using different parameters. In this example, you can see that two alternative implementations of the distance( ) method of the Point class are used. The version of distance( ) that requires no parameters calculates the distance of the point from the origin (0, 0). The version that takes another Point object calculates the distance between the two points.

```
class Point {
    public int m_x;
    public int m_y;

    public Point( ) {
        m_x = m_y = 0;
    }



    // Calculate distance from the origin.
    public double distance( ) {
        return Math.sqrt((m_x*m_x) + (m_y*m_y));
    }

    // Calculate distance from another Point.
    public double distance(Point p) {
        int dx = this.m_x - p.m_x;
        int dy = this.m_y - p.m_y;
        return Math.sqrt((dx*dx) + (dy*dy));
    }
}
```

When calling one or another of the overloaded versions of the distance( ) method of this Point class, the JVM automatically figures out which overloaded version to use based on which parameters are passed. That is, if you don't pass any parameters, the JVM knows to use the first version of distance( ). And if you pass a single Point object (or an object of a class derived from Point) then the JVM knows to use the second version of the distance( ) method.

Method Overriding

Overriding a class method means to provide a new implementation of a particular method other than the implementation inherited from a base class. In C++, you achieved method overriding by declaring a method as *virtual*, meaning a derived class may provide an alternative implementation. In this sense, all Java methods are virtual. For example, the toString( ) method implemented in the Object class (the ultimate base class of all other classes in Java) can be reimplemented, or overridden, in any class.

This example class, called the NamedPoint class, is derived from the Point class. This class does not have a public constructor, so external code cannot create named points. Instead, you must use the static NamedPoint class method lookupNamedPoint( ), providing a string name for the point. The thrust of this class is to ensure that only unique names are associated with individual NamedPoint objects. This is a relatively common design pattern in Java, in which references to extant instances of the class are stored by that class so they can be looked up later. (This class uses a Hashtable object to store references to extant named points. Hashtables are covered in Chapter 11 of this book, but it should be obvious the a Hashtable is a type of storage device that maintains a unique key associate with one or more objects.)

```
class NamedPoint extends Point {
    private static Hashtable s_hash;

    // Private constructor means you cannot use new operator
    // to create NamedPoints external to this class' code.
    private NamedPoint( ) {
        // Just call base class constructor.
        super( );
    }

    // Lookup method looks up extant NamedPoints. If name is
    // not recognized, then new NamedPoints is created. Since
    // you are within NamedPoint code, can invoke private
    // constructor using new operator. Method is static since
    // no non-static member variables are referenced.
    public static NamedPoint lookupNamedPoint(String strName) {
        Object objReturn;
        // Lookup name in private static hashtable.
        if(null == (objReturn = s_hash.get(strName)) {
            objReturn = new NamedPoint( );
            s_hash.put(strName, objReturn);
        }
        return objReturn;
    }
}
```

Abstract Methods

In C++, you have the concept of *pure virtual* class methods. These are methods that are declared in a base class, but not implemented. This means that the class is *abstract*, that it is a template or description of a class. The actual implementation of the method is left to be provided by overriding implementations in derived classes.

In Java, you have the same concept. The difference is just in the syntax. In Java, you use the keyword *abstract* to indicate that a method is abstract, as in this example:

```
abstract class Shape {
    // Abstract getArea( ) method to be implemented by derived classes.
    public abstract double getArea( );

    ...
}
```

Note that the Shape class had to be declared with the *abstract* keyword also indicating that the class include at least one abstract, or unimplemented, method. That means that you cannot actually instantiate any Shape objects, only objects of classes that are derived from Shape and provide implementations of the getArea( ) method. This sample code illustrates the point:

```
class Rect extends Shape {
    public int m_x, m_y, m_width, m_height;

    public Rect( ) {
        m_x = m_y = m_width = m_height = 0;
    }

    // Implementation of the Shape.getArea( ) abstract method. Required
    // if you want to actually create any Rect objects.
    public double getArea( ) {
        return (m_width * m_height);
    }

}

class MyProgram {
    public static void main(String astrArgs[]) {
        Shape s = new Shape( );   /* Illegal! Can't create object of abstract
                                   * class. Compiler will complain.
        s = new Rect( );          /* OK. Rect class is not abstract. Rect is a
                                   * Shape, so you can assign to Shape variable.
        System.out.println("Area of shape is: " + s.getArea( ));
```

        }
    }

In this example, the shape variable *s* is assigned to a Rect, which is an implicit cast that is allowed since Rect is derived from Shape. The reference to *s.getShape( )* is resolved to the Rect class implementation of the method.

Casting Variables

As in C++, a *cast* is when you tell the JVM to use an alternative type of a particular variable or object. For example, in the most recent example in which the Shape and Rect classes are used, an object of type Rect is cast into a variable of type Shape. This is allowed since the Rect class is derived from the Shape class, and thus all Rect objects are also Shape objects.

Unlike in C++, Java is a tightly typed language. This means that all such casting operations are checked either in the compiler or in the run-time JVM (usually in both) to ensure it is a legal cast. An illegal cast is when you cast an object to an incompatible type. This sample code demonstrates an illegal cast. In it, you are trying to cast a Rect object into a Parallelogram object. Since Rect derives directly from Shape, this is not a legal cast. It will cause the compiler to give an error message.

```
class Rect extends Shape {
    public int m_x, m_y, m_width, m_height;

    public Rect( ) {
        m_x = m_y = m_width = m_height = 0;
    }

    public double getArea( ) {
        return (m_width * m_height);
    }

}

class Parallelogram extends Shape {
    public Point m_vertex1, m_vertex2, m_vertex3, m_vertex4;

    public Parallelogram( ) {
        m_vertex1 = new Point( );
        m_vertex2 = new Point( );
        m_vertex3 = new Point( );
        m_vertex4 = new Point( );
    }
    public double getArea( ) {
        return (<calculate area of parallelogram here>);
```

The Java Language

```
    }

class MyProgram {
    public static void main(String astrArgs[]) {
        Rect r = new Rect( );
        r = new Parallelogram( );   /* Illegal! Can't cast to
                                     * unrelated class. */
    }
}
```

When casting between objects, the rules for legal casts are 1) you may implicitly cast if the object is being cast to a base class, and 2) you may explicitly cast if the object is being cast to a derived class.

An implicit cast is one such as

```
Shape s = new Rect( );
```

in which you simply assign a variable of a base class type to a reference of an object of a derived type. An explicit cast requires you to specify that you know a cast is going on. An explicit cast looks like the third line in this code segment:

```
Rect r = new Rect( );
Shape s = new Rect( );
r = (Rect)s;
```

You can see that a Rect is being assigned a reference from a shape variable. Since the variable *s* is a shape variable, an explicit cast is necessary to assign the Rect *r* a reference from *s*. An implicit cast will never cause a problem. An explicit cast may still be illegal, as demonstrated by this code segment:

```
Rect r;
Shape s = new Parallelogram( );   // OK. Parallelogram is derived from Shape
r = (Rect)s;                      /* Illegal! Ends up casting a Parallelogram
                                   * to Rect, which is not legal. */
```

This would not cause compiler error. Instead, at run-time the JVM will recognize the erroneous cast and immediately throw a ClassCastException. (Exceptions and exception handling are described in another section of this chapter.)

Casting Between Built-In Types

When casting between built-in types, there are also rules. Implicit casts are allowed if there is no *loss of precision*. That is, you may cast an int value to a double, since the double variable is more precise than the int. There will be no loss of information.

However, when casting from, say, double to int, you must perform an explicit cast. This indicates to the compiler that you are aware of the potential loss of information. (Since the double may have a fractional component, and the int variable will lose that fraction, then there is loss of precision.)

You may only cast between numeric built-in types. You may not cast from a numeric to a boolean, for instance. Unlike C/C++, the boolean type is completely differentiated from the numeric types. There is no conversion between the two. Neither may you cast from a char to a numeric value. Casting between any of these types is allowed as long as you follow the loss of precision rule for when to perform an explicit cast: byte, short, int, float, and double.

Run-Time Type Identification

The Java language has run-time type identification, unlike some implementations of C++. This allows you to discover an object's class given only a reference to the object. The *instanceof* operator is a boolean operator that tells you whether or not an object is a given type:

```
Shape s = new Rect( );
Shape s2 = new Parallelogram( );

if(s instanceof Rect) {        // true, object refed by s is a Rect
    // do something...
}

if(s instanceof Shape) {       // true, since Rects are Shapes
    // do something...
}

if(s2 instanceof Rect) {       // false, Parallelograms not Rects
    // do something
}
```

As this example demonstrates, the *instanceof* operator returns true if the referenced object's class is the same as, or is derived from, the class indicated by the second operand. Another way to think of this is that it returns true if the object could legally be cast to the indicated class.

Interfaces

Interfaces are a concept that Java borrows from the Objective-C language, and is foreign to C/C++. If you are familiar with OLE/COM, you will recognize the interface concept immediately, as the Java version is almost precisely the same.

An interface is basically a list of abstract method declarations. Since there are no implementations of abstract methods, an interface alone doesn't do much. This is an example interface declaration for a simple Advisable interface:

```
interface Advisable {
    public void advise(Object obj);
}
```

A Java interface is the same thing as a C++ pure virtual base class. That is, it is just a list of method signatures with no implementation attached. The previous example defines an interface with two member methods.

The *implements* keyword is used in a Java class declaration to indicate that a particular Java class implements all the methods of a particular Java interface, as in this example:

```
class Advisee implements Advisable {
    public void advise(Object obj) {
        System.out.println("Advisee advised about " + obj);
    }
}
```

The neat thing about interfaces is that they are allowable types in Java. You can declare variables of an interface type and cast objects to interface types. It is through interfaces that you can achieve something like C++'s multiple inheritance. You do this by declaring your class as implementing multiple interfaces. You can then cast objects of that class to any one of its interface types. This example demonstrates using interfaces:

```
interface Advisable {
    public void advise(Object obj);
}

interface WarmAdvisable extends Advisable {
    public void warmAdvise( );
}
```

```
interface Moveable {
    public void move(int x, int y);
}

class Thing implements WarmAdvisable, Moveable {
    private int m_x, m_y;


    public Thing( ) {
        m_x = m_y = 0;
    }

    // Methods of the WarmAdvisable interface
    public void advise(Object obj) {
        System.out.println("Thing advised about " + obj);
    }

    public void warmAdvise( ) {
        System.out.println("Thing given a warm advise.");

    }

    // Methods of the Moveable interface
    public void move(int x, int y) {
        m_x = x;
        m_y = y;
    }
}
```

And this class demonstrates how to cast an object to one of its interfaces:

```
class MyProgram {
    public static void MoveHalfwayTo(int x, int y, Moveable m) {
        /* m is an object that implements the Moveable interface,
         * so you are assured it implements a move( ) method. */
        m.move(x/2, y/2);
    }
}

    public static void AdviseAboutMove(int x, int y, Advisable a) {
        /* a is an object that implements the Advisable interface,
         * so you are assured it implements an advise( ) method. */
        a.advise(new Point(x, y));
    }

    public static void main(String astrArgs[]) {
        Thing = new Thing( );
        MoveHalfwayTo(10, 10, thing);    // casts thing to a Moveable
```

The Java Language

```
        AdviseAboutMove(5, 5, thing);    // casts thing to an Advisable
    }
}
```

As the previous example demonstrates, interface declarations look very similar to class declarations. Interfaces can be derived from other interfaces, just like WarmAdvisable extends from the Advisable interface. This means that WarmAdvisable declares everything the Advisable interface declares, plus some extra method declarations. Any class that implements WarmAdvisable also implements Advisable, demonstrated in the previous example by the fact that Thing objects can be cast to Advisable, even though the Thing class is declared as implementing WarmAdvisable.

In Microsoft's JVM, Java interfaces are used as the passageway between Java objects and COM objects. Using the Java/COM compiler, you can generate interfaces in Java that represent COM interfaces. By casting COM objects into these generated interfaces, you can call COM interface methods in Java! This makes for a very clean, extremely usable technique for communicating between Java and COM objects. Through appropriate interfaces, you could have your Java object control an Excel spreadsheet or Word document, which are implemented with COM interfaces. Alternatively, through appropriate COM interfaces you can control Java objects from your Visual Basic or C++ code. All of these communications are transparent; you never need deal with the underlying JVM or communications system.

You can see how in Java/COM communications alone, the interface concept is very important. Chapter 6 explains the techniques of Java/COM communications through interfaces in detail. In addition, using Java interfaces just within your own Java code can make for designs that are much simpler, and much easier to understand and program.

Packages

Java includes a system for arranging .CLASS files into associated groups, or *packages*, of classes. The *package* keyword indicates that a class belongs to a particular package. This has implications both for location of the .CLASS file on the local file system and for privileged access to copackage a class' member variables and methods.

To declare a class as part of a particular package, you use the *package* keyword, like this:

```
package com.osborne.VJ-Handbook;

class MyDemoClass {
   ...
}
```

which declares the MyDemoClass class as part of a package named "package.com.VJ-Handbook." So what? you say. Read on for an explanation of how packages are useful in Java.

A quick note: package names always take on the form <word>[.<word>][.<word>]..., as in the previous example. The individual words of package names should not have spaces or any character other than characters used for variable names.

.CLASS File Locations

A class' package name describes where the .CLASS file can be found. Each word in the package name is interpreted as a subdirectory name. Thus, the previous example defining the MyDemoClass class implies that the MyDemoClass.class file is found somewhere on the local file system in a subdirectory named com/osborne/VJ-Handbook. If the .CLASS file is not located in a subdirectory with this name, then the .CLASS file cannot be loaded by the JVM!

So, what is the root directory of the com/osborne/VJ-Handbook subdirectory? It can be any directory listed in your CLASSPATH environment variable. The CLASSPATH environment variable lists a set of root directories to be searched for .CLASS files. If the class being loaded is in a particular package, then the root directories are searched for a subdirectory of the appropriate name. The .CLASS file is expected to be in a subdirectory of the name indicated by the class' package name off of one of the root CLASSPATH directories. A common CLASSPATH value may look something like this:

```
set CLASSPATH=".;C:\Java\Classes;C:\Windows\java\classes"
```

which indicates that there are three root CLASSPATH directories: the current directory (indicated by "."), the directory C:\Java\Classes, and the directory C:\Windows\Java\Classes.

When accessing classes across the Internet (for example, you load an applet on a World Wide Web page) the package name is used as the base of a relative URL. For example, you look at a web page with an embedded applet at http://www.my.domain.com/java/demo/index.html. That applet refers to the MyDemoClass class. To load the MyDemoClass.class file, your web browser will automatically generate the URL http://www.my.domain.com/java/demo/com/osborne/VJ-Handbook/MyDemoClass.class, and it will try to load that file.

Copackage Access Privileges

Previously in this chapter, you read about the default access privileges for member variables and class methods. That is, the access restrictions applied to variables or methods that are not given either the *public*, *protected*, or *public* access specifier. For example, the *fFlag* member variable in this class has default access privileges:

```
package com.osborne.VJ-Handbook;

class Stuff {
    boolean fFlag;         // no access specifiers given.
    ...
}
```

The fFlag variable is given privileges called *private to package*. Only code that is part of classes within the package com.osborne.VJ-Handbook may directly access the fFlag variable of Stuff objects.

Default access privileges are similar to *friend* variables and functions in C++. They allow code in unrelated classes to access essentially private variables and methods. The C++ *friend* specifier similarly allows code not related by class hierarchy to access private or protected member variables or methods of C++ classes.

The Form of Java Programs

All Java program code is located within Java classes. That's it. Executable Java programs—applets, servelets, any kind of executable unit—are made up of one or more classes, defined for the JVM by an equal number of .CLASS files.

So, how do you write a Java program? In this case, it is best to start with an example. This will probably not be the last time in your life that you dissect yet another HelloWorld program. For those of you who have seen one too many HelloWorlds, here is a completely different introductory program called HelloUniverse. It is defined in a single source code file named HelloUniverse.java:

```
public class HelloUniverse {
    public static void main(String astrArgs[]) {
        System.out.println("Hello, Universe!");
    }
}
```

First, notice that this file declares a class named HelloUniverse. Remember, all Java executables consist of one or more classes. In this case, we have only a single class name, HelloUniverse.

The HelloUniverse class defines a single method called main( ). The only requirement of a Java program is a main( ) method declared as in this example. The main( ) method is the entry point of your program. When you run your program, it is this method that is invoked. If you were to diagram a Java program as a black box, its only external feature is a main( ) method declared as in the previous example.

It is not too much of a stretch to see that this single line of code writes the text "Hello, Universe!" to the Java program's standard output. There is a System class included as part of the Java run-time. One public static member of the System class is *out*, which is an output stream associated with the program's standard output stream. (In World Wide Web-based applets, the *System.out* output stream is associated with the Java Console of the web browser, if there is one.)

CHAPTER 2

The Visual J++ Environment

The Visual J++ integrated development environment (IDE) is the most advanced, up-to-date, and state-of-the-art development system for Java in existence. The features and capabilities of this IDE far outshine the competing products, such as Symantec's Café. By using VJ++, you will have a distinct advantage over your competition.

There are two distinct reasons for the advantage you will have using Visual J++ versus using other development environments and other languages. First, there's all the advantages Java itself has over other languages. It's platform-independent, so you can develop for multiple platforms at the same time. It's interpreted, so you never have to recompile your code for alternative platforms. And because it's interpreted, while your compiled code may not run today on some of the more exotic operating systems, as soon as a Java virtual machine (JVM) is developed in software for those systems (and rest assured there are legions of programmers porting the JVM to various new platforms even as you read this) your compiled code will run on them. No recompilation needed. Java is object-oriented. The benefits of object-oriented programming—which, when used correctly, decrease almost all phases of software development from initial design through legacy system maintenance—completely blows away non-object-oriented languages. Not to mention that Java is the de facto standard for Web-based programming even at this early stage of its release into the real world. Tons of professional developers and students of computer science, just like yourself, are tooling up with Java. The platform-independent virtues of the language virtually guarantee this fact.

In addition to the advantages Java itself brings to the table, Visual J++ adds a whole lot more. The sheer volume of online documentation included with the VJ++ package is almost overwhelming. Microsoft has put together thousands of pages of online documentation and linked them to the Visual J++ development environment. Context-sensitive language help is just a short keystroke away. Microsoft has also added something to the JVM: the power of OLE/COM technology. Using Java code, you can create your own COM objects, or you can instantiate and communicate with other COM object classes created by third parties. This Java/COM capability is actually easier in Java than in any other commercially standard language to date! Easier than C++ to use and more versatile than Visual Basic. The best of both worlds, and you can really only get it with Visual J++.

Visual J++'s built-in ResourceWizard can automatically generate user interface components for you, saving lots of time. VJ++'s AppletWizard generates applet code skeletons with helpful comments, taking away the more tedious aspects of applet development. This both removes the possibility of costly mistakes when initially creating applets and saves time.

Visual J++ also has all the features you would expect in an integrated development environment (IDE), that are mentioned here, though you should be more surprised not to see these features than to see them. Java has an integrated, visual Java debugger that works equally well debugging Java applications as applets. VJ++ has a built-in Project Manager to make working with large and complex projects so much easier. The Project Manager can also be easily integrated with source control programs, such as Microsoft's

The Visual J++ Environment

Visual SourceSafe, to make working in teams where source code control is an issue not only doable, but downright easy.

All of the features of Visual J++ mentioned above are covered in this chapter. First you will explore the Visual J++ CD, which includes directions on installing VJ++ on your system. Next, using VJ++'s InfoViewer you can get an overview of the tons of documentation included with Visual J++, which should help you find that crucial piece of information faster. After that, you will start working with projects by loading and compiling the sample Java applets and applications included with the VJ++ CD. You will then see how to debug your applets and applications. Finally, the VJ++ AppletWizard and ResourceWizard are introduced.

Exploring the Visual J++ CD

The Visual J++ CD has an autoloading program on it. So, when you place the CD into your CD-ROM drive on a Windows 95 or Windows NT machine, the CD's auto-starting program will begin immediately. Figure 2-1 shows what the auto-start program looks like when it is first launched.

The five lines of text to the right on this screen are *hyperlinks*. For example, click on the "Install Visual J++ 1.0" text to begin installing Visual J++.

Installing Visual J++

When you click on the "Installing Visual J++ 1.0" hyperlink from the Visual J++ CD's startup screen, the Visual J++ installation process will begin.

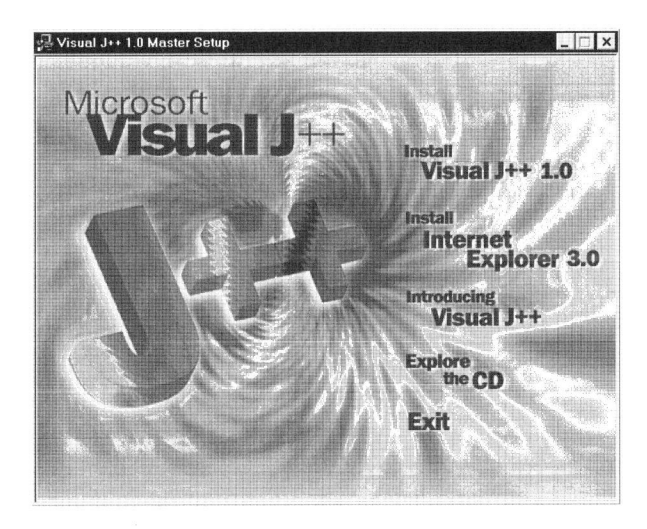

The Startup Screen of the Visual J++ CD
Figure 2-1.

Installing Visual J++ is a painless process, in which you are guided through a sequence of several dialogs. Figure 2-2 is a screen shot of the first dialog that will appear.

All of the installation dialogs have a wizard-like set of navigation buttons, which you can see at the bottom of the dialog in Figure 2-2. Hit the Next button to go to the next dialog on the installation sequence, and hit the Back button to return to the previous dialog. At any point you can return to a previous dialog and change any option you selected.

After you hit the Next button, Visual J++ displays its license agreement. You should read this agreement and make sure you can comply with it. Hit the Yes button to proceed to the next step in Visual J++'s installation.

In the next step, you type in your name and organization. This information is used for registration purposes. Once you fill in this dialog and install Visual J++, the software is licensed to *you*. Figure 2-3 is a screen shot of the Registration dialog you see at this step. Fill in your name, and your organization (the organization field is optional). Fill in the CD-key number located on the back of the Visual J++ CD jewel box (the little plastic case the CD came in). Without this CD-key, the installation process will not proceed.

Once you have filled in these fields, hit the Next button to proceed. If you typed in the CD-key wrong, or you left out a name in the Name field, then Visual J++ will tell you to fill in these fields again before it can proceed.

The next screen asks you basically what parts of Visual J++ you want installed on your system. You have four options. Figure 2-4 shows what this dialog looks like. The Typical installation option will load Microsoft's Developer Studio, Visual J++'s on-line documentation, and a few additional utilities that might make your life easier in the future (such as a File

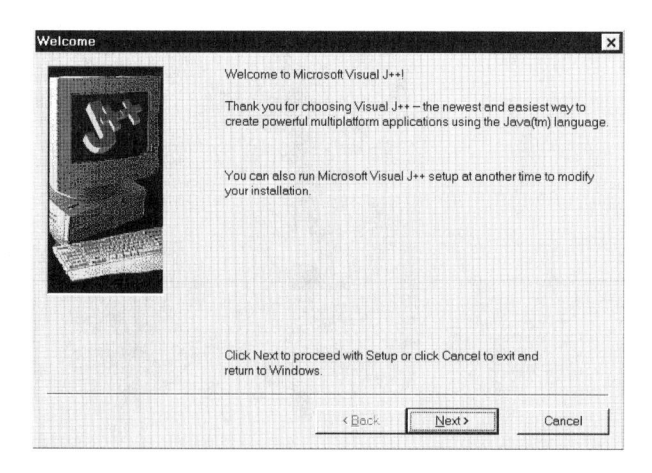

The first Visual J++ Installation Dialog
Figure 2-2.

The Visual J++ Environment

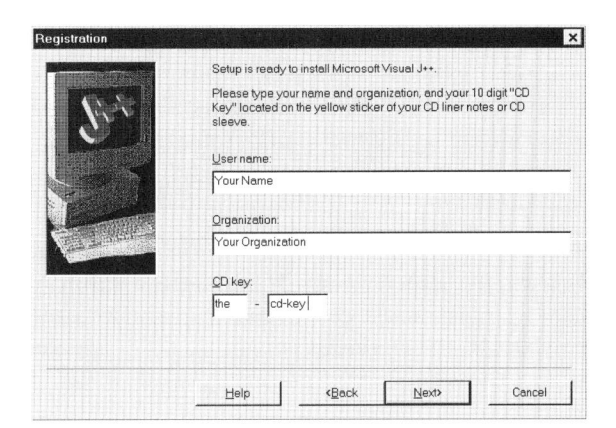

The Registration screen
Figure 2-3.

Compare program). With the typical installation, everything you need to begin Visual J++ development in Java will be copied to your hard drive.

The Minimum installation option just installs the Developer Studio and Microsoft's compiler. The on-line books will be access from your CD drive in the future. That is, you'll have to put the Visual J++ CD into your drive to look at Visual J++'s extensive on-line documentation. This option saves disk space, but means you have to use the CD to access any of the Java information included on the CD.

The CD-ROM installation option only installs the Developer Studio on your hard drive. The compiler, debugger, and any on-line documentation must be run from the CD-ROM drive. This is a good option if you have limited drive space, for example if you are installing Visual J++ on a small laptop computer.

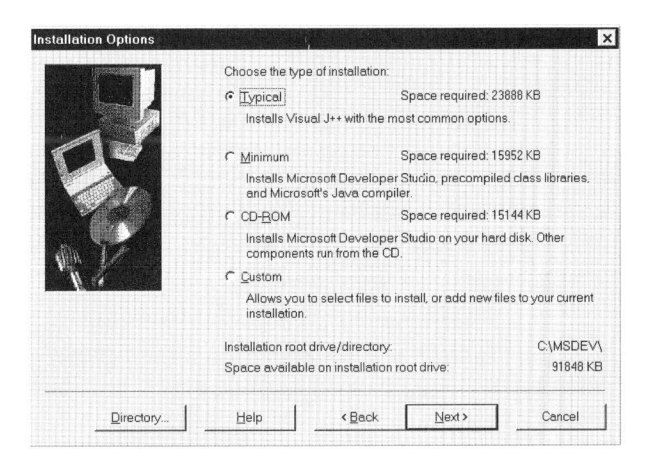

The Visual J++ Installation Options Dialog
Figure 2-4.

Finally, the Custom option allows you to select which parts of Visual J++ you want to install on your hard drive. Using the Custom option, you can install more or less than the Typical installation option will install. For example, you can make the installation program install the DAO components, which are needed to use the Data Access Objects capabilities of Visual J++. (DAO and database connectivity are topics covered in Chapter 7.)

After you press the Next button on the Installation Options dialog, Visual J++ will list exactly what it plans to install to your system in a confirmation dialog. This allows you to back-up and change the option in case you made a mistake in the previous screen(s). If you're confident of the choices you made, press the Next button.

At this point, the installation process must first install Microsoft's Internet Explorer from the Visual J++ CD. The Internet Explorer is used to show and debug Applets in Visual J++, so you cannot skip this step. A small dialog will appear telling you the Internet Explorer is about to be installed; press the Install button on this dialog:

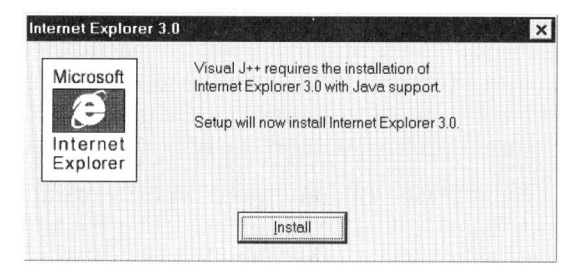

The installation program will install the Internet Explorer, and continue to install all the Visual J++ parts you specified in the Installation Options dialog. Once that is done, Visual J++ will allow you to register your copy of Visual J++ via modem immediately. You can follow the steps of the On-line Registration Wizard only if you have a modem connected to your machine. An Internet connection will not do. You need a modem connected to your machine to complete on-line registration. Luckily, you don't have to do on-line registration to use Visual J++. If you opt not to register your copy of Visual J++ on-line, remember to send off the registration card included with Visual J++. Until you register your copy of Visual J++, you can't receive any telephone support for the product (unless you call the phone support number and ask really nicely, in which case they'll probably help you anyway).

You must reboot your machine before you can use Visual J++. After your machine reboots, you will notice a new group in your desktop's startup menu: the Microsoft Visual J++ 1.0 group.

The Visual J++ Environment

Other CD Options

There are three other hyperlink options from the Visual J++ CD's autostarting screen. The Installing Internet Explorer 3.0 option will just install Microsoft's Internet Explorer. Remember that the Internet Explorer is also installed to your system as part of installing Visual J++ itself. This option is included so that you can install the Internet Explorer on alternative machines, other than your primary Java development system. The Visual J++ license agreement states that you can't install Visual J++ on more than one system at a time, but you can install the Internet Explorer on as many systems as you want legally.

The Introducing Visual J++ hyperlink will display some HTML documents about Visual J++ using your current web browser. You should take a look at these HTML documents, because they include last minute and other nifty information about Visual J++. For example, under the Other Topics of Interest links are some documents explaining the Liquid Reality and other third-party packages bundled on your Visual J++ CD. These additional packages include wizards for making some pretty cool applets without having to write a line of Java code!

The Explore the CD option will show you the actual contents of the CD. Through this option, you can install the additional third-party Java packages bundled with Visual J++, and the CAB and Code & Sign development kits off the Visual J++ CD. (CAB files and code signing are used to create "trusted" applets in Java. Chapter 6 explains what these things are, and how to use these two development kits for creating trusted applets in Java.)

Introduction to the Visual J++ Interface

Figure 2-5 is what Visual J++ looks like when you first start it up, with different parts of the UI labeled. The following explanation lists what each of these parts is used for.

- **Tip of the Day** This friendly dialog box pops up whenever you start Visual J++. It displays some quasi-interesting fact about Visual J++ that you may not know, or quickly describes some feature you may not have had the opportunity to explore yet. Unless it truly annoys you, while you are getting used to Visual J++ and the Microsoft Developer's Studio you should consider allowing this tip box to pop up when you start VJ++. If you take the time to actually read the tips, you will find yourself saying, "Uh! I didn't know I could do that!" more often than not. To disable the Tip of the Day, turn off the Show Tips at Startup checkbox in the lower-left corner of the Tip of the Day dialog.

- **InfoViewer toolbar** The InfoViewer toolbar is used to control the InfoViewer, which is the large pane on the right side of Figure 2-5, behind the Top of the Day dialog. The InfoViewer is very much like a web-browser for the Visual J++ online documentation, and the InfoViewer toolbar is its control pad. Through the toolbar you have access to the InfoViewer's search and bookmark lists, and if you hit the Home button (the button with the little picture of the house on it, appropriately enough), then the InfoViewer will display Visual J++'s online title page.

- **Output pane** The Output pane displays the program output from various parts of Visual J++. At the bottom of the pane are the five tabs used to separate the different types of output. The Build tab displays the compiler's output messages, including warnings and errors. The Debug tab displays debug output. The Debug Output tab is not to be confused with the Debug toolbar (shown later) used to control the debugger. The Find in File tab displays results from multifile text searches through your projects. The Java Type Library Wizard tab displays output from the Java Type Library Wizard. This Wizard is used to generate stub classes for using COM objects from within Java code. The Profile tab displays output from the Java profiler. The profiler is used while your program or applet is running to see how much time your program is spending in different methods of your Java classes. This information is quite useful when you are trying to optimize your code.

- **Standard toolbar** The Standard toolbar provides buttons to perform common operations: New file, Save file, Cut/Copy/Paste, Undo/Redo, Search, etc.

Project Toolbar

The Project toolbar includes buttons for performing common operations on your projects. This includes compiling individual files, rebuilding all your classes, starting a debug session, etc.

Using Toolbars

In addition to the toolbars listed above, there are several more toolbars available in Visual J++. In general, toolbars are provided to give you a faster way to perform common operations than by using the Main menu. Most toolbar buttons have a direct equivalent menu item. For example, the New Text File button on the Standard toolbar does the same thing as the File/New menu option when you select New Text File. The Project toolbar's Rebuild button does the same thing as the Build/Rebuild Main menu option.

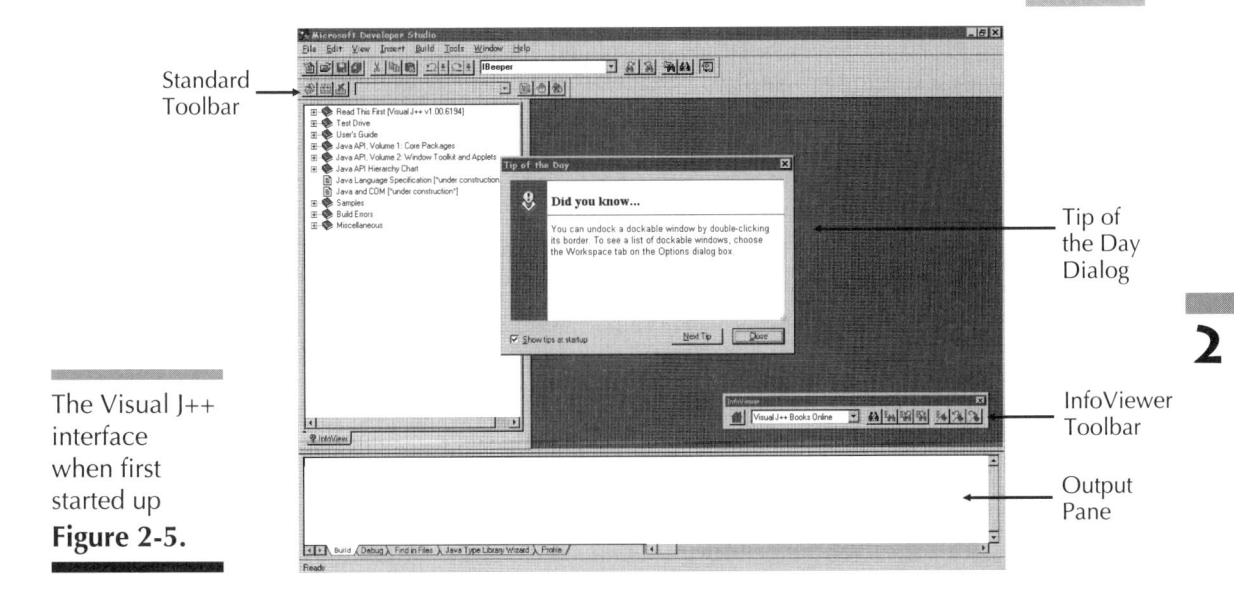

The Visual J++ Environment

Figure 2-5. The Visual J++ interface when first started up

Callouts: Standard Toolbar; Tip of the Day Dialog; InfoViewer Toolbar; Output Pane

All of Visual J++'s toolbars are *dockable*. That means you can move them around to different places in the IDE. The whole point of a toolbar is to make performing certain operations faster. If you can perform them fastest by having the toolbar located on the bottom of your screen as opposed to the top, then by all means simply click and drag the appropriate toolbar to the bottom of the screen. You will see the toolbar remove itself from its original location and reappear wherever you dragged it. Similarly, the various windows in the IDE are also dockable. For example, the InfoViewer pane can be moved from the left side of VJ++'s main window (its default location) onto the right side just by clicking and dragging the window to the left side. The Output window too can be dragged from the bottom of the screen to the top, or to any one of the four edges of the main window.

Dockable elements can also become floating windows. The picture of the initial VJ++ interface from Figure 2-5 shows the InfoViewer toolbar as a floating window. Try dragging this window against any of the four edges of the interface and it'll "dock" itself against the edge. The windows, such as the InfoViewer or Output window, can also be made into free-floating windows.

The Rest of the Visual J++ Toolbars

Here's a list and a short summary of the other toolbars available in the Visual J++ interface:

♦ **The Resource toolbar** The Resource toolbar has buttons for creating new resources of all types. Actually, the resource editor that comes with

Visual J++ is just the resource editor included with Microsoft's Developer's Studio. That is, it's the same resource editor that comes with Visual C++, so you'll see that the toolbar allows you to create all the same types of resources. Unfortunately, you can't actually use most of them in Java, at least not with the first version of Visual J++. The only resources you can really use are the Dialog and Menu resources, which VJ++'s ResourceWizard can turn into Java classes for you.

- **The Edit toolbar** The Edit toolbar includes commands for working with your source code. Commands include operations for working with a source file's bookmark list. (Yes, you can bookmark individual lines in Visual J++, which makes it much easier to jump between different sections of code than by using the scroll bar over and over.) It is through this toolbar that you can invoke the Find in Files command, which is also available under the File menu. Some buttons are also included in this toolbar so you can split, rejoin, tile, or cascade source code windows.

- **The Debug toolbar** The Debug toolbar includes buttons for the most common debugging operations. These operations will be covered in detail in another section of this chapter, the section on debugging using Visual J++. Such operations include start/stop debugging, step in/over/out of/ up to, quick-watch, as well as buttons for hiding or displaying all the various debugging windows: call stack, breakpoints, locals, variables, disassembly, etc.

- **The Browse toolbar** The Browse toolbar controls Visual J++'s integrated program database. Through it, you can jump to different files within your code. For example, you find a reference in one of your classes to another class' static variable *m_hash*, but you don't know the type of that variable. The browser database lets you highlight the variable and jump to the variable's definition. (That's the Goto Definition button on the Browse toolbar.) You can find any reference to or definition of any class' variable or method through the Browse toolbar.

As stated before, all the buttons on the various toolbars are just faster ways for completing commands available under the Main menu. You will probably find that even when starting to use Visual J++ it will be easier and more intuitive to use the toolbar than using the Main menu. You will find that you will resort to using the Main menu only for finding the most obscure or infrequently used commands. And, of course, once you become a Visual J++ master, you will use keyboard shortcuts since these are generally faster than using either the toolbars or the Main menu.

Customizing and Creating Toolbars

To make the toolbars potentially even more useful, they are completely customizable. You can remove the buttons you don't use from any of the toolbars, or add buttons you would like to be included to any of the toolbars. Check out the Toolbar tab of the Customize dialog, located by selecting the Main menu option Tools/Customize. Drag and drop items from this tab onto the appropriate toolbar to add new buttons, or drag the buttons from the toolbar to the Toolbars tab to remove them.

One more toolbar trick: you can actually create your own toolbars. These could include either any of the commands available in Visual J++ or invocations of your own programs. That is, if you had a Java decompiler and a few other utilities you use often, and you wanted a toolbar to make them more accessible, you could create a dockable one. The View/Toolbars Main menu option brings up the Toolbars dialog. The New button on this toolbar will allow you to create toolbars. The Tools tab of the Customize dialog (available through the Main menu's Tools/Customize option) allows you to make new VJ++ commands. These commands actually invoke programs external to VJ++.

By creating new tools, and adding buttons for them to dockable toolbars that you create, you can make a Java development environment that is highly tuned to you. It can provide the fastest access to the tools and commands you use most often.

The InfoViewer Window

The Visual J++ InfoViewer is the fancy name for the part of Visual J++ that lets you browse through all the online documentation included with the development environment. You can think of the InfoViewer as a specialized web-like browser dedicated to VJ++ documentation. Really, the InfoViewer is pretty much the same thing as a web browser, except that instead of getting the information from the World Wide Web, it gets it from the Visual J++ CD. The InfoViewer presents that online documentation as a hyperlinked set of pages, organized in a hierarchy of subject matter. Figure 2-6 shows the Visual J++ InfoViewer's top-level table of contents.

The topics included in the documentation are arranged hierarchically. Figure 2-6 shows the main subject areas, which have been arranged from top to bottom in the order a new user of VJ++ like yourself is likely to use them. When you double-click with your mouse on any of the top-level

The Visual J++ Handbook

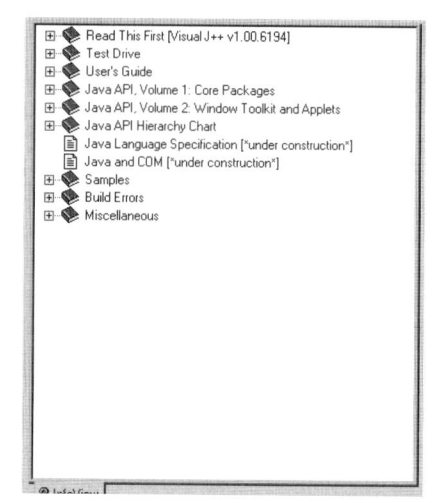

**The InfoViewer's table of contents
Figure 2-6.**

topics, the topic expands to show you the subtopics, which further expand as you click on them until you come to a page of documentation. Figure 2-7 is a screen shot of the entire VJ++ interface after a particular document is opened. Note the hierarchy of topics on the left pane of the screen, called the InfoViewer pane.

Getting to the InfoViewer is easy. Whenever Visual J++ is running, and you don't have a project opened up, then the InfoViewer pane is automatically

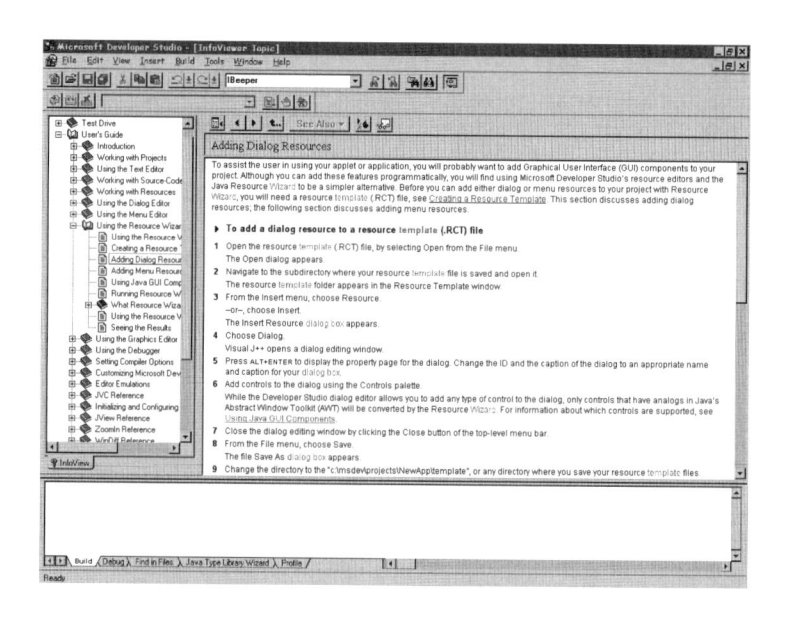

**A document opened up in the InfoViewer
Figure 2-7.**

The Visual J++ Environment

displayed on the left side of your screen (that is, unless you move it). See, the InfoViewer pane is a *dockable* window (indeed, all panes in Visual J++ are dockable windows). That means you can move them around your screen to wherever you like them best. Try starting up Visual J++, left-clicking on the InfoViewer pane and dragging it around your screen. You'll see that if you drag it near the bottom of your screen and let go, it automatically becomes like a status bar aligned across the bottom of VJ++'s main window. If you drag it toward the top of your screen it becomes like a toolbar. If you drag it to the middle of your screen it becomes a floating window over the VJ++ main window.

InfoViewer Navigation

There are four different ways of navigating through the online documentation using the InfoViewer: through the table of contents, through interdocument hyperlinks, by searching, and by using bookmarks. You can, as already discussed, trace through the InfoViewer's table of contents to find a document.

You can follow hyperlinks within online documents. Hyperlinks "jump" between related topics within the online documentation. Hyperlinks appear as underlined green text within an InfoViewer topic. Click on the green text to jump to the related topic. The InfoViewer also has another type of hyperlink. Text appearing in light gray will automatically bring up a term definition. Figure 2-8 is a screen shot of an InfoViewer topic with underlined hyperlinks and with light-gray definition links. The floating window next to the InfoViewer document is an example of a definition. A definition window is what pops up when you click on a light-gray piece of text.

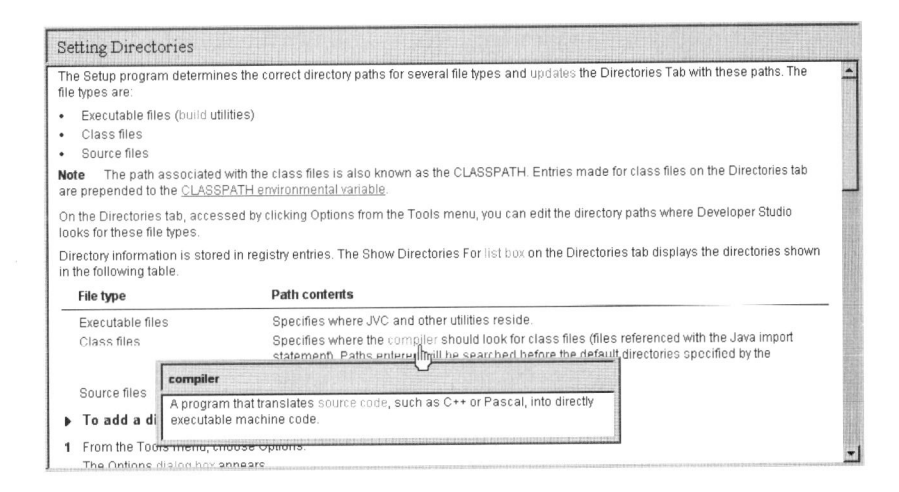

InfoViewer hyperlinks and definition links
Figure 2-8.

To search through the online documentation of a keyword, choose the Main menu's Help/Search... option. This will bring up the Search document, which is shown here:

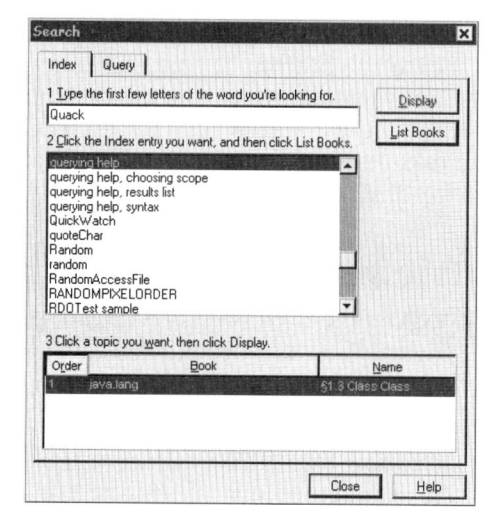

The InfoViewer toolbar's Search button will also bring up the same dialog. The hot key CTRL-F will also bring up this same dialog.

In the same way that you can bookmark your favorite World Wide Web sites in most web browsers, you can also bookmark topics in the InfoViewer. The InfoViewer keeps an internal list of bookmarks that you configure. This list is independent of project or current session, so your list is saved no matter what you are doing in Visual J++. Click on the InfoViewer toolbar's Bookmark button to bring up the current list of bookmarks. If you do this while you are viewing a topic you want to create a bookmark for, then simply press the InfoViewer Bookmark dialog's Add button to add a bookmark for the current document. Alternatively, you can right-click on the document and choose the Add Bookmark option.

To navigate through your list of bookmarks, use the same InfoViewer Bookmarks button, shown here in the margin. The full list of InfoViewer bookmarks will appear. By double-clicking on any of them, the InfoViewer will instantly open up the bookmarked document. You should bookmark documents you find interesting or find yourself frequently referring to.

Projects

A VJ++ project is a collection of source code and resources that are grouped together. A single project includes all the files necessary to develop a Java applet or application. This includes source files, resource files (such as dialog templates, menu templates, etc.), and a program database. The program database stores lots of useful information to make navigating through your code using the editor much faster: for example, navigating to where certain methods and variables are declared, and viewing the relationships between your Java classes. A single Java project can actually include subprojects. Thus you can break down larger projects into smaller and smaller ones, making each easier to develop. A project also includes a set of configurations that tell the VJ++ compiler and debugger how you want your classes created or debugged.

The Visual J++ project window displays the classes, files, and subprojects that make up a project. The project window displays what is called a Project Workspace. That is how you will see it referred to in the Visual J++ interface. For example, the File menu includes two commands called Open Workspace and Close Workspace, which mean the same thing as Open Project and Close Current Project. The Visual J++ developers thought the word "Workspace" was less intimidating than "Project." The word Workspace is reused in other contexts, even within Visual J++, however. For example, one important class in the Data Access Objects set of classes is a "Workspace". To avoid confusion, this book will use the word *project* interchangeably with Project Workspace.

Here's the time where you will create your first Java project. This book will save you the tedium of typing in a sample project by reusing one of the sample projects from the Visual J++ online documentation. Follow these steps to create your first Java project:

1. Open up Visual J++ so the InfoViewer window is displayed with the main table of contents. Open up the Samples topic, then open up the Sun Samples subtopic.
2. Double-click on the TicTacToe: A Simple TicTacToe Program document. This will automatically open up the InfoViewer to a document describing this sample applet provided by Sun.
3. You should now see a pushbutton in the upper-left corner of the document window with the caption "Click to open or copy the TicTacToe project files." Press that button.
4. A Sample Application dialog will open with a list of files. The samples all include the project description files, which would automatically make a project for you. Since you want to create your own project, highlight all the files except TICTACTOE.MDP and TICTACTOE.MAK. To select a range of files in this list box, hold the SHIFT key down while first clicking on the first file and then the last file in the range you want to copy. You can alternatively hold down the CTRL key while clicking with the mouse on each file you want to copy. Each file you click on

this way will remain highlighted as you click on other file names too. With example projects you copy from the Samples section of Visual J++'s InfoViewer later, you will want to copy all of the files (it would save you several of the remaining steps here), but for now just humor yourself by not getting these two files. After you select the files you want, press the Copy button.

5. Another dialog will appear asking you where you want the files created, and suggesting a directory under MSDEV\SAMPLES\SUN\TICTACTOE. Press OK to download the files to this directory, or select a new directory if you want. The downloader is capable of creating new directories of arbitrary depth, so type in any crazy directory you want here. Then press OK.

6. If the directory you choose does not exist yet, Visual J++ will ask you if you want it created at this point. Just press OK.

7. At this point, the TicTacToe sample applet files have been copied to your disk. Press the Close button to dismiss the Sample Application dialog box. Now that you have the source files, you just need to create a Visual J++ project (or Project Workspace) for the applet. From the Main menu, choose the File/New option. A dialog will appear asking you what type of new element you want to create. Select Java Workspace and click OK.

8. The New Project Workspace dialog will appear. Into the Name box, put TicTacToe. Into the Location box enter the parent directory of the directory where you loaded your files. That is, if you loaded the files to MSDEV\SAMPLES\SUN\TICTACTOE, then put MSDEV\SAMPLES\SUN into the Location box. If you press the Browse button next to the Location edit box, you can navigate to the desired folder using the mouse rather than typing in the full path name via the keyboard. Press Create.

9. Your project has been created and opened. This is indicated by the project window being shown where the InfoViewer table of contents was just a second ago. Figure 2-9 is a screen shot of roughly what you should be seeing at this point. You can read about the project window and how to use it in a minute. For now, follow the rest of these steps.

10. Your project exists, but you haven't added the project files to it yet. To do that, choose the Inset/Files Into Project Main menu option. A dialog should appear showing the contents of the directory where you loaded the TicTacToe files. You only need to select the file TicTacToe.java and press OK, since that file includes all the source code for the program.

That's it! You've just finished creating your first Java project. To satisfy curiosity, try building and running the TicTacToe applet. From the Build

The Visual J++ Environment

Right after TicTacToe is built
Figure 2-9.

menu, choose Rebuild All. Immediately you will see the compiler placing output in the output window's Build tab. After a few seconds, you should see the line "TicTacToe - 0 error(s), 0 warning(s)" appear in the output window, indicating the project has been completely built and is ready to run. Then run the applet by choosing the Build|Execute Main menu option (or pressing CTRL-F5).

At this point, a dialog reading Information for Running Class will appear. This is a one-time dialog asking how Visual J++ should run your project. At this point, VJ++ doesn't know if your project is for an applet or an application, or which class the applet or application class is to run. In the Class File Name box, type **TicTacToe.class**, then press OK. You should now see Microsoft's Internet Explorer running with the TicTacToe applet, as shown in Figure 2-10. Play around for a bit if you want.

ClassView

The project window uses a ClassView to display the classes included within your Java project. The ClassView is available under the Class tab in the project window. That's the left-most tab on the lower end of the project window.

The ClassView presents the classes of your project in a hierarchical manner. Under the root item of the project, which is labeled with the project name, is a list of the various classes within the project. For example, in the TicTacToe project there is a single class listed. It's called TicTacToe, of course. In

The Visual J++ Handbook

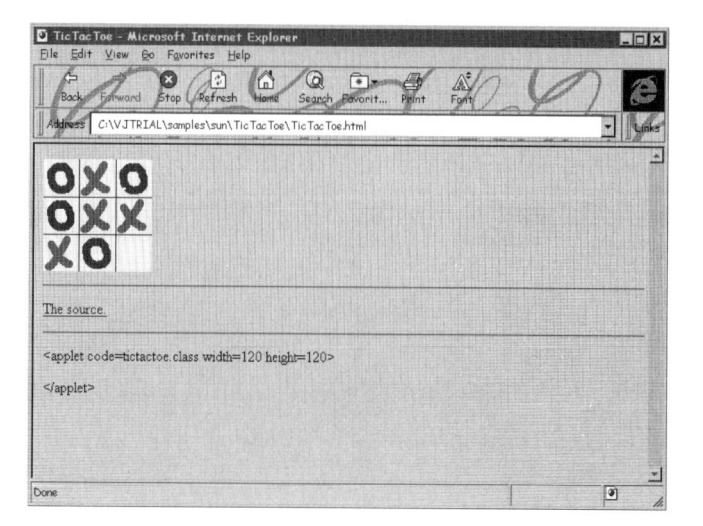

The TicTacToe sample applet
Figure 2-10.

projects with multiple classes, which you will see in other examples in this chapter, all of the project classes defined in any of the files added to the project are listed as separate items under the root node in the ClassView.

Under each class' entry in the ClassView is a listing of the various methods and variables defined within the class. Figure 2-11 is a screen shot of the ClassView of the TicTacToe sample applet fully expanded.

Here's a quick explanation of the symbols used to denote class methods and variables. Methods are denoted by a small red cube (actually, more like chartreuse), and variables by a blue cube (or perhaps more like turquoise).

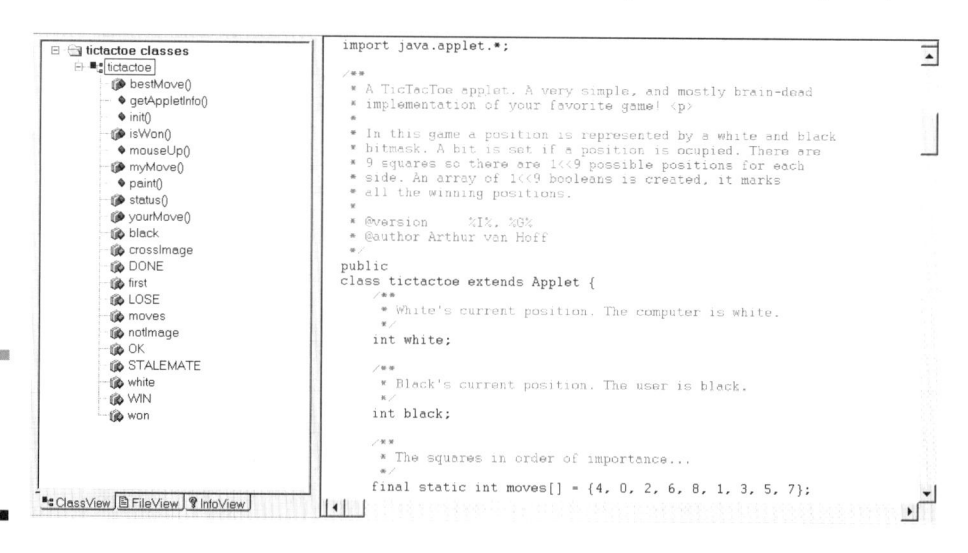

ClassView of the TicTacToe project
Figure 2-11.

Methods or variables with no access modifiers (which means they have default access) have a box behind the cube. The logic behind the "box" icon is to indicate that the member's scope includes the package in which the member exists (it's a wrapped box, like a holiday package). The protected members have the package plus a key for their icon; this indicates that the scope of a protected member is the entire package in which the member is defined, plus any classes derived from the class in which the member is defined. The private members have a padlock only, since the scope is restricted to the class in which the member is defined. Since the TicTacToe class has no private or protected methods or variables (all the ones with no access modifiers have default or *private to package* access protection), you won't see any of these symbols without changing the project a little.

In ClassView, you can double-click on any of the method or variable names in the ClassView and Visual J++ will jump to the method or variables declaration in the source code. From the ClassView, you can also add new variables or methods to a class. Do this by right-clicking on the class name and selecting the Add Method or Add Variable option. In either case, a handle dialog appears asking you for the particulars about your method or variable. For example, if you choose the Add Method option, the Add Method dialog appears. This dialog asks you for the new method's return type, declaration, or signature (the method name followed by the parameters in parentheses), and the various specifiers you want added to the class. After filling this dialog out and pressing OK, Visual J++ automatically adds the declaration to your source file and opens that file. The editor's cursor is positioned so that you can immediately begin typing the body of the method. Using Add Method and Add Variable saves a few keystrokes and some time for you, so go ahead and get used to using them.

You can also create new classes for your project from the ClassView tab. Right-click on the project root node and choose the Create New Class option. The Create New Class dialog appears, asking you for the new class' name, base class, and flags. Note that you cannot define which interfaces you want your class to implement. You'll have to directly edit the source code to do that.

Once created, Visual J++ automatically opens a new file for you with the appropriate name and adds the new class to your project. The class' declaration is automatically added to the new file, and you can start defining the class' methods and variables immediately. Note that in addition to adding any interfaces you want your class to implement to the class declaration, you will probably also have to modify or add to the imports statements at the beginning of the Visual J++-generated file. That's because Visual J++ only adds an imports statement for the base class of your class.

If you add a Frame-derived class, that means your imports statement will look like

```
imports java.awt.Frame;
```

Usually, you will want to change this imports statement to look like

```
imports java.awt.*;
```

and you may want to add more imports lines.

FileView

The project window can present your project in a file-centric manner, as opposed to the ClassView's class-centric display. The FileView tab is located next to the ClassView tab along the lower edge of the project window:

The FileView presents your project in a hierarchy, the same as the ClassView. The root node of the project is tagged with the project's name. Under this node is a list of the various files included in the project. Different types of files have different symbols next to the file names. Java source code files have a small document symbol with an arrow pointing down. The down arrow is supposed to look similar to the Compile button or the Go button on the Project toolbar, which also uses a down arrow to indicate action on source code or compiled bytecode. Shown here is the Project toolbar, with arrows pointing out from its Compile and Go buttons.

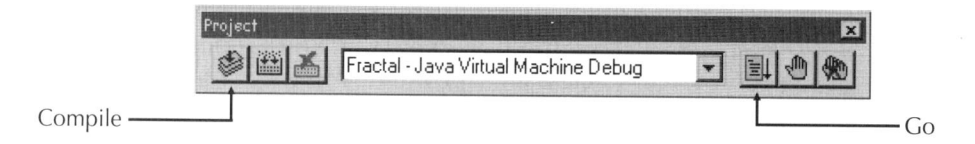

Compile ——— Go

The symbol used to indicate that a file is not a Java source code file is a document without the arrow.

The FileView is a bit less useful than the ClassView. Basically, from within the FileView you can open or compile any of the project files listed in the hierarchy. The FileView does not list any information about the contents of various project files, such as the classes defined within each file. The FileView only lists which files are part of the project. If you had added an

The Visual J++ Environment

HTML file to an applet project, then you could open that HTML file for editing quickly from the FileView. You couldn't do that from the ClassView since the HTML file does not define any classes that would be listed in the ClassView.

Say, for example, that you wanted to add the TicTacToe.html file to your project, which you may want to do if you had coordinating file archives such as is provided by Microsoft's SourceSafe. To do so, you would use the Main menu's Insert/|Files into Project Menu option, and select the file(s) you wanted to add to the project. If those files were Java source code files, then Visual J++ would automatically parse the files for class definitions and add the classes to the ClassView. The file will be added to the FileView regardless.

Building Projects

The buttons on the Project toolbar include most of the commands you will need at first for building and running your Java projects. To see a demonstration by example, you should now open another Sun Sample project from the Visual J++ InfoViewer. These steps will lead you through creating a new project for another sample project. After that, you will compile and run that project in Visual J++.

1. If you have it displayed, close the TicTacToe project from the previous section. Do this by choosing the File/Close Workspace option from the Main menu. Visual J++ may ask you if you want to also close all associated document windows (such as Java source code and HTML file windows). Press the Yes button to close those windows.

2. You will now have the InfoViewer again displayed. Open up the Samples subtopic from the main table of contents. Then open the Sun Sample subtopic. Then double-click on the node that is labeled "Fractal: A Fractal-drawing Program" (which is in fact not a program, but an applet).

3. The InfoViewer will display a page describing this sample project. Press the button to copy the project files.

4. This brings up the Sample Application dialog. Simply press the Copy All button on this dialog to copy all the files of the Fractals project, including the project definition files.

5. Another dialog will appear asking where you want the project files written to on your local disk. The suggested directory is MSDEV\SAMPLES\SUN\FRACTALS. Press OK unless you really want to load the files to another directory.

That's it. The project files have been written to your disk. There is no need to create a project, as the directions for loading the TicTacToe sample had you do. To open the Fractals project, use the File/Open Workspace Main menu option. A dialog will appear asking you for a directory and project file. Simply navigate to the directory where the project files were loaded and select the file named Fractals.

The ClassView of the Fractals project will appear in the project window. Believe it or not, the project is ready for compiling and running. (That's the great thing about prepackaged sample applications. I'm sure you wish all your professional projects were as easy to assemble!) From the Project toolbar, press the Build button. Shown below is the Project toolbar with this button labeled. This will cause the project to be built, compiling all classes defined in all files in the project into their respective .CLASS files. The compilation output will appear at the bottom of your screen in the output window, assuming you have not moved that window to another part of Visual J++'s interface. When the output window indicates that compilation is complete, then the project is ready to be run.

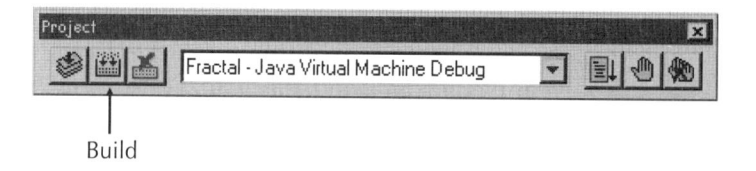

Build

From within Visual J++, there are two ways to run an application or applet. You can either run it in the debugger, or just run it without debugging using the standalone JVM (called the *Java interpreter* within Visual J++). The next section in this chapter discusses debugging in Visual J++; so, for now try just running the project using the standalone interpreter. To start the interpreter, either choose the Build/Execute option from the Main menu or press CTRL-F5. Note that there is no Execute button on the Project toolbar, though there is a Start Debugging ("Go") button. If you find yourself running the standalone interpreter a lot, you may want to add a button for it to the Project toolbar, which you can do using the instructions given previously in this chapter.

When you invoke the Fractals applet, Microsoft's Internet Explorer will automatically start up, running the Fractals applet (shown in Figure 2-12).

Debugging

The Visual J++ development environment includes an interactive debugger integrated with the interface. This debugger is pretty complete in its abilities, including single-step debugging, breakpoints, interactive variable

The Visual J++ Environment

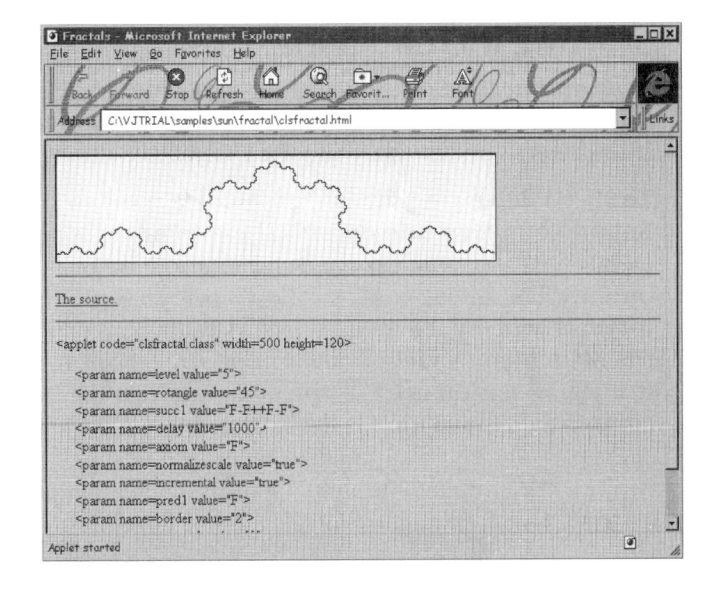

The Internet Explorer running the Fractals applet
Figure 2-12.

watching, multithreading, viewing the call stack, and a bytecode decompiler. This section discusses how to invoke and use all these aspects of the Visual J++ debugger.

You will use one of the Visual J++ sample applets in this section to explore the various debugger capabilities. The sample that will be used is Sun's JumpingBox example applet, an infuriating little game with not much purpose except to demonstrate mouse event handling in Java. Note that Chapter 3 discusses the AWT Component classes, details events, event handling, and the mouse.

To open the JumpingBox sample applet, open the Visual J++ InfoViewer and open the JumpingBox document under the Sun Samples topic, which is itself under the Samples topic in the main table of contents. Press the button in the InfoViewer for copying the JumpingBox project files and load the files into the suggested directory. Detailed instructions for copying and opening sample projects from the Visual J++ InfoViewer have been listed previously in this chapter.

Open the JumpingBox project so that you see the project window's ClassView, listing the classes of the JumpingBox applet. Actually, there is only one class in this project, and it is called JumpingBox. Build the JumpingBox applet. Now you are ready to proceed through the following demonstrations of Visual J++'s debugging features.

Starting a Debugging Session

As mentioned previously, you can run programs or applets in two ways from the Visual J++ interface: in a debugging session and through the standalone interpreter. You can only use the interactive debugger in a debugging session.

To start a debugging session, use the Main menu's Build/Debug/Go or Build/Debug/Step Into option. These commands are also available using the Debug toolbar, which is much faster and easier to use than the Main menu options. The Debug toolbar, shown below, is not displayed in the Visual J++ interface when VJ++ is started, by default. You can show this toolbar using the Main menu's View/Toolbars option. Yet another way to start a debugging session is to just press F5, which is the hotkey from the Go command, or F8, which is the hotkey for the Step Into command.

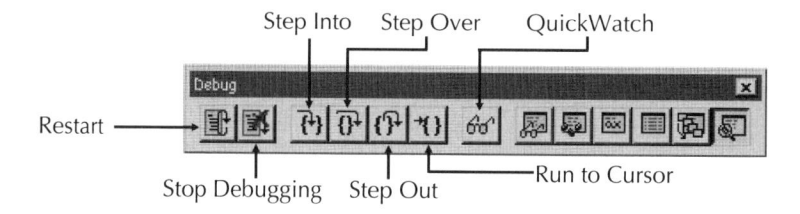

[Debug toolbar figure with labels: Step Into, Step Over, QuickWatch, Restart, Stop Debugging, Step Out, Run to Cursor]

The way the Visual J++ debugger works, which is similar to how most interactive debuggers work, is to run a program until a *breakpoint* is hit. A breakpoint is a special note, attached to a particular line of source code that says to the debugger "stop when the program's execution gets here." A step operation in the debugger says to the debugger "set a temporary breakpoint on the next line, and remove it after you stop there." That is, "step" to the next and stop.

Stopping a Debugging Session

To see the JumpingBox applet run in the debugger without any breakpoints set, which will accomplish about the same thing as just running the applet using the standalone interpreter, press F5 now. After a couple of minutes of chasing a little rectangle around the screen (that rectangle is the "jumping box" of the applet's title), you should get bored and stop the debugging session. You can stop the debugging session either by closing down the Internet Explorer, or through Visual J++'s interface: use the Main menu's Debug/Stop Debugging option, use the Debug toolbar's Stop Debugging button, or simply hit ALT-F5. (Get it? F5 means "start debugging", and ALT-F5 means "stop debugging.")

The Visual J++ Environment

Stepping Through a Program

Start your first real debugger session by stepping into the JumpingBox applet. Use the Build/Debug/Step Into option to do this, or just press F8. This will cause the debugger to start up the JumpingBox applet in Microsoft's Internet Explorer, and it will run the applet until the applet's first line of code is executed. The debugger will stop the applet just prior to executing that first line. Go ahead and press F8 now.

You will see the Internet Explorer pop up and display the JumpingBox project's HTML page with a gray rectangle where the JumpingBox applet will run. Soon thereafter, Visual J++'s debugger will detect that the first line of the applet's code is about to be run, and it will suspend the applet. You will see Visual J++ pop back up in front of the Internet Explorer, and it will look a little different than it did when you started the debugging session. See, now Visual J++ is in debugging mode, in which commands for debugging are available and windows to display the debugging state are also available. Figure 2-13 is a screen shot of the debugger at this point, where the applet's first line of code is about to be executed.

Here a quick description of the scene: First, you should notice the Debug toolbar has appeared as a floating window. That is, of course, if you haven't already shown the Debug toolbar using the View/Toolbars Main menu

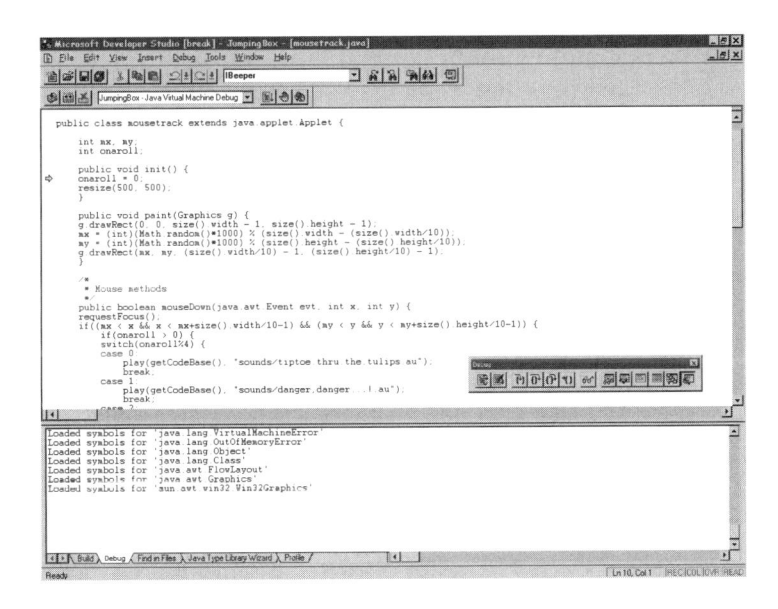

The debugger stops when JumpingBox is about to execute
Figure 2-13.

option. In that case, the Debug toolbar is just where you left it. The main window of Visual J++ is displaying the exact line of code in the JumpingBox applet that is about to execute. The little yellow arrow on the left margin of the code is pointing to that line. It is called the *execution point*. At the bottom of the screen, the output window is now displaying its Debug tab. Within the Debug tab is a list of all the Java classes that were loaded as part of the JumpingBox applet.

The execution point is right now pointing to the very first line of code in the first JumpingBox applet line of code that is to be executed. As you will learn in following chapters, the first method invoked for all applets is the Applet class' init( ) method, which is where the execution point is right now. Press F8 again to see the execution point jump to the next line of code, which reads

```
resize(500, 500);
```

You probably don't know what this line of code does, but that's not important right now. What's important is that you can see how to step through your Java applications or applets using the debugger.

There are four "step" operations in the Java debugger. Here's a quick description of each of them before you try to use them:

- **Step Into** steps to the next line of execution. If the current line of execution is a method invocation, then a Step Into will step into the first line of that method. For example, if you did a Step Into right now in the JumpingBox applet, then the debugger would step into the resize( ) method that is being called. The hotkey for Step Into is F8.

- **Step Over** is similar to Step Into. It steps to the next line of execution. The Step Over command, however, does not step into invoked methods. Instead, it steps over the method invocation to the next line of code in the same method. The hotkey for Step Over is F10.

- **Step Out** runs the debugger until you leave the current method. That is, you jump up the call stack to the previous method invocation in the call stack. The hotkey for Step Out is SHIFT-F7.

- **Run To Cursor** runs the debugger until the execution point reaches the line of code where the cursor is in Visual J++. This is like a temporary breakpoint on an arbitrary line of code. As soon as the debugger stops, the temporary breakpoint is removed. The hotkey for Run To Cursor is F7.

Here's a recipe for a debugging session that uses all four of these commands. It starts where you left off with the JumpingBox applet: with the execution point at the resize( ) call in the init( ) method.

The Visual J++ Environment

1. Click on the line of code where the execution point is in Visual J++. This moves the cursor to that line.
2. Press the down arrow until you move the cursor to the first line of code in the paint( ) method. That line reads

   ```
   g.drawRect(0, 0, size().width - 1, size().height - 1);
   ```
3. Do a Run To Cursor command by pressing F7 or by hitting the Run To Cursor button on the Debug toolbar. You will see the Internet Explorer momentarily pop up in front of Visual J++, indicating that it is running. Then Visual J++ will jump to the front, with the execution point moved to the first line in the paint( ) method.
4. Press F10 (Step Over) three times to advance the execution point stepwise to the last line in the paint( ) method.
5. Press F7 now, which will take you to the next line of code after the invocation of the applet's paint( ) method. If you are following these steps, you will probably right now say, "Yikes!," because Visual J++ now looks like Figure 2-14. Before you panic, here's what happened: The applet's paint( ) method was called by other class code, external to the applet. That means that Visual J++ doesn't have the source code files for where the execution point is now. So, instead of just choking and giving up, Visual J++ did the next best thing. It is now displaying the Visual J++ disassembler, with the disassembled bytecode for the code currently being executed. As you can see from Figure 2-14, disassembler bytecode is not very helpful if you don't know how to read it.
6. Select the Window/MouseTrack.java Main menu option, which will bring back the source code file for the JumpingBox applet. Click on the first line of code within the mouseDown( ) method, which is just under the paint( ) method code. This will place the cursor at that line. Hit F7 (Run To Cursor) again. You will see Internet Explorer pop up. Visual J++ will reappear with the execution point where you have the cursor when you hit F7 as soon as you click with the mouse on the applet. (The mouseDown( ) method is invoked whenever the mouse is clicked.) The line of code where the execution point is at this point reads

   ```
   requestFocus();
   ```
7. Press F8 (Step Into) at this point. You should see the execution point jump to the next line of code. But shouldn't the Step Into command have stepped into the first line of code in the requestFocus( ) method? Not in this case: the requestFocus( ) method is implemented in a base class of the JumpingBox applet's class, a base class for which Visual J++ does not have the source code. Therefore, instead of showing you a bunch of disassembly, Visual J++ just stepped to the next line of

executable code. In cases like these, the Step Into commands acts exactly the same as the Step Over command.

8. To stop this debugging session, press ALT-F5 (Stop Debugging). You will see Visual J++ return to the state it had before you started this debugging session, with the project window showing.

Breakpoints

As mentioned above, the Step commands essentially set temporary breakpoints. The Toggle Breakpoint command will create or remove a *permanent* breakpoint from the line of code where the cursor is in Visual J++.

You can invoke this command outside a debugging session. Visual J++ keeps a list of permanent breakpoints along with each VJ++ project, so your list of breakpoints remains persistent across debugging and editing sessions. To invoke the command, use the Debug toolbar's Toggle Breakpoint button. Note that outside a debugging session, there is no way from the Main menu to invoke this Visual J++ command. The hotkey for this command is F9.

Set a breakpoint in the paint( ) method of the MouseTrack class, which is the only class in the JumpingBox example applet. Do this by placing the cursor on the first line of that method in the source code and pressing F9. You will see a little stop sign appear to the left of the line, indicating that a permanent

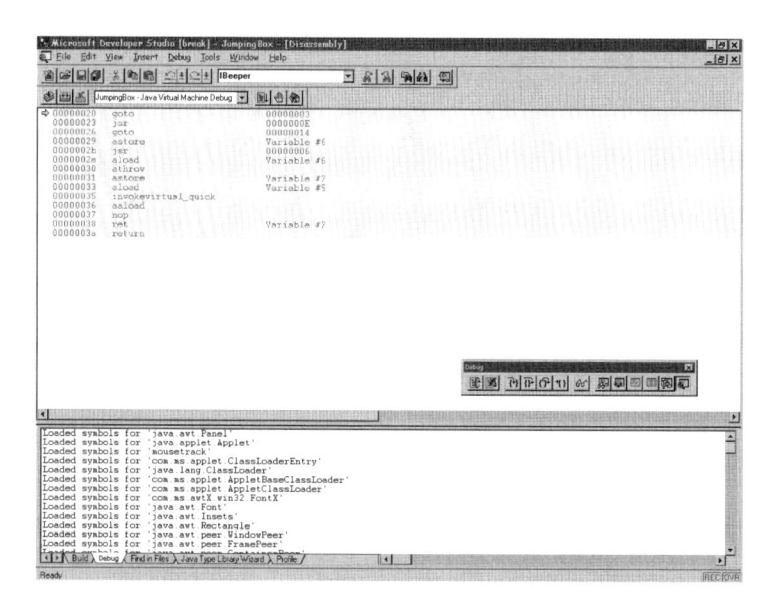

State of the debugger after step 5
Figure 2-14.

The Visual J++ Environment

breakpoint has been set there. Below is what this should look like. (Well, in this black-and-white reproduction it just appears as a black octagon. On your screen it will be red.)

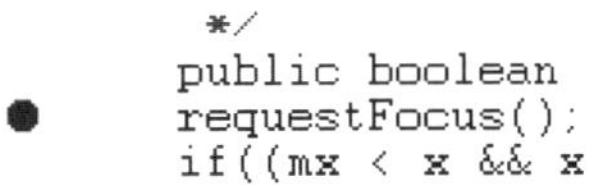

```
                    */
                    public boolean
              ●     requestFocus();
                    if((mx < x &&  x
```

Press F9 a couple more times, and you will see this symbol disappear and reappear. That's because the breakpoint is being toggled on and off every time you invoke the Toggle Breakpoint command.

Turn the breakpoint back on, then invoke the Start Debugging command by pressing F5. You will see the Internet Explorer appear as shown in Figure 2-15. You can see the execution point is on the same line you set a breakpoint previously. In fact, you can see that the breakpoint symbol is being overlaid by the execution point symbol in the left margin of the source code.

This example continues in the next section, so don't close down Visual J++ yet, or make sure you start it up again and go to the same breakpoint before reading the next section.

Performing a QuickWatch

If you've followed the example from the previous section, and you should have, then at this point you are stopped in the Visual J++ debugger

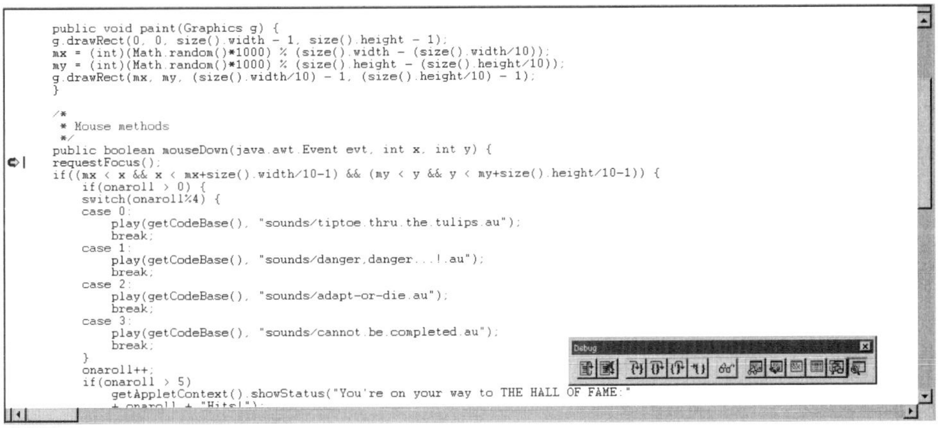

Visual J++ stopped at a breakpoint
Figure 2-15.

at the first call to paint( ) in the JumpingBox applet. The signature for this method is

```
public void paint(Graphics g)
```

From this you can see there is a variable named *g* that is local in this method. You know g is a Graphics object, so imagine that you wanted to actually examine the various member variables or g: that is, you wanted to examine the object's internal state. Of course, if you have been reading this book from the beginning to this point, then you probably don't know what a Graphics object is (the Graphics object and rendering graphics in general are covered in Chapter 5). But just pretend for now that for some reason you wanted to examine the state of g; for example, you had some assumption about its state that is not holding valid while your application is running, and you wanted to see how g was different from what you expected.

To do this quickly, use Visual J++'s QuickWatch feature. Highlight the variable g in the source code window, then use the Main menu's Debug/QuickWatch option. You will see the QuickWatch dialog appear, displaying everything that is known about the variable g at this point during program execution. Shown here is how the QuickWatch dialog looks at this point:

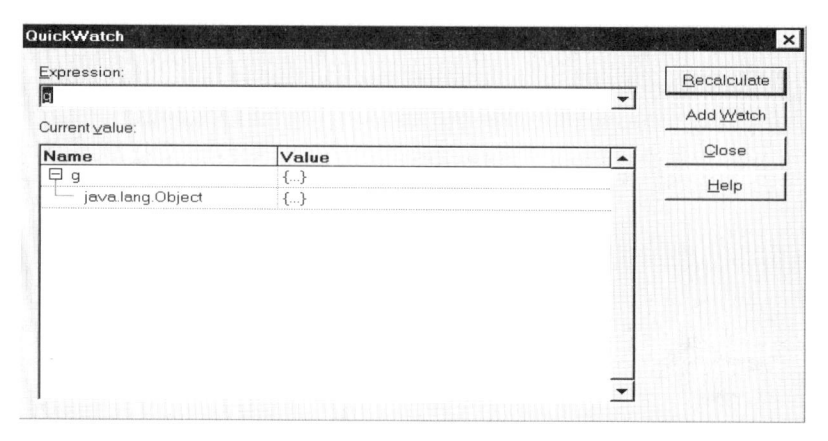

As you can see, you can type in a different expression into the Expression edit box of this dialog. You could, for instance, type in a mathematical expression using local variables that are in scope at this point during program execution. You could try these expressions, for example:

```
mx * my
this.width
this.height
```

The Visual J++ Environment

Notice the Add Watch button. Using this button, you can add the expression in the dialog to a permanent Watch window.

The Watch Window

The Watch window is like a permanent version of the QuickWatch dialog. To bring up the Watch window, choose the Main menu's View/Watch option. The Watch window is a dockable window with four tabs, labeled Watch1, Watch2, Watch3, and Watch4. Shown here is the Watch window while not docked (i.e., as a floating window):

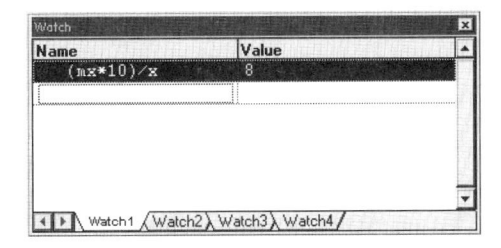

Within each of the Watch window tabs you can type an expression or variable name to evaluate. Thereafter, whenever the Visual J++ debugger pauses program execution, like at a breakpoint, the expression is reevaluated and its value is displayed.

The reason there are four separate tabs under the Watch window is so that you can separate related groups of expressions yourself. This is useful when you have a long list of watch expressions: you wouldn't want to have to continually scroll up and down through a single watch display, looking through a long list of expressions for the two or three you were interested in at the time. Instead, you can add individual expressions to any one of the four Watch window tabs.

There are three ways to add an expression to a Watch window tab. The first was mentioned previously: the Add Watch button of the QuickWatch dialog will add the expression being evaluated by the QuickWatch dialog to the currently (or most recently) viewed tab in the Watch window.

The second method involves you typing the expression in by hand directly in the Watch window. To do so, just click in the Name column of a blank row in the Watch window. An edit box will appear, into which you can type any available expression, much the same as you can type available expressions into the QuickWatch dialog.

You can also drag and drop expressions directly from the source code window to the Watch window, or from the variables window to the Watch window. That's the third way to add expressions to the Watch window. This will save you a bit of typing. Highlight some expression of code in the source code window, then drag it over the Watch window. A new row is automatically created in the Watch window with your expression in it. Click on the Name column to modify the expression at any time.

The Variables Window

More often than not, you'll be using the QuickWatch dialog or Watch window to examine the value of variables within some method. Visual J++ has a special window dedicated to just displaying the value of local variables. It's called the Variables window, and it is shown undocked in Visual J++ here:

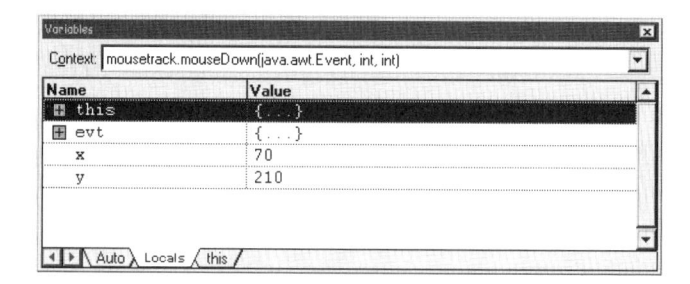

To bring up the Variables window, use the Main menu's View/Variables option. The window is, as are all windows in Visual J++, dockable. The window has three tabs that display overlapping sets of information about the local variables. The Locals tab displays all declared local variables, as well as the *this* variable if the method you are in at the time you are viewing this window is nonstatic.

The Auto tab displays only the variables and expressions that are needed to evaluate the current line of code. For example, when concatenating several String objects together using the + operator, a temporary object of the class StringBuffer is actually created to accomplish the concatenation. While the Locals tab would not display this temporary object, the Auto window would.

The This tab just displays the *this* variable. The *this* variable is also included in the Locals and Auto windows, but the This tab might make it easier to examine. It is very common to examine the *this* variable in nonstatic methods while debugging, and that's why the Visual J++ designers added the convenience of the This tab to the interface. In static methods, the evaluation of the *this* variable in the This tab writes a message that looks like

```
J0017: Error: symbol "this" not found
```

The Call Stack Window

The Call Stack window shows the chain of method calls that lead to the current execution point for the current thread. Use the View/Call Stack Main menu option to bring up the Call Stack window. The Call Stack window is shown here at a typical breakpoint:

```
Call Stack
⇨ mousetrack.mouseDown(java.awt.Event {...}, int 247, int 148) line 26
  java.awt.Component.handleEvent(java.awt.Event {...}) + 175 bytes
  java.awt.Component.postEvent(java.awt.Event {...}) + 10 bytes
  sun.awt.win32.MComponentPeer.handleMouseDown(long 841165677770, int -6
  sun.awt.win32.MToolkit.callbackLoop() address 0x00000000
  sun.awt.win32.MToolkit.run() + 68 bytes
  java.lang.Thread.run() line 292
```

If you double-click on a line in the Call Stack window, the source code window will display that point in the source code where the execution point is located. Note that the best way to jump up the call stack to a specific method call is to double-click on that method call in the Call Stack window and press F7 (Run to Cursor).

The contents of the Locals, Auto, and This tabs of the Variables window adjust to show the variables local to the method call you choose in the Call Stack window. That's what the green arrow in the ilustration above indicates: which method's variables (or *stack frame*) are being displayed right now. The Watch window contents are also reevaluated whenever the stack frame is modified in the Call Stack window.

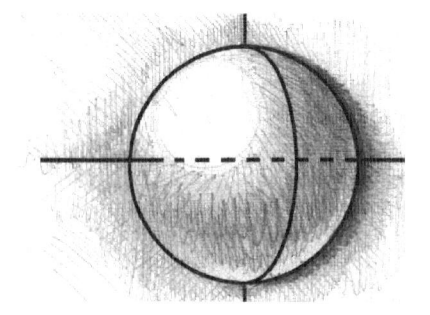

CHAPTER 3

GUI Basics

GUI stands for graphical user interface, and it is a term that has been appropriated to mean windowing interface. The top-selling desktop applications in use today are applications built with GUIs to work within a native windowing operating system, such as Windows 95, X-Windows, or Macintosh.

Java's major design goal, that of being platform-independent, means that Java programmers must be able to create windowing programs to work on these popular operating systems using the paradigms computer users have grown to appreciate and trust. To that end, one of the most important parts of the core Java class library is the *AWT*, or Abstract Windows Toolkit. The AWT is a (somewhat) idealized abstraction of a windowed operating system, describing the functionalities and capabilities common to all of them. For example, the AWT contains a Window class to abstract a generic window. When a Java program with a GUI is run on a windowed operating system, Window objects are represented as native windows to the user. All four of the major windows-based desktop operating systems (Windows 95, Macintosh, X-Windows and O/S2) use pretty much the same windowing metaphor. And that's good, because it makes your Java GUIs act pretty predictably on operating systems you've never used or even seen before.

GUI Example: HelloX

Though the name implies it, the HelloX program is not a Java ActiveX control. (Although, using Visual J++ you can turn it into one very easily, as you'll see in Chapter 7. If you read and remember the HelloWorld application from Chapter 1, or from the ad nauseum examples you've been exposed to in your computer science schooling and career, you'll recognize the purpose of this program. The HelloX program displays a string, "Hello, X!," where X is some string you supply. This example program uses a graphical user interface that includes the basic elements you will learn about in this chapter: top-level windows (a type of container), layout managers, and components. Here's the listing for the HelloX program:

Listing 3-1
The HelloX
program

```
import java.awt.*;

// HelloX: The program class. It contains the program's main entry point, and
//   each instance creates a HelloX GUI.
public class HelloX {
    // Static main method: program entry point.
    public static void main(String[] astrArgs) {
        if(1 == astrArgs.length)
            HelloX gui = new HelloX(astrArgs[0]);
        else
            System.err.println("Usage: java HelloX <display-string>");
    }

    // HelloX constructor: takes the display string as its parameter.
    // Constructs GUI made of a top-level window and a HelloXComponent.
    public HelloX(String strDisplay) {
        // Create top-level window and its layout manager.
        Frame f = new Frame("HelloX Example Program");
        f.setLayout(new BorderLayout());
        f.resize(300, 200);
```

GUI Basics

```
            // Create the string display component.
            HelloXComponent c = new HelloXComponent(strDisplay);

            // Put together these two pieces.
            f.add("Center", c);
        }
    }

    class HelloXComponent extends Canvas {
        // Class constructor takes the display string and stores it away.
        public HelloXComponent(String strDisplay) {
            m_strDisplay = new String(strDisplay);
        }

        // The paint() method is called when the component is to display itself.
        public void paint(Graphics g) {
            String strDisplay = "Hello, " + m_strDisplay + "!";
            int cxText = (size().width / 2) - (g.textWidth(strDisplay) / 2);
            int cyText = (size().height / 2) - (g.textHeight(strDisplay) / 2);
            g.drawText(cxText, cyText, strDisplay);
        }

        // Private members.
        private String m_strDisplay = null;
    }
```

Building HelloX in Visual J++

Follow these steps to build the HelloX application in Visual J++.

1. Start up Visual J++.
2. Create a new Project Workspace using the File | New menu command, specifying that you want a new Project Workspace to the Choose Type dialog box. Specify a new directory, in the file system location of your choosing (try "msdev\Projects" if you can't think of a better one), called "HelloX" (no extension is necessary, Jakarta will use the appropriate file extension automatically).

You should now see the Workspace window with a folder named HelloX classes in the left pane of the MS Developer's Studio. If you expand the folder, you will see that your project has no classes in it yet. The third step is to create the HelloX class.

3. From the Insert menu, select the New Java Class option. The Create New Class dialog box will appear. In the Name field, input **HelloX**. Leave the Extends field blank. Leave the Package field alone, too. The only modifier you should check is Public, indicating you want the HelloX class to be a public class. Click OK.

4. You should see the HelloX class appear in an edit screen. Fill in the class with the code for the HelloX class above.
5. Again, from the Insert menu, select the New Java Class option. Fill out the dialog for a new public class named **HelloXComponent**, based on the Canvas class. That is, fill in the name **Canvas** in the Extends edit box.

When you are done typing in the program, select the Build menu's Rebuild All option. HelloX is now ready to run!

Components

The HelloX application defines a class to handle the displaying of the "Hello, X" string, and that's the HelloXComponent class. This class is derived from the Canvas class, a core class that is part of the java.awt package. The Canvas class is derived from the Component class. Figure 3-1 illustrates the class hierarchy of these classes.

In AWT, the base class for all GUI elements is the Component class. In HelloX, Component is the base class of Canvas. It is also the base class for list boxes, push buttons, scrollbars, and all custom controls. This class

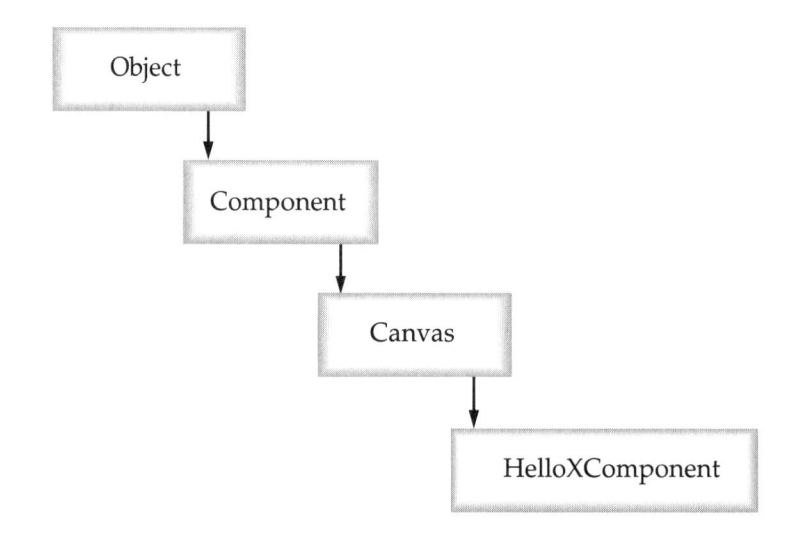

HelloX-Component class hierarchy
Figure 3-1.

defines the basic functionalities and capabilities common to all GUI elements. The basic functionalities can be broken into four groups:

- Component/container hierarchy
- Size and position
- Event handling
- Graphics operations

The subject of graphics operations will be discussed in Chapter 5. The remaining three categories of Component class functionalities are discussed here.

Component/Container Hierarchy

All components exist within a parent container. For example, both an OK and a Cancel push button within a dialog are components, and their parent container is the dialog window. In the HelloX example program, the HelloXComponent object's container is a Frame, or top-level window, created by the program.

Just as components are described by the Component class, containers are described by the Container class. And here's something a little strange at first glance: the Container class is derived from the Component class. Actually, that's not very strange if you think about it. What is a container but a component that can "contain" other components? It still does all the things a component does; it has a bounding rectangle, handles events, can be drawn on, etc.

So, every component must be contained by exactly one parent container. But, since the Container class extends the Component class, all containers must also be contained by exactly one container (which in turn must be contained, and so on, and so on). This component/container relationship defining container and contained relationships defines an infinitely spanning tree, or hierarchy of components. Well, *infinite* is just an approximation of *finite* in this component/container hierarchy, as shown in Figure 3-2. Following this discussion of AWT components, you will see that there are such things as top-level containers in AWT, such as the Frame used in the HelloX example program. Top-level containers are containers that do not have parent containers.

To get a Component object's parent container, use the component's getParent( ) method. In the following section on containers, you can see how to get a list of a container's components.

The component/container hierarchy of a simple Java GUI
Figure 3-2.

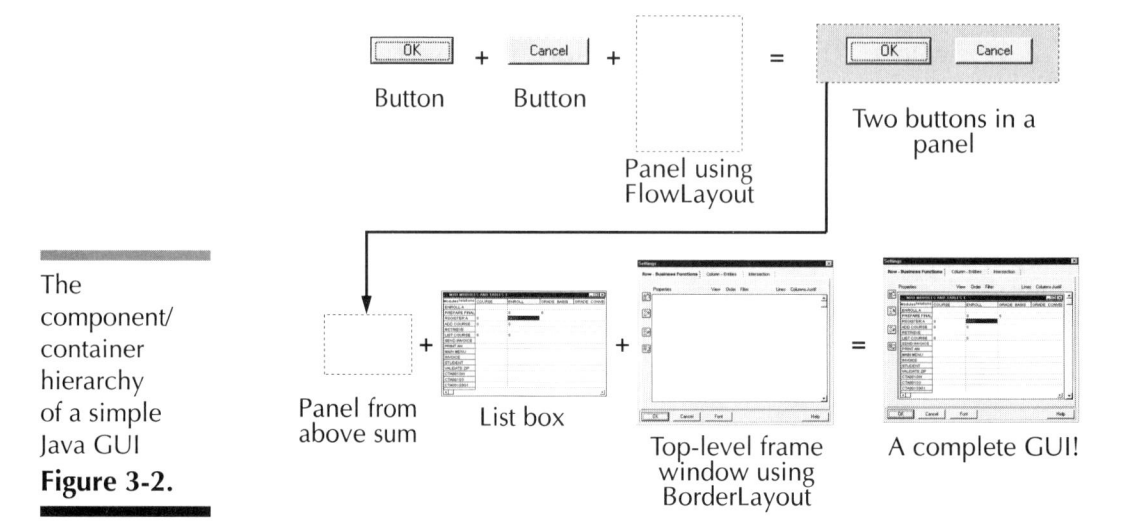

Size and Position of Components

Put simply, a GUI element, or component, is a rectangle of desktop space dedicated to some visual purpose. That purpose can be the displaying of a single string, a push button for the user to push, a complex animation sequence, etc. The rectangle that defines the desktop real estate of a component is called the component's *bounds*, or *bounding rectangle*. The dimensions of the component's bounds are called the component's *size*. The bounding rectangle is further defined by an origin, which is generally the component's upper-left corner. The Component class methods bounds( ) and size( ) return a Rectangle and Dimension object, respectively, that define the bounding rectangle of the component.

In the HelloXComponent's paint( ) method in the preceding HelloX program example, you can see that the size( ) method is used to determine the centerpoint of the component in order to place the HelloX string. The bounds( ) method could also have been used. In that case, the x and y coordinates of the bounding rectangle's origin would have to be taken into account. Component origins are always expressed in terms of the component's container's origin, and you can read more about component origins in the following section on containers. For now, suffice it to say that the Component class method location( ) returns a point that describes the component's upper-left corner. Taken together, the size( ) and location( ) methods give you the same information that the bounds( ) method's return rectangle gives you.

GUI Basics

Components can be positioned and resized using Component class methods. The move( ) method changes the origin of the component without changing the component's dimensions. The resize( ) method, on the other hand, changes the component's dimensions without modifying its origin. Note that while you can specify negative x or y arguments for a component's position, effectively placing the upper-left corner of the component to the left and above the origin of the component's container, a component's dimensions are always positive. The reshape( ) method allows you to change any aspect of the component's bounding rectangle: either its origin or its dimensions.

In general, you don't actually move components around much using the move( ), resize( ), or reshape( ) method. Often, the task of placing components within containers can be very tedious. The Java designers created layout managers to free you from performing this task all the time. A following section in this chapter discusses layout managers. You should be aware that a layout manager is responsible for moving and resizing a container's components to fit some layout criteria. For example, the BorderLayout object used in the HelloX example program is used to ensure that the HelloComponent object is always positioned and sized to fill up the top-level Frame's full client area. Notice how you don't see a single line of code resizing or other changing of the bounding rectangle of the HelloXComponent object, yet the component is continually reshaped to fill the Frame's client area. So, in general, you do not have to move or reposition your GUI components very often in Java. Instead, you create layout managers to do the task for you.

Components have two additional boolean states that define the component's appearance and actions. A component can either be *enabled* or *disabled*. Components are, by default, enabled. Disabled components lose their interactive capabilities. For example, a push button cannot be pushed while it is disabled. Most components take on a grayed-out look to indicate they are disabled. The Component class methods enable( ) and disable( ) are used to toggle the component's state between enabled and disabled. The isEnabled( ) method tells you whether or not the component is enabled.

Components can be *visible* or *hidden*. When a component is visible, it can either be *showing* or *not showing*. Any component you see on the screen is visible and showing. If a component exists, but you can't see it on the screen, then it is either hidden or not showing. Whether or not a visible component is showing is a matter of the component's onscreen position. A component placed too far to the right or left, or above or below the bounds of the parent container is said to be not showing. If it is visible and falls within the bounds of the parent container, it is showing. The Component class method isShowing( ) tells you whether or not the component is showing (that is, whether or not it is within its parent's bounds and is visible).

A hidden component, on the other hand, is always invisible on the screen, no matter what its position or size. The ability to hide a component is nice to have. For example, let's say you have a panel of buttons that should only be visible when another checkbox is checked by the user. The easiest way to accomplish this is to hide the component when the checkbox is unchecked. The Component class methods hide( ) and show( ) allow you to force a component to be hidden or visible. (It is unfortunate that the method show( ) is named so. Make sure you have no confusion: show( ) makes the component visible, while only by positioning the component within its parent container can the component be said to be showing.)

Event Handling

Java has built-in methods for generic event handling. *Events* are synchronous or asynchronous notification messages, commonly passed around between GUI elements in most windowed operating systems. In Java, all events are instances of the Event class. One of the basic functionalities of all Java components is that they can handle events. An example of a type of event is a mouse movement event. That is, say you move the mouse so that the cursor moves around within the bounding rectangle of your component. The component then would receive several asynchronous notifications indicating that the mouse movement had occurred. Similarly, if you clicked the mouse, or typed on the keyboard, or engaged in any kind of I/O with your GUI component, that component would receive asynchronous event notification.

The Component class method handleEvent( ) is called whenever a synchronous or asynchronous event notification is sent to the component. Take the mouse movement example again: when you moved the mouse over your Component object, the component's handleEvent( ) method would be called automatically by the Java system. An Event object would be passed to that method. The public member variables of the Event object describe exactly what type of event occurred, and what the parameters are.

The HelloX program from Listing 3-1 is quite boring. Let's add some interactivity to it by having the program react to mouse events. In Listing 3-2, the HelloXComponent class is modified to handle mouse cursor movement events. The HelloX string appears to follow the mouse cursor around whenever the cursor enters the component's bounding rectangle.

GUI Basics

Listing 3-2
Adding mouse event handling to the HelloX-Component

```java
import java.awt.*;

class HelloXComp2 extends Canvas {
    // Class constructor takes the display string and stores it away.
    public HelloXComponent(String strDisplay) {
        m_strDisplay = new String(strDisplay);
    }

    // Let handleEvent determine whether or not the event is a mouse move
    // event, and call a subsequent handler function if so.
    public boolean handleEvent(Event evt) {
        if(Event.MOUSE_MOVE == evt.id)
            return mouseMove(evt, evt.x, evt.y);
        return false;
    }

    // mouseMove stores away the coordinates of the move, and then forces the
    // component to repaint.
    public boolean mouseMove(Event evt, int x, int y) {
        m_cxText = x;
        m_cyText = y;
        repaint();
        return true;
    }

    // The paint() method is called when the component is to display itself.
    // Displays the string over the last mouse movement coordinates.
    public void paint(Graphics g) {
        String strDisplay = "Hello, " + m_strDisplay + "!";
        g.drawText(strDisplay, m_cxText, m_cyText);
    }

    // Private members.
    private String m_strDisplay = null;
    private int m_cxText = 0;
    private int m_cyText = 0;
}
```

Figure 3-3 is an actual screenshot from a session with this new version of HelloX. Note that the text's display baseline is right where the mouse cursor is. Note that in the HelloXComp2 class of this example that the handleEvent( ) method was overridden to detect what kind of event had occurred and to call an appropriate member method to handle the event. That method is called an *event handler*.

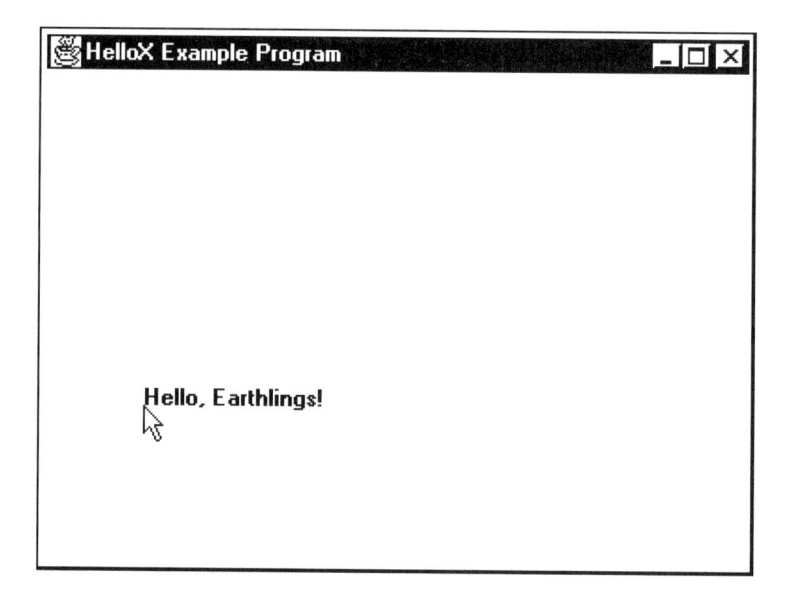

Screenshot of the modified HelloX program
Figure 3-3.

There are a number of event handlers built into the Component class already. The default implementation of the handleEvent( ) method acts as a large switch statement, calling the appropriate Component class event handler for the type of event. In the HelloXComp2 class (the second version of the HelloXComponent class), you can see that this was done explicitly for *mouse move* events. In fact, it was not necessary to override the handleEvent( ) method at all, since the default implementation already calls the Component class method mouseMove( ) whenever a mouse event occurs.

An event's *type* is defined by the value of the Event object's public *id* member variable. The Event class defines several static integer values to represent the common types of events. Several other Event class members describe additional information about the event. The *x* and *y* members define where certain events occurred. For example, mouse move events typically have *x* and *y* values specifying where the mouse move was detected. The *key* member variable is used to specify keyboard keys associated with the event.

Key press and key release events use this member. In addition, the *modifiers* member tells whether or not the SHIFT, CTRL, ESC (also called the META key in Java), or the ALT key was pressed. The Event class constants SHIFT, CTRL, META, and ALT can be ORed with the modifiers member bitwise to tell which special key was held during the keyboard event.

The *clickCount* member is used only for mouse click events, and it tells how many mouse clicks occurred. For double-clicks, the clickCount member's value will be two. One more member, the *arg* member, is used as a general-

GUI Basics

purpose information variable. The arg member is any object. For example, action events such as button pushes or menu selections use the arg member to pass a string holding the title of the item that was selected. Table 3-1 lists all the event types, the associated Event class static integer used to define events of that type, and any event-handle procedure called by handleEvent( ) in response to the event. Note that not all event types have event handlers in

Event Class Constant	Event Description	Event Handler
ACTION_EVENT	Used to describe button pushes or menu item selections	action(Event, arg)
GOT_FOCUS	The component received "keyboard focus," meaning all keyboard presses will be sent to the component	gotFocus(Event, arg)
KEY_PRESS	A key press was detected. Examine the *modifiers* member to tell what special keys are pressed	keyPress(Event, key)
KEY_RELEASE	The key was released. *Modifiers* tell what special keys are down	keyRelease(Event, key);
LIST_SELECT	Used with list boxes. Tells list box's container that a list item was selected	None
LIST_DESELECT	Used with list boxes. Tells list box's container that a list item was deselected	None
LOST_FOCUS	The component has lost keyboard focus. Keyboard events will no longer be sent to the component	lostFocus(Event, arg)

The Common Event Types
Table 3-1.

MOUSE_DOWN	The user clicked the mouse button down	mouseDown(Event, x, y)
MOUSE_DRAG	The user moved the mouse cursor while the mouse button was held down	mouseDrag(Event, x, y)
MOUSE_ENTER	The cursor has just entered the bounding rectangle of the component	mouseEnter(Event, x, y)
MOUSE_EXIT	The cursor has just left the bounding rectangle of the component	mouseExit(Event, x, y)
MOUSE_MOVE	The user moved the mouse cursor (without the mouse button held down)	mouseMove(Event x, y)
SCROLL_LINE_UP, SCROLL_LINE_DOWN, SCROLL_PAGE_UP, and SCROLL_PAGE_DOWN	These special event identifiers are used only with Scrollbar objects. They indicate what type of actions the user is performing on the scrollbar	None

Table 3-1. The Common Event Types *(continued)*

the Component class, only the events that are likely to be common to most components in general.

You may have noticed in the preceding HelloXComp2 code that the handleEvent( ) method returns a boolean value. What's that for? Well, you indicate that you have completely "handled" the Event by returning a true value from handleEvent( ) (or one of the event-handling procedures called by handleEvent( )). A false value indicates that the event was not handled, or it was only handled partially.

Unhandled events are automatically passed on to a component's container for possible handling. If the container does not handle it (or at least return true from handleEvent( )), the container's container is given a shot at the event, and so on. This is actually quite convenient, because it means you can centralize all your event-handling code within a single class instead of having to spread it out over several Component classes. That is, a single Container class that you create could have several push buttons contained within it. Instead of putting the action event-handling methods within the various button components, you can place the code in your Container class. The action events that are generated when you press on your buttons are automatically routed up to your container, where you can handle them appropriately. Note also that the various event-handling methods, such as mouseMove( ) and keyDown( ), also return a boolean value the same as handleEvent( ).

Custom Components

Before you are presented with the boring, ordinary components that come with Java, such as push buttons and list boxes, you should first see what goes into making a custom component of your own. Once you see what effort it takes to make one, those boring components may not look so ordinary after all.

AWT defines a single Component class called *Canvas*. Canvases are simply blank, unreactive components that can be placed within any container. These are very malleable components that you can use as the basis for custom components. Here are the three steps to take for making any custom component class in Java:

1. Derive your custom component class from the Canvas class in the java.awt package.
2. Add state information in the form of member variables, and appropriate public methods allow external code to control your custom component objects. For example, a status bar (the 0–100% bars commonly seen in windowing applications) would include a private integer or floating point member variable that held the current percentage of the bar. Two public methods named something like setPercentage( ) and getPercentage( ) could be used to control the status bar component.
3. Override the default (Component class) implementation of the event handlers in your class to react appropriately to user interaction with the component. Also, override the paint( ) method of your Component class to draw the component.

An example would be a two-state component. A functional example of a two-state component would be the AWT's Checkbox class. Two-state components have an internal state that is either "0" or "1." Based on its state, the button draws itself differently. In the example implementation of the TwoStateComp class demonstrated in Listing 3-3, you pass the component's constructor two images. One image is drawn when the component is in state "0," and the other is drawn when the component is in state "1."

Listing 3-3
Implementation of a TwoState Comp Custom Component class

```java
import java.awt.*;

class TwoStateComp extends Canvas
{
    /* ********
     * Constructors/destructors
     ******** */
    public TwoStateComp(Image imgState0, Image imgState1) {
        m_aimgStates[0] = imgState0;
        m_aimgStates[1] = imgState1;
    }

    /* ********
     * Public instance methods
     ******** */

    public void setState(int nNewState) {
        if((nNewState < 0) || (nNewState > 1))
            throw(new IllegalArgumentException(s_strErrorInvalidStateValue));
        m_state = nNewState;
        repaint();
    }

    public void paint(Graphics g) {
        // See Chapter xx "Graphics" for a discussion
        // of drawing to the desktop.
        g.drawImage(m_aimgStates[m_state], 0, 0, this);
    }

    //////////
    // Event handling methods.

    public boolean mouseDown(Event evt, int x, int y) {
        m_fMouseDown = true;
        repaint();
        return true;
    }

    public boolean mouseEnter(Event evt, int x, int y) {
        m_fMouseInBounds = true;
        repaint();
        return true;
    }

    public boolean mouseExit(Event evt, int x, int y) {
        m_fMouseInBounds = false;
```

GUI Basics

```
        repaint();
        return true;
    }

    public boolean mouseUp(Event evt, int x, int y) {
        if(m_fMouseDown && m_fMouseInBounds) {
            Event evt2 = new Event(this, Event.ACTION_EVENT, null);
            getParent().postEvent(evt);
        }

        m_fMouseDown = false;
        return true;
    }

    /* ********
     * Private instance members
     ******** */

    private Image[]         m_aimgStates = new Image[2];
    private int              m_state = 0;
    private boolean         m_fMouseDown = false;
    private boolean         m_fMouseInBounds = false;

    /* ********
     * Private static members
     ******** */

    private static final String s_strErrorInvalidStateValue =
            "Error: TwoStateComp may only have states 0 or 1.";
}
```

Containers and LayoutManagers

As stated previously, all components (except top-level windows) have a parent container. The Container class is the base class for all containers. The Container class is derived from the Component class, since containers are just a type of component that can *contain* other components. The additional methods of the Component class are of two categories:

♦ Child component management methods
♦ Child component layout methods

To parent a component with a particular Container object, use the Container class method add( ). This method adds the component as a child of the container, like so

```
myContainer.add(myComponent);
```

This removes the component from its current container, if any, and adds the component as a child of the container. In order to appear on the desktop at all, a Component object must be contained within a container. The exception to this rule is top-level windows, which are specific containers that do not require a parent container. Note that the HelloX example application listed earlier in this chapter used a version of the add( ) method to add a child component to the application's main frame window.

To remove a component from a container, use the Container class method remove( ). Several other Container class methods exist to help manage child components, and those methods along with a short description of each are listed in Table 3-2.

LayoutManagers: Placing Components Within Containers

Once a component is added to a container, where does it get placed on the screen within that container? Java uses a very simple set of classes called *LayoutManagers* to arrange child components within parent containers. Every container has a LayoutManager object associated with it. To the LayoutManager is delegated the job of placing the child components on the screen, based on some algorithm.

There are several different types of LayoutManagers included with the Java core class libraries. Each one uses a different algorithm for placing the child components, and each one thus is appropriate for use in different situations. For example, the FlowLayout LayoutManager places all child components in the parent container in a left-to-right, top-to-bottom manner starting at the container's upper-left corner.

Method	Description
removeAll	Removes all the components of a container. After a call to this method, the container has no child components
getComponent	Get the *n*th child component in the container
getComponents	Get an enumeration of all the child components in the container
locate	Given a point (x, y), returns a reference to the child component that occupies that point in the container

Additional Container Class Methods for Managing Child Components
Table 3-2.

The container, its child components, and its LayoutManager interact through a mechanism called *validation*. A container keeps an internal state flag indicating whether it is *valid* or *invalid*. An invalid state indicates that the container needs to be laid out, usually because a child component needs to be resized or a child component has been added or removed from the container. The Container class method validate( ) can be called to explicitly force the container's LayoutManager to rearrange the container's child components. The validate( ) method does nothing if the container is marked valid. On the other hand, if the container is marked as invalid, then the container's LayoutManager's layoutContainer( ) method is called. Different LayoutManagers implement this method differently, but they all generally perform the same steps:

1. Get the current size of the target container.
2. Get each child component's preferred size. The Component class method preferredSize( ) returns a Dimension object describing the component's preferred height and width.
3. The LayoutManager uses some algorithm to fit the child components into the parent container as best it can.

Note that the size returned from the preferredSize( ) Component class method is just a suggestion. The LayoutManager may ignore this size preference altogether. The Component class method minimumSize( ) returns a minimum size requirement describing the smallest dimensions the component can be and still remain useful to a user. Layout managers always try to keep components at least as large as the Component object's minimumSize( ) method indicates.

The advantage of the LayoutManager method of placing components over the normal Windows technique should be apparent. In Windows, you must place each child component yourself, by hand. This can cause quite a few problems for interfaces that allow the user to resize the interface a lot. Visual J++'s ResourceWizard uses a layout manager called a *DialogLayout* that uses this exact method. Wherever the child controls are defined in the dialog template is exactly where the DialogLayout places those controls in the parent container. But what happens if the parent container is resized? Or, what if the dialog was designed for a larger area than your application can provide (say, if you have a much smaller screen than you did when you created your dialog). Solving this problem is what layout managers are good at. When the container is resized or initially sized, the layout manager uses its algorithm to use the space provided as best it can.

You use the Container class method setLayout( ) to specify which layout manager should control a container's interface. Here is the germane code from the previous HelloX example application, which associates a BorderLayout object with the main frame window of the application:

```
Frame f = new Frame("HelloX Example Program");
f.setLayout(new BorderLayout());
```

The Various LayoutManagers

Here's a quick description of each of the layout managers included with the Java runtime libraries. In addition, the DialogLayout class used by Visual J++'s ResourceWizard when converting dialog resources into Java classes is described.

FlowLayout

The FlowLayout is the simplest layout manager. It arranges a container's components in a left-to-right, top-to-bottom manner within the parent container. The component's preferred size is always used. Sometimes that means components are placed outside the parent container's bounding rectangle. The FlowLayout manager places components in the same order they were added to the parent container. Figure 3-4 illustrates a Java GUI that uses the FlowLayout manager to arrange six push buttons. The buttons are placed all in a row, going from left-to-right in the order they were added to the parent container.

BorderLayout

The BorderLayout layout manager can only take five or less child components. Each one is designated "North," "South," "East," "West,"or "Center." The north, south, east, and west components are each placed against one of the container's four edges (top, bottom, left, and right). The center component is centered within the parent container. The north and south components are allowed to be as tall as their preferred size indicates,

Sample GUI that uses a FlowLayout object as the layout manager
Figure 3-4.

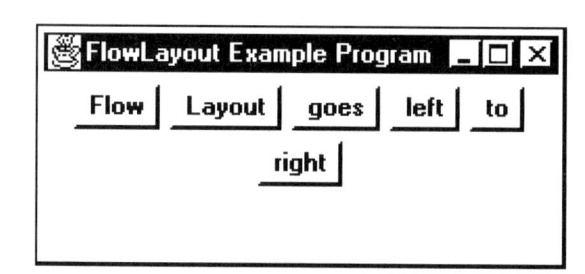

GUI Basics

and they are forced to be exactly as wide as the parent container. The east and west components are given their preferred width and made as tall as the container minus the height of the north and south components. The center component is given all the remaining area. Use the Container class add( ) method that takes two parameters to indicate the position of the component you are adding. For an example, look to the HelloX example program given previously in this chapter; specifically, when the HelloXComponent object is added to the GUI, it is added as the "Center" component to the main frame window:

```
HelloXComponent c = new HelloXComponent(strDisplay);
f.add("Center", c);
```

GridLayout

The GridLayout layout manager places the child controls in a grid of equally sized cells. You need to specify to the GridLayout constructor how many rows and columns of cells you want the GridLayout layout manager to create. For example, the following code uses a GridLayout object to arrange six push buttons in a two-by-three grid as shown in Figure 3-5. Grid cells are filled in a left-to-right, top-to-bottom order, where the first component added to the container occupies the upper-left cell.

```
Panel p = new Panel();
p.setLayout(new GridLayout(3, 2));
p.add(new Button("Upper Left"));    p.add(new Button("Upper Right"));
p.add(new Button("Middle Left"));   p.add(new Button("Middle Right"));
p.add(new Button("Lower Left"));    p.add(new Button("Lower Right"));
```

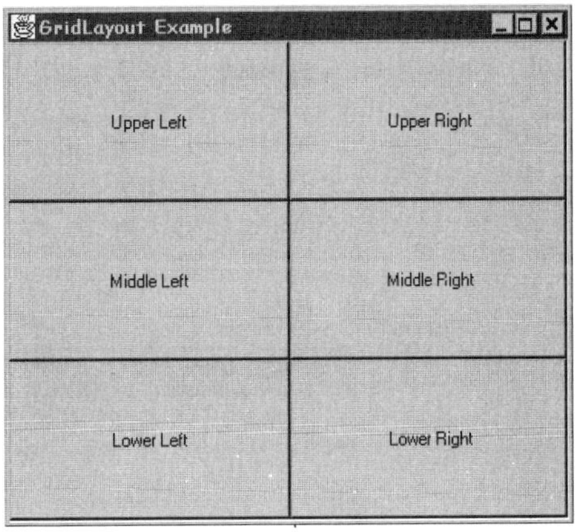

Sample GUI that uses a GridLayout layout manager
Figure 3-5.

CardLayout

The CardLayout layout manager places all cards on top of each other, like cards in a deck. Only one child component is made visible at a time, just like only the face of the top card of a deck is visible at any one time. Use the CardLayout class methods first( ), next( ), last( ), and show( ) to tell the CardLayout object which card, or component, to show. All cards are resized to the container's full surface area when visible. The TabbedPanel example program in a following section demonstrates the use of a CardLayout layout manager in creating a "tabbed dialog"-type container, called a TabbedPanel class.

GridBagLayout

The GridBagLayout is by far the most complex of the layout managers included with the Java runtime libraries. Think of the GridBagLayout as laying out components in a grid of joinable and stretchable cells. That is, similar to the GridLayout, the GridBagLayout is based on a grid pattern. The GridBagLayout, however, is able to "join" consecutive columns and rows, and is able to stretch the width of columns and the height of rows to fill a container. Figure 3-6 shows a GUI that uses a GridBagLayout to arrange some components.

When adding a component to a container controlled by a GridBagLayout object, you must also specify a GridBagConstraints object to the GridBagLayout for each child component in the container. The GridBagConstraints object describes how the GridBagLayout is to size and place a component. The GridBagConstraints class has several public member variables you set with values describing where and how to lay out a component. After adding the component to the container, you must also call the GridBagLayout's setConstraints( ) method to associate the constraint values with the component. Here is a list of the various GridBagConstraints member variables and a description of each.

Anchor   Describes where within the cell to place the component if the cell is larger than the component. Any one of these self-explanatory constants can be used: GridBagConstraints.NORTH, GridBagConstraints.EAST,

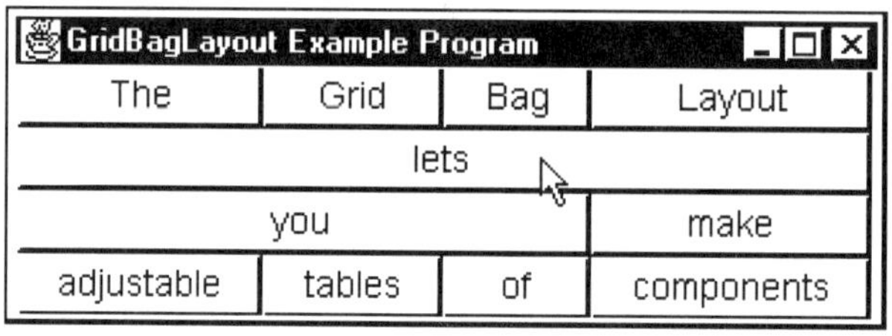

Sample GUI that uses a GridBagLayout layout manager
Figure 3-6.

GridBagConstraints.WEST, GridBagConstraints.SOUTH, GridBagConstraints.NORTHEAST, GridBagConstraints.NORTHWEST, GridBagConstraints.SOUTHEAST, GridBagConstraints.SOUTHWEST, and GridBagConstraints.CENTER.

Insets An Insets object telling how much padding to leave between the top, left, right, and bottom edges of the cell and the edges of the component.

ipadx X-Indicates how much padding to add to the left and right of the component within its cell.

ipady Y-Indicates how much padding to add to the top and bottom of the component within its cell.

gridx and gridy The column and row number, respectively, of the cell the component is to occupy. If the component spans several columns and/or cells, then these variables describe the upper-left cell.

gridwidth The number of columns the component is to span. The special value GridBagConstraints.REMAINDER means "all the way to the right edge." The special value GridBagConstraints.RELATIVE means "all but the last column."

gridheight Same as gridwidth, only it indicates the space of rows.

weightx Specifies whether this component's width will be increased if the row must be made wider. If more than one component has a nonzero value, then each component is made wider in relative proportion to its weightx constraint value. This is a floating point number. At least one component of the row must have a nonzero value.

weighty Same as weightx, only this specifies by how much the component's height is to be stretched if needed.

DialogLayout

When using Visual J++'s ResourceWizard to change a dialog resource into a Java class, you should notice that the resultant Dialog class uses a DialogLayout to place the components. DialogLayout is not included with the standard Java libraries.

The DialogLayout is a simple XY layout manager. That is, you specify to the DialogLayout precisely where you want your components in XY coordinates and in width and height. All numbers are in *dialog units*. A dialog unit is the number of pixels equal to 1/8th of the width of the average rendered character, and 1/4th the height of the average rendered character. Those familiar with Windows dialog will recognize this unit. Those unfamiliar may be struck by its definition. The purpose of a dialog unit is to make exact XY measurements not quite so dependent on the display size. See, dialog units are larger on systems using higher resolution screens. That means your components will get larger on higher resolution screens. This layout manager is really only good for nonresizing dialogs. If your dialog can resize, use one or more of the other layout managers to lay out your GUI.

Designing Custom LayoutManagers

Sometimes the standard layout managers just don't provide enough flexibility for you to make the GUI you want. When this happens, you might consider making your own layout manager. In addition to solving your immediate problem, this has an added benefit: reusability. Once you have created a new layout manager to solve your particular problem, you need never rewrite that code. Better yet, you can show off to your Java buddies by giving them your new layout manager.

Consider, for example, creating a SplitterLayout that can turn any container into a splitter window. A splitter window is a flexible grid of components that sometimes lets the user "drag" the grid boundaries to adjust the sizes of columns or rows. To build this beast, your SplitterLayout object would have to keep track of the individual column widths and row heights, and it would have to provide public member methods for adjusting them, as the partial class code in Listing 3-4 demonstrates.

Listing 3-4 The state members of a SplitterLayout class

```
public class SplitterLayout implements LayoutManager {
    public SplitterLayout(int cRows, int cCols) {
        m_cRows = cRows;
        m_cCols = cCols;
        m_anRowHeight = new int[m_cRows];
        m_anColWidth  = new int[m_cCols];
    }

    /* ********
     * Public instance methods
     ******** */

    public void setColWidth(int iCol, int cxWidth) {
        m_anColWidth[iCol] = cxWidth;
    }
```

GUI Basics

```
    public void setRowHeight(int iRow, int cyHeight) {
        m_anRowHeight[iRow] = cyHeight;
    }
    ...

    /* ********
     * Private instance members
     ******** */

    private int m_cCols = 0;
    private int m_cRows = 0;
    private int[] m_anColWidth = null;
    private int[] m_anRowHeight = null;
}
```

The LayoutManager interface defines the following methods to be implemented by each layout manager. After each is a sample implementation for the SplitterLayout layout manager.

addLayoutComponent(String name, Component comp)   Provided in case your layout manager needs to maintain state information on a per-component basis. The GridBagLayout layout manager, which keeps GridBagConstraint information for each of the target container's child components, provides an implementation of this method. The BorderLayout also must keep track of which component is north, south, etc.

The SplitterLayout doesn't keep per-component state information, so the SplitterLayout class would provide a null implementation:

```
public void addLayoutComponent(String name, Component comp) {}
```

removeLayoutComponent(Component comp)   As with addLayoutComponent( ), this method is provided for per-component state information maintenance. SplitterLayout provides a "no-op" implementation (that is, an empty implementation that does nothing):

```
public void removeLayoutComponent(Component comp) {}
```

preferredLayoutSize(Container parent)   Returns a Dimension object set to the preferred dimensions for the parent container. Generally, the preferred dimensions are determined by examining the preferredSize( ) of each of the target container's child components. The layout manager must take into account the container's *insets*, which are the padding along each border the container does not want components to appear in. The SplitterLayout only need use its column width and row height values to determine the preferred size:

```
public Dimension preferredLayoutSize(Container parent) {
    Dimension d = new Dimension(parent.insets().left + parent.insets().right,
                    parent.insets().top  + parent.insets().bottom);
    for(int i=0 ; i<m_anColWidth.length ; i++)
        d.width += m_anColWidth[i];
    for(int j=0 ; j<m_anRowHeight.length ; j++)
        d.height += m_anRowHeight[j];
    return d;
}
```

minimumLayoutSize(Container parent)   Similar to the preferredLayoutSize( ) method, this method also returns a dimension describing a preference for the size of the target container. In this case, it returns the minimum size below which the layout manager will begin to fail to lay out child components within its algorithm's parameters. Since the SplitterLayout's algorithm is only defined to work for a single size, its implementation of this method can return the same dimension as the preferredLayoutSize( ) method:

```
public Dimension minimumLayoutSize(Container parent) {
    return preferredLayoutSize(parent);
}
```

layoutContainer(Container parent)   This method is called as part of the validation mechanism. When called, the layout manager must set the positions and sizes of the target container's child components. Here's SplitterLayout's implementation:

```
public void layoutContainer(Container parent) {
    Component[] aComps = parent.getComponents();

    int xAccum = 0;
    int yAccum = 0;
    for(int i=0, int y=0 ; ((i<aComps.length) && (y<m_cRows)) ; i++, y++) {
        for(int x=0 ; ((i<aComps.length) && (x<m_cCols)) ; i++, x++) {
            aComp[i].reshape(xAccum, yAccum, m_anColWidth[x], m_anRowHeight[y]);
            xAccum += m_anColWidth[x];
        }
        xAccum = 0;
        yAccum += m_anRowHeight[y];
    }
}
```

Using null for the LayoutManager

In a few cases, you know exactly where you want to place components within the container, down to the exact pixel in position and dimension. In such cases, layout managers are essentially useless. Instead of adding components and telling the layout manager where to place them, you want to use the Component class methods move( ) and resize( ) or reshape( ) to place the Component objects where you want them.

To accomplish this kind of pixel-by-pixel control over your components, you set the container's LayoutManager to null:

```
myContainer.setLayout(null);
```

Then, use a series of move( ), resize( ), and reshape( ) calls on the individual components to place them where you want them, like this:

```
myContainer.add(myComp1);
myContainer.add(myComp2);
...

myComp1.move(0, 0);
myComp1.resize(100, 75);

myComp2.reshape(80, 0, 100, 75);
...
```

And that's all there is to it. Almost. There are a couple of caveats you should be aware of. First, one of the container's ancestors must be a top-level window already in order for the component move( ), resize( ), or reshape( ) calls to take effect. The top-level window must be showing (use the show( ) method to make sure this has been done). That is, make sure your entire hierarchy of container and child components has been created before moving or resizing your components. Otherwise, you'll find your components are not where you want them, or are simply missing from your GUI when it is eventually created.

Second, if you find yourself resorting to using null for the layout manager a lot, you're probably not implementing your GUI as efficiently as you could. As stated previously, this technique is appropriate for a *few* cases. That means only a small minority of cases. Take a look at your GUI and see if it can be broken down into a hierarchy of panels that each use one of the LayoutManagers included with the Java libraries. Chances are, it can. Take, for example, the TabbedPanel presented in Listing 3-5. It uses two subpanels that each use different LayoutManagers to arrange components within their respective portions of the TabbedPanel.

Even if you can't think of a way to use the standard LayoutManagers, then chances are you can create your own custom layout manager to do the job. For example, consider the implementation of a simple vertical list. If each element of the list were a component, then in fact there is no easy way to use the existing LayoutManagers to accomplish a vertical arrangement. (Think about it. If you have a solution, then you're smarter than the author.) Instead of placing each component individually in the vertical list, you could create a VerticalLayout class. The implementation of the VerticalLayout would be very much like the FlowLayout, with the X and Y axes reversed.

A Comprehensive Example: TabbedPanels

One very useful visual metaphor is that of the "tabbed dialog." That's the name given to the nifty dialogs used widely in Windows 95 and Windows NT 4.*x*, wherein a single dialog, with several labeled "tabs," is used in replacement of many dialogs. Tabbed dialogs are very useful for saving desktop space when you want to communicate a lot of information. Unfortunately, the Java class libraries do not include any sort of tabbed panels.

In this section, you will see how to create a TabbedPanel class that implements the tabbed dialog metaphor. The TabbedPanel class is quite reusable. To add a new tab, pass a unique tab name string to the TabbedPanel's addTab( ) method, along with the component you want shown when the user selects the appropriate tab. Figure 3-7 is a screen

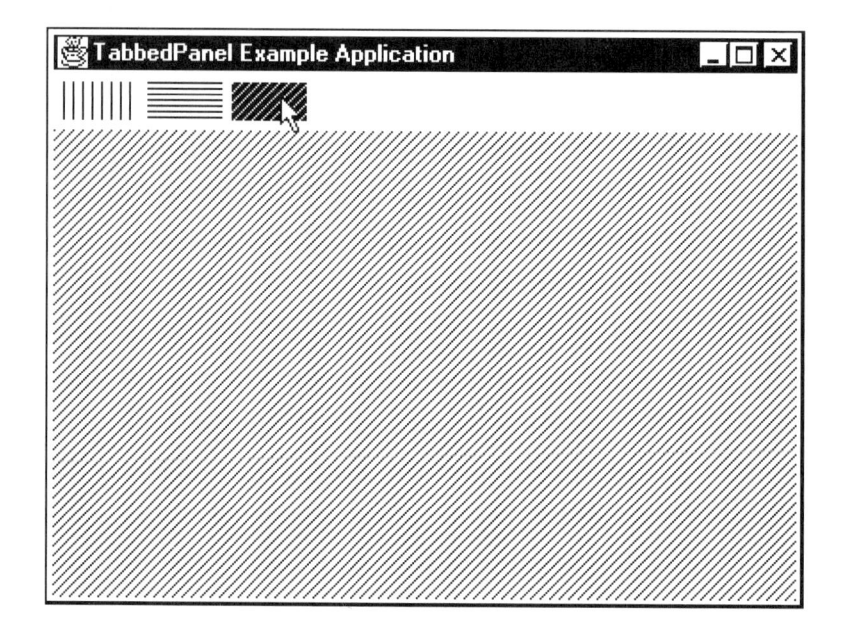

A sample TabbedPanel
Figure 3-7.

GUI Basics

shot of a simple application that uses the same TabbedPanel. The other TabbedPanel methods are removeTab( ), selectTab( ), getSelectedTabName( ), and getSelectedTabPanel( ).

Before looking at the TabbedPanel code, here is a quick architectural overview of the TabbedPanel class. A TabbedPanel is a panel with just two child components arranged in a BorderLayout. One child component is a panel holding all the tabs. This is the *north* component. The second child is a panel holding all the tab panels. This is the *center* component. Remember, the north component of a BorderLayout occupies the topmost area of the parent container. In a TabbedPanel, this means the row(s) of tabs will be at the top of the TabbedPanel. The center component gets all the rest of the space, which means all the tab panels will be fit over the top of each other to take up the rest of the TabbedPanel space.

In this TabbedPanel implementation, TwoStateComp objects are used to represent the actual tabs. These two-state components are managed by the TabbedPanel so that only one at a time is in state "1," representing the currently selected tab. Listing 3-5 lists all the code for the TabbedPanel class, with periodic descriptive text explaining what's going on.

Listing 3-5
The TabbedPanel class

```java
import java.awt.*;

public class TabbedPanel extends Panel
{
    /* ********
     * Constructors/destructors
     ******** */

    public TabbedPanel() {
        // Create a flow-layout panel to hold the tabs.
        Panel m_panelTabs = new Panel();
        m_panelTabs.setLayout(new FlowLayout(FlowLayout.LEFT, 0, 0));

        // Create a card-layout panel to hold the comp panels.
        Panel m_panelPanels = new Panel();
        m_CardLayoutForPanels = new CardLayout(0, 0);
        m_panelPanels.setLayout(m_CardLayoutForPanels);

        // Add both these panels to this TabbedPanel.
        setLayout(new BorderLayout());
        add("North", m_panelTabs);
        add("Center", m_panelPanels);
    }
```

```
/* ********
 * Public instance methods
 ******** */

public boolean addTab(String strName, Image imgSelected,
    Image imgUnselected, Component compPanel) {
    String strNameCopy = new String(strName);

        // Make sure name is not in use.
        if(m_hashNameToTab.contains(strNameCopy))
            return false;

        // Create the TwoStateComp, to be used as the tab.
        TwoStateComp tsc = new TwoStateComp(imgSelected, imgUnselected);
        m_hashNameToTab.put(strNameCopy, tsc);
        m_hashNameToCompPanel.put(strName, compPanel);
        m_panelTabs.add(tsc);
        m_panelPanels.add(strNameCopy, compPanel);

        // If this is the first component, select it.
        if(1 == m_hashNameToTab.size())
            selectTab(strNameCopy);

        return true;
}

public boolean removeTab(String strName) {
    // Make sure tab name is in use.
    Component tsc = (Component)m_hashNameToTab.get(strName);
    Component compPanel =
            (Component)m_hashNameToCompPanel.get(strName);
    if(null == tsc)
        return false;

    // Remove hastable entries, tab, and associated comp panel.
    m_hashNameToTab.remove(strName);
    m_hashNameToCompPanel.remove(strName);
    m_panelTabs.remove(tsc);
    m_panelPanels.remove(compPanel);

    // If that was the selected component, select another.
    // Arbitrarily choose the first available name in the
    // names hashtable.
    if(m_strSelectedTab == strName) {
        m_strSelectedTab = null;
        Enumeration enumKeys = m_hashNameToTab.keys();
        if(enumKeys.hasMoreElements()) {
```

GUI Basics

```
                    String strNewSelectedTab =
                            (String)enumKeys.nextElement();
                    selectTab(strNewSelectedTab);
            }
        }

        return true;
    }

    public boolean selectTab(String strName) {
        // If this tab is already selected, ignore this call.
        if(strName == m_strSelectedTab)
            return true;

        // Get the tab component, return false if none with
        // this name.
        TwoStateComp tsc = (TwoStateComp)m_hashNameToTab.get(strName);
        if(null == tsc)
            return false;

        // Get currently selected tab component. Unselect it.
        TwoStateComp tscOldSelectedTab =
                    (TwoStateComp)m_hashNameToTab.get(m_strSelectedTab);
        if(null != tsc) tsc.setState(0);

        // Select new tab, bring comp panel to front.
        tsc.setState(1);
        m_CardLayoutForPanels.show(m_panelPanels, strName);
        m_strSelectedTab = new String(strName);

        // give an action event to the parent container indicating
        // the new selection.
        Event evt = new Event(this, Event.ACTION_EVENT, strName);
        Container parent = getParent();
        if(null != parent) postEvent(evt);

        return true;
    }

    public String getSelectedTabName() {
        return new String(m_strSelectedTab);
    }
    public Component getSelectedTabPanel() {
        return (Component)m_hashNameToCompPanel.get(m_strSelectedTab);
    }
```

An ACTION_EVENT is passed to the TabbedPanel through the normal event-passing mechanism, described in preceding sections of this chapter, whenever the user selects one of the TwoStateComp objects that are the tabs. The TabbedPanel is designed to post another ACTION_EVENT to the TabbedPanel's parent container whenever the user selects a new tab. That is the purpose of the action( ) event-handler method:

```java
public boolean action(Event evt, Object what) {
    // If target is one of our TwoStateComps, then
    // find the associated key string and select it.
    if(!(evt.target instanceof TwoStateComp))
        return false;

    TwoStateComp tsc = (TwoStateComp)evt.target;
    if(!m_hashNameToTab.contains(tsc))
        return false;

    Enumeration enumKeys = m_hashNameToTab.keys();
    String strName = null;
    for(strName = null ; enumKeys.hasMoreElements() ; ) {
        String str = (String)enumKeys.nextElement();
        if(tsc == m_hashNameToTab.get(str)) {
            strName = str;
            break;
        }
    }

    selectTab(strName);
    Event evt2 = new Event(this, Event.ACTION_EVENT, strName);
    getParent().postEvent(evt2);

    return true;
}

/* ********
 * Private instance members
 ******** */

private Panel        m_panelTabs;
private Panel        m_panelPanels;
private CardLayout   m_CardLayoutForPanels;
private Hashtable    m_hashNameToTab;
private Hashtable    m_hashNameToCompPanel;
private String       m_strSelectedTab;
}
```

Parts Is Parts

GUIs are made up of Component objects arranged in a hierarchy. Each component must be "contained" within a container. Containers are a special type of component with the added capability of being able to contain other components. However, even containers (being components themselves) must be contained within other containers. At the root of the GUI hierarchy is a top-level frame or dialog. Top-level containers are containers that don't have to be contained.

A layout manager is an object that uses a specific algorithm or production rules to arrange components within a parent container. The Java libraries include a few general-purpose layout managers, each using a different algorithm for arranging components. The standard layout managers include the FlowLayout, the BorderLayout, the CardLayout, the GridLayout, and the GridBagLayout. Most GUIs can be broken down into a hierarchy of panels, each one using one of these standard layout managers. VJ++'s ResourceWizard also includes a DialogLayout layout manager to place components at specific x, y, width, and height positions within a parent container. The DialogLayout expresses these bounding rectangles in terms of "dialog units." Replacing this DialogLayout with more dynamic layout managers is often preferable, especially if you don't know how large or how small the overall container is going to be. In a few cases, it is appropriate to use null for your layout manager, and to place your components "by hand," using a series of component move( ), resize( ), and reshape( ) calls. Consider also creating reusable custom layout managers.

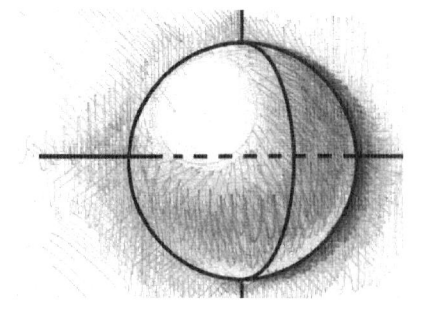

CHAPTER 4

AWT Controls and Menus

Graphical user interfaces (GUIs) can be one of the most important parts of a commercial-grade computer program. No matter how fast, efficient, or powerful your tool is, if it doesn't have a user interface (UI) that is both easy to use and visually stimulating, then your program has no legs. It just won't survive the market. This is even more true when talking about distributed programs in the World Wide Web (WWW). Web surfers are becoming as discriminating and impatient as MTV viewers during the early 1980s.

You have precious few seconds to grab the user's attention. After that, your program must be intuitive and efficient to use.

Luckily, most GUI tasks can be described using a small family of window controls. The push button, the checkbox, the list box, the menu: these and other controls are time-tested GUI devices that windowing adepts understand, and that every major windowed operating system provides native support for. A push button looks and acts pretty much the same in Windows 95 as it does on a Macintosh, and as it does on X-Windows and O/S2. The user knows and understands the paradigm as the same thing on the various platforms.

Unfortunately, while to the user these devices look similar on the various windowed operating systems, to the developer they look very different in native code. The Windows programmer could hardly be expected to be able to recreate a GUI on the Macintosh that she developed for Windows.

Enter Java (and the saving of a lot of duplicate work). The Java designers were not the first people to recognize the value of crossplatform development tools for windows. The popular Galaxy development suite has been used for a few years to create crossplatform-compatible windows programs. The not-so-popular Coconet development suite defined a crossplatform-compatible GUI environment for use across a network, much the same as Java can be used to make WWW applets. The Java developers were not the first, but they were the first to do it well and for cheap (two properties you can't create a programming revolution without).

This chapter describes the built-in Abstract Windows Toolkit (AWT) classes for creating GUIs in Java, and Visual J++'s ResourceWizard that makes designing GUIs even faster. The standard GUI devices you would expect to be present in a windowed operating system are included as Component class derived classes in the java.awt package. Menu classes are not Component classes, but are instead a different stem of the AWT class tree. Menus are also explained in this chapter.

VJ++'s ResourceWizard can automatically generate Java classes from dialog and menu resources defined in a resource file, such as an .RCT file or an .RES file. You will see how to do this, and how it saves you a lot of time.

The Built-in AWT Controls

The java.awt Component classes include classes that define push buttons, labels, checkboxes, radio buttons, list boxes, edit boxes, text boxes (multiline edit boxes), and drop-down list boxes. Each of these classes is derived from the Component class. Figure 4-1 shows the class hierarchy of the various classes described in this section of this chapter.

AWT Controls and Menus

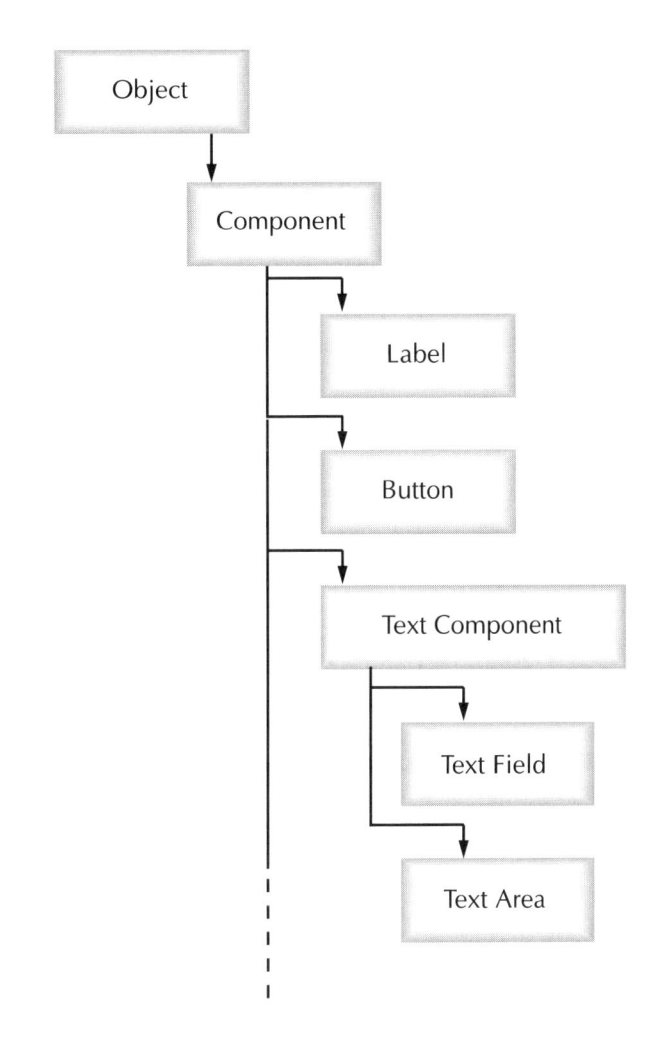

```
                    Object
                      │
                      ▼
                  Component
                      │
          ┌───────────┼───────────┐
          ▼           ▼           ▼
        Label       Button    Text Component
                                  │
                          ┌───────┴───────┐
                          ▼               ▼
                      Text Field      Text Area
```

Class hierarchy of the AWT Component classes
Figure 4-1.

The built-in Component classes notify your program about user interactions using the Component class event-handling procedures. For example, when the user clicks a push button that you've defined, the button's Container object's action( ) method is called to notify you that the button push has occurred. If you are not sure about component/container interactions and the event-handling procedures of AWT, take a look at Chapter 3, which discusses them in detail.

The Label Class

A label is the simplest of built-in Java Component classes. A label is merely a component that displays a single string of text. Labels are generally placed next to other GUI components to label what they do. The illustration below shows two labels describing the use of two different sets of components. In general, you will want to consider placing a label in the proximity of list boxes, drop-down list boxes, edit boxes, text boxes, or groups of related components. Checkboxes and buttons automatically get a label, but those other classes do not.

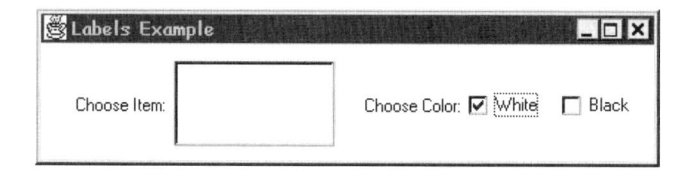

To create a label, you specify the title string to the Label class constructor. Place the resulting Label object in your GUI, and it will display your text to the user. Note that labels can only take a single line of text. Either use multiple vertically aligned labels or a multiline edit box to approximate a multiline label in Java.

The Label class methods getText( ) and setText( ) are used to modify the text string that appears on a Label object. You might want to use these methods to change displayed text on the UI when the program's state has changed. Alternatively, you could have two or more labels in your UI, where only one of them is not hidden at any one time.

A label is not a very interactive device. In Java, you receive no events from Label objects describing user interactions with the object. That is, you will not receive mouse messages when the user clicks on or moves the cursor over a label. Labels are really only meant to label other devices. You can easily make a custom component that is an interactive label using the techniques for making custom components described in Chapter 3.

Here is the code that creates the GUI from the preceding illustration (the Frame object must be resized just right to recreate the layout from that illustration):

```java
import java.awt.*;

public class MyFrame extends Frame {
    public MyFrame(String strTitle) {
        super(strTitle);

        // Make the UI elements.
        setLayout(new FlowLayout(FlowLayout.RIGHT, 5, 10));

        add(new Label("Choose Item:", Label.RIGHT));
```

AWT Controls and Menus

```
            m_list = new List();
            add(m_list);

            add(new Label("Choose Color:", Label.RIGHT));
            m_radioWhite = new Checkbox("White");
            m_radioBlack = new Checkbox("Black");
            add(m_radioWhite);
            add(m_radioBlack);
        }

        private List m_list;
        private Checkbox m_radioWhite;
        private Checkbox m_radioBlack;
}
```

Notice that in this example the Label class constructor took two parameters. The first is the string to display, and the second is an alignment parameter. The three Label class public static constants LEFT, CENTER, and RIGHT are used to explain how to align the text string within the label. The method setAligment( ) can be used to change the alignment after the label has already been created.

The Button Class

The push button is probably the best known windowing UI device, along with the menu. Hardly a Windows program exists that does not have some version of a menu and a toolbar of push buttons as part of the basic UI. Take a look at the most popular Windows programs: Netscape Navigator, Microsoft Office products, Microsoft Internet Explorer, etc. Notice that all these GUIs include push buttons. Below is a screen shot of Netscape Navigator 2.0 in which you can see several push buttons in the basic user interface.

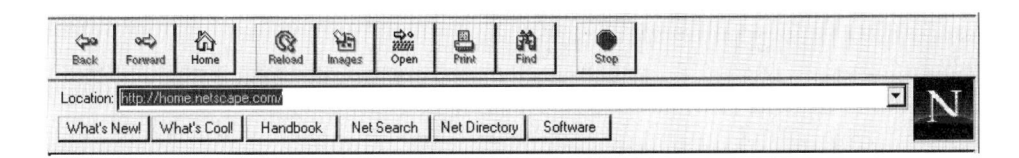

The Button class abstracts push buttons in the AWT. A Java Button object can display a single line of text on top of the button. Usually, programs will place a single verb or descriptive word in this space to describe what the button does. For example, "OK" or "Cancel." Specify the label you want to display to the Button class constructor.

Similar to the Label class' setText( ) and getText( ) methods, the Button class methods getLabel( ) and setLabel( ) are used to get or set the text displayed on the button. (You cannot account for the discrepancy in the names, except to say that maybe the Label class designers thought the names "getLabel" and "setLabel" would be too confusing when used within that class.)

The following defines a Toolbar class approximating Netscape Navigator's Directory Button's toolbar (the toolbar starting with the "What's New" on the left):

Listing 4.1
A Navigation Toolbar class

```java
import java.awt.*;

public class NavToolbar extends Panel {
    public NavToolbar() {
        setLayout(new FlowLayout(FlowLayout.LEFT, 3, 3));
        add(m_buttonWhatsNew = new Button("What's New!"));
        add(m_buttonWhatsCool = new Button("What's Cool!"));
        add(m_buttonHandbook = new Button("Handbook"));
        add(m_buttonNetSearch = new Button("Net Search"));
        add(m_buttonNetDirectory = new Button("Net Directory"));
        add(m_buttonSoftware = new Button("Software"));
    }

    public boolean action(Event evt, Object arg) {
        if(m_buttonWhatsNew == evt.target)
            getParent().postEvent(new Event(this,
                    WHATS_NEW, null));
        else if(m_buttonWhatsCool == evt.target)
            getParent().postEvent(new Event(this,
                    WHATS_COOL, null));
        else if(m_buttonHandbook == evt.target)
            getParent().postEvent(new Event(this,
                    HANDBOOK, null));
        else if(m_buttonNetSearch == evt.target)
            getParent().postEvent(new Event(this,
                    NET_SEARCH, null));
        else if(m_buttonNetDirectory == evt.target)
            getParent().postEvent(new Event(this,
                    NET_DIRECTORY, null));
        else if(m_buttonSoftware == evt.target)
            getParent().postEvent(new Event(this,
                    SOFTWARE, null));
        else
            return false;
```

```
        return true;
    }

    // Private variables and constants
    private Button m_buttonWhatsNew;
    private Button m_buttonWhatsCool;
    private Button m_buttonHandbook;
    private Button m_buttonNetSearch;
    private Button m_buttonNetDirectory;
    private Button m_buttonSoftware;

    public static final int WHATS_NEW = -1;
    public static final int WHATS_COOL = -2;
    public static final int HANDBOOK = -3;
    public static final int NET_DIRECTORY = -4;
    public static final int NET_SEARCH = -5;
    public static final int SOFTWARE = -6;
}
```

As you might have gleaned from this example, action events are posted to a Button object's container whenever the user clicks on the button. The *arg* parameter contains the same value as the *arg* variable of the Event object, which is the string label of the Button object. For example, if the "What's Cool!" button of the NavToolbar is clicked, then the *arg* parameter to the action( ) method of the Toolbar class will be the string "What's Cool!". You might prefer to identify the target of a user click using this *arg* parameter, but it is better to test the *target* variable of the Event object instead, as demonstrated in the preceding NavToolbar class implementation. Several Button objects could have the same label and your action( ) method would not gain much information by finding out what the label of the clicked button was.

The Checkbox Class

A checkbox is a two-state object, much like a light switch. The user, by clicking on the checkbox, toggles its state. Checkboxes are often used to indicate on/off options to users.

They can also be used to give the user a one-of-many selection. In the Windows environment, when AWT Checkboxes are used to specify a one-of-many selection, radio buttons are used instead of regular Windows checkboxes. Of course, your Java code is unaware of this distinction, but you should be aware of the interface considerations. The illustration below shows a simple interface that has both a simple checkbox, and several checkboxes involved in a one-of-many selection.

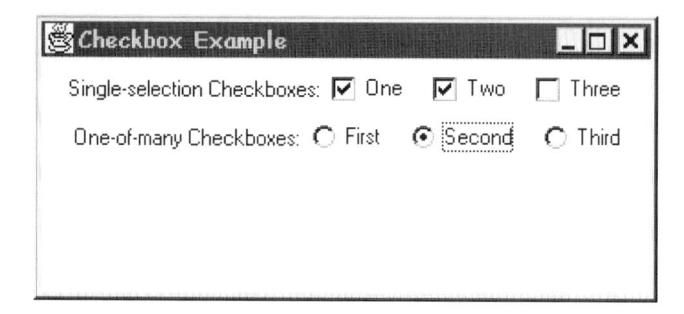

A single-selection checkbox acts much like a push button, except that it maintains a single boolean-state variable. Also, like push buttons, a checkbox has its own label. You do not then need to design your UI with additional Label objects.

The simplest constructor requires no parameters, and it creates a single-selection checkbox with no label initialized to an unchecked state. The second constructor takes only a string to use as the checkbox's label. Similar to the Button class, the setLabel( ) and getLabel( ) Checkbox class methods are used to modify the checkbox's displayed string. Use the Checkbox class methods getState( ) and setState( ) to modify the state of the checkbox between "true" (checked) and "false" (unchecked).

A one-of-many selection is accomplished in Java by associating several different Checkbox objects with a single CheckboxGroup. The CheckboxGroup class is not a graphical class, but is just an organizer for Checkboxes. Checkboxes must be created with an association to their CheckboxGroup using the third version of the Checkbox class constructor:

```
CheckboxGroup group = new CheckboxGroup();

Checkbox chkbxOne = new Checkbox("One", group, false);
Checkbox chkbxTwo = new Checkbox("Two", group, true);
Checkbox chkbxThree = new Checkbox("Three", group, false);
```

When more than one checkbox is associated in a group this way, then only one of the checkboxes may be in a checked state at a single time. If you use the Checkbox class setState( ) method to check one of the checkboxes in a group, then any other that happens to be checked will automatically be turned off. Note that the CheckboxGroup class has the public convenience methods getCurrent( ) and setCurrent( ) so that you may change the checked item using the CheckboxGroup object instead of the individual Checkbox objects.

The CheckboxGroup class is not very versatile, however. You cannot, for example, get a list of the checkboxes within a group from the

AWT Controls and Menus

CheckboxGroup object. You cannot add or remove checkboxes from the group, either. To approximate adding and removing checkboxes from a group, remove unwanted checkboxes from your UI temporarily by hiding them, and bring them into your UI by unhiding them at the appropriate time.

The following example class was used to build the UI you see in the preceding illustration:

Listing 4.2 A Checkbox example application

```java
import java.awt.*;

public class MyFrame extends Frame {
    public MyFrame() {
        setLayout(new FlowLayout(FlowLayout.RIGHT, 5, 5));
        add(new Label("Single-selection Checkboxes:"));
        add(new Checkbox("One"));
        add(new Checkbox("Two"));
        add(new Checkbox("Three"));

        add(new Label("One-of-many Checkboxes:"));
        add(new Checkbox("First"));
        add(new Checkbox("Second"));
        add(new Checkbox("Third"));
    }
}
```

The Scrollbar Class

A scrollbar device allows the selection of a subrange from a range of values. Like push buttons and menus, scrollbars are probably some of the most universally known UI elements. Generally, they are used to control the horizontal or vertical scrolling of a list box, an edit box, or custom document view windows. Below is a scrollbar used as a select-one-of-range input device. You would create scrollbars yourself to control the scrolling for custom view windows or as a device so the user can select a value within a range. An example of the latter case would be the "Slow...Fast" range selector in the illustration.

The Scrollbar class represents scrollbar items in Java programs. The Scrollbar class includes several public methods to control how the scrollbar looks and acts, and the Scrollbar class also has a few Event IDs dedicated just for it. For example, there is an Event class value SCROLL_LINE_UP that is used only when a scrollbar's Line Up button is clicked by the user.

The Scrollbar object's state is defined by seven internal-state variables:

- **Orientation**: A scrollbar is oriented either vertically or horizontally. All scrollbar terms are built around vertical scrollbars. The SCROLL_LINE_UP value is also used for horizontal scrollbars that are scrolled to the left. SCROLL_LINE_DOWN is used for horizontal scrolls to the right. The two possible values are Scrollbar.HORIZONTAL and Scrollbar.VERTICAL.

- **Value**: The current value of the scrollbar. This value lies somewhere between the scrollbar's minimum and maximum values.

- **Minimum**: The value of the least-valued end of the scrollbar. When the thumb of the scrollbar is farthest to the top of vertical scrollbars and to the left of horizontal scrollbars, then the value of the scrollbar is equal to its minimum.

- **Maximum**: The value at the most-valued end of the scrollbar. When the thumb of the scrollbar is farthest to the bottom of vertical scrollbars and to the right of horizontal scrollbars, then the value of the scrollbar is equal to its maximum.

- **Page Size**: The size of a page increment on the scrollbar. When the user does a page-down operation either by clicking on the lower part of the trackbar or by hitting the Page Down button while the scrollbar element has keyboard focus, then the value of the scrollbar increments by this value.

- **Line Size**: The size of a single line on the scrollbar. When the user does a line-down operation either by clicking on the Line Down button of the scrollbar or by hitting the line-down key when the scrollbar has keyboard focus, then the value of the scrollbar increments by this value. Unless changed by an explicit call to the Scrollbar class method setLineIncrement( ), this value is assumed to be one.

- **Visible Size**: The size of the thumb. This is indicated in the range from zero to the difference of maximum minus minimum.

One of the three Scrollbar class constructors takes initial values for five of these values:

```
public Scrollbar(int orientation, int value, int visible,
                 int minimum, int maximum)
```

You must specify at least the orientation of the scrollbar when you create a Scrollbar class object. The version of the constructor that takes no arguments

AWT Controls and Menus

assumes that the scrollbar is oriented vertically. The only other version of the constructor takes the scrollbar's orientation as its only parameter.

In addition to specifying initial values for the other four internal-state variables, you can also set these state values at any time using the Scrollbar class method setValues( ). In fact, if either the no-parameter or the single-parameter constructor is used, then the internal-state values must be set explicitly. setValues( ) is the simplest method for doing that:

```
public void setValues(int value, int visible, int minimum, int maximum)
```

These methods allow you to change the value, line or page increment internal-state variables of a scrollbar: setValue(int value), setLineIncrement(int line_inc), setPageIncrement(int page_inc). Get methods also exist so you can examine the internal state of a scrollbar: getMinimum( ), getMaximum( ), getLineIncrement( ), getPageIncrement( ), getValue( ), and getVisible( ).

Here is the source code for the program displayed in the preceding illustration.

Listing 4.3 An example application that uses scrollbars

```java
import java.awt.*;

public class ScrollbarExample extends Frame implements Runnable {
    public ScrollbarExample() {
        super("Scrollbar Example Application");

        setLayout(new BorderLayout(5, 5));
        m_scroll = new Scrollbar(Scrollbar.HORIZONTAL, 0, 10, 0, 100);
        add("South", m_scroll);
        m_label = new Label("Scroll val: move scrollbar");
        add("Center", m_label);
    }

    public boolean handleEvent(Event evt) {
        switch(evt.id) {
            case Event.SCROLL_LINE_UP:
            case Event.SCROLL_LINE_DOWN:
            case Event.SCROLL_PAGE_UP:
            case Event.SCROLL_PAGE_DOWN:
            case Event.SCROLL_ABSOLUTE:
                updateValue(m_scroll.getValue());
                return true;
        }
        return false;
    }
```

```
    private void updateValue(int val) {
        m_label.setText("Scroll val: " + val);
    }

    // private member fields
    private Scrollbar  m_scroll = null;
    private Label      m_label  = null;
}
```

You have already heard about the SCROLL_LINE_UP/DOWN and SCROLL_PAGE_UP/DOWN Event IDs. The SCROLL_ABSOLUTE Event indicates that the user has moved the thumb by hand. This event is sent after the scrollbar's thumb has been moved. The event's *arg* member holds the scrollbar's new value.

The TextField and TextArea Classes

An edit box can be either a single or multiline device in Windows. In Java, these are broken up into two different classes. The TextField class is a single-line edit box. The TextArea class is a multiline edit box. Edit boxes are devices that allow users to enter text from the keyboard into your program. Edit boxes are also fully featured simple text editors, with cut, paste, copy, and select functionalities.

Both the TextField and TextArea classes are derived from the TextComponent class, which defines most of the functionality of both classes. You can refer to either a text field or a text area as a text component.

The state of a text component is defined by several internal-state variables. These variables can each be examined and modified using the various public methods of the TextComponent class. In addition, extra state information is added to each of the TextField and TextArea classes, which can also be examined and modified by the specific public member methods of the respective classes. Here are the state variables of text components in general:

- **isEditable**: Edit boxes can either be editable or not. Noneditable edit boxes are functionally the same thing as labels, although they may appear slightly different. You can use a noneditable TextArea as a multiline label. Edit boxes are editable by default, so you must make them noneditable programmatically.
- **Text**: The text contents of the text component. Text characters are given a *position* within the text component. The position is the same thing as the zero-based index of the character in the text component's text. That is, the first character has position zero, the second has position one, etc.

- **Selection Range**: None, some, or all of the text in a text component is part of the selection range. When you set the selection range, it is usually presented to the user by highlighting the text in the selection range. The user may also set the selection range (for editable text boxes) using the mouse or through the keyboard. The selection range is defined by a start character position and an end character position. The start character position indicates that the beginning of the selection range starts at (and includes) the character at the selection start position. The character at the selection end position is also included within the selection.

As stated above, there are circumstances when a noneditable text component is useful (in a minority of cases). Text components are assumed to be editable, but you can use the TextComponent class method setEditable( ) to change the text component to being either editable or not at any time. getEditable( ) tells whether or not the text component is editable currently.

Of course, you will want to change the text in a text component in some programs, and so, of course, the TextComponent class provides methods for doing this. You can use getText( ) to get the full text within the text component. And, symmetrically, the setText( ) method is used to completely replace the text within the text component. (You can see how the getText( ) and setText( ) methods of the Label class are similar to these TextComponent class methods.)

Text selection can be examined and modified as well using the public methods of the TextComponent class. The TextArea class implements some convenient methods to make this even easier. The TextComponent methods to get the selection start and end positions are getSelectionStart( ) and getSelectionEnd( ). If the values returned by these two methods are the same, then the value indicates the location of the insertion point. A start position that is greater than an end position indicates that the insertion point is at the beginning of the selection. Otherwise, the insertion point is at the end.

The getSelectionText( ) method returns a string copy of the selection. The select( ) method is passed a start and an end position, and it is used to select text programmatically. selectAll( ) causes the entire text string of the TextComponent to become selected.

The TextField Class

A TextField is a single-line text component. It is derived from the TextComponent class, so it has all the internal-state elements the text component does: an editable flag, a displayed text string, and a selection range that may include none, some, or all of the text string. In addition, a

TextField has a column count, indicating the maximum number of characters in the TextField.

There are four TextField constructors. This table explains which state variables are initialized by which available TextField class constructors:

Constructor Signature	Text Initialized	Rows Initialized
TextField( )	No	No
TextField(int rows)	No	Yes
TextField(String strText)	Yes	No
TextField(String strText, int rows)	Yes	Yes

The first and third constructors create a TextField without explicit text length restrictions. That is, the maximum length of the text in the TextField is dependent on the maximum length of text in an edit box according to the underlying operating system.

A TextField may also act as something like a password entry field. When you are entering a password into a computer, you don't want someone to be able to look over your shoulder at the password you type in. In most computer programs based in a windowing operating system that involve typing in a password, usually the edit box you type the password into does not display the characters you type. Instead, it displays some sort of "echo" character, like an asterisk or a period, for each character you type in. The TextField class allows you to configure your TextField like a password entry field. The character that is displayed instead of the actual character you type in is called the TextField's *echo character*.

To make your TextField a password entry field like this, use the TextField method setEchoCharacter( ) to set the Text field's echo character. Note that making a TextField a password entry field is an irreversible process. You cannot remove the use of an echo character once you have used the setEchoCharacter( ) method. getEchoCharacter( ) returns what the character is, and echoCharIsSet( ) tells you whether or not the TextField is set up to be a password-entry TextField.

Even when a TextField uses an echo character, the TextComponent class methods getText( ) and getSelectedText( ) return the actual contents of the TextField, not just a string of echo characters. Remember that if you really want to restrict access to the contents of a password-entry TextField, use of an echo character is not enough, since another object could use the

TextField's getText( ) method to get the actual content of the TextField. To prevent this kind of unsecure access, you must prevent any other class from getting even a reference to your TextField.

The TextArea Class

A text area is a multiline edit box. Like the TextField class, it is derived from the TextComponent class, so it has all the internal states of that parent class: an editable flag, a string of text, and a selection region. In addition, the TextArea class includes a count of the number of lines in the text area and a count of the number of columns. The number of rows and columns indicates the size of the text area on the screen. The maximum length of the text within the text area is defined by the maximum length of text within the edit boxes of the underlying operating system. The TextArea class cannot be configured as a protected-entry edit box like the Text field can. If you have ever had, or can think of, a need for protected-entry multiline edit boxes, please write to the author in care of the publisher because you probably have imagined the rarest of things: something no one else has dreamed up before.

The TextArea class provides methods for examining the number of rows and columns a text area was created with. There are no methods, however, for modifying these values. The TextArea class methods for examining these values are getRows( ) and getColumns( ).

The TextArea class still addresses text characters using character position values, just like the TextComponent and TextField classes do. There is no addressing text by row and column number. In fact, there is no easy way to divine what row a particular character is in without running through the text area's text string and counting up the line return characters. That's unfortunate in some cases, but true.

Anyway, as mentioned previously, the TextArea class includes extra methods for modifying the text area's text that are not included with the TextComponent class. For example, the TextArea class method insertText( ) can insert a string of text at a specific text position within the text area. The TextArea class method appendText( ) will append a string of text to the end of the text area's text string. And the TextArea class method replaceText( ) will replace the text between a specified start and end position with an alternative string of text. Of course, the TextComponent class methods getText( ) and setText( ) are still valid. The TextArea class does improve the capabilities of its base class, however.

If the text string in the text area is too large to display within the text area's given number of rows and columns, then the text area automatically creates scrollbars so the user can scroll through the entire text area's contents.

The List Class

A list box is a device that lets the user select from a list of strings. List boxes are used, for example, to let the user select a filename from a directory list or select a channel name from a list of Chat channels. The list box is a common UI device in all the main windowing operating systems, and so has a class dedicated to it in the java.awt package. That is, the List class. Below is a simple GUI that uses a list box.

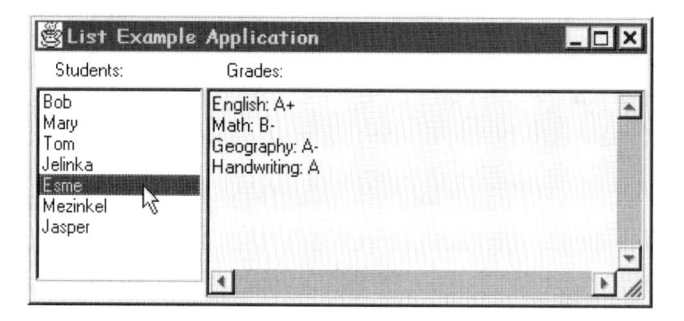

A list box can be either a multiple- or single-selection list box. A multiple-selection list box allows the user to select more than one of the items in the list, usually by holding down special character keys while clicking on more than one item in the list.

The no-parameter constructor of the List class constructs a single-selection List object that will stretch in size to match whatever area it is supposed to take up on the screen. The only other constructor makes you specify the number of visible rows in the list, and whether the list is a single- or multiple-selection list box. The isMultipleSelect( ) method of this class returns true if the list is a multiple-selection list. setMultipleSelect( ) can be used to switch a List object between single- and multiple-selection after the list has been created.

The List class' public interface actually looks a lot like the public interface of a linked list class. After all, what is a List but an ordered queue of strings. The graphical interface details of the List class are abstracted away behind the List class' public interface, so you can see how it would look like a linked list.

This table shows the functionalities that you would expect from a linked list class, and the equivalent function in the public interface of the List class. Every functionality you could reasonably expect is included in the List class.

Functionality	List Class Method
Get count of elements in the list	countItems( )
Empty the list	clear( )
Append an item to the list	addItem(String)
Insert an item in the list	addItem(String, index)
Replace an item in the list with another item	replaceItem(String, index)
Delete an item from the list	delItem(index)

As the second of the two List class constructors implies, List objects have a set number of rows. The getRows( ) method returns the number of rows specified to the List class constructor. A value of 0 indicates that the no-parameter constructor was used, and the List object will be as large as it needs to be to fill whatever desktop bounds it is given.

There are additional methods in the List class' public interface to manage the selections of the list, whether in single- or multiple-selection mode. The methods meant to be used with single-selection lists are a little simpler, so you should read about them first. This simple method will print out a single-selection list's selected string to System.out:

```
public void displaySelection(List list) {
    System.out.println("Item #" + list.getSelectedIndex() + ": " +
                    list.getSelectedItem());
}
```

which demonstrates the getSelectedIndex( ) and getSelectedItem( ) methods of the List class.

The multiple-selection list is a little more complicated. This code does essentially what the previous method did; it prints out the selected indexes and strings of a multiple-selection list component to System.out:

```
public void displaySelection(List list) {
    int[] an = list.getSelectedIndexes();
    String[] astr = list.getSelectedItems();

    for(int i=0 ; i<an.length ; i++)
        System.out.println("Item #" + an[i] + ": " + astr[i]);
}
```

So, you can see that the getSelectedIndex( ) and getSelectedIndexes( ) methods do essentially the same things, the only difference being that the latter returns an array of indexes. Similarly, the getSelectedfItem( ) and getSelectedItems( ) methods do about the same thing, the only difference being that getSelectedItems( ) returns an array of strings.

For both single- and multiple-selection lists, you use the same methods to change the selected items programmatically. The select( ) method takes an index as its only parameter. When called, it causes the specified item to become selected if it is not already. In a single-selection list, calling this method will cause the currently selected item to be deselected, since you can't have more than one item selected in a single-selection list. In a multiple-selection list, you call this method for each of the items you want to select. The deselect( ) method unselects the item at the specified index, and it works in the same way for single- and multiple-selection lists. isSelected( ) tells whether or not an item at a particular index is selected.

When the number of items in a list is longer than the list can display on the screen with its given bounding rectangle, then the list automatically creates a scrollbar and adds it to the list's interface. You have a limited control over the scrolling from within your programs. The makeVisible( ) method will cause the list to move its scrollbar either up or down to ensure that the item at the specified index is shown on the screen. This can be useful if you wanted to coordinate the actions of a TextField and a list. The following example code does just that, and shown here is a screen shot of the working program.

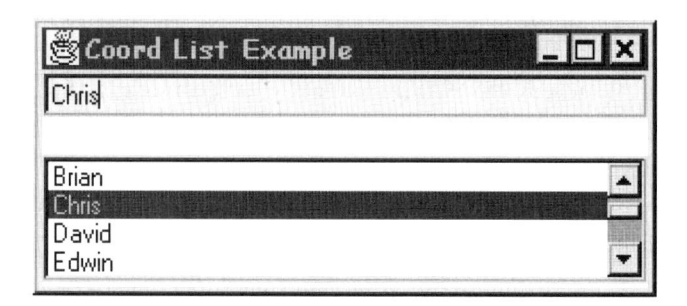

Listing 4.4
A coordinated list box and text field example

```
import java.awt.*;
import java.util.*;

public class CoordExample extends Frame {
    public static void main(String astrArgs[]) {
        CoordExample ce = new CoordExample();
        ce.show();
    }
```

AWT Controls and Menus

```java
public CoordExample() {
    super("Coord List Example");
    m_list = new List();

    m_vect.addElement("Albert");
    m_vect.addElement("Brian");
    m_vect.addElement("Chris");
    m_vect.addElement("David");
    m_vect.addElement("Edwin");
    m_vect.addElement("Frank");
    m_vect.addElement("Gershom");
    m_vect.addElement("Hank");
    m_vect.addElement("Igor");
    m_vect.addElement("Justin");

    // Add strings to the list.
    Enumeration enum = m_vect.elements();
    while(enum.hasMoreElements())
        m_list.addItem((String)enum.nextElement());

    // Modify strings in the vector so they are all lower case.
    enum = m_vect.elements();
    while(enum.hasMoreElements())
        ((String)enum.nextElement()).toLowerCase();

    // Now that list and vector are initialized,
    // create our UI.
    setLayout(new BorderLayout(5, 5));
    add("North", m_text = new TextField());
    add("South", m_list);
}

public boolean keyUp(Event evt, int key) {
    if(evt.target == m_text) {
        int i = m_vect.indexOf(m_text.getText().toLowerCase());
        if(-1 != i)
            m_list.select(i);
    }

    return super.keyUp(evt, key);
}

public boolean handleEvent(Event evt) {
return false;
}

// Private instance members.
private TextField m_text;
```

```
    private List m_list;
    private Vector m_vect;
}
```

One thing is not demonstrated by this program: how to detect user interactions with the list element. When the user double-clicks on a list element, the List object will automatically send an ACTION_EVENT to the list's parent container. When the user single-clicks on list items, then the parent container receives an Event with a special Event ID reserved for use only by the List class. The Event ID is LIST_SELECT. Thus, if the user double-clicks on a list item, then your program will receive first a LIST_SELECT event, then an ACTION_EVENT event. There is one more specially reserved Event ID for use by multiple-selection lists: LIST_DESELECT. When one of a multiple-selection list's items become unselected, then the parent container receives a LIST_DESELECT event indicating what the user has done.

The Choice Class

A drop-down list box is very similar to a list box. Functionally, they are about the same. The difference is in appearance. Drop-down list boxes usually only take up a single line of room on the screen. When the user selects the element, however, its list *drops down*, revealing a selectable list. Only while the drop-down list has keyboard focus does the list stay exposed. Once the keyboard focus leaves the element, it collapses to a single line that displays the selected item. Figure 4-2 shows a program that uses a drop-down list element. There is also a slight difference in capability. Drop-down list boxes in Java cannot be multiple-selection lists.

In Java, the java.awt.Choice element is used for drop-down lists. There is only a single constructor to the Choice class, and it takes no arguments. Basically, your Choice object will be as wide on the screen as the room it is given. Its preferred size will be wide enough to accommodate the widest string that's been added to it.

Unlike the list element, the choice element's public interface includes only those methods that are absolutely necessary to manage the contents of the Choice object. The addItem( ), getItem( ), and countItems( ) methods are all you get for polling the contents of the Choice object. As you can infer from this limited interface, there is no way to remove an item from a choice once it has been added. Instead, you must create a whole new Choice object and replace the one in your interface with it.

You actually have more methods in the interface that can be used to manage the single selection of the choice than you do to help you manage the contents. The getSelectedIndex( ) and getSelectedItem( ) methods mirror the

AWT Controls and Menus

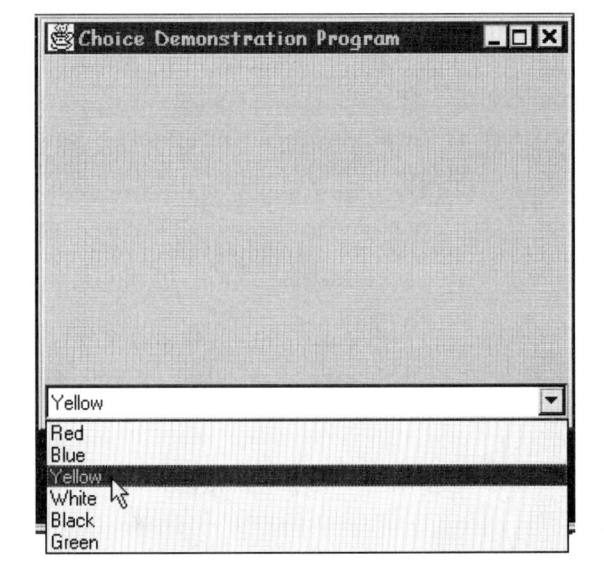

Figure 4-2.
A drop-down list box, or Choice object, in use

methods of the same name in the List class. Two overloaded versions of the select( ) method exist so that you may select an item either by index or by its string value. This program demonstrates using a choice element:

Listing 4.5 Example program demonstrating the Choice class

```
import java.awt.*;

public class ChoiceDemo extends Frame {
    public static void main(String[] astrArgs) {
        ChoiceDemo cd = new ChoiceDemo();
        cd.show();
    }

    public ChoiceDemo() {
        super("Choice Demonstration Program");

        Canvas canvRed = new Canvas();
        Canvas canvBlue = new Canvas();
        Canvas canvYellow = new Canvas();
        Canvas canvWhite = new Canvas();
        Canvas canvBlack = new Canvas();
        Canvas canvGreen = new Canvas();

        canvRed.setBackground( Color.red );
        canvBlue.setBackground( Color.blue );
        canvYellow.setBackground( Color.yellow );
        canvWhite.setBackground( Color.white );
        canvBlack.setBackground( Color.black );
```

```java
            canvGreen.setBackground( Color.green );

            m_panelCanvases = new Panel();
            m_panelCanvases.setLayout(m_cardlayout = new CardLayout());
            m_panelCanvases.add("Red", canvRed);
            m_panelCanvases.add("Blue", canvBlue);
            m_panelCanvases.add("Yellow", canvYellow);
            m_panelCanvases.add("White", canvWhite);
            m_panelCanvases.add("Black", canvBlack);
            m_panelCanvases.add("Green", canvGreen);

            setLayout(new BorderLayout());
            add("North", m_choice = new Choice());
            add("Center", m_panelCanvases);

            m_choice.addItem("Red");
            m_choice.addItem("Blue");
            m_choice.addItem("Yellow");
            m_choice.addItem("White");
            m_choice.addItem("Black");
            m_choice.addItem("Green");
        }

        public boolean handleEvent(Event evt) {
            if((evt.id == Event.ACTION_EVENT) && (evt.target == m_choice)) {
                m_cardlayout.show(m_panelCanvases, (String)evt.arg);
                return true;
            }
            return false;
        }

        // Private instance members.
        private Choice m_choice;
        private Panel m_panelCanvases;
        private CardLayout m_cardlayout;
}
```

This program demonstrates how to handle item selections by the user. Item selections are represented as ACTION_EVENT events, where the event's *target* member variable is a reference to the choice element. This is the same event that is passed to the container of Lists when the user double-clicks on one of the List's items.

Creating GUIs with the ResourceWizard

If you are a Windows C/C++ programmer familiar with either the Windows SDK or the VC++/MFC development environments, then you no doubt are

AWT Controls and Menus

familiar with the idea of *dialog resources*. A dialog resource is a definition of sorts. It defines a GUI made up of built-in windows components, such as the ones I have described above.

Visual J++ is a personality module of the Microsoft Developer Studio. So, you can use the resource editor built into the Developer Studio. The resource editor is great at helping you dummy up, define, or refine GUIs that use standard windows controls. If you are one of Microsoft's army of Windows developers, then you no doubt have seen a dialog editor before. Figure 4-3 is a screen shot of the Visual J++ dialog editor with a dialog being edited in it.

What Visual J++ adds to the dialog editor is a ResourceWizard that can turn your dialog resource into a working Java class. It's very easy to do, and can save you a lot of time. Figure 4-4 is a screen shot of the dialog as an applet interface after the ResourceWizard has made a Dialog class out of the dialog being edited in Figure 4-3. It only took about 15 minutes to generate the entire interface using the Visual J++ dialog editor and the ResourceWizard. While ResourceWizard-generated dialogs are usable in Java applications, you will find they work best as interfaces to embedded applets. You can read about the reasons why in the following paragraphs of this section.

In order to get the ResourceWizard to generate a Dialog class like this, you must start the Visual J++ dialog editor. The dialog editor is kick-started whenever you create a new dialog resource in your Java project. Below are the VJ++ toolbar buttons that create a new dialog resource in your project.

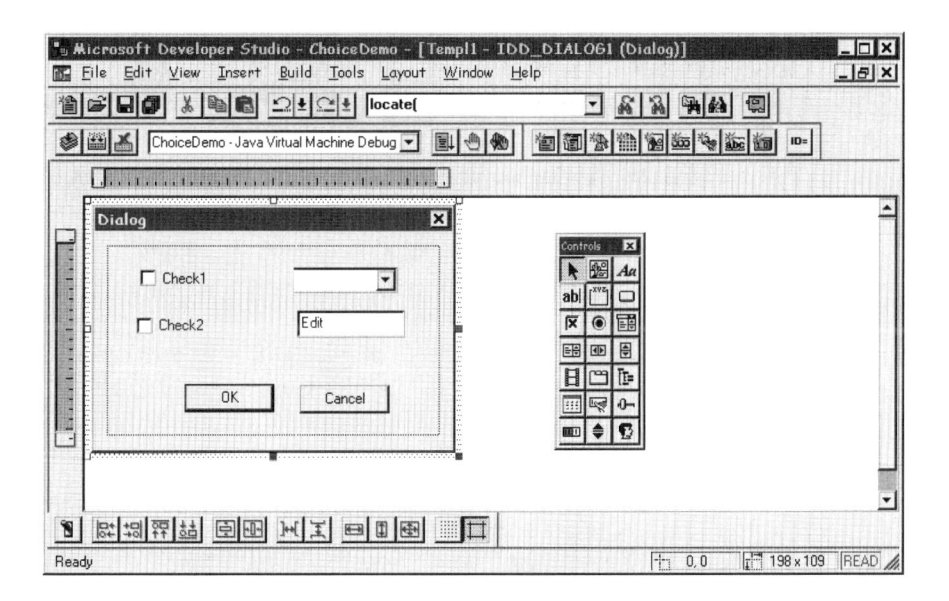

The Visual J++ dialog editor
Figure 4-3.

A ResourceWizard generated dialog as an applet interface
Figure 4-4.

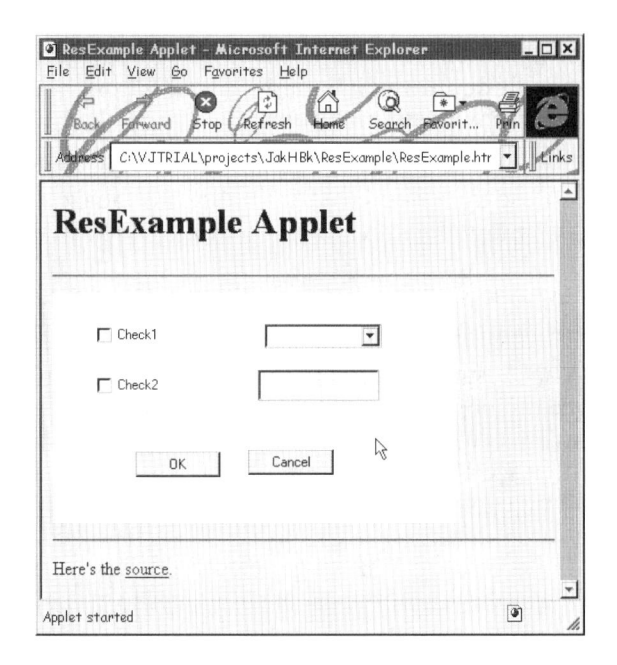

You can either click on this button or use the File|New menu option to create a new dialog in your project.

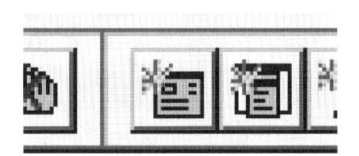

You edit the dialog by adding new visual elements to your dialog's surface, then positioning and resizing them using the dialog editor. That's really all there is to it.

When you have finished editing your dialog resource, you must name it. By double-clicking on any exposed portion of the dialog window's surface in the dialog editor, or by using the Edit/Dialog menu option, you will get to the dialog's property sheet. The identifier of the dialog will become the dialog class' name (though you will have the option of changing this value during the conversion), and the dialog's text will become its title.

Save the resource file. Use the File/Save menu option. If the dialog resource is the first resource in the new resource file, then you will be prompted for a filename. You might find it easiest to use a name that is the same as the main class filename in your project. All your dialog and menu resources can

AWT Controls and Menus

be saved to this same file. The file will have an .RCT extension; if the "Save as type:" edit box does not say "Resource Template (*.rct)", click on the drop-down box's arrow and change the selection to "Resource Template."

You are now ready to use the Java ResourceWizard to convert your dialog resource into a Java class. From the Tools menu, select the Java ResourceWizard menu option. The Java ResourceWizard will then prompt you for the name of the resource template (.RCT) or compiled resource (.RES) file containing the dialogs and menus you want to use in your Java application(s). Select the resource template with the dialog you created, then hit the Next button. The ResourceWizard then displays a table of dialogs and menus defined in your resource template. The purpose of this table is both to allow you to select the dialogs or menus you want changed into Java classes and to allow you to give names for the Java classes that are created. For example, the default name for dialogs created by the resource editor looks something like "IDD_DIALOG1." That's not a very pretty name for a Java class, so you may want to change it. Change it by double-clicking on the Class Name column of the table and typing in the name you want to use for the class. Figure 4-5 shows this step of converting a sample dialog into a Java class using the ResourceWizard.

The Java ResourceWizard will then generate two classes for you. The first class is your Dialog class. The second class is called DialogLayout (more on that in a second). You will need to add these two classes to your Java project. To add the classes, use the File/Insert Into Project menu option from VJ++'s

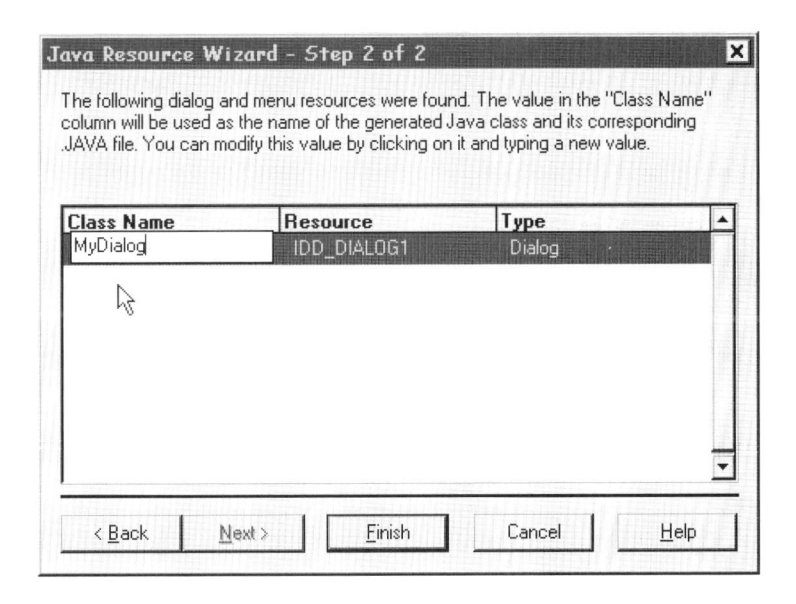

Changing the class name of a ResourceWizard generated class
Figure 4-5.

main menu. The two files to add to your project are: DialogLayout.java and
<your-class-name>.java. (You will only have to add DialogLayout.java to your
class once. If you make more than one ResourceWizard-generated Dialog
class, don't bother adding DialogLayout.java to your project again after
the first time.)

The Dialog class you created has a constructor that takes a single parameter:
a container. Create the dialog, passing the container you want the dialog
interface to be created on. After you have created the Dialog object, use its
CreateControls( ) method to place the dialog controls onto your container.
When you do this, the container will automatically have the dialog's
interface recreated on it. This sample code demonstrates how to use a
ResourceWizard-generated Dialog class named MyDialog:

```
Panel p = new Panel( );              // Container to place dialog UI on.
MyDialog dlg = new MyDialog(p);      // associated dialog with Container.
dlg.CreateControls( );               // Creates controls and places them on p.
```

What ResourceWizard-generated Classes Look Like

Figure 4-6 is a screen shot of a dialog that was generated using the
ResourceWizard following the steps outlined previously. Following that
screen shot is the actual ResourceWizard-generated code for the dialog. If

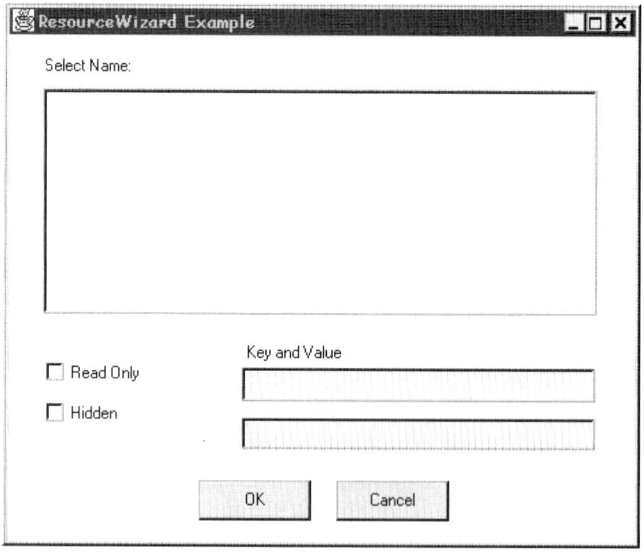

Dialog interface generated by VJ++'s ResourceWizard
Figure 4-6.

AWT Controls and Menus

you can follow any of the other GUI code samples in this chapter, then you certainly can follow the code that the ResourceWizard has generated for us.

Listing 4.6 ResourceWizard-generated Dialog UI class

```java
public class MyDialog
{
    Container   m_Parent       = null;
    boolean     m_fInitialized = false;
    DialogLayout m_Layout;

    // Control definitions
    //---------------------------------------------------------------
    Button      IDOK;
    Button      IDCANCEL;
    List        m_listNames;
    Label       m_labelNames1;
    Checkbox    m_chkbxReadOnly;
    Checkbox    m_chkbxHidden;
    TextField   m_tfKey;
    TextField   m_tfVal;
    Label       m_labelKeyVal;


    // Constructor
    //---------------------------------------------------------------
    public MyDialog (Container parent)
    {
        m_Parent = parent;
    }

    // Initialization.
    //---------------------------------------------------------------
    public boolean CreateControls()
    {
        // CreateControls should be called only once
        //-----------------------------------------------------------
        if (m_fInitialized || m_Parent == null)
            return false;

        // m_Parent must be extended from the Container class
        //-----------------------------------------------------------
        if (!(m_Parent instanceof Container))
            return false;
        // Since a given font may not be supported across all platforms, it
        // is safe to modify only the size of the font, not the typeface.
        //-----------------------------------------------------------
        Font OldFnt = m_Parent.getFont();
```

```java
        if (OldFnt != null)
         {
            Font NewFnt = new Font(OldFnt.getName(), OldFnt.getStyle(), 8);

            m_Parent.setFont(NewFnt);
         }

        // All position and sizes are in dialog logical units, so we use a
        // DialogLayout as our layout manager.
        //---------------------------------------------------------
        m_Layout = new DialogLayout(m_Parent, 310, 230);
        m_Parent.setLayout(m_Layout);
        m_Parent.addNotify();

        Dimension size  = m_Layout.getDialogSize();
        Insets    insets = m_Parent.insets();

        m_Parent.resize(insets.left + size.width  + insets.right,
    insets.top  + size.height + insets.bottom);

        // Control creation
        //---------------------------------------------------------
        IDOK = new Button ("OK");
        m_Parent.add(IDOK);
        m_Layout.setShape(IDOK, 94, 195, 55, 18);

        IDCANCEL = new Button ("Cancel");
        m_Parent.add(IDCANCEL);
        m_Layout.setShape(IDCANCEL, 161, 195, 55, 18);

        m_listNames = new List (1, false);
        m_Parent.add(m_listNames);
        m_Layout.setShape(m_listNames, 17, 23, 271, 107);

        m_labelNames1 = new Label ("Select Name:", Label.LEFT);
        m_Parent.add(m_labelNames1);
        m_Layout.setShape(m_labelNames1, 17, 7, 116, 12);

        m_chkbxReadOnly = new Checkbox ("Read Only");
        m_Parent.add(m_chkbxReadOnly);
        m_Layout.setShape(m_chkbxReadOnly, 19, 140, 69, 16);

        m_chkbxHidden = new Checkbox ("Hidden");
        m_Parent.add(m_chkbxHidden);
        m_Layout.setShape(m_chkbxHidden, 19, 158, 69, 16);
```

AWT Controls and Menus

```
            m_tfKey = new TextField ("");
            m_Parent.add(m_tfKey);
            m_Layout.setShape(m_tfKey, 114, 145, 173, 16);

            m_tfVal = new TextField ("");
            m_Parent.add(m_tfVal);
            m_Layout.setShape(m_tfVal, 114, 167, 173, 15);

            m_labelKeyVal = new Label ("Key and Value", Label.LEFT);
            m_Parent.add(m_labelKeyVal);
            m_Layout.setShape(m_labelKeyVal, 116, 134, 115, 10);

            m_fInitialized = true;
            return true;
        }
    }
```

Notice that the ResourceWizard has generated code and provided methods for you to handle certain events within your Dialog class. That's really very convenient, since for the most part that skeleton code always looks the same. And don't get spoiled by the ResourceWizard-generated comments: there are far too many Windows programs out there whose only source code comments were generated by development "wizards" like VJ++'s ResourceWizard or AppletWizard, and VC++'s AppWizard.

The DialogLayout Class

When you use the ResourceWizard to generate a Dialog class for you, the ResourceWizard automatically adds a DialogLayout class to your project. This class is capable of laying out the components that make up your Dialog class' interface in exactly the same way you designed the dialog in the dialog editor.

The DialogLayout class is given the dimensions of a bounding rectangle for each component to be added to the dialog's interface. The values of that rectangle are not pixel distances on the screen. Instead, they are in *dialog units*. A dialog unit is a scalable unit that has a different value depending on the resolution of the screen the program is running on. On screens with higher resolution, a dialog unit is equal to a larger number of pixels. On lower resolution screens, a dialog unit is equal to a lower number of pixels.

The idea is that you want your dialog to scale in size so that its components remain visible to the user. For example, imagine designing a dialog resource in the dialog editor on a screen that is 800 × 600 in dimension. At a later time, after you've completed what you believe to be the seminal GUI to end all GUIs, a user tries to use your program on a system with a $1,120 \times 800$ screen. Suddenly, the list boxes and edit boxes you laid out so carefully are 25 percent smaller, and suddenly your GUI doesn't look so fantastic anymore!

The DialogLayout class avoids this problem by scaling the dialog units relative to the size of the *dialog font*. On any system, the dialog font is the font used to display labels, checkbox titles, and so on by default. On windowing systems, the size of this font will change relative to the resolution of the screen, so that larger font sizes will be used on higher resolution screens, and smaller font sizes will be used on systems with lower resolution screens. A dialog unit is defined as equal to 1/8 of the width of the average character of the dialog font in the X direction, and 1/4 of the height of the dialog font. (Unlike with width of a font, which varies by the character, the *height* of a font is constant across all characters even if the individual characters do not have the same height.)

So, you can see how the DialogLayout class is quite useful. If you read Chapter 3, which covers layout managers, you might also have guessed one of the biggest drawbacks of the DialogLayout class: it doesn't scale based on the dimension of the container. That is, your dialogs are defined in the dialog editor to be one single size (in dialog units). If the container your dialog interface finds itself in changes in size, however, then your dialog will not look so nice any more. In a worst case, your child components will be clipped by the right or bottom edge of the container, which might render the interface completely useless.

You will find that this problem with dialog layouts is minimal for embedded applet interfaces. When an applet is embedded, it is given a specific width and height as defined by the HTML document the applet is embedded in. That means you can guarantee the size of an applet container, and so you may design your dialog interfaces around that specific size. (Or, conversely, you may define your applet's size based on the size of your dialog resource.)

In this case, the DialogLayout class will still use dialog units when specifying the sizes of your components. Just make sure your applet is slightly larger than what the dialog resource calls for. Only users with screen resolutions towards the extremes will find any difficulties at all. If you find you really need to reach users with these types of screens without any UI problems, you can modify the DialogLayout class generated by the ResourceWizard for your project to use more hard-coded units than dialog units.

Menus

Along with push buttons, one of the most recognized GUI elements is the window menu. Certainly if you have ever done any interface design or building before, then you have seen window menus. Here is a sample Java application with a menu:

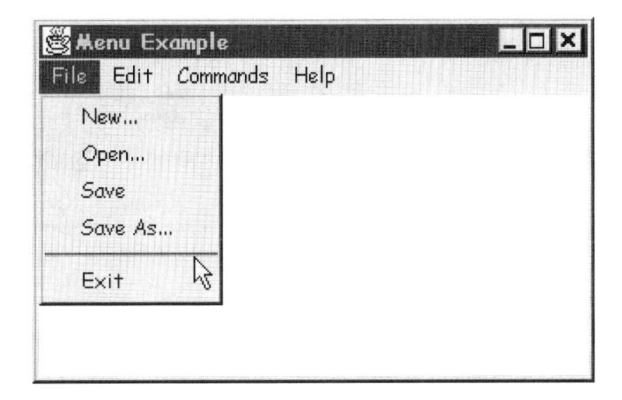

A menu is essentially a list of commands arranged hierarchically. At the top of the hierarchy is the large categories of commands. The unwritten standard menu command categories that should be present in almost every menu are "File," "Edit," and "Help." Take again, for example, the menu displayed above. Note that it has these three major menu categories, as does just about every piece of Windows software Microsoft releases.

So, a menu is a hierarchy of commands. Under the main categories of commands, called *menus* in the *menu bar*, are either individual commands or submenus. You can see in Figure 4-7 an example of a Menu Bar menu with commands and submenus under it.

Visual J++'s ResourceWizard is able to generate menu classes from your menu resources. In much the same way that ResourceWizard can convert dialog resources into source code, it can also convert your menu resources into source code. The time savings is substantial.

Menus, MenuItems, and Menu Bars

The hierarchy of objects used in Java to represent menus is actually quite similar to the hierarchy Java uses to represent an interface's container/component hierarchy. In the UI hierarchy, all elements are derived from components. Similarly, in Java the MenuComponent class is the cornerstone of the Menu classes.

The java.awt.Component class defines the functionalities that are the same for all visual elements. The MenuComponent class does the same in Java.

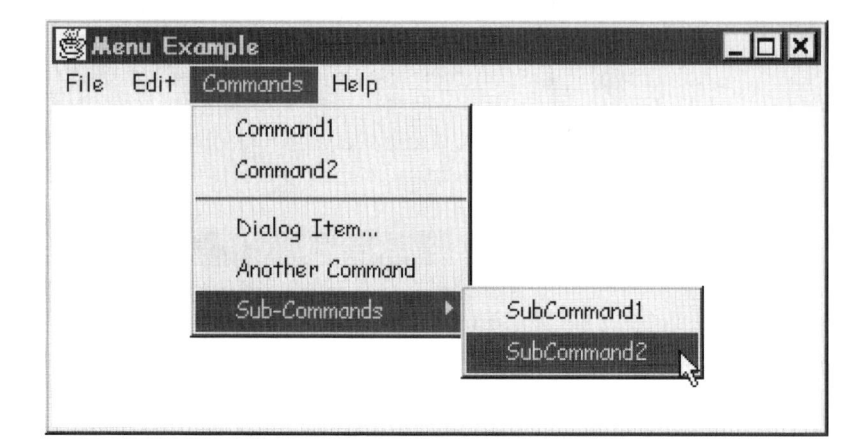

Menu with commands and submenus
Figure 4-7.

The simplest, nonabstract MenuComponent class is the MenuItem class. A menu item represents a simple command in Java.

Additionally, you have the Container class in Java's AWT that can contain zero or more components. There is similarly a Menu class (derived from the MenuComponent class) that can contain other menu components, including other menus. Therefore, using Menu and MenuItem class objects, you can build up a hierarchy of commands and submenus within parent menus.

The top-level Menu class in Java is called the Menubar class. The highest level sibling menus must all be contained within the same menu bar. Only a menu bar can be associated with a top-level Frame to create a full-fledged menu using Java's AWT. This is always true: you can only create a menu in a top-level window, and that does not include Dialog class–derived windows. The Frame must be a true top-level, unparented window in order to have a working menu bar. The Frame.setMenubar( ) method associates a menu bar with a top-level Frame window.

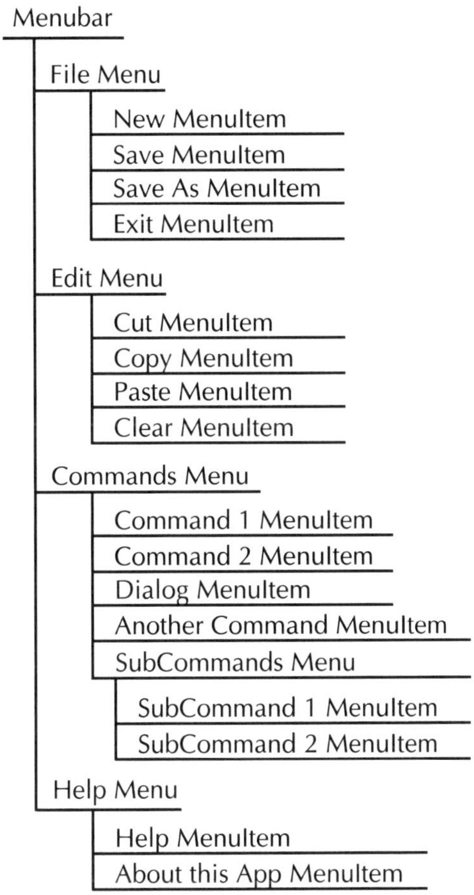

AWT Controls and Menus

Sample hierarchy of an application menu
Figure 4-8.

```
Menubar
├── File Menu
│   ├── New MenuItem
│   ├── Save MenuItem
│   ├── Save As MenuItem
│   └── Exit MenuItem
├── Edit Menu
│   ├── Cut MenuItem
│   ├── Copy MenuItem
│   ├── Paste MenuItem
│   └── Clear MenuItem
├── Commands Menu
│   ├── Command 1 MenuItem
│   ├── Command 2 MenuItem
│   ├── Dialog MenuItem
│   ├── Another Command MenuItem
│   └── SubCommands Menu
│       ├── SubCommand 1 MenuItem
│       └── SubCommand 2 MenuItem
└── Help Menu
    ├── Help MenuItem
    └── About this App MenuItem
```

Figure 4-8 is the hierarchy of a sample menu. You can see it holds the quasi-standard File, Edit, and Help menus. The Java code for creating this menu is included here:

Listing 4.7 A sample method that creates a Menubar

```
public Menubar createMenu() {
    Menubar mbar = new Menubar();

    // Make the File menu
    Menu menuFile = new Menu("File");
    menuFile.add(new MenuItem("New..."));
    menuFile.add(new MenuItem("Open..."));
```

```
    menuFile.add(new MenuItem("Save"));
    menuFile.add(new MenuItem("Save As..."));
    menuFile.add("-"); // seperator
    menuFile.add(new MenuItem("Exit"));

    // Make the Edit menu
    Menu menuEdit = new Menu("Edit");
    menuEdit.add(new MenuItem("Cut"));
    menuEdit.add(new MenuItem("Copy"));
    menuEdit.add(new MenuItem("Paste"));
    menuEdit.add(new MenuItem("Clear"));

    // Make the Commands menu
    Menu menuCommands = new Menu("Commands");
    menuCommands.add(new MenuItem("Command1"));
    menuCommands.add(new MenuItem("Command2"));
    menuCommands.add("-"); // seperator
    menuCommands.add(new MenuItem("Dialog Item..."));
    menuCommands.add(new MenuItem("Another Command"));
    menuCommands.add("-"); // seperator

    // Submenu under the Commands menu.
    Menu menuSubCommands = new Menu("SubCommands");
    menuSubCommands.add(new MenuItem("SubCommand1"));
    menuSubCommands.add(new MenuItem("SubCommand2"));
    menuCommands.add(menuSubCommands);

    // Make the Help menu.
    Menu menuHelp = new Menu("Help");
    menuHelp.add(new MenuItem("Help"));
    menuHelp.add("-"); // seperator
    menuHelp.add(new MenuItem("About this app..."));
    // Add the menu items to the Menubar.
    mbar.add(menuFile);
    mbar.add(menuEdit);
    mbar.add(menuCommands);
    mbar.add(menuHelp);

    return mbar;
}
```

MenuItems

Individual MenuItem objects, which represent single commands on a menu, have two pieces of state information:

AWT Controls and Menus

- **Label** The text displayed on the menu. Usually this is a verb for simple commands (Open, Paste, Help). For more complex commands that require a modal dialog to configure, an ellipsis after the command label indicates that a modal dialog will appear when the menu item is selected (Open..., "About this application...").
- **isEnabled** Whether or not the menu item is currently enabled. A disabled menu item is indicated to the user by a grayed-out label on the menu. This item is not selectable by the user.

The MenuItem class has several methods for examining and modifying these state variables. The setLabel( ) method can be used to changed the displayed text of a menu item at any time. The getLabel( ) method returns the label string currently being used to display the menu item. Use the isEnabled( ) method to poll for whether or not the menu item is currently enabled. Use the enable( ) and disable( ) methods to toggle the enabled state of the menu item.

The MenuItem constructor creates a menu item with these internal-state variables already initialized. The first version of the constructor requires that the label string be passed to the constructor:

```
public MenuItem(String strLabel)
```

When an enabled menu item is selected by the user, the menu bar's Frame window receives an ACTION_EVENT. The target of the action is the menu item selected, and the *arg* variable of the Event object is equal to the string label of the menu item. Here's some example code that handles menu events for a top-level Frame:

Listing 4.8 A smart way to handle Menu events

```
public boolean action(Event evt, Object arg) {
    if(evt.target instanceof MenuItem)
        return handleMenuAction(evt, (MenuItem)evt.target, (String)arg);
    ...
}

public boolean handleMenuAction(Event evt, MenuItem target,
                String strLabel) {
    if(evt.target == m_menuitemCommand1) {
        doCommand1();
        return true;
    } else if(evt.target == m_menuitemCommand2) {
        doCommmand2();
        return true;
    } else
        return false;
}
```

Menus

Menu objects include the same internal-state information that the MenuItem class does. Specifically, a menu has a label and an enabled flag. Like the MenuItem class, a menu's label can be changed using the getLabel( ) and setLabel( ) methods. In fact, the Menu class is derived from the MenuItem class, so the methods isEnabled( ), enable( ), and disable( ) are present for all Menu objects just the same as they are for menu items.

A menu is a container for other menus and for menu items. As such, the public interface of the Menu class includes methods for examining and modifying the submenus and command items under the menu. As you have seen in previous examples, the add( ) method adds a menu or a menu item to the menu. Menus added as children under a menu are called submenus. Not shown in the previous examples is the overloaded version of add( ) that creates your menu item for you, as in this example:

```
Menu menu = new Menu("Menu");
menu.add("Sample MenuItem"); // MenuItem made automatically
```

The Menu class' public interface does not allow you to get a reference to this created menu item when you use this version of add( ), so you will not want to use it if you need to maintain a reference to your menu items.

The companion method to add( ) is remove( ). Specify the zero-based index of the menu item or menu to remove an item from this menu. A child item's index is determined by the order it was added to the menu. That is, the first element to be added to the menu has index zero. The second has index one, and so on. You may also remove an item given just a reference to it, instead of its zero-based index within the parent menu. An overloaded version of the remove( ) method takes a reference to the menu or menu item to remove. Thus, this piece of sample code

```
Menu menu = new Menu("Menu");
menu.add(new MenuItem("Remove Me!"));
...
menu.remove(0);
```

does exactly the same thing as this:

```
Menu menu = new Menu("Menu");
MenuItem mi = new MenuItem("Remove Me!");
menu.add(mi);
...
menu.remove(mi);
```

Using ResourceWizard to Make Menu Classes

In the same way that the ResourceWizard can generate Dialog classes from dialog resources, the ResourceWizard can generate a Menu class from menu resources. Visual J++'s resource editor facilities allow you to create a menu visually. The ResourceWizard then takes the menu resource you have created and saved, and it generates a Menu class from it. This can be a great timesaver. Take a look at some of the menu examples given previously. See that they are not an insignificant amount of code. Letting the ResourceWizard generate menus from your menu resources is much more efficient than trying to type all the boring menu creation code in by hand.

To have ResourceWizard generate a Menu class for you, start by creating a menu resource. Use the Insert/Resource... Main Menu option in VJ++, and select Menu as the type of resource you'd like to add. The menu editor will appear. By using the menu editor, you can define menus much more quickly than you could by defining the menu in Java source code by hand.

The menu editor has space on the menu properties dialog for you to type in the label and the identifier of each menu item (though you may only specify the label of menus and submenus). The identifier will be used as the generated class private member variable for the menu item. Use the Seperator checkbox to specify a seperator in your menu.

Once you have defined your sample menu, save the menu resource. You may save multiple menu and dialog resources to the same .RCT file, which makes project management much easier. Don't forget to give the generated class name: the menu's identifier in the menu editor is used as the generated class' name. For example, if I use an identifier "MyMenu" for a menu resource, then when called to generate a Menu class from this resource the ResourceWizard will create a file named MyMenu.java that defines a MyMenu class. You must add this file to your project. Here is some sample source code generated by the ResourceWizard for the same sample menu given in code previously:

Listing 4.9 ResourceWizard-generated MenuBar code

```
public class MyMenu
{
    Frame     m_Frame       = null;
    boolean m_fInitialized = false;

    // MenuBar definitions
    //-------------------------------------------------------------
    MenuBar mb;

    // Menu and Menu item definitions
    //-------------------------------------------------------------
    Menu m1;    // File
```

```java
    MenuItem m_miNew;          // New...
    MenuItem m_miOpen;         // Open...
    MenuItem m_miSave;         // Save
    MenuItem m_miSaveAs;       // Save As...
    MenuItem ID_FILE;          // -
    MenuItem m_miExit;         // Exit
    Menu m8;         // Edit
    MenuItem m_miCut;          // Cut
    MenuItem m_miCopy;         // Copy
    MenuItem m_miPaste;        // Paste
    MenuItem m_miClear;        // Clear
    Menu m13;        // SubCommands
    MenuItem m_miCommand1;     // Command1
    MenuItem m_miCommand2;     // Command2
    Menu m16;        // SubCommand2
    MenuItem m_miSubCommand1;  // SubCommand1
    MenuItem m_miSubCommand2;  // SubCommand2
    Menu m19;        // Help
    MenuItem m_miHelp;         // Help
    MenuItem m_miAbout;        // About this Application...

    // Constructor
    //-------------------------------------------------------------
    public MyMenu (Frame frame)
    {
        m_Frame = frame;
    }

    // Initialization.
    //-------------------------------------------------------------
    public boolean CreateMenu()
    {
        // Can only init controls once
        //---------------------------------------------------------
        if (m_fInitialized || m_Frame == null)
            return false;

        // Create menubar and attach to the frame
        //---------------------------------------------------------
        mb = new MenuBar();
        m_Frame.setMenuBar(mb);

        // Create menu and menu items and assign to menubar
        //---------------------------------------------------------
        m1 = new Menu("File");
        mb.add(m1);
            m_miNew = new MenuItem("New...");
            m1.add(m_miNew);
```

AWT Controls and Menus

```
            m_miOpen = new MenuItem("Open...");
            m1.add(m_miOpen);
            m_miSave = new MenuItem("Save");
            m1.add(m_miSave);
            m_miSaveAs = new MenuItem("Save As...");
            m1.add(m_miSaveAs);
            m1.add("-");
            m_miExit = new MenuItem("Exit");
            m1.add(m_miExit);
        m8 = new Menu("Edit");
        mb.add(m8);
            m_miCut = new MenuItem("Cut");
            m8.add(m_miCut);
            m_miCopy = new MenuItem("Copy");
            m8.add(m_miCopy);
            m_miPaste = new MenuItem("Paste");
            m8.add(m_miPaste);
            m_miClear = new MenuItem("Clear");
            m8.add(m_miClear);
        m13 = new Menu("SubCommands");
        mb.add(m13);
            m_miCommand1 = new MenuItem("Command1");
            m13.add(m_miCommand1);
            m_miCommand2 = new MenuItem("Command2");
            m13.add(m_miCommand2);
            m16 = new Menu("SubCommand2");
            m13.add(m16);
                m_miSubCommand1 = new MenuItem("SubCommand1");
                m16.add(m_miSubCommand1);
                m_miSubCommand2 = new MenuItem("SubCommand2");
                m16.add(m_miSubCommand2);
        m19 = new Menu("Help");
        mb.add(m19);
            m_miHelp = new MenuItem("Help");
            m19.add(m_miHelp);
            m_miAbout = new MenuItem("About this Application...");
            m19.add(m_miAbout);

        m_fInitialized = true;
        return true;
    }
}
```

Notice that the menus and submenus have been given stock member variable names *m1*, *m2*, etc. It will be easy for you to go through this class and replace those member names with more appropriate ones, such as *m_menuFile*, *m_menuEdit*, etc.

Use this class by creating an instance, passing the constructor a reference to the Frame you want this menu to be used by. At some point, you must call the Menu class method CreateMenu( ), which generates a menu bar and associates it with your Frame window, like this:

```
Frame f = new Frame();
MyMenu menu = new MyMenu(f);
...
menu.CreateMenu();
```

Summary

A quasi-standard for interface components exists across most major windowed operating systems. This standard includes such elements as push buttons, labels, list boxes, scrollbars, and so on. You cannot hope to create usable GUIs without having familiarity with these common windowing elements.

The java.awt package includes Component classes for these quasi-standard windowing elements. They act just like any other component. That is, they have a bounding rectangle, they receive and handle messages, they are contained within a container, etc. These classes are provided so you do not have to "reinvent the wheel" for common GUI tasks. The java.awt control classes are Label, Button, Scrollbar, Checkbox, List, Choice, TextField, and TextArea.

Similar to Java's Component/Container classes is Java's Menu|MenuItem hierarchy for creating menus on top-level Frame windows. Menu item elements, however, are much simpler elements than components. A menu item is just a label and a little bit of state information (isEnabled, etc.).

Visual J++'s ResourceWizard makes it easy for you to generate dialog interfaces and menubars from resources. The dialog and menu resource editors included with VJ++ make it easy for you to define dialog interfaces or menus in .RCT files. The ResourceWizard can then create classes from those resources. Using the ResourceWizard is much faster and easier than trying to create dialogs or menus by hand using Java.

CHAPTER 5

Graphics

The ability to use Java across the World Wide Web in applets is one of the driving forces behind Java's meteoric rise in popularity. Most Web-based applets involve displaying interactive, animated visual elements and sounds: two things that are difficult to do in a platform-independent manner across the Web without Java. Therefore, interesting, visually grabbing visuals are one of the most exploited capabilities of Java today.

This chapter describes how to perform graphics renderings in Java: text rendering, drawing graphical elements, and drawing images are all covered. By the time you have finished the examples and read through the explanations of this chapter you will be able to add the kind of eye stimuli to your applets that will attract and grab World Wide Web users. By adding the same sorts of graphics to your Java applications, you will find that Java is your preferred language for creating interesting user interfaces (UIs). You will find it easier and faster to create your UIs in Java than in other languages you have used to date for windows-based operating systems.

Of course, graphics and UI work are just window dressing for most programs. The real meat of your applications and applets should still be in the middleware level. Not many programs ever made it to the big time on fancy images or animations alone. But certainly without these features, your programs won't have "legs." They won't hold a user's attention, and consequently the user will move on to the next program (your competitor's) that does. For this reason, a thorough knowledge of Java's graphics system should be a basic tool in your programming toolbox. Luckily, the graphics system is simple, easy to use, and easy to learn. Most of the complexities commonly associated with programming graphics have been abstracted or simplified for you in Java. On the other hand, for those times when you need more raw power, you can get it.

Graphics and Display Surfaces

When you render graphics or text in Java, you render it to some sort of *display surface*. A display surface is, in general, a two-dimensional plane of pixels. Some examples of display surfaces are an in-memory bitmap, the desktop itself, or even a page in a printer. Each of these examples is essentially a 2D surface that can be drawn to.

You can appreciate, however, that each of these example surfaces is very different as far as the system sees it. The in-memory bitmap is actually an array of bytes in memory. So, when you set a particular pixel's color, this translates into setting the value of a particular byte or bytes in regular memory.

But the desktop that the user sees is a more complex beast. At its most basic, it is an array of bytes in the machine's video memory. The operating system generally manages the desktop, so that when you set the color of a particular position on the desktop, it translates into a complex series of operating system calls that eventually modifies the value of video memory; that is, if the desktop position you are trying to modify is not clipped by a child or sibling window, and if the color you are trying to paint can be rendered by the system hardware at all.

A page in the printer, while still being conceptually similar to the in-memory bitmap and the desktop surface, requires special operating system drivers to render anything to it at all. And different printers act completely differently in hardware and in the form of its driver software. So when you try to set the color of a particular position on the page in the printer, that operation is almost indescribably complex. (It could take another whole chapter added to this book just to describe it!)

You would like to have a single, abstract set of method calls (also known as an API, or Application Programming Interface) for rendering text or graphics to any display surface. That way, you wouldn't have to learn multiple different APIs for each different type of surface you want to draw on. Imagine having to write different code for laser printers versus dot matrix printers versus bubble-jet printers. How absurd!

The Java Graphics class contains the single API you want for manipulating all the different types of display surfaces there are. (Well, it may not have the ideal API, but it has a pretty basic and generic one that works.) This is how it works: each Graphics object is *associated with* or *attached to* a single display surface. To render your custom Components on the desktop, you use a Graphics object attached to the Component's bounding rectangle on the desktop surface. To render a figure on a bitmap in memory, you use a Graphics object attached to the in-memory bitmap. Similarly, when you draw on a printer page, you go through the public API of a Graphics object attached to the printer's display surface. The same API is used to draw on these essentially very different, but conceptually very similar, display surfaces. Figure 5-1 shows how different types of surfaces are all manipulated through the Graphics class' public API.

Getting a Surface's Graphics Object

When displaying graphics on the desktop, you are only going to be able to render anything onto a component-derived object. That's because the entire desktop is a hierarchy of components and containers. Even the desktop itself can be thought of as a giant container that contains all other component elements. When you draw on the desktop, you do it onto a particular component's bounding rectangle.

As explained somewhat in Chapter 3, the update( )/paint( ) methods of the Component class are where all desktop rendering takes place. You see, the Java runtime system, in cooperation with the native operating system, manages the desktop. It keeps track of which component occupies what bounding rectangle on the desktop. It keeps track of which components are

Figure 5-1. The Graphics class' API is used to draw on any surface

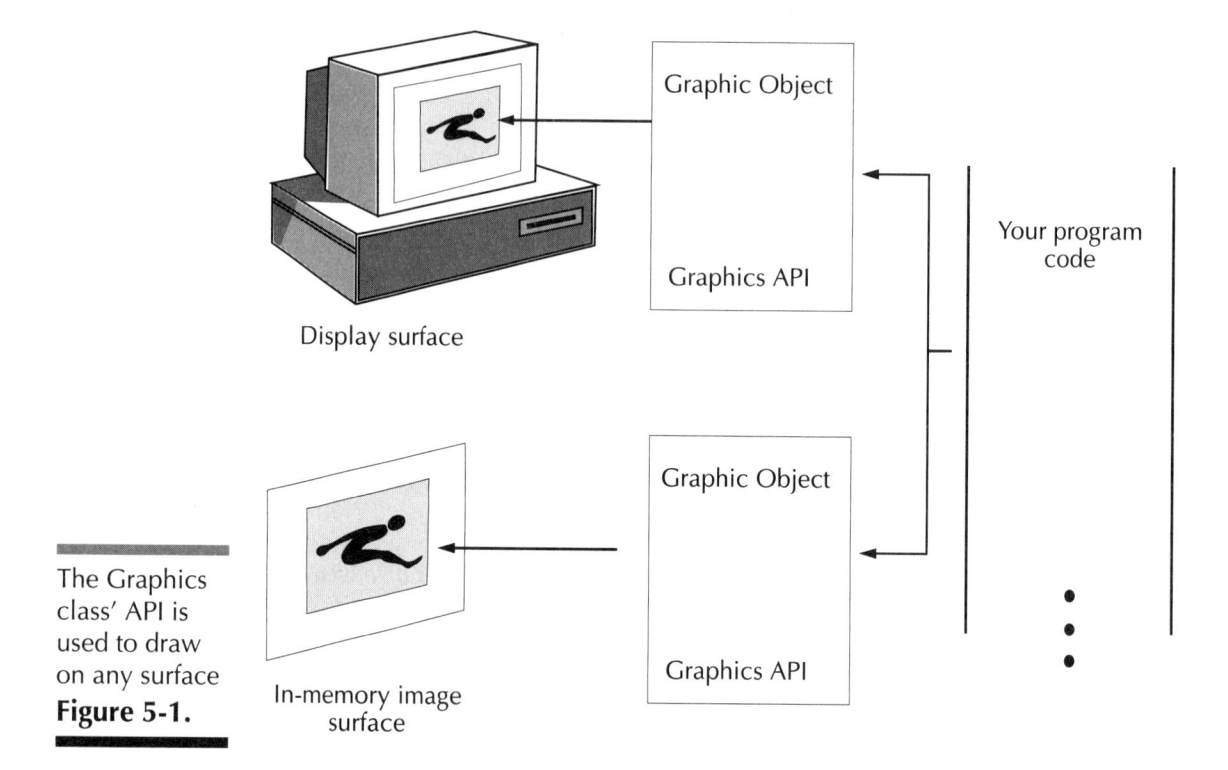

clipping siblings, and exactly when different areas of the desktop have been repainted last. When the Java system detects that a particular area of the desktop needs to be updated (or "painted"), it creates a Graphics object attached to just that rectangle of the desktop and hands the Graphics object to the appropriate component's or components' update( ) method. Here's the signature of update( ):

```
public void update(Graphics g)
```

which has as its only parameter a Graphics object. That Graphics object is attached to some area of the component's bounding rectangle that the system has determined needs to be painted.

There are a couple of different reasons why the system would want to get a component to paint its bounding rectangle on the desktop. For example, say your program creates and displays a modal dialog box until the user hits its OK button. When the OK button is hit, you dismiss the dialog box. At that point, the system is going to get any (and every) component under the modal dialog box to repaint itself as quickly as possible. The area where the dialog box was on the display surface is said to be *invalid*, and it needs to be validated.

Graphics

To validate a component's rectangle, the system calls the component's update( ) method. When the method returns, the rectangle is automatically marked as valid by the system.

Instead of waiting for the system to determine that an area of the screen is invalid and needs to be repainted, you can also force the system to mark a component as invalid using the component's repaint( ) method. The implementation of the method causes the Java system to mark the component as invalid and schedule a call to the component's update( ) method as soon as possible.

The default implementation of the update( ) method calls the component's paint( ) method. Generally, you'll want to do all your rendering within a paint( ) method, not update( ). There are times when the Java system calls paint( ) explicitly, instead of going through update( ). In order to make your component handle those situations as well as the situations where update( ) is called, just implement the paint( ) method, since it gets run in either case.

Anyway, the way to get the Graphics object associated with a particular area of the desktop is to implement the paint( ) method of the component(s) whose bounding rectangles contain the area in question. Use the component's repaint( ) method to force an update( ) as soon as possible.

Graphics Objects

Think of a Graphics object as a toolbox of drawing tools dedicated to a particular drawing surface. With these tools you can draw lines, rectangles, ovals, arcs, polygons, text, and even the contents of some other surfaces (that is, you can even draw a copy of an in-memory image onto another display surface). Using these elemental graphics operations, you can create much more complex figures when drawing.

A Graphics object has an internal set of variables that describes how it is going to draw. For example, a Graphics object has an internal *current color* that is used when drawing simple figures. When you draw those figures, the current color is used to render them. Draw a line on a display surface, and the line will be drawn with the Graphics object's current color. Draw a filled rectangle, and the Graphics object's current color will be used. About the only thing the current color is not used for is to draw other images onto a display surface. In that case, the original colors of the source image are faithfully reproduced on the target display surface without regard to the current color of the Graphics object.

The following table lists the various internal state variables of the Graphics class, and provides a short description of each. After that, you can read more fully about how these variables affect how you use the Graphics object.

State Variable	Description
Surface	The surface attached to the Graphics object. All Graphics objects are attached to and operate on a single display surface. A single surface, however, may have more than one Graphics object attached to it.
Current color	The color used when drawing on the attached surface.
Clipping rectangle	The rectangle of the drawing surface that the Graphics object can draw in. The Graphics object will only draw within this rectangle, and will leave the surface alone outside this rectangle.
Current font	The font used when rendering text on the display surface. Text is rendered in the current color using the current font.
Painting mode	Either *paint* or *XOR* mode. Graphics operations in paint mode overwrite the current pixel values of the display surface. Operations in XOR mode perform a bitwise XOR with the current pixel values of the display surface using an *alternate color*.
Origin	The origin of the X and Y axes in the graphics coordinate system. The origin is the point (0, 0), and is usually the upper-left corner of the display surface, though it can be moved.

The Current Color

The current color is the color used by the Graphics object when drawing anything (except other images) onto a display surface. Any lines you draw, text, rectangles, polygons, etc. are all drawn using the Graphics object's current color.

Colors are described in Java using Color objects. A Color object simply describes a red, green, and blue component. That is, a point in the RBG color space.

To create a Color object, simply pass red, green, and blue component values to the Color class constructor, like this:

Graphics

```
Color colorRed = new Color(255, 0, 0); // full red, no green or blue
```

As you can see, each of these components is described using a byte value, which leaves you room to describe roughly 16 million colors. However, your system is still limited to the number of colors supported by the current hardware configuration; if the color specified is not available, a mapping will be done to find the closest match. You may also create a color using a packed 32-bit integer of RGB color information. Such an integer is described by the mask *0x00rrggbb*. That is, the lower byte is the blue color component, the next byte is the green color component value, and the third byte is the red color component value. The highest byte is termed the *alpha* or transparency component value, though it is not currently used in Java. Here's an example of creating a color using a packed 32-bit integer:

```
Color colorYellow = new Color(0x00FF0000 /* red */ | 0x0000FF00 /* green */);
```

To get the individual red, green, and blue component values of a particular Color object, use the Color class methods getRed( ), getGreen( ), or getBlue( ). The Color class method getRGB( ) returns the packed 32-bit integer for the color, using the same 0x00rrggbb packing scheme described above.

The Color class has several public static color instances you can use for convenience. The Color class defines these Color objects for colors you would commonly use, such as red, green, blue, gray, white, black, magenta, cyan, black, etc. To use these, simply refer to them like this:

```
Color myRedRef = Color.red;
Color myWhiteRef = Color.white;
```

So enough about colors. Here's how you actually use them in a Graphics object. The Graphics class getColor( ) method returns the graphic's current color. And the Graphics class setColor( ) method sets the current color. It's that simple. Here's an example paint( ) method implementation of a hypothetical Component. This method uses a slightly lighter color than the Component's foreground color to do its drawing:

```
public void paint(Graphics g) {
    // Get the current color.
    Color colorCurrent = g.getColor( );

    // Make a new color that is slightly lighter.
    Color colorLighter = new Color(
        colorCurrent.getRed( ) + 5,
```

```
                colorCurrent.getGreen( ) + 5,
                colorCurrent.getBlue( ) + 5)
    );

    ...
}
```

The Clipping Rectangle

A Graphics object is restricted to operating only within a clipping rectangle of the display surface. That is, graphics drawing operations that would affect pixels outside the clipping rectangle end up having no effect.

One place where the clipping rectangle can be seen to be particularly useful is when painting a component on the desktop. The component's paint( ) method is handed a Graphics object attached to the desktop for the component to use to draw itself. Without a clipping rectangle, the component could draw arbitrarily outside its bounding rectangle. That means the component's paint( ) method could draw over neighboring components, over the title bar of your application's main Frame window, or even over any part of the entire desktop. That could be a real mess.

In this case, however, the graphics' clipping rectangle is set to, at largest, the bounding rectangle of the component. If the component tries to draw anything outside this clipping rectangle, the drawing operation results in a no-op. Nothing except the component's rectangle can be drawn by the component. Figure 5-2 illustrates a component's clipping rectangle being the same size as its bounding rectangle.

Incidentally, you can see now that a component's update( )/paint( ) methods may be called several times while the system is trying to update it just once. This would happen in the case where the component is being clipped by, say, a sibling component. The system will in this case break the surface of the component into several rectangles, as illustrated in Figure 5-3. For each of these smaller rectangles, the system will call update( )/paint( ) once, setting the clipping rectangle of the graphics to one of the smaller rectangles. That way, the component can draw all of its exposed surface area, but it still cannot draw over any part of the sibling component, or any other part of the desktop.

The Graphics class' getClipRect( ) method returns a Rectangle object whose x, y, width, and height member variables describe the current clipping rectangle. These coordinates are expressed in terms of the graphics' current origin point.

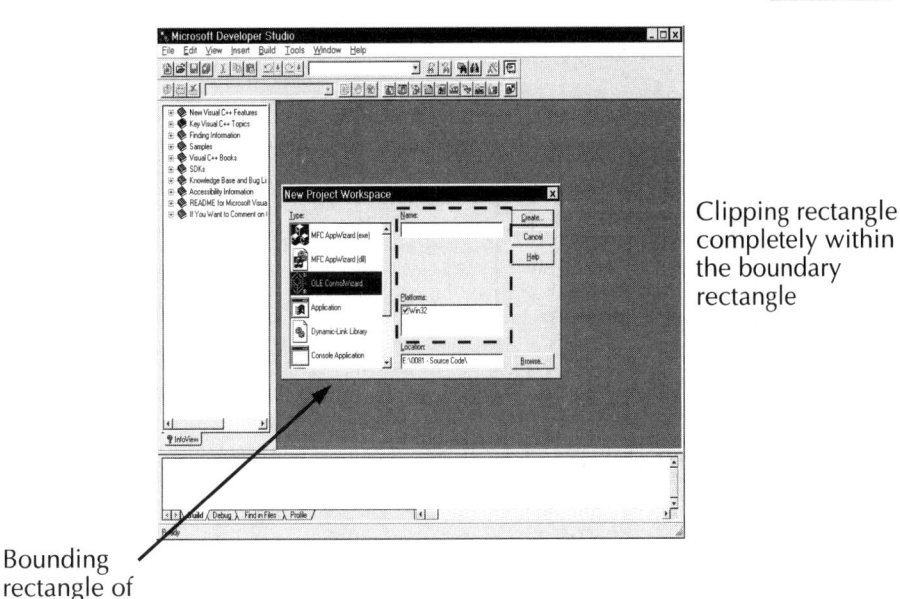

Graphics

A component's clipping rectangle is no larger than its bounding rectangle
Figure 5-2.

Clipping rectangle completely within the boundary rectangle

Bounding rectangle of this component

Use the Graphics class setClipRect( ) method to change the clipping rectangle of a Graphics object. Obviously, you cannot make a clipping rectangle larger than it already is. That would violate the whole idea of a

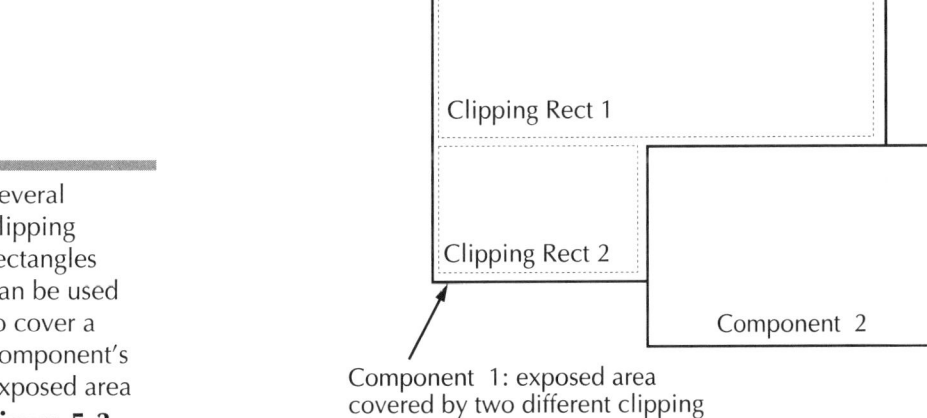

Several clipping rectangles can be used to cover a component's exposed area
Figure 5-3.

Clipping Rect 1

Clipping Rect 2

Component 2

Component 1: exposed area covered by two different clipping rectangles.

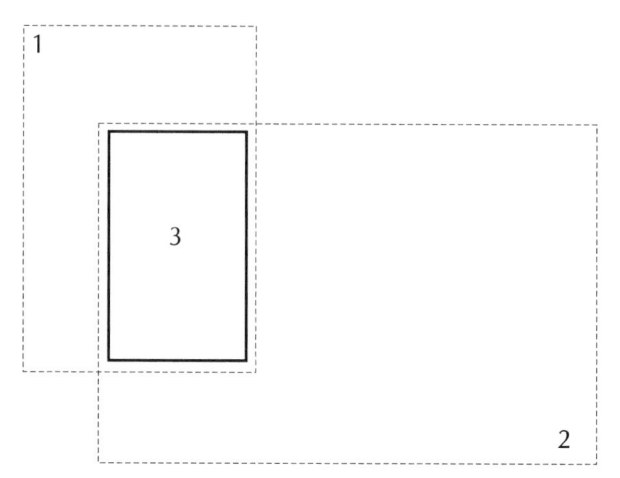

Clipping rectangles always get smaller
Figure 5-4.

1 Original clipping rectangle
2 Call to Graphics object( ) tries to make this clipping rectangle
3 Resulting clipping rectangle is intersection of 1 and 2, always no bigger than the original clipping rectangle 1.

clipping rectangle. Remember the component, which you don't want to let paint outside of its bounding rectangle: if it was possible to make the clipping rectangle of the Graphics object passed to paint( ) arbitrarily larger, then it would be able to draw outside its bounding rectangle. A Graphics object's clipping rectangle, after a call to the object's setClipRect( ) method, is equal to the geometric intersection of the clipping rectangle before the call and the rectangle passed to the setClipRect( ) method. Figure 5-4 shows how the resulting clipping rectangle is formed using this rule.

A good way to use the clipping rectangle to your advantage is speeding up the time to render a component: only draw that which is necessary *within the clipping rectangle*. For example, suppose you had a component that draws a grid over its surface on every repaint. If the Component only tries to paint the grid hashes that appear within the clipping rectangle, that could potentially save a lot of graphics calls that would just be wasted. Here's some painting code to demonstrate this principle using this example. First, we'll cover how you would draw a grid while ignoring the clipping rectangle:

```
public void paint(Graphics g) {
    Dimension size = size();

    // Draw vertical hashes every 10 pixels, starting at column 5.
    for(int col = 5 ; col<size.width ; col+=10)
```

Graphics

```
        g.drawLine( /* from point */ col, 0,
                    /* to point   */ col, size.height);

    // Draw horizontal hashes every 10 pixels, starting at row 5.
    for(int row = 5 ; row<size.height ; row+=10 )
        g.drawLine( /* from point */ 0, row,
                    /* to point   */ size.width, row);
}
```

This will get the job done. But, if you have a lot of updating to do in a short amount of time, you may be wasting processor cycles with unnecessary drawLine( ) calls. Instead, only draw those lines that pass through the clipping rectangle, like this:

```
public void paint(Graphics g) {
    Dimension size = size();
    Rectangle rectClip = g.getClipRect( );

    // Draw horizontal hashes every 10 pixels w/i clipping rect
    for (int col=((rectClip.x+4)/10)*10+5; col < rectClip.x+rectClip.width; col+=10)
            g.drawLine( /* from point */ col, 0,
                        /* to point   */ col, size.height );

    // Draw vertical hashes every 10 pixels w/i clipping rect.
    for(int row=((rectClip.y+4)/10)*10+5; row<rectClip.y+rectClip.width; row+=10)
            g.drawLine( /* from point */ 0, row,
                        /* to point   */ size.width, row);
}
```

The Current Font

A font is a typeface, size, and style for drawing text. When you draw text on a surface using a Graphics object, the Graphics object's current font is used to render the text.

What is a typeface? A typeface is a description of exactly how each letter in the alphabet should look. For example, the Courier typeface is a fixed-width typeface, used in this book for displaying code:

```
The Courier typeface looks like this.
```

A font's size is the measure of how large the individual letters are rendered. The larger the size, the larger the letters are rendered. Java has basically borrowed the font size concept from typesetters, who have had a lot of experience with font sizes (as you can imagine). Unfortunately, Java has also inherited a typesetter's antiquated way of describing font sizes. In Java, we use the *point* unit for describing font sizes. A point is roughly equal to 1/72 of an inch. That's a weird unit, and it makes measuring rendered text in Java a little unwieldy, though not that hard. (It's just a little harder than it had to be, though.) Of course, if you have any experience programming for Microsoft Windows, where you had to render text to a window, you're familiar with points and font sizes and probably know what a pain they can be. You'll be relieved to know that in Java it is quite a bit easier than when using the Windows SDK and the Visual C++ MFC classes.

Font Size

As mentioned before, font size is measured in *points*. A font is measured for height from the baseline of text to the top of ascending characters in the alphabet. Figure 5-5 shows this and other key font measurements, or *metrics*. When you create a font, you specify the font's size (i.e., height) as one of the font constructor parameters.

This table describes these metrics:

Metrics	Description
Ascent	Distance, in points, between the baseline and the top of ascending characters. Ascending characters, such as *h*, *A*, and *t* rise higher above the baseline than characters such as *a*, *c*, and *v*.
Descent	Distance, in points, between the baseline and the bottom of descending characters. Descending characters, such as *g*, *j*, and *q* fall below the baseline.
Leading	Distance between concurrent lines of text. This is a suggested value, measured in points.
Height	Combination of the Ascent, Descent, and Leading distances of the font.

Translating between points and pixels could be a painstaking bit of boredom, especially if you had to write code to do this operation into every

The metrics on rendered text
Figure 5-5.

application or applet you wrote. That's why in Java you have a companion class to the Font class: the FontMetrics class. A FontMetrics object describes how rendered text will be in pixels, given a particular font and a particular Graphics object that will be used to render the text.

Note that a font may be rendered in a different actual pixel size on two different Graphics objects. Say one Graphics object is attached to a rectangle of the desktop, and another is attached to a dot matrix printer page. Since all single-line fonts on the dot matrix printer really render to the same size, the same font could have different pixel sizes for the same text on the two different Graphics objects. That's why the FontMetrics object describes sizes for a particular font on a particular Graphics object.

The Graphics method getFontMetrics( ) returns the FontMetrics for the graphic's current font as rendered on the graphic's attached display surface. That is, the FontMetrics returned by this method describes the size in pixels of text rendered on the Graphics object using the Graphics object's current font.

You use the FontMetrics methods to extract measurements of rendered text in pixels. The getAscent( ) method returns the ascent of the font in pixels. The getDescent( ) method returns the descent. The getLeading( ) method returns the suggested distance between the bottom of descending characters and the top of ascending characters in subsequent lines of text. That is, it is the additional space to add between baselines of consecutive lines of text. The getHeight( ) method returns the sum of getAscent( ), getDescent( ), and getLeading( ), which is the distance you should use between baselines of text. The charWidth( ) method returns the width, in pixels, of a single text character. The stringWidth( ) method returns the width of an entire string of text when rendered. Various other similar methods also exist, so you do not have to pass in a String object, but instead can pass in either an array of chars (charsWidth( )) or an array of bytes (bytesWidth( )). Finally, the getWidths( ) method returns an array of 256 integers that describes the widths of all the individual characters in order.

Here's an applet that uses the FontMetrics class to figure out where to render text on the screen. It takes an arbitrary number of parameters named "line*X*." The applet renders these lines, one after the other, with the FontMetrics' suggested leading distance between subsequent lines. Lines that are wider than the applet are rendered in red, while shorter ones are rendered in the foreground color of the Applet object. Figure 5-6 is a screen shot of this applet with some typical lines of text as the values of the line*X* parameters. To create this applet using Visual J++, start a new Java Project Workspace with a single .JAVA file, and copy this code to that file before compiling the project. You will have to create your own HTML file and add in parameter lines to the <APPLET> container tag to see it run, or use the Build/Settings

The Visual J++ Handbook

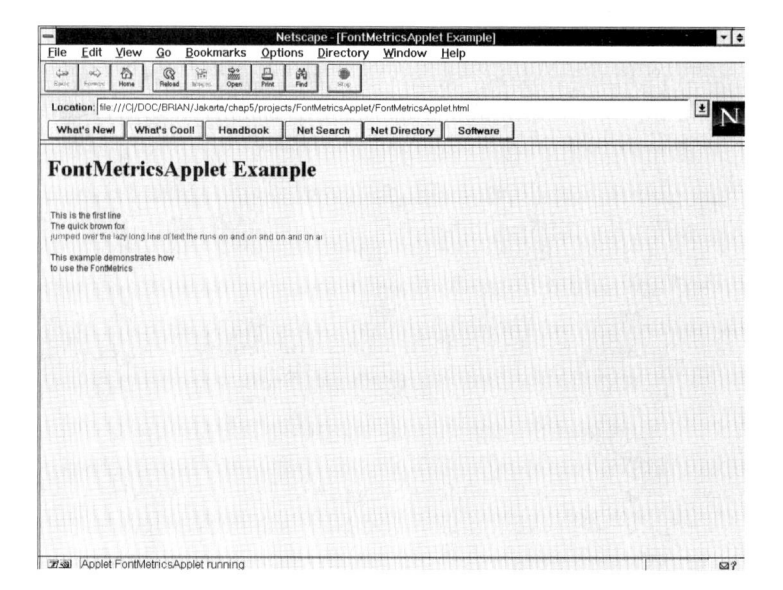

The FontMetrics-Applet
Figure 5-6.

dialog's Debug tab to set the parameters when the applet is invoked in the Visual J++ debugger.

```
import java.applet.*;
import java.awt.*;

public class FontMetricsApplet extends Applet {
    String[] m_astrLines;

    public void init() {
        int cLines;
        for(cLines=0 ; null != getParameter("line"+cLines) ; cLines++)
            ;

        m_astrLines = new String[cLines];
        for(int ii=0 ; ii<cLines ; ii++)
            m_astrLines[ii] = getParameter("line"+ii);
    }

    public void paint(Graphics g) {
        FontMetrics fm = g.getFontMetrics( );
        Dimension size = size();
        for(int ii=0 ; ii<m_astrLines.length ; ii++) {
            int cx = fm.stringWidth(m_astrLines[ii]);
            g.setColor( getForeground() );
            if(cx >= size.width)
                g.setColor( Color.red );
```

```
            g.drawString(m_astrLines[ii], 5, fm.getHeight()*(ii+1));
        }
    }
}
```

Here's the HTML file used to produce Figure 5-6:

```
<HTML>
<HEAD>
<TITLE>FontMetricsApplet Example</TITLE>
</HEAD>

<BODY>
<H1>FontMetricsApplet Example</H1>
<HR>
<APPLET CODE="FontMetricsApplet.class" WIDTH="400" HEIGHT="300">
<PARAM NAME="line0" VALUE="This is the first line">
<PARAM NAME="line1" VALUE="The quick brown fox">
<PARAM NAME="line2" VALUE="jumped over the lazy long line of text that runs on
and on and on and on and on and on and on">
<PARAM NAME="line3" VALUE="">
<PARAM NAME="line4" VALUE="This example demonstrates how">
<PARAM NAME="line5" VALUE="to use the FontMetrics">
</APPLET>

</BODY>
</HTML>
```

Font Styles

Fonts have extra style attributes that can be added to the typeface. You of course recognize what italics (*like this*) and bold (**like this**) attributes are. These are the only two style attributes understood by Java right now. The two Font class constants Font.ITALICS and Font.BOLD can be ORed together logically to describe either one or both of these attributes for a font.

The style attributes, along with the typeface name and the font size, are passed to the Font constructor when you are creating new fonts.

Typefaces

As previously stated, a typeface is a name applied to fonts describing how the various letters of the alphabet look when rendered. The example of the Courier typeface, given previously, is also an example of a typeface that is generally available for all platforms. That means that no matter what platform your Java application or applet is running on, you can be pretty sure the Courier typeface is available.

AWT's Toolkit single-instance class has a method that returns an exhaustive list of typefaces available on the system. The Toolkit class method to use is getFontList( ), and it returns an array of strings. Each element of this array is the name of one of the typefaces available on the system. Here's a program that lists out all the typefaces available on the current system:

```
import java.awt.*;

public class ListFonts {
    public static void main(String astrArgs[]) {
        String astrFonts[] = Toolkit.getDefaultToolkit().getFontList();

        for(int ii=0 ; ii<astrFonts.length ; ii++)
            System.out.println("Font " + ii + ": " + astrFonts[ii]);
    }
}
```

Creating Fonts

Given all the above background information, it's pretty easy to see how to use fonts in Java, as soon as you know how to create new fonts. The Font class constructor takes three arguments: the name of the typeface you want, the size (that's the size in points, more specifically the ascent of the font in points), and the style attributes to apply to the font. This line creates a 10-point, italics font using the Courier typeface:

```
Font f = new Font("Courier", Font.ITALICS, 10);
```

The Graphics class method setFont( ) is passed a Font object. That Font object becomes the current font for the Graphics object, and all subsequent text rendering operations use that font to draw text to the attached display surface.

Here's an example that puts all the font information you have read so far into one big program. The FontGallery applet uses a modified version of the TabbedPanel from Chapter 3 as the primary interface. The code for that class is not included here, though it can be found on the World Wide Web at the *Visual J++ Handbook* site. The big difference between this modified version and the version from Chapter 3 is that this one allows you to pass in any old component to act as a tab, instead of requiring you to create images. The various tabs of the TabbedPanel are made from buttons, where each button has the name of one of the typefaces available on the system. When you click on a typeface's button, the panel showing example lines of text using that font is displayed in the lower portion of the applet. Figure 5-7 is a screen shot of this applet in action.

Graphics

```java
import java.awt.*;
import java.applet.*;

class FontDisplayPanel extends Panel {
    Font m_font;
    Font m_fontItal;
    Font m_fontBold;
    Font m_fontBoldItal;
    private String m_strSampleText;

    public FontDisplayPanel(Font f, String s) {
        m_font = f;
        m_fontItal = new Font(f.getName(),
                f.getStyle() | Font.ITALIC, f.getSize());
        m_fontBold = new Font(f.getName(),
                f.getStyle() | Font.BOLD, f.getSize());
        m_fontBoldItal = new Font(f.getName(),
                f.getStyle() | Font.BOLD | Font.ITALIC, f.getSize());
        m_strSampleText = s;
    }

    public void paint(Graphics g) {
        // Select in the font
        g.setFont(m_font);

        // Get the font's metrics.
        int cy = g.getFontMetrics().getHeight();

        // Display the sample text in normal, italics
        // and bold, and bold italics.
        g.drawString(m_strSampleText, 5, cy);

        setFont(m_fontItal);
        g.drawString(m_strSampleText, 5, cy*2);

        setFont(m_fontBold);
        g.drawString(m_strSampleText, 5, cy*3);

        setFont(m_fontBoldItal);
        g.drawString(m_strSampleText, 5, cy*4);
    }
}

public class FontGallery extends Applet {
    public void init() {
        TabbedPanel tp;

        // Make our interface a TabbedPanel.
```

```
        setLayout(new BorderLayout());
        add("Center", tp = new TabbedPanel());

        // Get list of Fonts. For each font, create normal
        // (non-bold, non-italics) instance and make tab for it.
        String[] astrFonts = Toolkit.getDefaultToolkit().getFontList();
        for(int ii=0 ; ii<astrFonts.length ; ii++) {
            Font f = new Font(astrFonts[ii], Font.PLAIN, 10);
            tp.addTab(astrFonts[ii], new Button(astrFonts[ii]),
                    new FontDisplayPanel(f, "The slow gray fox sneezed."));
        }
    }
}
```

Painting Mode

There are two possible graphics painting modes. You are intuitively familiar with the first of these, called *paint mode*. The second takes just a little bit of explanation, and it is called *XOR mode*.

When in paint mode, any graphics operation you perform will copy the current color of the graphics to some pixels in the display surface. For example, when you draw a line on the display surface (assuming some part of the line lies within the graphic's clipping rectangle), then the current color value is copied into the memory associated with the pixels that lie along the line you are drawing. If you draw a line across the top of the clipping rectangle, then all the pixels along that edge will contain the current graphics color, no matter what their previous values were.

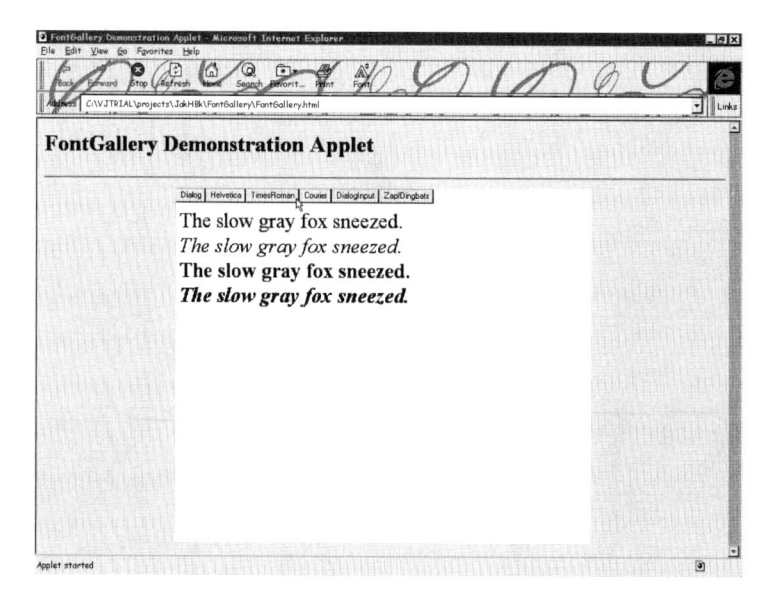

The FontGallery Applet in Action
Figure 5-7.

Graphics

You may say at this point, "What's the big deal with that?" Well, nothing's very exciting about this mode. When in this mode, the Graphics object overwrites pixels with the current color. That's what you would expect to happen when you draw something: you would expect the current color to be used. That's what happens in paint mode.

XOR mode, however, is a little different. In XOR mode, three different colors are combined to create the new color of affected pixels. Those three colors are: the graphics' current color, another color stored in the Graphics object called the *XOR alternate color*, and the color of the pixel before the graphics operation. These three values are all XORed together, bitwise, to form a new 32-bit packed RGB color value for the pixel.

XOR mode can be used for a variety of specialty drawing operations that just can't be as easily done in paint mode. Here's an example: how would you draw a selection rectangle over a generic image? You could draw the rectangle by picking a color, such as black or white. That would work for most cases, but what would it look like if the image you were selecting from was also predominantly (or entirely) the same color? The user wouldn't even be able to see the rectangle at all!

In this case, you can easily use XOR mode when drawing your selection rectangle. This would cause the section rectangle to be black where the underlying image was white, and it would be white where the underlying image was black. Similarly, the selection rectangle would be yellow where the underlying image was green, and blue where the underlying image was orange. Figure 5-8 is a screen shot of just such a selection rectangle Applet. The code following the figure was used to create the image.

Using graphics XOR mode to draw a selection rectangle
Figure 5-8.

```java
import java.awt.*;
import java.applet.*;
import java.net.*;

public class SelectionRect extends Applet {
    Rectangle m_rectSelection;
    Image m_img;

    public void init() {
        // Assume a "image" parameter is present.

        try{
          m_img = getImage(new URL(getDocumentBase().toString() +
getParameter("image")));
          m_rectSelection = null;

        } catch (MalformedURLException e) { /* handle exception here*/ }
    }

    // Override update() to prevent inherited implementation
    // from erasing the background with this Applet's
    // background color.
    public void update() {
        paint(g);
    }

    public void paint(Graphics g) {
        // Draw the image. Make sure you are in
        // paint mode at this point.
        g.drawImage(m_img, 0, 0, this);
        g.setPaintMode();

        // If there is a selection rectangle, draw it
        // in XOR mode.
        if(null != m_rectSelection) {
            Color colorAlt = new Color(~getForeground().getRGB());
            g.setXORMode(colorAlt);
            g.drawRect(m_rectSelection.x, m_rectSelection.y,
                     m_rectSelection.width, m_rectSelection.height);
        }
    }

    /**********
     * Mouse handling to track the selection rectangle.
     **********/

    public boolean mouseDown(Event ect, int x, int y) {
```

Graphics

```
        m_rectSelection = new Rectangle(x, y, 0, 0);
        repaint();
        return true;
    }

    public boolean mouseUp(Event evt, int x, int y) {
        m_rectSelection = null;
        repaint();
        return true;
    }

    public boolean mouseDrag(Event evt, int x, int y) {
        m_rectSelection.width  += x - m_rectSelection.x;
        m_rectSelection.height += y - m_rectSelection.y;
        repaint();
        return true;
    }
}
```

Drawing Graphics

The Graphics class exposes public methods so that you can draw lines, rectangles, filled rectangles, polygons, filled polygons, ovals, filled ovals, arcs, filled arcs, and images. How these elements are rendered and where on the drawing surface is a matter of the internal state of the Graphics object at the time the element is drawn. For example, filled rectangles are drawn as a rectangular block using the current color of the Graphics object. The position and dimensions of the rectangle to draw are specified relative to the current origin of the Graphics object. The painting mode can also affect how the rectangle is rendered on the display surface. The following sections detail how to draw each of these elements.

Drawing Lines

Drawing a line is the simplest operation in any graphical programming environment. To draw a line in Java, use the Graphics method drawLine( ). The four parameters to this method define two points, in terms of individual *x* and *y* parameters of each of the two points, you want a line segment drawn between. It's really very simple:

```
public void paint(Graphics g) {
    // Draw an X between this component's four corners.
    g.drawLine(0, 0, size().width-1, size().height-1);
}
```

Drawing Rectangles

While a rectangle is a special case of a polygon, the Graphics class includes methods specifically for rendering both polygons and rectangles. This is probably because the underlying native operations for filling or drawing a rectangle are a whole lot more efficient than those for drawing or filling generic polygons.

To draw the outline of a rectangle, use the Graphics drawRect( ) method. Pass the x, y, width, and height parameters of the rectangle you want to draw. The fillRect( ) method draws a filled-in rectangle, or a rectangular block, in the Graphics object's current color. For example, this code fragment draws a rectangle centered over a component's bounding rectangle as part of the Component's paint method:

```
public class MyCanvas extends Canvas {
    ...

    public void paint(Graphics g) {
        Rectangle rectBounds = bounds();

        // Shrink rect by 10 on each side, but not more than width
        // of this Component.
        rectBounds.grow(Math.max(-size().width/2, -10),
              Math.max(-size().height/2, -10));

        // Draw the rectangle.
        g.fillRect(rectBounds.x, rectBounds.y, rectBounds.width,
              rectBounds.height);
    }
}
```

Drawing Polygons

Java can also draw any generic polygon. You can define a polygon you want to draw in two different ways. The first technique involves providing two arrays specifying the X and Y coordinates of the points of your polygon to the Graphics drawPolygon( ) or fillPolygon( ) method, as in

```
int aXCoords[] = {10, 50, 50, 15};
int aYCoords[] = {10, 15, 50, 50};

g.drawPolygon(aXCoords, aYCoords, 4);
```

Graphics

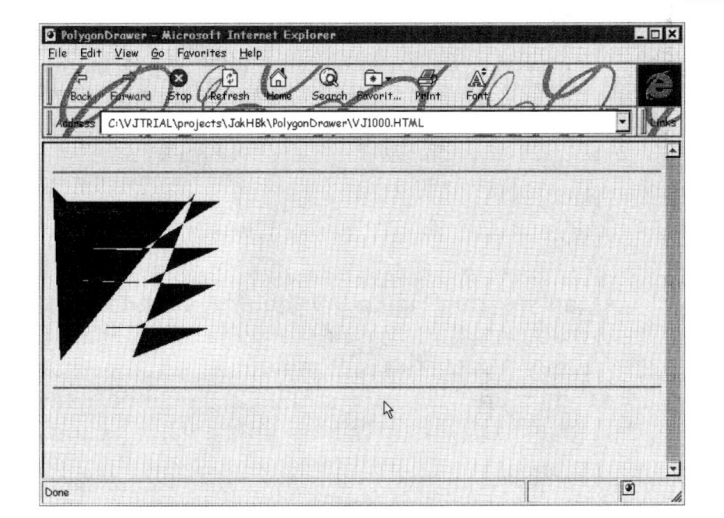

A polygon drawn by a graphics object
Figure 5-9.

The above code would draw the polygon shown in Figure 5-9. Note that the third parameter tells how many vertexes there are in your polygon. Note also that you don't have to repeat the first point twice; the graphics will automatically close your polygon by joining the first and last vertexes.

The AWT package also includes a Polygon class you can use to define a polygon shape. An overloaded version of the drawPolygon( ) and fillPolygon( ) methods of the Graphics class takes Polygon objects instead of the arrays of X and Y coordinates shown in the previous example. The Polygon class' constructor is handed two arrays defining the X and Y coordinates of the polygon's vertexes. The Polygon class' addPoint( ) method can also be used to add vertexes to the polygon dynamically. The following example applet tracks the user's mouse clicks and uses them to define a polygon dynamically. Every new mouse click is a new vertex of the polygon for the applet to draw.

```
import java.awt.*;
import java.applet.Applet;

public class PolygonDrawer extends Applet {
    int x[] = { 0, 10, 15};
    int y[] = { 0, 10, 15};
    Polygon m_poly = new Polygon(x, y, 3);

    public void paint(Graphics g) {
        // Draw the polygon filled in.
        g.fillPolygon(m_poly);
    }
```

```
        // For each mouse click from the user, add a new
        // point to the polygon where the mouse clicked.
        public boolean mouseDown(Event evt, int x, int y) {
            m_poly.addPoint(x, y);
            repaint();
             return true;
        }
}
```

You can see from Figure 5-9 that the method Java uses to draw filled polygons only fills areas of the polygons that are fully surrounded by the polygon's edges. That is, if you draw, say, a pentagram, the arms of the pentagram are filled in, but the center is not because the edges of the figure cross over each other. The algorithm used is called the "odd-even" algorithm.

Polygon objects are useful for two different reasons. First, they allow you to keep your sets of X and Y coordinates within a single object. Then you don't have to write extra code to manage storing associated arrays of X and Y coordinates together. Second, the Polygon class includes a few convenient methods you may find useful. The getBoundingBox( ) method of the Polygon class will return the smallest rectangle that completely encloses the polygon. The inside( ) method of the Polygon class returns true if a given point falls within the edges of the polygon. The same odd-even algorithm used when filling in polygons by the Graphics class' fillPolygon( ) method is also used to determine if a point lies within a polygon in the inside( ) method.

In addition, you can extend the Polygon method in useful ways. You could, for example, write a move( ) method and add it to a Polygon-derived class. This method would translate all the vertexes of the Polygon by some distance along the X and Y axes. Similarly, you could implement rotate( ) or scale( ) methods, too. The public member variables of the Polygon class *npoints*, *xpoints[]*, and *ypoints[]* define the vertexes of the polygon, and can be manipulated directly by derived class methods, as in this example implementation of the move( ) method:

```
class SuperPolygon extends Polygon {
    public SuperPolygon(int xpoints[], int ypoints[], int npoints) {
        super(xpoints, ypoints, npoints);
    }

    public void move(int dx, int dy) {
        for(int ii=0 ; ii<npoints ; ii++) {
            xpoints[ii] += dx;
            ypoints[ii] += dy;
        }
    }
}
```

Drawing Ovals

Using the Graphics class methods drawOval( ) and fillOval( ), you can render an oval or a circle. The ovals are oriented with their axes along the X and Y axes. This means you can't draw an oval oriented diagonally on the graphic's drawing surface. Well, you could, but you would have to draw it as either a set of connected lines or as a polygon with many vertexes. That is, you would have to draw diagonally-oriented ovals "by hand".

When you draw an oval, you define the rectangle that bounds the oval. If the bounding rectangle is a square, then the oval happens to be a circle, since the X and Y extents of the oval are equal. Figure 5-10 shows an oval and its bounding rectangle drawn using this code:

```
public void paint(Graphics g) {
    Rectangle r = new Rectangle(10, 10, 50, 100);
    g.setXORMode(Color.red);
    g.fillRect(r.x, r.y, r.width, r.height);
    g.drawOval(r.x, r.y, r.width, r.height);
}
```

Drawing Arcs

An arc is a segment of an oval. The Graphics class methods drawArc( ) and fillArc( ) are used in much the same way as drawOval( ) and fillOval( ). That is, you specify the bounding rectangle of an oval. In addition you specify the starting angle and angular distance of the arc you want to draw. (Angles are

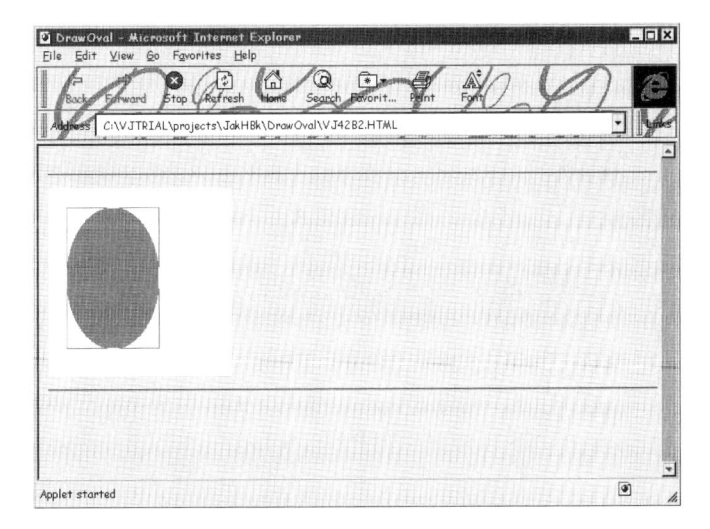

An oval drawn with its bounding rectangle
Figure 5-10.

specified in radians.) If you say you want an arc of 2π radians, you just draw the whole oval. If you tell the Graphics to draw an arc of π radians, you'll draw half the oval.

The starting angle of the arc, also specified in radians, is measured relative to the three o'clock position around the oval. Positive angles move the starting point clockwise around the oval, while negative values move counterclockwise. Similarly, positive values specified for the arc distance extend the arc for that distance in a clockwise direction around the oval from the starting angle, and negative values extend it a distance counterclockwise from the starting angle.

The signatures of the fillOval( ) and drawOval( ) methods both look the same. They are

```
public void drawArc(int x,  int y,  int width,  int height,    // defines rect
       double startAngle,  double arcDistance);
public void fillArc(int x,  int y,  int width,  int height,    // defines rect
       double startAngle,  double arcDistance);
```

Drawing Images

Using the Graphics class method drawImage( ) you can copy an image to the display surface attached to a Graphics object. Copying images in memory to a surface like this is also sometimes referred to as *bitblting* ("bit bliting"), or just *blting*. (The word is an acronym of the term "bit block transfer"). This custom component, the ImageCanvas, is a component that just displays an image. Note that its minimumSize( ) and preferredSize( ) methods have been overridden to return the size of the image passed to its constructor:

```
import java.awt.*;

public class ImageCanvas extends Canvas {
    private Image m_img;

    public ImageCanvas(Image img) {
        m_img = img;
    }

    public Dimension preferredSize() {
        return new Dimension(m_img.getWidth(this), m_img.getHeight(this));
    }

    public Dimension minimumSize() {
        return preferredSize();
    }
```

Graphics

```
    public void paint(Graphics g) {
        g.drawImage(m_img, 0, 0, this);
    }
}
```

Note that the Graphics class drawImage( ) method takes *four* parameters. The first three parameters are easy to understand: an image to draw, and the X and Y coordinates of where to place the image on the drawing surface attached to the Graphics object.

The fourth parameter is an *ImageObserver* object. You can read Visual J++'s on-line description of ImageObservers for a more detailed description of what they are, but here's a quick explanation: an image can be downloaded from across the Internet. Since images are defined by .GIF or .JPG files that can be quite large, Java downloads the image file asynchronously. The ImageObserver is a special object that receives updates of this asynchronous downloading operation. For example, the above example ImageCanvas code uses the Image methods getWidth( ) and getHeight( ) to determine the width and height of the image to be displayed. Since the width and height may not be known at the time these methods are called (because the Java system has not finished downloading the image from the Internet), you pass an ImageObserver to the method. As soon as the width or height of the image becomes known, then the ImageObserver is notified. Of course the width and height may already be known as of the time the getWidth( ) or getHeight( ) method is called, in which case the ImageObserver parameter is ignored. The Component class is defined as implementing the ImageObserver interface, and so the ImageCanvas class (which is a type of component) also inherits the ImageObserver interface implementation.

Animation

Animation is the term commonly applied to displaying a series of images in a seamless, time-sequenced manner. The effect you want to achieve with animation is that of a "moving picture," a display of animated parts that make up a single visual experience for the user. Examples of animation could be a cartoon made up of interacting characters, the display for a video game like pinball or a shoot-em-up space fighter game, or a display of chemical molecules reacting together to form new compounds.

There are a couple of examples of pretty good animation included in Visual J++'s Sun samples. Figures 5-11, 5-12, and 5-13 are screen shots of the Animator, GraphLayout, and MoleculeViewer applets, respectively. Each one of these applets displays a time-sequenced series of images using animation.

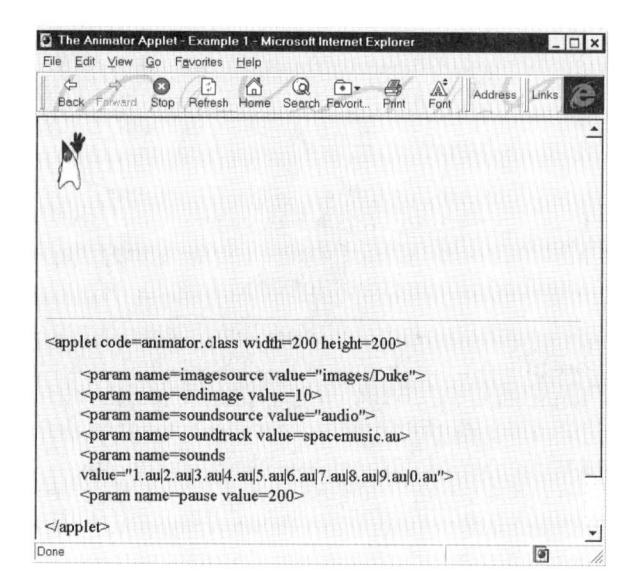

The Visual J++ Handbook

[Screenshot: The Animator Applet - Example 1 - Microsoft Internet Explorer]

```
<applet code=animator.class width=200 height=200>
    <param name=imagesource value="images/Duke">
    <param name=endimage value=10>
    <param name=soundsource value="audio">
    <param name=soundtrack value=spacemusic.au>
    <param name=sounds
    value="1.au|2.au|3.au|4.au|5.au|6.au|7.au|8.au|9.au|0.au">
    <param name=pause value=200>
</applet>
```

The Animator applet
Figure 5-11.

The techniques for achieving animation in Java are pretty simple. There are only two coordinating pieces of code you must implement to achieve good animation in Java. You will be examining the Animator Sun sample applet to see how these two coordinating techniques work, and how to implement

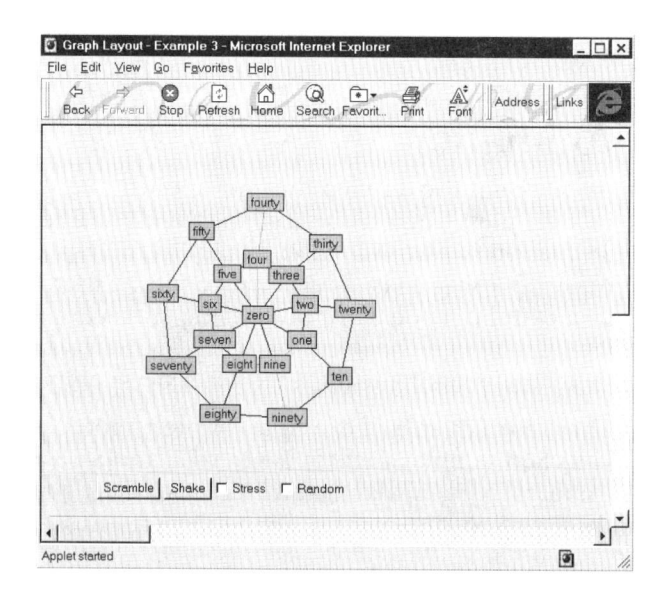

[Screenshot: Graph Layout - Example 3 - Microsoft Internet Explorer]

The GraphLayout applet
Figure 5-12.

Graphics

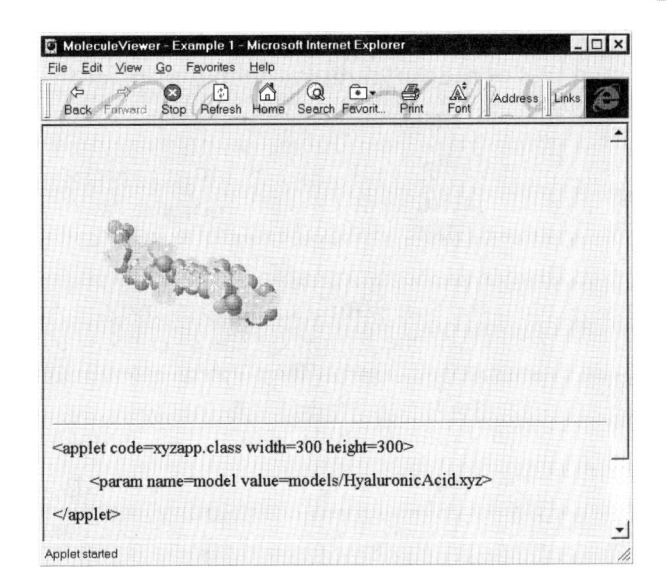

The Molecule-Viewer applet
Figure 5-13.

them. The first thing to learn is how to time-sequence a series of pre-loaded images using background threads. A second, more complex technique involves coordinating more than one background thread to generate and display successive animation frames. Sun's Animator applet is pretty much a simple example of the first technique, so first take a crack at decomposing that code in the following section.

Animation Frame Time-Sequencing: The Animator Applet

The Sun sample Animator applet displays a series of downloaded images in a single time-sequenced animation. Each frame of the animation is defined by a frame number (0 through *N*), an image, a duration to display the image in milliseconds, a position to display the image in the applet, and an audio file to play while displaying each frame. In addition, you can specify several *global* parameters for the Animator applet, including an HREF for the entire applet so that the applet will act like a hyperlink if the user clicks on it, a background color to use for the applet, and a background music file to play while the applet is running (the background and frame-by-frame audio files are automatically mixed together to formed the audio of the applet). All you need to see of this applet is how it uses a background thread to sequence the display of the animation frames.

First, you should copy the Animator sample and open it up. Start by copying the files of the Sun sample Animator Applet from Visual J++'s InfoViewer. Follow these steps to copy the files and open the Animator project:

1. Start Visual J++. Close any project workspace that is open by using the Main menu's File|Close Workspace option. You will then see the InfoViewer's top-level table of contents.

2. Under the Samples topic in the InfoViewer's main table of contents, open the Sun Samples subtopic, and the Animator document under that. Click the button on the document to download all the files of the Animator Applet project. Visual J++ will ask you where to download the files, and it will suggest the directory MSDEV\SAMPLES\SUNSAMPLES\ANIMATOR.

3. Now, open the project you have just copied using the Main menu's File|Open Workspace... option. Visual J++ will ask you for the directory where the project exists in an Open File dialog. You must browse to the directory where you copied the project files (MSDEV\SAMPLES\SUNSAMPLES\ANIMATOR from step 2). Open the Animator project file.

Open up the class view for the Animator project, which lists these three classes: Animator, DescriptionFrame, and ParseException. You don't have to be concerned with the DescriptionFrame or ParseException classes right now. Only the code that the Animator Applet class uses to display a sequence of images in an animated manner is of interest.

The Animator applet uses a background thread to perform a very simple animation loop. The same method can be used by any of your animation applets to sequence a series of animation frames. Here's a pseudo-code description of what the background thread does:

```
public class Animator extends Applet implements Runnable {
    Thread engine;
    int framenum = -1;

    // In init(), download all images, audio files, other things
    // you need to perfrom the animation. Start the background
    // animation engine thread too.
    public void init() {
    // get list of images, audio file, other resources to download

        //    download images and stuff for animation
    }
```

Graphics

```
// In start(), start up the background engine thread.
public void start() {
    engine = new Thread(this);
    engine.start();
}

// In stop(), drop reference to the background engine thread.
// The thread itself recognizes when this has occurred, and gracefully
// kills itself when it happens.
public void stop() {
    engine = null;
}

// The run() method is run by the background engine thread. It handles
// all the actual animation.
public void run() {
    store reference to the current thread, which should be engine thread

    if not done downloading images etc. yet, wait

    while reference to current thread == thread referenced by engine var {
        increment framenum by 1
        repaint();
        make current thread sleep for some duration
    }
}

// In paint(), just paint the framenum-th image.
public void paint(Graphics g) {
    if(framenum >= 0)       // will be -1 while initializing
        draw the framenum-th image onto surface attached to g
}
```

So, you can see that there is code in five coordinating methods:

- init( ) downloads the images and other data that make up all the animation frames
- start( ) starts the background thread running
- stop( ) stops the background thread from running any more
- paint( ) paints the *current* animation frame
- run( ), which is executed by a background thread, continuously updates the *current* frame after sleeping for some duration

If you look at the list of methods in the Animator class using Visual J++'s class view, you will see a whole lot of methods not listed here. Those are mostly helper methods that assist each of the above five controlling methods in their activities. For example, there are five parsing methods in the Animator class. These parsing methods are called only by the init( ) to parse the Applet's parameters so init( ) knows what images and audio files to download: parseImages( ) parses a list of images that make up the animation frames; parseDurations( ) makes a list of duration values, one for each animation frame; parseSounds( ) parses a list of sound file names, one for each animation frame; etc. The point is that the init( ) method still carries out the same tasks outlined in the pseudo-code: it downloads all the images and other associated data required to display each of the frames in the animation sequence. Similarly, most of the other helper methods in the Animator class are used by one of the five coordinating methods init( ), start( ), stop( ), paint( ), and run( ).

Avoiding "Flicker"

There is one important technical note you'll need to know for all your animations, and even for most intensive drawing you'll want to do using Java in general. That is that Java has a built-in flaw causing problems with high-speed rendering. The update( ) method of all components, which is what calls your paint( ) methods, automatically erases your entire component using the background color before calling your component's paint( ) method. The unfortunate effect of this when trying to do animation is that you will experience "flicker" in your animations if you don't override the update( ) method.

To get rid of this flicker, override the update( ) method with this code in your animation applets:

```
public void update(Graphics g) {
    paint(g);
}
```

Double Buffering

The Animator applet is a fine implementation of animation for the cases where you have a fully defined, finite set of animation frames. But what if you have dynamic animations? For example, what about a video game such as Space Invaders, in which the user may move his or her piece around the

Graphics

screen at will? Surely you can see that having a fixed number of performed images played in sequence can't achieve anything like an interactive animation sequence. Sure, each of the individual pieces of the animation can be stored in a static image, but these small images or glyphs must be composited together on the fly to create a dynamic animation sequence.

You can use the same basic framework used in the Animator applet to construct a dynamic animation sequence using a technique called *double buffering*. In double buffering, instead of downloading a series of images to be displayed in sequence, you construct the individual animation frames on the fly in memory. The same time-sequencing engine thread can be used to display these in-memory frames. As the display engine thread is sleeping, you construct your animation frames in memory. The animation thread wakes up and displays the next constructed frame instead of displaying a downloaded image.

Instead of five methods coordinating to create animation, you have six coordinating methods when using double-buffered animation. In addition to the five methods from the time-sequencing, you have on additional method run by another background thread. This runFrameGeneration( ) method is responsible for generating successive animation frames and storing them in a class variable. The two background threads, the display engine, and the frame generator coordinate in this way: The frame generator fills the buffer in memory and waits for the animation engine to display it (possibly indefinitely). The animation engine thread waits until the in-memory buffer is filled, then wakes up and displays it, after which it goes back to sleep until the buffer is filled again.

Using a single in-memory buffer makes for pretty simple programming, but it's not the best use of your computer's processor. It is more efficient to let the frame generator run full bore, generating as many frames as it can and storing them away. The animation engine uses a timer then and wakes every so often, takes the next frame from the top of the stack and displays it, then goes back to sleep. See, this way the frame generator never sleeps, so precious time isn't wasted.

Since you don't have unlimited memory, the last technique I gave actually isn't practical. You can't just let the frame generator run until all memory is taken up with generated frames. Instead, you could hook the frame generator up to a storage device that can only store up to N frames. When the frame generator tries to store $N+1$, it is blocked until the animation engine grabs a frame out of the storage device. This way, you know there are at most N frames taking up space in memory.

Using a Graphics Object Attached to an In-Memory Image

Drawing on an in-memory surface is just like drawing on the desktop: you use a Graphics object attached to the in-memory surface. Here are the cookbook steps:

1. First, create the in-memory image. Any component can create such an image using its createImage( ) method, which just requires a width and a height.

   ```
   Image img2blBuffer = createImage(width, height);
   ```

2. Next, get the image's graphics. Use the Image class' getGraphics( ) method:

   ```
   Graphics g2blBuffer = img2blBuffer.getGraphics( );
   ```

The graphics you get out must still have its color and font set. The origin of the graphics is the upper-left corner of the in-memory image. The clipping rectangle is the exact same size as the entire in-memory image.

Here's pseudo-code that demonstrates how an animation thread and a frame generator thread would cooperate using multiple in-memory images to do double-buffered animation. Only the run methods of the two threads are given; the init( ), start( ), stop( ), and paint( ) methods are pretty much the same as given previously.

```
public class MyAnimator extends Applet implements Runnable {
    Vector m_vectFrames = new Vector();
    Thread m_threadAnimator;
    Thread m_threadFrameGenerator;
    Image m_imgNextFrame;

    // init( ) downloads any resources we need.

    // start() creates and starts the two background threads running.

    // stop() halts the two background threads by dropping references.

    // paint() grabs and removes the 0-index frame from m_vectFrames
    // and displays it.

    // run() differentiates which thread is running and calls the
    // appropriate method.
    Public void run() {
        if(Thread.currentThread() == m_threadAnimator)
            runAnimator();
        if(Thread.currentThread() == m_threadFrameGenerator)
            runGenerator();
    }
```

Graphics

```
// runAnimator() is run only by the animator thread.
public void runAnimator() {
    while current thread == m_threadAnimator
        if there is at least one frame in m_vectFrames
            remove zero-th frame from m_vectFrames.
            store zero-th frame in m_imgNextFrame.
            repaint()
        Sleep for some duration.
}

public void runFrameGenerator() {
    If initialization isn't done, wait until its done.

    while(m_threadFrameGenerator == current thread)
        generate next frame
        add next frame to the N-th position of m_vectFrames
  }
}
```

As an exercise for the reader, you can take a look at the GraphLayout Sun sample applet, included with the Sun samples in Visual J++. This applet uses a double-buffering technique like this to generate successive frames of a dynamic animation sequence.

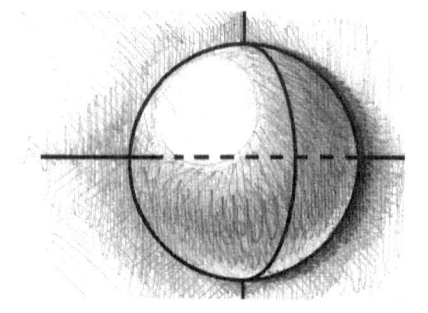

CHAPTER 6

Applets

Java is a versatile, networked, secure, object-oriented programming language and architecture. But other than these features, what is Java other than just a new programming language? Certainly there are other object-oriented, interpreted languages that either already do or could easily be augmented to have these same features. Visual Basic, for example, compiles down to P-Code, which is also an interpreted instruction set not unlike Java bytecodes (although now you can also compile your VB code down to executable files directly, too).

So why did Java become so popular, achieve such hype and wide acceptance so quickly?

Undoubtedly one of the main reasons was that Java had applets. Applets are embeddable executable objects that can be distributed across the Internet and incorporated into World Wide Web pages. Applets gave to Internet programmers what they had been waiting for for quite a while: easily distributable, platform-independent executable content for the Internet.

An applet is a Java object. In concept, it is similar to a Windows OCX or ActiveX control. An applet lives within a container program, and interacts with that container program to give custom interactive content to the user. For example, an applet can be a simple interface to a remote database, or it can be something to display a complex animation sequence in. It could display charts and graphs like up-to-the-minute stock market information or waterflow volumes.

An applet is embedded in a browser, such as a Web browser. Although, there are also experimental e-mail-based browsers out there that let you send interactive applets through e-mail! While this chapter will deal exclusively with applets in Web browsers, you might want to keep in mind that the applet architecture is not tied to just the Web. There are potentially lots of other ways for sending applets around the world.

As the ability to distribute applets was one of the most popular features of Java, your Visual J++ Java development environment has many features added to it to make applet development quicker and easier. Most notably, Visual J++ comes with an **Applet Wizard** that guides you through the initial stages of Applet creation. The Applet Wizard is very similar to Visual C++'s AppWizard: it creates for you a skeleton of your applet that you fill in with your specific code. It saves you a lot of time in creating this skeleton code, since most of it is exactly the same for all applets.

Visual J++ also comes bundled with demonstration versions of other types of applet creation programs. This chapter will demonstrate the use of these alternative "wizards," not so that you can decide to buy them or anything like that, but only to show you how Visual J++ can be extended with third-party wizards and development tools to make Java applet (and application) development even easier. A lot of people just like you are getting into Java, and there's no reason why Visual J++ wouldn't bring as many developer's skills to your disposal as possible. Visual J++'s extensibility makes this possible.

The Anatomy of Applets

What is an applet? Start with the Applet class: The Applet class is part of the core Java class libraries. It is located in the java.applet package. So, whenever you want to create your own applet, you will want to make sure to include an import statement in your custom Applet class source code that looks like this:

```
import java.applet.Applet;
```

or this:

```
import java.applet.*;
```

Figure 6-1 shows the class hierarchy of the Applet class. It shows that an applet is a type of container. (Containers are explained in detail in Chapter 3.) Remember that a container is a type of component that (a) can contain other components, and (b) must be contained by another container. An applet, which Figure 6-1 shows is also derived from the Component class, takes up some rectangle of display surface within its parent container. For applets, the parent container is the Web browser, and the applet is visible within the browser's page display. Figure 6-2 shows Microsoft's Internet Explorer showing a page with an applet in it.

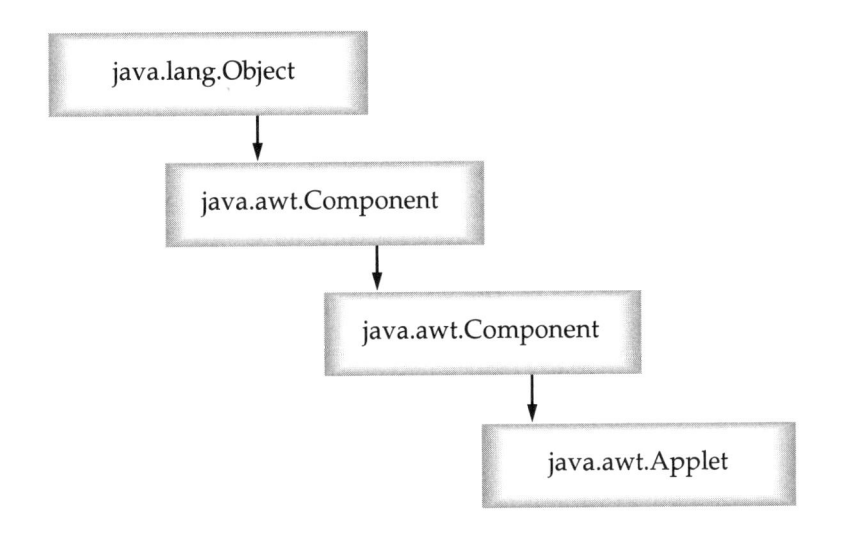

```
java.lang.Object
      ↓
java.awt.Component
          ↓
    java.awt.Component
              ↓
        java.awt.Applet
```

The Applet class hierarchy
Figure 6-1.

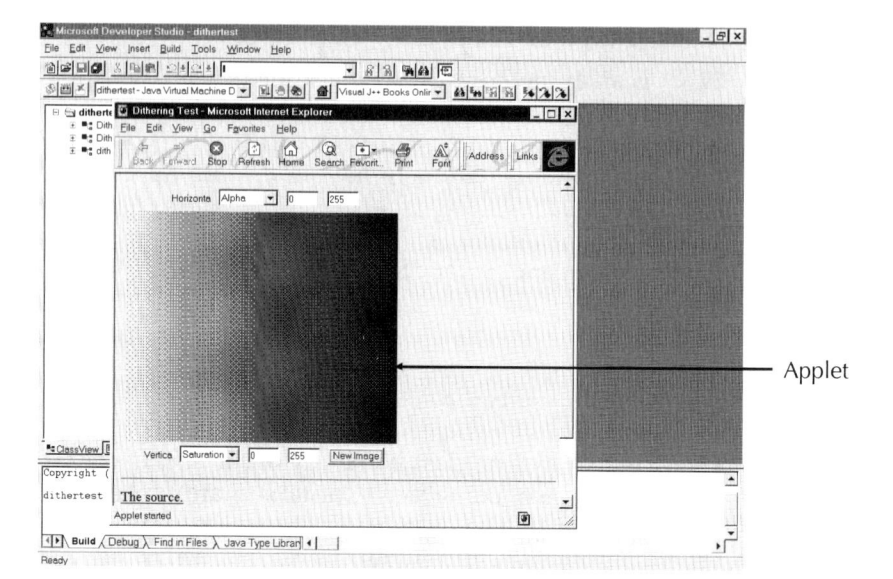

A Web browser displaying an applet
Figure 6-2.

Applet-Aware Browsers

What differentiates an applet from a simple container is the fact that applets exist to display interactive content across the Internet. The Applet lives within its browser, and the state of the browser can vastly affect what your applet does.

For example, say you placed an applet at the top of a long Web page. Your applet displays up-to-the-minute stock market data and takes buy and sell orders for a broker. This may seem like a space-age use of applets, but these are exactly the types of applications most people are (and you should be) thinking of using applets for. Anyway, your applet keeps an open socket connection back to the broker's server machine, through which buying and selling orders will take place. So, this applet might be using up a decent amount of the user's Internet bandwidth by constantly downloading stock market quotations and other information. Now, imagine that the user scrolls down this rather large Web page, and scrolls your brokering applet right off the active display. Should the applet continue downloading and trying to display stock market data? Since the applet is scrolled off the screen, at least for the moment, should the applet continue to burn Internet bandwidth for information that will never be seen or used?

The answer is, of course, no. This example demonstrates one of the big differences between applets and plain-old containers. An applet must be aware of the state of the browser it's in. It must "know," and react positively to, the normal types of things a Web browser user is going to do to it. The

Applets

applet also is able to interact in special ways with its Web browser. For example, the applet can force the browser to display a specific URL in one of the browser's frames. The applet can also tell the browser to display a particular message in its status bar. The point is, an applet is a container with special functions made for browser-embedding.

An applet-aware browser is a browser that is able to download and run applets. Since applets are Java objects, you can see that the browser must have a Java Virtual Machine implemented in it. That is, part of the browser must include a JVM to run the applets in. Some operating systems have incorporated or will soon incorporate JVMs as part of the operating system itself. When this happens, the browser will no long have to have an internal JVM, but will be able to use the operating system's JVM. When your applet runs, it is run within the context of the browser' JVM.

Embedding Applets in Web Pages

You use the <APPLET> container tag to embed applets in HTML Web pages. The sample applets from Visual J++ are filled with various examples of applets embedded in HTML pages, and in each case you can also see an example of the HTML <APPLET> tag. For example, Sun's Animation example applet, which is available under the InfoViewer under the Samples/Sun Samples./Animation Applet topic, has an HTML file with the embedded applet in it. This is the <APPLET> container tag in that HTML file:

```
<applet code=Animator.class width=460 height=160>
    <param name=imagesource value="images/Beans">
    <param name=backgroundcolor value="0xc0c0c0">
    <param name=endimage value=10>
    <param name=soundsource value="audio">
    <param name=soundtrack value=spacemusic.au>
    <param name=sounds
value="1.au|2.au|3.au|4.au|5.au|6.au|7.au|8.au|9.au|0.au">
    <param name=pause value=200>
</applet>
```

This demonstrates the format of the <APPLET> tag container in HTML files. The entire container is made up of a set of tags, the <APPLET> tag and the </APPLET> container closing tag. As you can see in this example, the <APPLET> tag itself has three different fields: the *Code* field, the *Width* field, and the *Height* field. The Code field of the applet tag tells the class of the applet you want embedded. The Width and Height fields tells the dimensions of the rectangle to place the applet in on the Web page.

In this example, the Code field indicates that the applet's class is Animator. Note that in this example the Code field's value is "Animator.class," which is a .CLASS file name, not a simple class name. In fact, you may use either the .CLASS file name of the class, or just the class name alone. That is, in the example above, the value of the Code field could be either "Animator.class" or just "Animator."

The value of the Width and Height fields is the width and height, in pixels, of the rectangle to place the applet in. Since HTML pages are statically laid out, you need these parameters. The applet cannot resize itself or move itself with the Web page. It is specified in the <APPLET> tag's Width and Height fields exactly what size the applet is to be, and the browser places the applet within the Web page according to the other contents of the page.

There are two other tags that you can also include in the <APPLET> tag. A *Name* field gives the applet a string name within the Web page. This name is used within Java by allowing your applet to get a reference to any other applet that is also running at the same time within the Web page. As is explained in greater detail in a following section of this chapter, the AppletContext method getApplet( ) allows you to pass a name string. If an applet is running that has a Name field that matches the string that you pass this method, then a reference to that applet is returned. Through this mechanism, you can communicate between concurrently running applets in a Web page.

How Applets Are Loaded by Browsers

The other possible field of the <APPLET> tag is a *Codebase* field. The codebase field tells the browser where to look for applets on the remote HTTP server. By default, when the browser attempts to load your applet, it must download the .CLASS file for your applet's class from the same HTTP server it got the encapsulating Web page from. For example, you have an applet-containing Web page on your Web server "www.myserver.com" with the URL "http://www.muserver.com/MyAppletPage.html." The <APPLET> container tag in this page looks like this:

```
<APPLET CODE=MyApplet WIDTH=100 HEIGHT=200>
</APPLET>
```

To load the MyApplet class into the browser's JVM, the browser will automatically generate the URL "http://www.myserver.com/MyApplet.class." This URL is generated by combining the URL of the applet-containing Web page with the expected .CLASS filename of your applet's class ("MyApplet.class"). If the classfile's URL that the browser generates does not exist on your Web server, you will probably see a message in the status bar of the browser that look something like this:

```
ClassNotFoundException: class MyApplet not found.
```

Applets

See, the browser generates a URL for your applet's classes by using the HTML page's URL as a base. Your classfile's name ("MyApplet.class") essentially becomes a relative URL that is combined with the HTML page's absolute URL. Figure 6-3 shows how the browser looks for a class' .CLASS file across the Web.

The CODEBASE tag allows you to specify an alternative location for the browser to look for your applet's .CLASS files. This <APPLET> container tag example demonstrates the use of a codebase field in the <APPLET> tag:

```
<APPLET CODE=MyApplet CODEBASE="/java/classfiles/" WIDTH=100 HEIGHT=200>
</APPLET>
```

The browser that reads this <APPLET> container tag will not look for the MyApplet.class file in "http://www.myserver.com/MyApplet.class," but instead will look in "http://www.myserver.com/java/classfiles/MyApplet.class." The browser will combine the server name with the value of the codebase field and the expected name of the .CLASS file to generate a URL. Figure 6-4 shows how a browser combines the HTML page's URL, the codebase field, and the class' .CLASS filename to look for class files across the web.

The codebase field can be quite useful for saving space on your server. Instead of having to keep duplicate copies of commonly used .CLASS files in different locations on your server, you can keep them all in one central location. For each <APPLET> tag, point the codebase field to this central location. Otherwise, each directory on your Web server that contains an

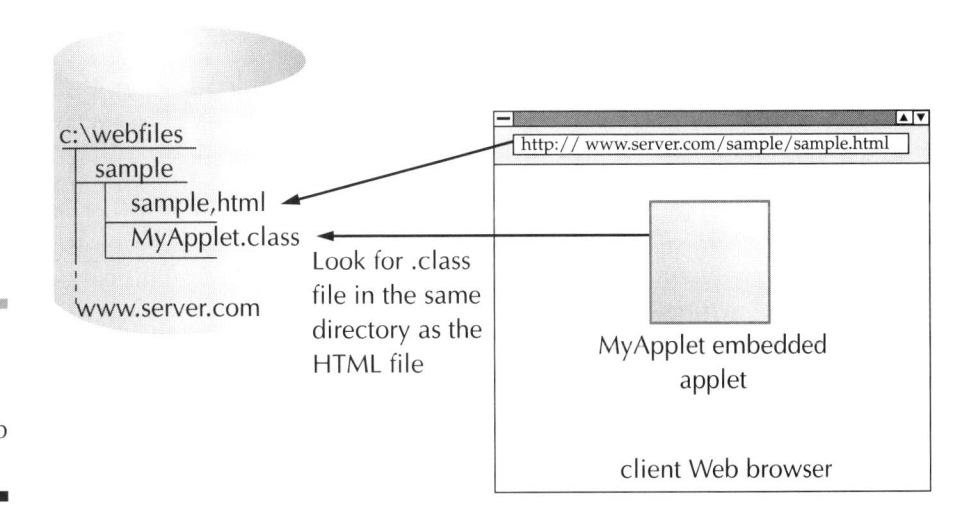

Figure 6-3. A browser looking for a .CLASS file across the Web

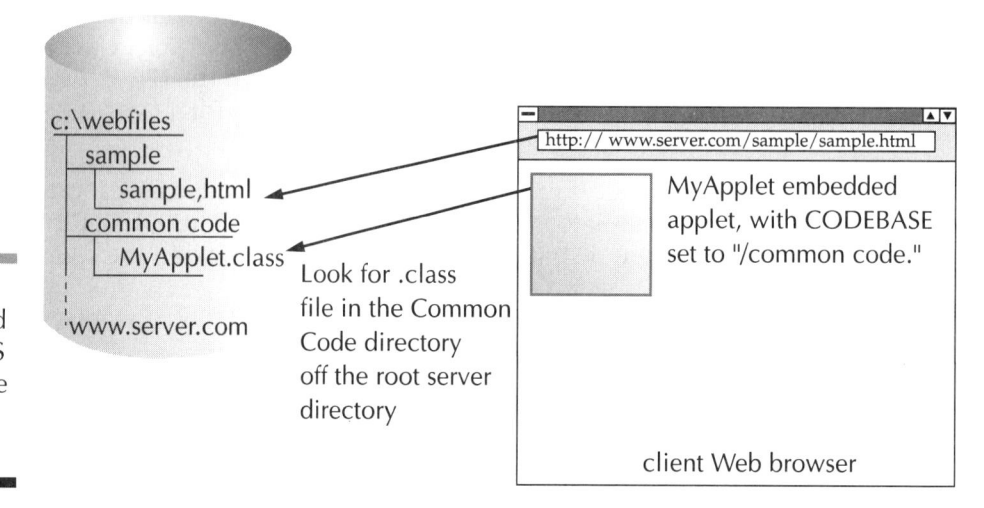

Using the codebase field to find .CLASS files across the Web
Figure 6-4.

applet-containing Web page will have to keep copies of all needed .CLASS files within the same directory.

Note that, as part of loading your applet's .CLASS file into the browser's JVM, the virtual machine will also load all classes that your applet needs to run. For example, if your MyApplet class refers to a special display panel class MyPanel, then the browser's JVM will also attempt to download the .CLASS file for the MyPanel class. It will look for the MyPanel.class in the same directory that it found the applet's .CLASS file on the server. If the URL for MyApplet.class was "http://www.myserver.com/java/classfiles/MyApplet.class," then the URL the browser will generate for the MyPanel .CLASS file will be "http://www.myserver.com/java./classfiles/MyPanel.class."

Applet Archives

Each .CLASS file the browser needs to download causes the browser to make a whole new URL and HTTP session to download the associated .CLASS file. If your applet has 20 classes that it needs to run, then that's 20 different HTTP requests the browser must make. Considering that just to set up an HTTP session can take several seconds across the Internet, then the browser will waste half a minute or more just setting up these multiple HTTP requests to download your .CLASS files. This can cause a significant delay in downloading your files.

Also, remember that you can't compress .CLASS files before they are downloaded, which is really a bit of a shame. In experiments, it has been shown that the average .CLASS file can be compressed by 50 percent or more using PKZIP or some other similar compression software.

Applets

What a waste of precious bandwidth for 28.8 modem home users that the browser not only must set up and connect to the same Web server 20 or more times, but in addition must download uncompressed files: files that easily could be made must smaller.

To solve this pair of problems, two different (but essentially the same) mechanisms have been created. The good people at Microsoft have included with your Visual J++ development environment a CAB creation kit for use when sending applets across the web. This archiving capability is included with Visual J++ and works with Microsoft's Internet Explorer v3.0 and greater. That is, using CAB files is available today and works today.

A similar mechanism is also included in Java v1.1. Added to the core set of Java classes are JAR files, or "Java ARchive" files. Most browsers working with the Web today do not have the Java v1.1 core classes in them, although they will be updated soon. You can read about the JAR archive file classes and format on JavaSoft's Web pages. JavaSoft's main Web page is located at "http://www.javasoft.com."

CAB files and JAR files are conceptually the same thing, so for the purposes of this discussion you can call them generic "archive" files. An archive file is a compendium of .CLASS and other resource files all wrapped into one archive. The individual files that make up the archive are each compressed individually, and the compressed versions of the files are placed together in a single file. This compendium file is the archive. Figure 6-5 illustrates how archive files are made.

The big difference between CAB archive files and JAR archive files is just the format of the files themselves. CAB files use Microsoft's CAB (short for

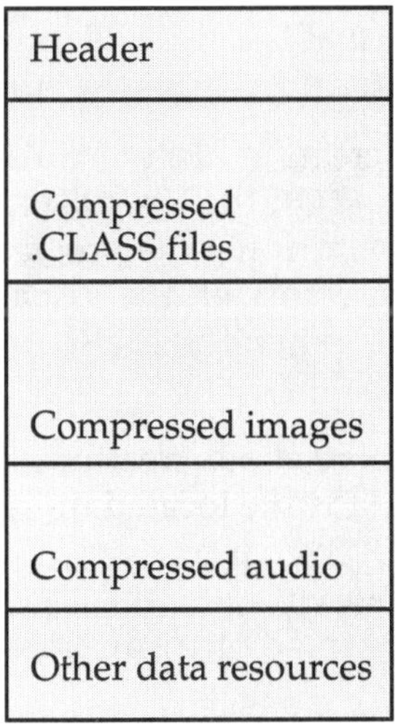

Archive files
Figure 6-5.

| Header |
| Compressed .CLASS files |
| Compressed images |
| Compressed audio |
| Other data resources |

"cabinet") file format, which has been used by Microsoft products and installation packages for quite some time. The format uses Lev-Zimpel algorithm-based compression to compress individual files within the archive. (The Lev-Zimpel algorithm is the same algorithm used by the popular PKZIP compression software.) JAR files use another compression format based on the ZLIB standard. CAB files also use a different mechanism for arranging individual files within the CAB archive than JAR files do. Other than compression standards and specific format, however, CAB files and JAR files are essentially the same.

So, how can you use archive files? Well, by bundling an applet's .CLASS files and other resources (like sound files and image files) into a single archive file, you can significantly reduce the impact of the problems with .CLASS file downloading given previously. Using an archive file, the browser need only initiate a single session with the Web server in order to download all the needed Java classes. Instead of downloading each .CLASS file individually, the browser downloads the archive file that contains all the individual .CLASS files. And, since archive files store .CLASS files compressed within them, the compression problem is mitigated quite a bit. Using archive files, download times can be reduced significantly for the users of your Web-based applets.

Using CAB Files

Java's JAR files are not currently ready for prime-time, real-life Web development yet. The Java v1.1 core class files have not been added to most Web browsers, and most browsers have not yet been updated to use the JAR files.

Microsoft's Internet Explorer has been outfitted to work with CAB files, however. And Visual J++ v1.0 includes a CAB file creation utility. Later versions of Visual J++ also will have a CAB Wizard, which will make it even easier to create and distribute CAB files for your applets.

The CAB file creation utility instructions and executables are distributed with Visual J++. On the Visual J++ CD, you can install the CAB file creation kit by running the program CABDEVKIT.EXE, located under the CAB&SIGN directory off the Visual J++ CD's root. Installation of the CAB file development kit is also one of the options available when installing Visual J++.

To find out more about creating and using CAB files, read the OVERVIEW.HTM file located in the CAB&SIGN directory off the root of your Visual J++ CD. In that overview file are the instructions needed to create and use CAB files in your Visual J++-generated applets. That overview file also contains pointers to other information about CAB files and code signing.

Applet Parameters

Applet's are essentially Web page-embeddable Java programs. As you shall read about below, an applet has init( ), start( ), stop( ), and destroy( ) methods that act analogously to a Java program's main( ) method. Other applet features also make the applet quite similar to an application.

In an application, you pass the application command-line parameters. These parameters are passed on to your application's static main( ) method in the *astrArgs[]* String array, which is the only argument passed to the main( ) method. But an applet has no command line. That is, the user does not type anything in to get the applet started. The applet comes prebundled with an HTML page. How to pass parameters to applets as you would an application?

You may have noticed in one of the <APPLET> container tag examples given previously that there were a series of <PARAM> tags contained by the <APPLET> container tag. It is through the use of these <PARAM> tags that you give parameters to your HTML-embedded Applet objects.

Between the <APPLET> and </APPLET> tags you can place zero or more of these <PARAM> tags. Each tag is passed on the applet. The format of the <PARAM> tag is

```
<PARAM NAME="paramname" VALUE="paramvalue">
```

A <PARAM> tag lets you specify a single key/value pair of strings that the applet can use. Using applet parameters, you can make your applets much more versatile. For example, instead of creating an applet to perform a specific animation sequence, Sun's Animator sample applet takes a group of parameters and can be used to perform almost any animation sequence. Here, again, are the <PARAM> tags from the Animator sample applet's HTML file:

```
<param name=imagesource value="images/Beans">
<param name=backgroundcolor value="0xc0c0c0">
<param name=endimage value=10>
<param name=soundsource value="audio">
<param name=soundtrack value=spacemusic.au>
<param name=sounds
value="1.au|2.au|3.au|4.au|5.au|6.au|7.au|8.au|9.au|0.au">
<param name=pause value=200>
```

Using this series of <PARAM> tags, the Animator applet is given a parameter with the name "imagesource" whose value is "images/Beans"; a parameter with the name "backgroundcolor" whose value is "0xc0c0c0"; a parameter with the name "endimage" whose value is "10"; etc. In all, seven parameters are passed to this Animator applet. Using the values of these named parameters, the Animator applet is able to use different image sequences, different background colors, different audio sequences, and display the animation at a faster or slower frame rate. So, instead of creating an applet that could only display a particular, hard-coded series of images in a specific order with specific background music, this Sun sample applet can display almost any animation sequence, using any background color and background music. Similarly, you will want to make your applets to be as generic as possible, and to take parameters to tell them specifically what to do. One of the Applet class methods is called getParameter( ). This method takes a string as its only argument, which is the name of one of the HTML parameters contained in the applet's <APPLET> container tag. This method returns the string value of that particular parameter. If the parameter does not exist, then this method returns null. Here's some example code that tries to create a URL from the string value of the applet's parameter named "URL."

```
class MyApplet extends Applet {
    // Other Applet code...
    ...

    // Method to get the URL specified by the "URL" Applet parameter.
    public URL getURLParam() {
        URL url;
        try {
            url = new URL( getParameter("URL") );
        } catch (MalformedURLException mue) {
            url = null;
        }

        return url;
    }

    ...
    // Rest of Applet's code
}
```

The Four Applet Lifetime Methods

Once the applet is created within the browser, its lifetime is controlled by four Applet class methods. These methods are init( ), start( ), stop( ), and destroy( ). Most custom applets implement one or more of these inherited methods.

The init( ) method is called by the browser's JVM when the applet is first loaded, but before it is displayed to the user. Within your custom implementation of this method is the appropriate place to do any applet initialization, such as computing lookup tables or downloading images, sounds, and data from the remote server that your applet needs to run. The init( ) method is called only once during the lifetime of your applet by the browser's JVM.

The start( ) and stop( ) methods tell your applet when it is being displayed to the user. Whenever the page of the HTML page that contains your applet is shown on the user's screen, the start( ) method is called. When the applet is removed from the screen, either by being scrolled off the top or bottom of the browser's view by the user or when the browser goes to display a different HTML page, then the stop( ) method is called.

Your implementation of the start( ) and stop( ) methods should be used to control when your applet performs actively. For example, if your applet has an active background thread that computes the movement of a character in some applet-based video game, then that thread should only start running after a call is made to the applet's start( ) method, and that background thread should cease after any call to the applet's stop( ) method.

This is just part of your applet being a polite Web citizen. If you maintained a background thread that kept processing, even while the applet was not being displayed to the user, then the applet is taking up system resources unnecessarily. If all applets did that, then users would find that applets run slow in general, and your applets in particular were just not nice to use.

Note that calls to the start( ) and stop( ) methods are paired. Every call to the applet's start( ) method is matched by exactly one subsequent call to the applet's stop( ) method at some time in the future. Furthermore, the start( ) method is always called after the call to init( ), and is always called before the stop( ) method.

The last applet lifetime method is the destroy( ) method. This method is called just once, and just prior to the applet being terminated permanently. A call to this method is made when the browser is about to display a different HTML page, or when the user is closing the browser application down. Resources that were allocated during init( ) should be deallocated during destroy( ). Of course, because of Java's garbage collection mechanisms it is not necessary to deallocate objects since the garbage collector will destroy those anyway. You should get rid of resources that might delay the destruction of your applet in the destroy method: background threads that were not destroyed by stop( ) (maybe you just put them to sleep, to be reawakened at the next call to start( )), or socket connections made back to the server that were created as part of the applet's running.

Figure 6-6 shows the sequence of calls to an applet's init( ), start( ), stop( ), and destroy( ) methods.

The sequence of calls to an applet's init( ), start( ), stop( ), and destroy( ) methods

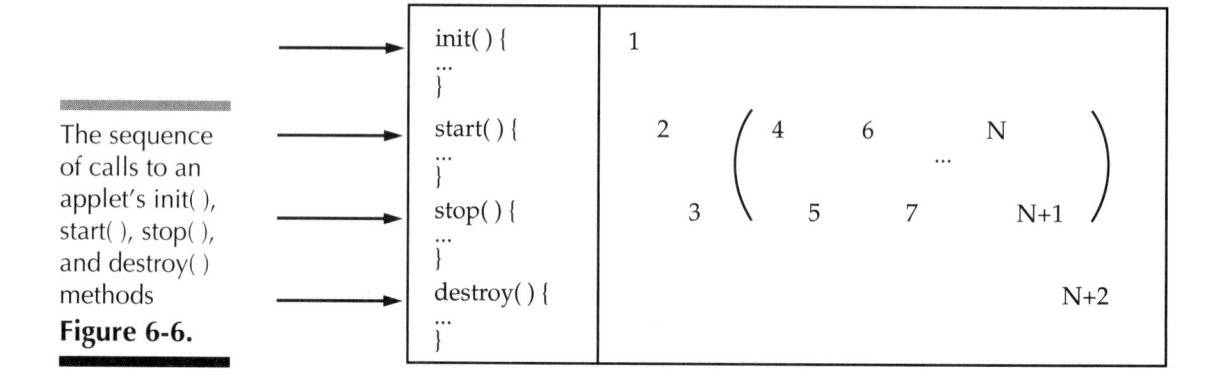

Figure 6-6.

```
init( ) {
   ...
}
start( ) {
   ...
}
stop( ) {
   ...
}
destroy( ) {
   ...
}
```

$$\begin{pmatrix} 1 & & & & & \\ 2 & 4 & 6 & & N & \\ & & & \cdots & & \\ 3 & 5 & 7 & & N+1 & \\ & & & & & N+2 \end{pmatrix}$$

Here is an example Applet class. This applet just displays a timer value. The timer is controlled by a background thread, which sleeps for one-second durations before waking up and causing a repaint( ) of the applet's surface. This code demonstrates one very common technique for controlling the life of background threads: the Applet class member variable m_threadTimer maintains a reference to the timer thread that is supposed to keep running. Each time through its timer loop, the timer thread makes sure that this member variable still refers to itself. When the value of this member variable changes, that is the signal for the background thread to terminate.

```
import java.applet.Applet;
import java.awt.*;
import java.util.*;

class TimerApplet extends Applet implements Runnable {
    // Private state includes a reference to the timer thread that is
    // currently running.
    private Thread m_threadTimer;

    // In init(), the Font that will be used to display the current
    // time is created and set up as this Applet's font.
    public void init() {
        Font f = new Font("Helvetica", Font.BOLD | Font.ITALIC, 15);
        setFont(f);
    }

    // In start(), the timer thread is created and is kick-started.
    public void start() {
        m_threadTimer = new Thread(this);
        m_threadTimer.start();
    }
```

Applets

```java
// In stop(), timer thread is made to stop. This is done by clearing
// the reference to the thread (m_threadTimer). On its next iteration
// in the timer loop in run(), the thread will see that this reference
// has changed, and quit the run() method immediately.
public void stop() {
    m_threadTimer = null;
}

// In destroy(), get rid of any reference to a running timer thread, in
// case the browser accidentally did not call stop() priorly.
public void destroy() {
    m_threadTimer = null;
}

// In the run() method, which is run by any background timer threads,
// run through a small timer loop. At each iteration, call repaint().
// When m_threadTimer no longer refers to currently running thread, then
// quit.
public void run() {
    do {
        repaint();
        try {
            Thread.currentThread().sleep(1000);
        } catch (InterruptedException ie) {
            System.out.println("Timer thread was interrupted: " + ie);
            break;
        }
    } while(m_threadTimer == Thread.currentThread());
}

// Display current time in paint().
public void paint(Graphics g) {
    g.setFont(getFont());
    FontMetrics fm = g.getFontMetrics();

    Date date = new Date(System.currentTimeMillis());
    String strTime = "" + date.getHours() + ":" + date.getMinutes() +
            ":" + date.getSeconds();

    int cx = fm.stringWidth(strTime);
    int cy = size().height/2;

    g.drawString(strTime, cx, cy);
}
}
```

Using the Applet Wizard

Visual J++ includes an Applet Wizard for quickly creating applet code. The applet code that the Applet Wizard generates is a complete skeleton for you to fill in with your specific applet's behavior. The Applet Wizard has facilities for specifying an applet's parameters, creating a default HTML page for viewing and debugging the applet, features for running your applet either in a browser or as a standalone application in its own top-level window, and basic multithreading animation support. The time you will save using the Applet Wizard, both in time saved from having to type in all the Applet Wizard-generated code and in time saved by not having to debug and correct the skeleton code, makes the Applet Wizard one of Visual J++'s best features.

To create an applet using the Applet Wizard, start by creating a new project workspace in the Developer's Studio. Do this by selecting the File|New... Main menu option, and selecting the Project Workspace type in the New dialog. Following is a screen shot of the New dialog, with the Project Workspace item highlighted.

Do not worry if your Visual J++ does not have all the same options as shown here. The items in this dialog reflect just the types of elements you can create if you have Visual J++ installed on your system.

The New Project dialog will appear at this point. To create an Applet Wizard-generated applet, select the Applet Wizard project type in the Type list of this dialog. The Name field indicates the name of the project you want to create. The Location field indicates the directory you want the new project to reside in. In the following illustration, the New Project Workspace dialog's fields have been filled in to create a new Applet Wizard-generated applet named "AppletWizExample", in the "C:\MSDEV\Projects\AppletWizExample" directory.

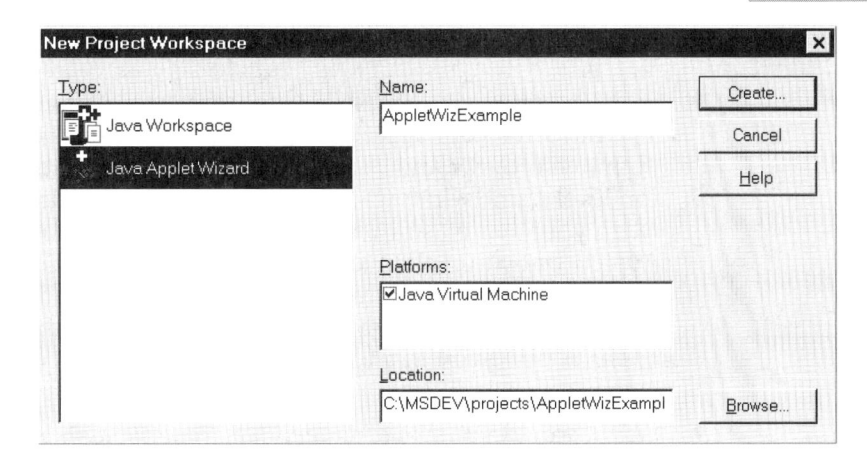

Applets

[Screenshot: New Project Workspace dialog with Java Applet Wizard selected, Name "AppletWizExample", Java Virtual Machine platform checked, Location C:\MSDEV\projects\AppletWizExampl]

Press the Create button on the New Project Workspace dialog to start the Applet Wizard. The Applet Wizard will guide you through a series of five dialogs through which you specify the features and specifics of the applet you want the Applet Wizard to create.

The first Applet Wizard dialog, which is titled "Java Applet Wizard - Step 1 of 5," specifies some overall parameters to the Applet Wizard. The following is a screen shot of the first Applet Wizard dialog.

[Screenshot: Java Applet Wizard - Step 1 of 5 dialog. Options: How would you like to be able to run your program? — As an applet only (selected) / As an applet and as an application. What would you like to name your applet class? AppletWizExample. Would you like to generate source file comments? Yes, please (selected) with Explanatory comments and TODO comments checked / No, thank you.]

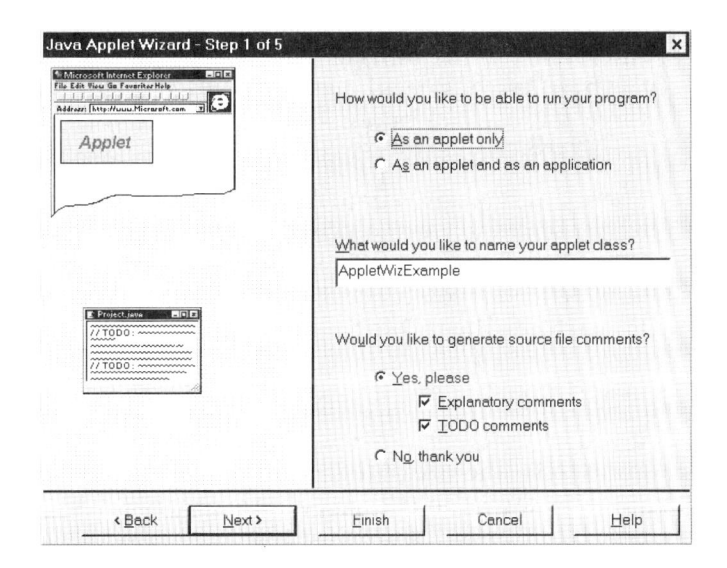

These are the three things you specify on this dialog:

- "How would you like to be able to run your program?" has two options. You can have your applet generated to only run in a browser, or to run both in a browser and as a standalone Java application in its own top-level frame window. Note that if you choose the second option, then when your applet is run as an application it will not have access to an AppletContext (explained in detail in a following section). Without an AppletContext, some of the inherited applet methods won't work, such as showStatus( ) and showDocument( ). These methods assume the applet is being run in a browser, and will cause exceptions to be thrown when the applet is instead run as a standalone Java application.
- "What would you like to name your Applet class" defaults to using the project name as the applet's name. You can specify any valid class name you want.
- "Would you like to generate source file comments?" will add Applet Wizard-generated comments to your applet's source files automatically. The Explanatory Comments option adds comments that explain each method and member variable of your Applet's class. The TODO Comments option adds placeholder comments that tell you where to add your own implementation to the Applet Wizard-generated Applet class. For example, it adds this comment within the init( ) method:

```
// TODO: Place additional initialization code here
```

After filling in the fields of this dialog, press the Next button to move on to the next Applet Wizard dialog. Note that on all the Applet Wizard dialogs there is also a Back button, which will take you back one dialog so that you can change options if you want to.

The second Applet Wizard dialog asks you about the HTML file you want to use while viewing and debugging your applet in Visual J++. The Applet Wizard will automatically generate a simple HTML file in which your applet is embedded if you select the Yes option under, "Would you like a sample HTML file?" The HTML file that is generated is given the same name as your project, with a .HTML extension. Even after generating this file, you can go in and modify it in the future in any way you wish.

If you let the Applet Wizard generate an HTML file for you, then you must also specify the size of the embedded applet in that HTML file. The default value, as shown in the next illustration, is 320 by 240. The exact values you type into this dialog are used to fill in the Width and Height fields of the <APPLET> tag in the HTML file. You can always edit the HTML file directly later to change this size. Press the Next button to move on to the next Applet Wizard dialog.

Applets

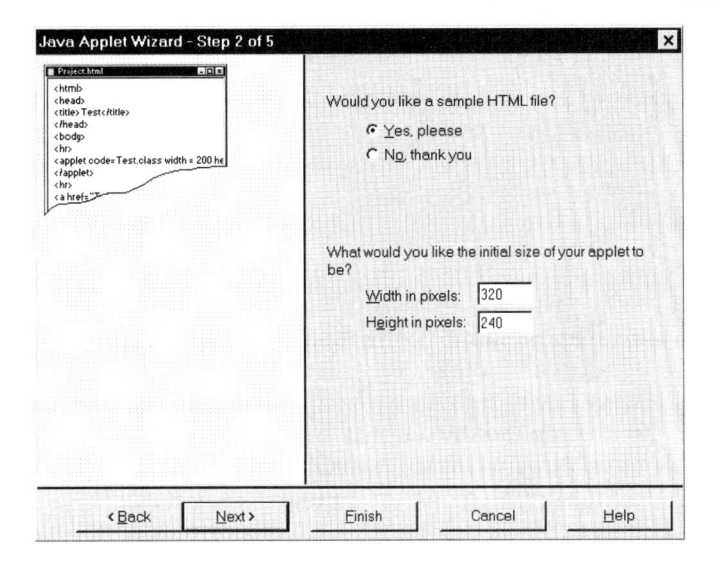

The third Applet Wizard dialog asks you two different questions:

◆ Do you want multithreaded support in your applet, and if so do you want code for displaying an animation sequence added also?

◆ Do you want mouse event handlers for mouse movement, mouse clicking, and mouse enter/exit events?

When you add AppletWizard's multithreading support, the Applet Wizard will generate an Applet class that implements the Runnable interface, i.e. with a run( ) method that background threads run on. The run( ) method implementation that the Applet Wizard will generate for you is a simple repaint( )/sleep( ) loop that repaints your applet every 50 milliseconds. Here is Applet Wizard-generated code for the run( ) method created if you specify that you want multithreaded support in your Java applet:

```
public void run()
{
    while (true)
    {
        try
        {
            repaint();
            Thread.sleep(50);
        }
```

```
        catch (InterruptedException e)
        {
            // InterruptedException is thrown by Thread.sleep(),
            //         meaning that another thread has interrupted this one
            stop();
        }
    }
}
```

When you specify that in addition to multithreaded support you also want animation support, the Applet Wizard adds code to display an animated sequence of images in your applet. The added code works by downloading a sequence of images in the run( ) method before the repaint( )/sleep( ) loop is run. Each iteration of the repaint( )/sleep( ) loop causes another one of the animated images to be displayed in your applet. The Applet Wizard comes bundled with a default animation sequence (a spinning globe made up of 18 different .GIF files) that your Applet Wizard-generated applet will display. The next screen shot shows an Applet Wizard-generated applet displaying this default sequence. You can change the number of images and their file names to replace this animation sequence with another one.

Click on the individual mouse event options in this third dialog to have the Applet Wizard add skeleton mouse event handling methods to your applet. Clicking on the mouseUp( ), mouseDown( ) option adds an empty mouseUp( ) and mouseDown( ) method to your applet, which you can fill in with code for what you want your applet to do when the mouse is clicked or released within your applet. Similarly, the mouseMove( ), mouseDrag( ) option adds

Applets

these event handlers so you can have your applet react to mouse movements or mouse drags. The mouseEnter( ) and mouseExit( ) event handlers are called whenever the mouse enters or exits your applet's bounding rectangle in the browser. Note that these six methods, and Java event handling in general are discussed in Chapter 4.

The fourth Applet Wizard dialog, shown in the next illustration, allows you to specify the parameters your applet recognizes.

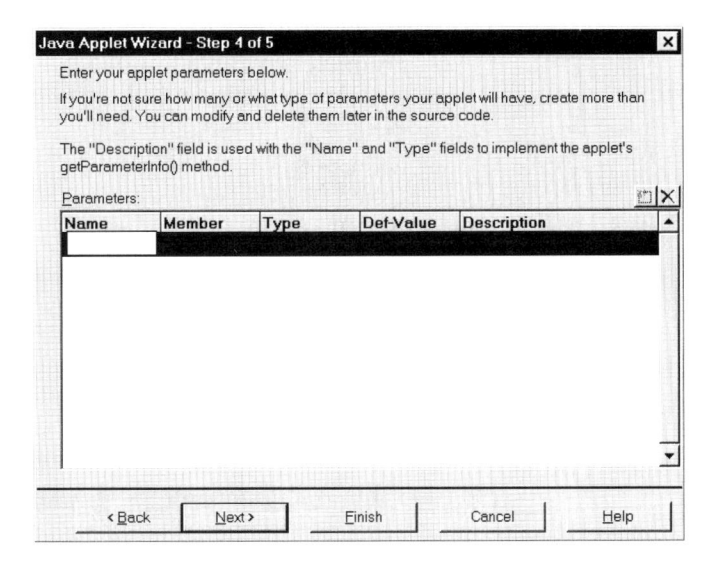

Fill in each row of the following table with this information:

Field	Description
Name	String name of the parameter. This is the string in the Name field of the HTML file's <PARAM> tag for this parameter.
Member	Name of a member variable that you want to hold this parameter's value. Applets generated by the Applet Wizard automatically read in all parameters to their respective member variables.
Type	This is the type of the member variable. This dialog only allows you to specify built-in types: boolean, double, float, int, long, and string. Booleans are read in from a "true" or "false" value. For more complex types, like colors or URLS, start off by making the member a string, and changing the Applet Wizard-generated code later.

Field	Description
Def-Value	This is an optional field that specifies what you want the default value of this parameter to be, in case there is no <PARAM> field in the HTML file.
Description	Returned by the getParameterInfo( ) method (explained in following section) so users of your Applet class can know which parameters the applet supports, and what valid values there are. Gives a brief description of the parameter and an allowable range of values. For example, "number of prime numbers to generate: 0–10."

The Applet Wizard will use this table to generate code that reads in your applet's parameters. Note that if your applet can also be run as a standalone application, then you will specify the parameters to the applet on the command line, like this:

```
jview MyAppletClass param1=val1 param2="val2 with spaces" param3=number
```

The final step is the Applet Wizard, which is the fifth dialog, shown in the next illustration:

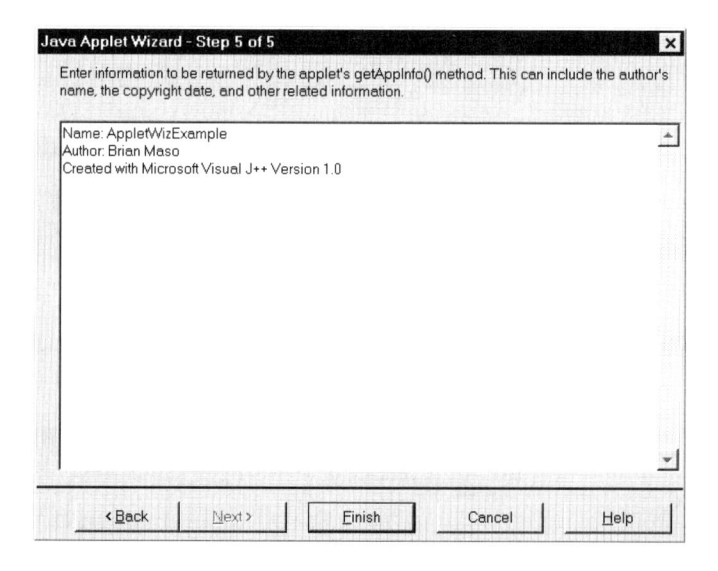

In this dialog, you specify the string returned by the applet's getAppletInfo( ) method. The getAppletInfo( ) method is a public method used to gather information about an applet externally, maybe by the browser or by some other Java object. In this string you should include such information as your name, the copyright message you want, etc. The Applet Wizard automatically throws in a plug for itself here, suggesting by default that you add the line

```
Created with Microsoft Visual J++ Version 1.0
```

to your applet's AppletInfo. Unless you like giving away free advertising, you might want to consider removing this line from your applet's AppletInfo.

You can hit the Finish button in the Applet Wizard at this point. The Applet Wizard will generate the applet for you, create a project workspace for it, and open up that workspace in the ClassView. The applet skeleton is ready to run. You can compile and run the applet right away, if you want to. Of course, as a skeleton it doesn't really do much. But after perusing the Applet Wizard-generated code for your Applet class(es), you can certainly agree that the Applet Wizard has gotten you a long way towards making a useful applet. Now the real work begins. You must add custom initialization, destruction, event handling, and background thread code to your applet. Good luck!

The Applet Class

You already know about the four "lifetime" methods of the Applet class, which control the lifetime of the applet: the init( ), start( ), stop( ), and destroy( ) methods. The Applet class also includes several other methods for making working with applets easier.

Applet Information Methods

There are two semistandard methods that allow you to detail how your applets work to the outside world. Anyone who can instantiate an instance of your Applet class may want to know, for example, who created the applet so that they can contact you and give you lots of money. (Anything's possible, after all.)

You should override the getAppletInfo( ) method in your Applet class to return a human-readable string that tells about the ownership and legal details of your applet. In this string, you may want to include your name, copyright information, and a URL pointing to some home page where the user can find out more about your applet, other applets and software you make, or more documentation on the Applet class. The Applet Wizard, for example, generates by default a getAppletInfo( ) method implementation that returns a string that looks like this:

```
"Name: <Applet class name>\r\n" +
    "Author: <your name here>\r\n" +
    "Created with Microsoft Visual J++ Version 1.0";
```

Of course, you may want to add copyright and additional information to this string, and to take out the reference to Visual J++.

The getParameterInfo( ) method of the Applet class is the appropriate place for you to return a list of the parameters the applet recognizes, and what format those parameter values should have. The getParameterInfo( ) method has this signature:

```
public String[][] getParameterInfo();
```

The return value from you overriding implementation of this method is an array of three-string arrays. That is, each element in the array returned is an array of three strings. Each three-string array should have this format:

```
{ "parameter name", "parameter data type", "description" }
```

The parameter name string is the string that will be used in the HTML <PARAM> tag's Name field. The data type is some descriptive string indicating the format of the data you're expecting for this parameter. For example, you may have a simple type like int, long, or url. There are no standards for the format of these type strings. Something short and to the point should do the trick. The description string can have anything you want in it, although it is a good idea to include both a description of how the parameter is used by the applet and a range of valid values. For example, the parameter info string array describes a parameter named "numFrames," which is some integer value between the range on 1–100:

```
{"numFrames", "int", "Number of animation frames: 1-100" }
```

Here is a typical implementation of the getParameterInfo( ) method:

```
private static String[][] m_aastrParamInfo = {
    { "numFrames", "int", "Number of animation frames: 1-100" },
    { "backcolor", "0x00rrggbb",
            "Background color to use: in packed red/green/blue hex format" },
    { "imageBaseName", "string", "Base to use for generating image filenames" +
            ": <basename>00.gif is used for first image" }
};

public String[][] getParameterInfo() {
    return m_aastrParamInfo;
}
```

Browser/Applet Communication Methods

An applet is typically run within the context of a browser. Each Applet object is handed an AppletContext instance when it is created within a browser. Through the AppletContext, the applet can talk to the browser and control it to a limited extent. For example, it is through the AppletContext that the applet can download images and audio files from the Internet. The applet can make the browser display a string in its status bar by passing that string to the AppletContext's showStatus( ) method.

Downloading Images and Audio Files

A following section listing applet security restrictions states that an applet cannot communicate with any other machine across the Internet other than the Web server that served up the applet in the first place. Before you even read that section, however, you get to first find out that it's not true. An applet can communicate with any other server on the Internet for the purposes of downloading image and audio files.

The Applet class method getImage( ) is passed a URL as its input argument. The return value is an image made up of the downloaded image file the URL referred to. (This method is actually a wrapper around the AppletContext.getImage( ) method, so it is really the AppletContext that is downloading the Image.) Whether or not the image file exists, or the URL points to anything at all, the Image object is returned from this method. However, once you try to draw the image or use it in any way, then the downloading process actually starts. If the URL passed to getImage( ) was bad, then the later operation will throw an exception.

Similar to getImage( ), the getAudioClip( ) method is used to download an audio file from anywhere on the Internet. (Note that, as it is implemented today, audio clips can only be created from .AU files with a sampling rate of 8kHz, mono sound, µ-law encoding. If you don't know what that means or can't create that kind of file, try downloading a shareware conversion program such as GoldWave from the Internet. GoldWave and other audio editing programs can convert the common Windows .WAV format to the appropriate .AU format for Java audio clips.) The getAudioClip( ) method of the Applet class is a simple wrapper around the AppletContext's getAudioClip( ) method.

An audio clip is represented by an AudioClip object in Java. The AudioClip's interface includes three methods—play( ), stop( ), and loop( )—which you can use to start playing and stop playing downloaded audio clips.

The Applet class includes some shorthand methods for working with AudioClips, too. The play( ) method of the Applet class takes a URL and starts playing the audio file the URL points to. The implementation of this method simply creates an AudioClip from the passed URL and calls its play( ) method.

Getting Parameters

The Applet class method getParameter( ) is used to get parameter values from the browser. These parameter values are the same values taken from the applet's <PARAM> tags in the HTML file. The GetParameter( ) method takes the name of an applet parameter and returns that parameter's value in a string. If there is no such named parameter for the applet, then this method returns null.

getDocumentBase( ) and getCodeBase( )

The URL for the HTML file that the applet is embedded in is returned by the getDocumentBase( ) method. This is really the only method you have for figuring out the name of the server that the applet came from. For example, if you wanted to download an image named "img0001.gif" from the "images" subdirectory under that directory where the HTML file came from, you would use a line like this:

```
Image img = getImage(new URL(getDocumentBase(), "images/img0001.gif"));
```

which uses the document base URL as a base for a relative URL to the "images/img0001.gif" URL.

If your Applet class was accessed from the Codebase field URL, not from the HTML file's directory on the server, then you may need to use the code base and not the document base to access files. In that case, use the Applet class method getCodeBase( ) instead of getDocumentBase( ) in the previous example to download files from the server.

AppletContext Methods

An applet's AppletContext is an object that abstracts the browser the applet is running in. Through the AppletContext, the applet can find out more about the browser, and to a limited extent control the browser.

Use the getAppletContext( ) method of the Applet class to get a reference to the applet's AppletContext object. This reference is stored as a private member variable of the Applet class, so your custom applets need to use the method to access the AppletContext.

The AppletContext's showStatus( ) method places a string into the browser's status bar. (This of course assumes the browser has a status bar. If it doesn't, then the AppletContext will probably ignore any calls to this method.) Here's an example of placing a string in the browser's status bar:

```
getAppletContext().showStatus("Attempting to download files.");
```

You can also tell the browser to display a new HTML file. The AppletContext's showDocument( ) method takes a URL, and the browser immediately begins downloading, displaying that URL in the Applet's browser frame. An overloaded version of this method also exists that takes a second string parameter. The string parameter is the name of the browser-frame where you want the new HTML document displayed. This, of course, assumes the browser is "frames-capable." If it isn't, then the actions of this method are undefined. You use the <FRAMESET> contain tag in HTML to define a set of named browser frames. The applet can then place new HTML documents into any one of them.

Communicating with Other Applets

Through the AppletContext, you can also get a reference to any other applet that is currently running. Using this mechanism you could have coordinated applets on one or more different HTML pages. For example, you could have a gas gauge applet that displayed the progress of another applet's downloading.

The AppletContext( ) method getApplet( ) takes a string as its only parameter. This string is the value of another applet's Name field (taken from the <APPLET> tag in the other applet's HTML file). The method returns an applet reference to the other applet. You can then call any one of the other applet's methods, check its class using the *instanceof* operator, or interact with the other applet in any way you choose.

Some browsers don't support the Name field of the <APPLET> tag. Never fear. The AppletContext also has a method called getApplets( ). This method returns an enumeration of applets, filled with references to *all* the other applets currently running within the browser. Here's an example applet that tries to find all other applets of the same class that are running at the same time, and passing a reference of itself to all those other applets of the same type:

```
import java.applet.Applet;
import java.awt.*;
import java.util.*;

class CooperativeApplet extends Applet {
    // References to all other CooperativeApplets currently running.
    private Vector m_vectOtherApplets = new Vector();

    // addRef() and removeRef() are used to pass references between instances
    // of CooperativeApplet objects.
    public void addRef(CooperativeApplet a) {
```

```
            if(!m_vectOtherApplets.contains(a))
                m_vectOtherApplets.addElement(a);
        }

        public void removeRef(CooperativeApplet a) {
            if(m_vectOtherApplets.contains(a))
                m_vectOtherApplets.removeElement(a);
        }

        // init() finds all other Applets of the same type, and sends a reference
        // of itself to them.
        public void init() {
            Enumeration enumApplets = getAppletContext().getApplets();
            while(enumApplets.hasMoreElements()) {
                try {
                    CooperativeApplet a =
                            (CooperativeApplet)enumApplets.nextElement();

                    m_vectOtherApplets.addElement(a);
                    a.addRef(this);
                } catch (ClassCastException cce) {
                    // Caused by enumerated Applet not derived from
                    // CooperativeApplet. Just ignore and continue in loop.
                }
            }
        }

        // When being destroyed, tell other CooperativeApplets to remove
        // reference to this object.
        public void destroy() {
            Enumeration enum = m_vectOtherApplets.elements();
            while(enum.hasMoreElements())
                ((CooperativeApplet)enum.nextElement()).removeRef(this);
        }
}(Yes, the CooperativeApplet example here does not have appropriate thread-safe
code. It demonstrates the use of the AppletContext.getApplets() method, however,
which is the whole point.)
```

Special Security Restrictions on Applets

Applets are distributed executable code. As distributed code, an Applet would seem to be the perfect conduit for distributing viruses, worms, or any other type of malicious executable code that you don't want running on your system. That's how viruses are usually transmitted from computer to computer: the virus hides within executable code, and when the time is right it transfers itself onto the newly infected machine. Executable code that is transferred, say by disk or over the Internet, from the newly infected machine will further infect other machines.

It's not hard to imagine viruses using applets to transfer from machine to machine. It seems like the perfect setup: executable code being transferred from the Web server machine to the Web browser's machine, across the Internet. Any innocent Web surfer could be infected!

That's why a whole host of special security restrictions have been arrayed against applets being able to *infect* the target system. If these security restrictions are properly implemented in the browser's Java Virtual Machine, it is virtually impossible to use applets to transfer viruses between machines across the Web. Unfortunately, these restrictions can hamper what your applets can do. This section details what the specific applet security restrictions are, and how you can compensate for some of the restrictions in a safe manner.

What's Not Allowed

Probably the most important security restriction placed on applets is that they cannot write any data whatsoever to the local file system on the browser's machine. Applet code cannot open files on the client's machine, they cannot create files on the client's machine, and they cannot open nor create directories on the client's machine.

If you try to make or open a File object or a FileInputStream or FileOutputStream object on the client's machine (the machine the applet is running on), then your attempt will cause a security exception to be thrown. For example, this code will cause a security exception to be thrown if the applet is embedded in an HTML page:

```
import java.applet.Applet;
import java.awt.*;

public class BadApplet extends Applet {
    public void init() {
        try {
            FileInputStream in = new FileInputStream(
                    getParameter("fileToOpen"));
        } catch (SecurityException) {
            System.out.println("SECURITY PROBLEM TRYING TO OPEN FILE!");
        }
    }
}
```

The SecurityManager and Applets

The object responsible for stopping applets from doing anything potentially dangerous is the Java SecurityManager. The SecurityManager is explained in detail in Chapter 11.

A quick explanation of how the SecurityManager does this: The System object has a single security manager. As part of each attempt to do a potentially dangerous operation, the SecurityManager is asked, "Is this OK?" If the SecurityManager determines that the operation is allowed, then it allows program execution to continue.

If the SecurityManager determines that the operation is not allowed, however, then it throws a security exception. As the previous applet example shows, the exception that was thrown by the attempt to open a file within an applet is a security exception. That security exception was thrown by the SecurityManager.

When Java applications are run, there is no SecurityManager. The potentially sensitive operations are all allowed to be done. There's nothing wrong with that, because you expect that any application the user starts running is "trusted" by the user, and so is allowed to do just about anything it wants.

Applets, however, are not specifically loaded nor started by the user, and thus are not trusted. The browser's JVM automatically is started with a very restrictive security manager. This security manager does not allow any suspect operation to take place. And that is how applet security is maintained in Java.

How to do File-Base Operations in Java

So, you can't perform any persistent operations in Java. That could be a problem, especially if your applet needs to maintain persistent information between sessions. For example, let's say you create an applet that plays chess with the user. Most chess-playing programs can take several minutes, or even several hours, to generate a computer-based move in chess. If the user doesn't want to wait around for such a long time to play chess, she may want to be able to save the game for later, and continue it at that time. But without the ability to store the game on the client's machine, how can you allow the user to postpone the game until later?

Well, if you can't store the game information on the client's file system, where else can you store it? On the *server* machine! You know, the machine the applet was served from; the IP address or machine name of that machine is included as part of the URL returned from the getDocumentBase( ) method. Through the Internet, you can send the information from the client applet back to the server machine, and the incomplete chess game can be stored on the server's machine. When the user comes back to the page with

Applets

the embedded chess applet in it, she could specify some identifying number for a chess game that was previously saved. At that point, the server would send the game information to the applet, and the game could continue. Figure 6-7 illustrates how data can flow from the applet back to the server, and then from the server back to the applet at a later time.

As Figure 6-7 shows, you need a program or server running on the server machine that is prepared to accept the data from the applet. The HTTP protocol, which is the protocol Web servers use, does not provide a mechanism for storing data on the server. Therefore, you must create some sort of executable program that runs on the server machine specifically to store, and send back out, data to be stored persistently.

There are all sorts of different ways to send data from an applet to a remote point on the Internet. As is explained in a following section, however, an applet is only allowed to make a socket connection to the server machine that served it in the first place. So, when trying to send data from an applet

(a) <send data token>, "bob," <data bytes ...>

(b) <retrieve data token>, "bob," <data bytes ...>

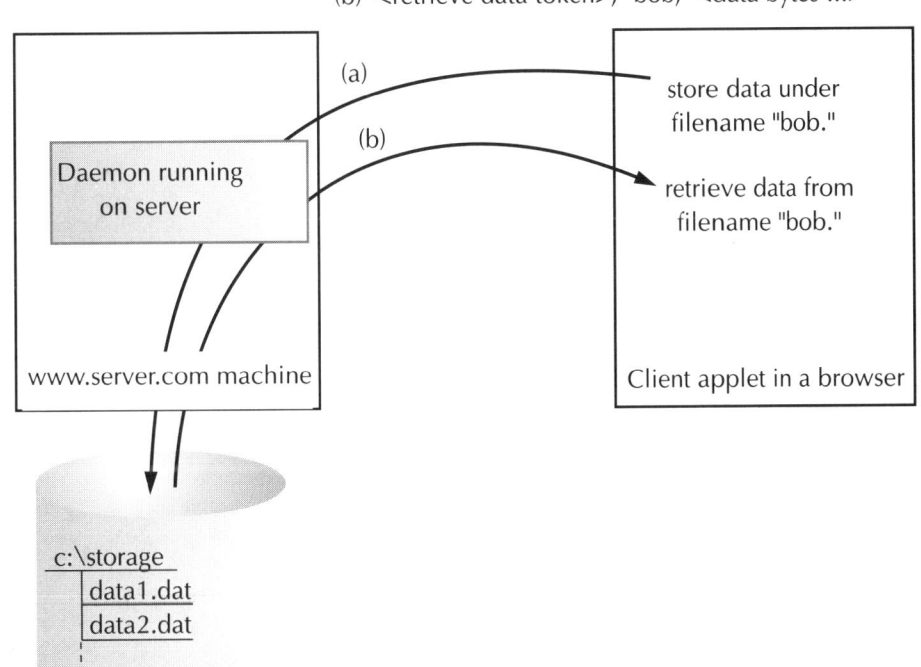

(a) Saving data persistently on the server machine, and (b) retrieving that data at a later time
Figure 6-7.

to a remote system, you can only directly connect to the Web server where the applet came from.

Here is one simple implementation of a persistent file mechanism that works across the Internet. The applet makes a socket connection to a server program and sends a "save file" token across the socket. This tells the server application that the applet is sending data to be stored. The applet then sends a file identifier under which the file data is to be saved. Then, the applet sends all the file data that is to be stored.

To get the data back at a later time, the applet connects to the server application again. It first sends a "send data" token across the socket connection, followed by a file identifier used previously to store the data. The server program then streams the data it has stored in a local file back across the socket connection to the applet. Here's the code you must add to an applet class to allow it to save data to this type of server program:

```java
import java.applet.Applet;
import java.awt.*;
import java.net.*;
import java.io.*;

public class MyStoringApplet extends Applet {
    public static final int m_nStorageServerPort = 1001;

    // Other Applet code...
    ...

    // The saveRemoteData() method takes an array of bytes that is to be stored
    // on the remote server machine, and a file name to store the data under.
    public void saveRemoteData(String strFilename, byte[] abData, int offset,
            int length) {
        // Open a socket connection to the host that served this Applet,
        // using the member m_nStorageServerPort as the port number to
        // connect to.
        DataOutputStream out = null;
        try {
            InetAddress addr = InetAddress.getByName(
                    getDocumentBase().getHost());
            Socket sock = new Socket(addr, m_nStorageServerPort);
            out = new DataOutputStream(sock.getOutputStream());
        } catch (UnknownHostException uhe) {
            System.out.println("Could not lookup host.");
            return;
        } catch (IOException ioe) {
            System.out.println("Could not connect back to host.");
            return;
```

Applets

```java
            }

            try {
                // Send "save data" token, which is an 0 int.
                out.writeInt(0);

                // Send the file name to store the data under.
                out.writeUTF(strFilename);

                // Write out the data.
                out.write(abData, offset, length);

                // Close socket stream, which flushes data out.
                out.close();
            } catch (IOException ioe) {
                System.out.println("Problem writing data to server: " + ioe);
                return;
            }
        }

        // The getRemoteData() method takes just a filename that data
        // has been stored under on the server machine. Returns a byte
        // array that is the data.
        public byte[] getRemoteData(String strFilename) {
            // Open a socket connection to the host that served this Applet,
            // using the member m_nStorageServerPort as the port number to
            // connect to.
            DataOutputStream out = null;
            InputStream in = null;
            try {
                InetAddress addr = InetAddress.getByName(
                        getDocumentBase().getHost());
                Socket sock = new Socket(addr, m_nStorageServerPort);
                out = new DataOutputStream(sock.getOutputStream());
                in = sock.getInputStream();
            } catch (UnknownHostException uhe) {
                System.out.println("Could not lookup host.");
                return null;
            } catch (IOException ioe) {
                System.out.println("Could not connect back to host.");
                return null;
            }

            // Send a "send data" token, which is a 1 int, and the name
            // of the filename to retrieve. Then just record everything that
            // is sent back across the socket connection.
            ByteArrayOutputStream bytes = new ByteArrayOutputStream();
            try {
```

```
                out.writeInt(1);
                out.writeUTF(strFilename);

                int n;
                while(true) {
                    n = in.read();
                    bytes.write(n);
                }
        } catch (EOFException eof) {
        } catch (IOException ioe) {
            System.out.println("Problem reading data from remote server.");
        } finally {
            try {
                in.close();
            } catch (IOException ioe) {
            }
        }

        // Return the byte array.
        return bytes.toByteArray();
    }
}
```

The server application, which must be explicitly started and left running on the Web server machine, listens for socket connections. When a new connection is made, the file server program listens for a "save data" or a "send data" token, and a file identifier string. Once the file identifier string is received, the server either sends the data in the specified file or creates the specified file and stores any information sent across the socket connection to that file. Here is the implementation:

```
import java.net.*;
import java.io.*;

// Each instance of the SimpleFileServer object is created to handle
// a single connection to the server. The static methods and members
// control the server program and the ServerSocket, and creates individual
// SimpleFileServer object instances to handle individual connections.
public class SimpleFileServer {
    // Port to connect to is hardcoded here.
    private static final int m_nServerPort = 1001;

    // Static class members hold the ServerSocket.
    private static ServerSocket m_socketServer;

    // main() method creates server socket, waits for connections and creates
    // SimpleFileServer instances for each connection made.
```

Applets

```java
public static void main(String[] astrArgs) {
    // Create server socket.
    try {
        m_socketServer = new ServerSocket(m_nServerPort);
    } catch (IOException ioe) {
        System.err.println("Problem creating server socket: " + ioe);
        System.exit(-1);
    }

    // For each connection to the server socket, create a handler object
    try {
        Socket s;
        while(null != (s = m_socketServer.accept())) {
            new SimpleFileServer(s);
            s.close();
        }
        m_socketServer.close();
    } catch (IOException ioe) {
        System.err.println("Server socket problem: " + ioe);
    }
}

// Constructor for the individual SimpleFileServer objects. The entire
// file exchange is completed within this constructor code.
private SimpleFileServer(Socket socket) throws IOException {
    // Get the socket's input and output streams.
    DataInputStream in = new DataInputStream(socket.getInputStream());
    DataOutputStream out = new DataOutputStream(socket.getOutputStream());

    // Read the request type and file name.
    int nType = in.readInt();
    String strFilename = in.readUTF();

    // If are supposed to read in file, then create FileInputStream and read
    // in the data.
    if(0 == nType) {
        try {
            FileOutputStream file_out = new FileOutputStream(strFilename);

            for(int n ; -1 != (n = in.read()) ; )
                file_out.write(n);
        } catch (EOFException eof) {
        }

    // If are supposed to write out file, then open the file and write it
    // out.
    } else if (1 == nType) {
        try {
```

```
                FileInputStream file_in = new FileInputStream(strFilename);

                for(int n ; -1 != (n = file_in.read()) ; )
                    out.write(n);
            } catch (EOFException eof) {
            }
        }

        // close socket connections.
        in.close();
        out.close();
    }
}
```

OK, so you may have noticed there are some problems with this server program. It is not in any way secure, so anyone could connect up to this server and download or upload any file she wanted to. Also, anyone could connect up to the server program and overwrite a file that someone uploaded earlier. And probably the biggest problem of all with this server is that you can't shut it down! All those bugs aside, this server program code illustrates essentially what you want a server to do when recording data from an applet. These types of servers are necessary if you want to preserve data persistently from your applets.

Socket Connection Restrictions on Applets
Just like local file system files are not the sort of things you want randomly downloaded executable code to be able to access, you also don't want the same executable code to be able to make socket connections around the network willy-nilly.

Imagine that you download an applet onto your machine and start viewing it. Suddenly, the machine on the desk next to yours seizes up, then you notice your accounting and financial data software server across the room is being accessed. You go to the financial server to see who could be connecting to it. And it tells you your machine is! Even though you are just innocently viewing a Web page, your sensitive company data is being rummaged through and going who knows where.

This is exactly the sort of thing that could happen if applets were not secured against being allowed to make arbitrary socket connections. There are several well-known, and probably even more not-so-well-known, techniques for attacking machines across the Internet through socket connections. In the example above, what happened was that the applet you downloaded as part of a Web page started attacking the machines within your office from within your browser's JVM. Luckily, Java's security restrictions on applets lock out these kinds of attacks from applets.

Applets

The only machine an applet can make a socket connection to is the Web server machine that the applet came from. This security restriction prevents the types of remote attacks described previously, but still allows the applet to send and get necessary data from across the Internet.

The MyStoringApplet class given previously demonstrates how to connect your applet back to the Web server that served it up. Here is the line of code you'll need to do it:

```
Socket s = new Socket(InetAddress.getByName(getDocumentBase()), nPort);
```

Your applet can't set up a server socket on the client machine, either. Only simple socket connections from the client machine to the Web server that served up the applet in the first place are allowed.

COM Restrictions

On Microsoft's Internet Explorer, applets are not allowed to instantiate or communicate with COM objects in general. This is to preserve Java's security, since COM objects are essentially security-less object that can do just about anything they want on the user's system.

For example, an applet could create an MS Word application object, which is a valid COM object. Just using Word Basic calls, the applet could tell the Word application to find all financial documents on the local machine, copy them, and send them through e-mail to some unknown destination. To preserve Java security, communications with COM objects cannot be allowed in Java Applets.

The solution to this problem is called *digital signatures*. Using a form of public-key encryption technology, you can "sign" a .CAB file with your own digital signature. If the user of your remote applet wants to, she can accept your digital signature as valid. Once the user does this, your applet will be able to go around all of the applet security restrictions. That is, your applet can instantiate and use COM objects, access the local file system, and connect to machines on the Internet other than the machine from which the applet was originally served.

The Visual J++ online documentation fully describes how to build and affix a digital signature to a CAB file. Look under the InfoViewer topic "Java and COM/Using Java with COM/Using Java and COM Together/Creating a Signed CAB File" for a description of how to do this. You will first have to install the CAB&SIGN toolkit from the Visual J++ CD before you can create digitally signed CAB files.

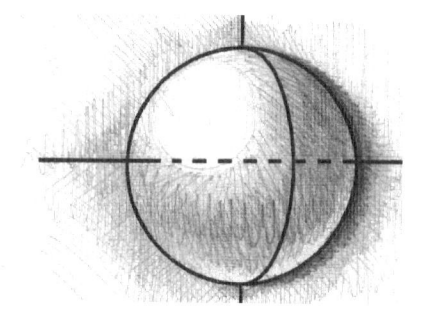

CHAPTER 7

Java and COM in Visual J++

Microsoft's Component Object Model (COM) has a surprising amount of symmetry with the Java object model. The similarities are close enough that Microsoft has added to its Java Virtual Machine for Windows the ability to create and use COM objects within Java. You can now incorporate the use of COM objects, implemented in whatever other language, in your Java code.

For example, the Data Access Objects (DAO) API and the Remote Data Objects (RDO) API included with visual J++ are actually implemented as COM objects. Yet, you can instantiate and use these objects as if they were Java objects. Almost any type of COM object can be used as part of your Java applications and applets in Windows now.

Since the two models are so similar, and it is now so easy to use COM objects in your Java code, shouldn't you be able to use Java objects in your COM applications? Well, you can! Using Microsoft's Java Virtual Machine (and associated executables), you can now create and use Java objects as if they were COM objects. This means you can implement, say, your user interface completely in Java, but have the rest of your application implemented completely in C++, or Visual Basic, or whatever other COM-capable language you want.

Those readers who are familiar with Java native programming probably won't be too impressed with this new capability. After all, since COM is a binary-executable standard, isn't the use of COM objects just another way of programming so-called native code in Java? It is true that using COM is functionally equivalent to programming using some other binary standard, such as Netscape's JRI standard (the standard recently adopted by JavaSoft as the standard for native platform programming in Java), but with COM you get so much, and it is so easy, that it almost seems like a trick.

COM is a very popular standard on Windows platforms. By implementing some libraries in COM, developers allow their classes to be used in different COM-aware applications. Of course, that's one of the big features of Java: distributability and portability. COM objects, unlike Java objects, are actually native-executable programs or DLLs, which means that they can run a lot faster than interpreted Java bytecode-based classes. By integrating COM, you can add a tremendous amount of value to your Java applications and applets.

Here's a quick example: Let's say you have a mathematics engine implemented in COM. You have a Mathematics COM coclass that implements an IMathematics interface. In Java (after some preliminary work that you will read about in this chapter), the code you would write to make this Mathematics COM class part of your Java application would look something like this:

```
// Import Mathematics COM class library package.
import math.*;

...
// Create Mathematics COM object and get a reference to it.
IMathematics math = (IMathematics)new Mathematics();
```

Java and COM in Visual J++

```
// Call Mathematics class functions.
int result = math.someFunction(10, 100, 1000);
int product = math.multSomeNumbers(45, 67.8);
```
...

Doesn't this look a lot like normal Java program code? It looks exactly like normal Java code. That's what Microsoft's Java Virtual Machine for Windows gives you: truly seamless integration of Java and COM. Similarly, you can integrate Java objects into other languages that are COM-aware, because Java objects can be exposed as COM objects by the Java Virtual Machine for Windows. The integration of Java and COM adds to both technologies immensely.

The Java and COM Models

In the Java model, you have a class of objects. That class defines a set of variables and methods that can be called by other Java objects. The classes can also implement Java interfaces, where an *interface* is a set of method declarations. A single Java class can implement multiple different interfaces, where each interface describes some set of related methods. Figure 7-1 shows a simple notation commonly used to indicate a Java class implementing several different interfaces.

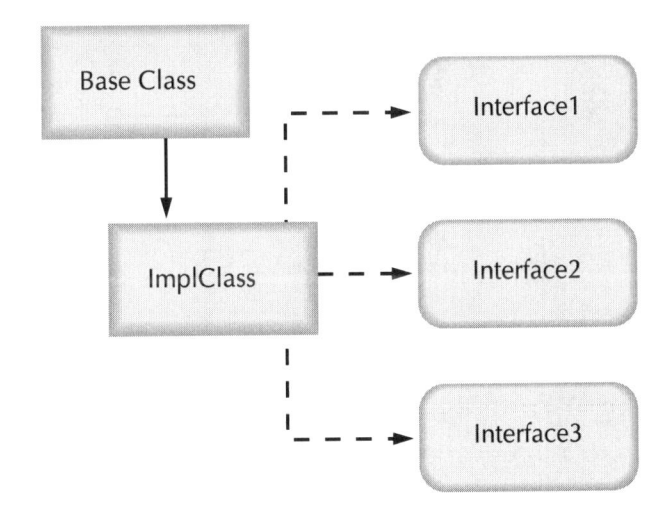

Notation for a Java class implementing Java interfaces
Figure 7-1.

Each little connector symbol in this diagram indicates a callable method of the class. Some of these methods are bundled together into groupings of related functionality, and those methods implement certain interfaces. Other objects now can refer to an instance of the class not by a class name, but instead by an interface name.

In COM, you also have classes. In COM, these are sometimes called *coclasses*, which is a strange compacting of the words *Component Object class*. Classes in COM have no member methods or variables. That is, given a reference to a COM object, you can't simply call one of its member methods. Instead, you must get a reference to the object *as an interface instance*. The interface definition describes which methods the object actually implements. So, once you have an interface reference to the COM object, you can call its methods that are defined within that interface. Figure 7-2 shows how a single COM object can (and usually does) implement several different COM interfaces.

Notice the similarities between Figures 7-1 and 7-2? Both of them have classes that implement interfaces. They are almost interchangeable. Well, there is a very big difference between the actual definition of COM objects versus Java objects, but the overall descriptions of the two different models look pretty similar, because both have objects that implement interfaces.

And that's how the Java Virtual Machine for Windows lets you create and call COM methods from within your Java code. Through the use of interfaces, a COM object can be represented within your Java code as an object that implements one or more different interfaces.

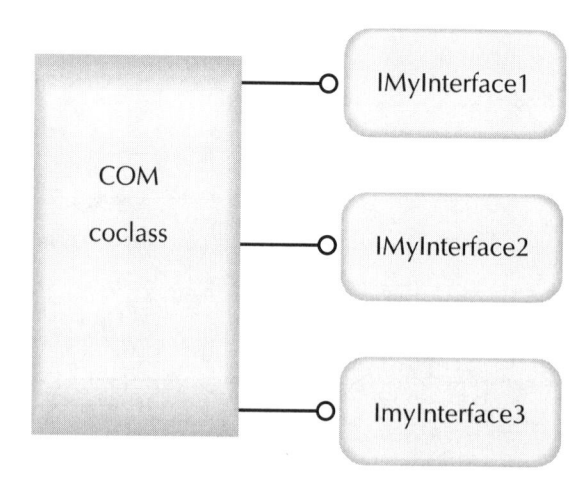

Notation for a COM class that implements several COM interfaces
Figure 7-2.

When you create a COM object in your Java code, you immediately get a reference to the object as an interface. The Java Virtual Machine keeps track of the fact that you don't have a reference to a bona fide Java object, but rather to a COM object. All of those details are abstracted away from you. All you have to do is create the COM object and call one of the various methods in one of its interfaces.

In COM Terms

In COM terms, whenever a Java object creates a COM object using the *new* operator, the Java Virtual Machine for Windows creates the COM object and increments its reference count once for each Java variable that holds a reference to the COM object. When in the Java code the object is cast to one of its interfaces, the Java Virtual Machine actually performs a QueryInterface( ) call on the object's IUnknown interface to get the new reference.

The Java Virtual Machine really does most of the dirty work here. When a Java program calls one of the COM object's methods, the JVM translates the parameters of the call, and the method being called into the proper COM call to the appropriate interface. As far as the Java code is concerned, the COM object "looks" just like any Java object. But under the table, in the JVM, the system is translating calls to the COM object's methods into calls to the correct COM interface method after translating the parameters' values into something that COM can understand. Figure 7-3 is an illustration of what happens when a COM object's method is called from within Java.

When each reference to the COM object is made in the Java code, the JVM calls the COM object's AddRef( ) method in its IUnknown interface. When the reference is deleted (either by the referring variable being reassigned or by dropping out of its scope), the object's Release( ) method is called. In this way, the lifetime of the COM object is controlled in much the same way as Java objects' lifetimes themselves are controlled. The object stays valid and in memory as long as at least one reference to the object exists. When all references are dropped, then the object is automatically cleaned up. Of course, in COM it is up to the COM object to destroy itself when its reference count goes to zero. This is unlike in Java, where the garbage collector is responsible for determining which objects to destroy because they have no more references to them.

Typelibs and Java/COM Shim Classes

The COM standard is a binary standard in which the method signatures of an interface are known at compile time. In a hypothetical non-Java program that uses the COM Mathematics object from the introduction to this

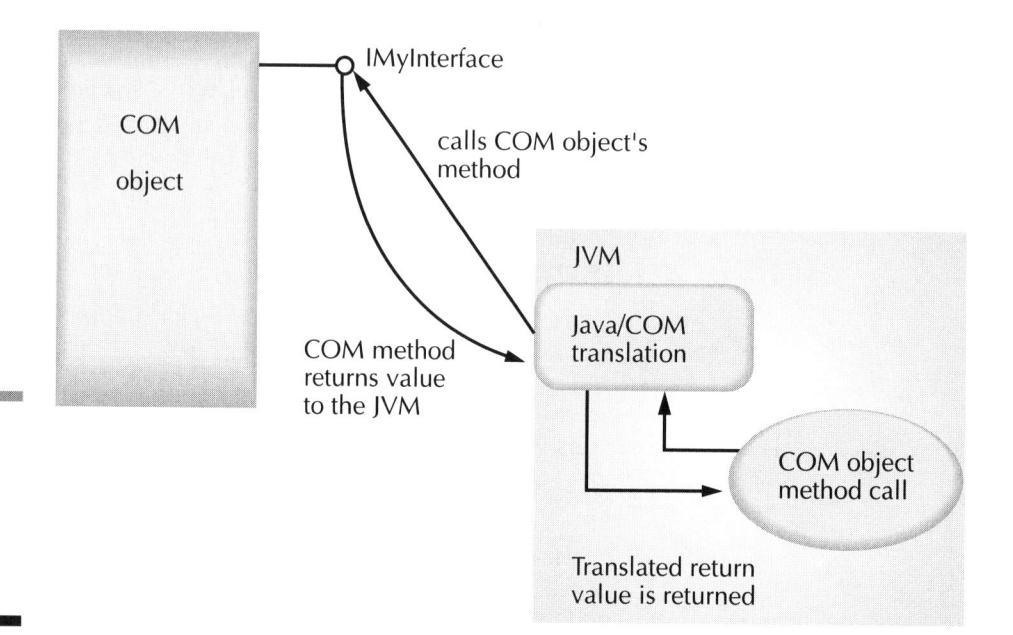

Figure 7-3.
How COM methods are called from within Java code

chapter, you would have to compile your program with the definition of the IMathematics interface definition. Without this definition, it would be impossible to call the COM object's methods correctly. That's just how COM works.

There is a way, however, for a class or an interface to publish to the outside world exactly what the methods and parameters to those methods are. And this public distribution of the interface's methods uses what are called *typelibs* in Windows. A typelib is essentially a file, in a special format, that describes all the methods and COM classes implemented in a particular COM library.

Generating Java/COM Shim Classes

The Visual J++ Java Type Library Wizard tool (javatlb.exe) is used to generate the Java/COM shim classes for a COM library. To invoke this tool, select the Tools/Java Type Library Wizard option from the main menu. The following illustration shows a screen shot of the Java Type Library Wizard dialog that is brought up when you start the tool:

Java and COM in Visual J++

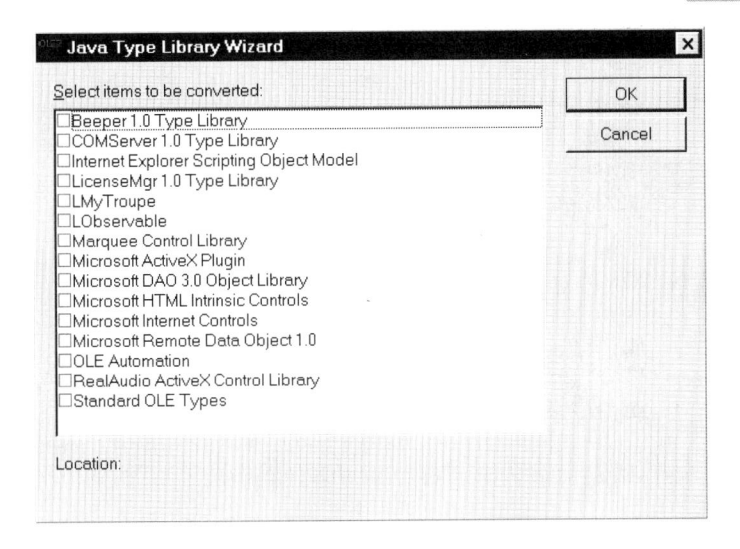

This dialog shows all the COM libraries that have typelibs and are registered in the Windows registry. The Java Type Library Wizard can generate the Java/COM shim classes for any one of these libraries. If you installed the DAO support when you installed Visual J++ (available under the Custom installation option in Visual J++ setup), you will see the "Microsoft DAO 3.0 Object Library" entry in this list. You should also see several other libraries, though not necessarily the same ones shown in the previous illustration.

To generate the shim classes for any (or all) of these libraries, check the checkbox to the left of the item in this listbox, then hit the OK button. The Java Type Library Wizard will then go about generating your shim classes. You will see the progress of the wizard in the Java Type Library Wizard tab of the Output pane. The next illustration shows the output when generating the DAO library's shim classes.

Note that the first line of output is a Java import statement. You must add this statement to the beginning of any of your Java code files that use the COM library. This import statement tells the compiler where to look for your shim classes. For example, the import statement shown in the previous illustration tells the compiler that your code uses the classes in the dao3032 package. That package is automatically created by the wizard.

You can see the actual .class files that the wizard generated in the \Windows\Java\Trustlib\<packagename> directory on your system. After generating the DAO library shim classes, a dao3032 directory is created in the Trustlib directory, and the shim classes (.class files) for all the various DAO library COM classes are placed there. Since the Trustlib directory is one of the directories the JVM for Windows looks in for class files, these classes are available to any Java program you run as long as the correct import statement is added to your Java files.

Taking a Look at COM Interfaces

The OLE Object View tool in Visual J++ lets you look at the descriptions of COM object classes and interfaces. Without such a tool, you would have to know beforehand the methods and constant values that are part of COM interfaces. For example, if you didn't know that the IBeeper interface had a method named Beep( ), the Beeper object you create in your Java code would be kind of useless. You need to know the methods and interfaces declared in order to use that object. Use the OLE Object View tool to look at the declarations of COM interface methods and constants.

To start the OLE Object View tool, choose the Tools/OLE Object View option from the Main menu bar. Figure 7-4 shows what this tool looks like when it is first brought up. It basically lists all the registered COM libraries with typelibs on your system. (A *typelib* is a binary description of a COM object's interfaces, enumerations, etc.) To view the classes and interfaces described in a library, double-click on the library name in the left panel.

When you view a library's classes and interfaces, it brings up another dialog, which is the ITypelib information viewer. Figure 7-5 is a screen shot of this dialog viewing the IBeeper interface of the Beeper 1.0 library. Use this feature to find which methods are implemented in a particular interface so that you can use them in your Java code.

Note that when you use the Java Type Library Wizard to generate the shim classes, the wizard also creates a file filled with the class and interface definitions for you. This file is located in the same directory as the generated .class files, under the Trustlib directory in the \Windows\Java directory of your local file system. This is a simple text file that has the filename "summary.txt". For example, if you generate the DAO 3.0 Object Library's

Java and COM in Visual J++

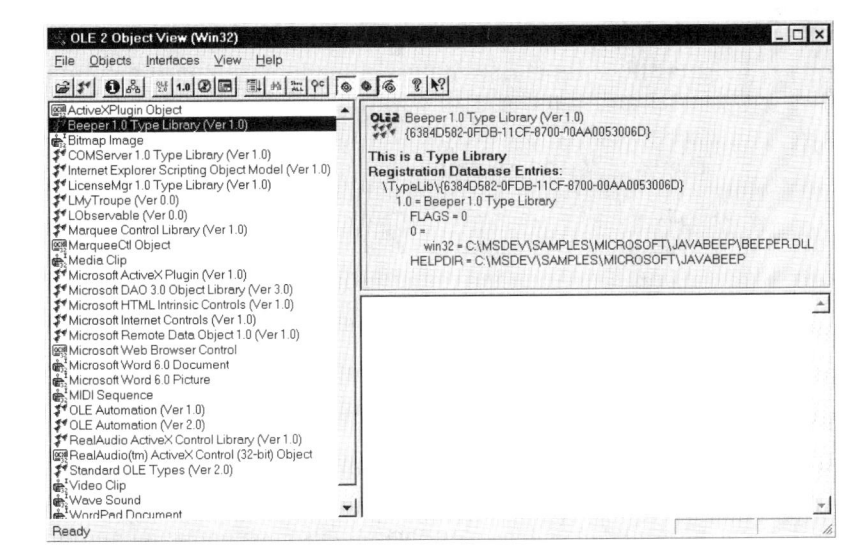

The ITypelib viewer viewing the Beeper library
Figure 7-4.

shim files using the Java Type Library Wizard, a file named dao3032.txt is generated in your \Windows\Java\Trustlib\summary.txt directory. This text file contains a summary of all the classes and interfaces defined in the COM library. You may find it easier to use the OLE Object View tool to get the same information, however. The text file can be long and awfully boring, while the OLE Object View tool organizes and allows you to navigate through all the methods and interfaces.

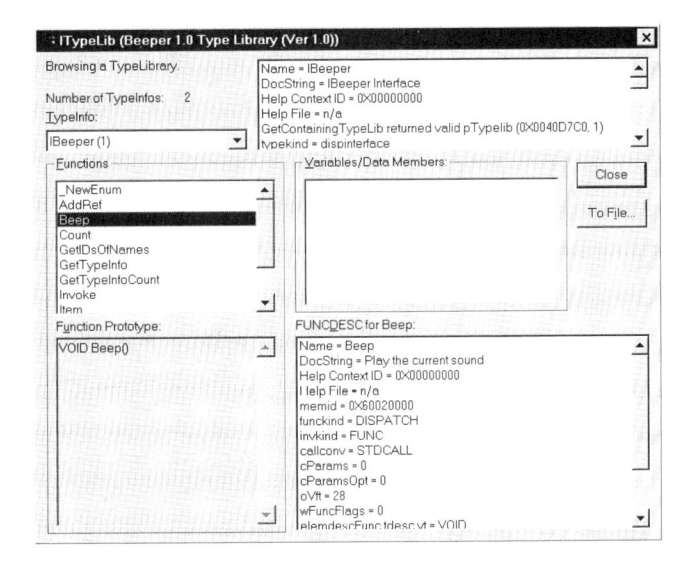

The OLE Object View tool examining the IBeeper COM interface
Figure 7-5.

Using COM Objects in Java

After the shim classes have been generated, you can now use the COM classes and interfaces in your Java applications and applets. Actually, there are restrictions on the use of COM objects in applets, which are discussed a little later in this section.

To create a COM object, simply use Java's new operator with the COM coclass name. Remember, you should use the import statement generated by the Java Type Library Wizard so that you can use the COM class' short name. Otherwise, you would have to prepend the package name to the COM class name, like this:

```
IMyCOMObj m = new thepackage.MyCOMObj();
```

The COM object class constructor always takes no arguments. You must immediately cast the object returned from the new operator to one of the COM object's COM interfaces. This is imperative, and will cause a run-time error if you do not. For example, this code won't work:

```
MyCOMObj m = new MyCOMObj();
```

But the example line above it does, because the MyCOMObj instance just created is immediately cast to a IMyCOMObj (which ostensibly is an interface).

Now you have a reference to the COM object in your Java code. Call any of the COM interface's methods. Here is the COM code for the javabeep sample application included with Visual J++. All the COM calls are located in the mouseDown( ) event handler, which is of course called whenever the mouse is clicked.

```
public boolean mouseDown(Event evt, int x, int y)
{
    String BeeperString = new String();

    // Check if the Beeper object exists, and create it if necessary
    if(m_Beeper==null)
        m_Beeper = (IBeeper) new Beeper();

    // Call Beeper object 'Beep' method. Note that the Beep object has
    // been written such that on the sixth call to Beep(), the Beep object
    // will return an OLE error code which gets thrown as a Java exception.
    // This sample catches the exception, Releases the Beeper object,
    // creates a new Beeper object, and continues
    try
    {
```

Java and COM in Visual J++

```
            m_Beeper.Beep();
    }
    catch(com.ms.com.ComException e)
    {
        // Release the Beeper object by setting m_Beeper=null
        m_Beeper=null;
        // Create a new Beeper object
        m_Beeper = (IBeeper) new Beeper();
        m_Beeper.Beep();
    }

    // Call the Beepers getCount and getItem methods
    for(int i=1;i<=m_Beeper.getCount();i++)
    {
        // Build a message string from the strings that getItem returns
        BeeperString+=m_Beeper.getItem(i)+" ";
    }

    // Display the string
    m_Graphics.drawString(BeeperString,x,y);

    return true;
}
```

Look first at how the Beeper object is created, and how a reference to it is kept within the program. A Beeper is created, but it is immediately cast as an IBeeper interface object (IBeeper is a COM interface defined in the Beeper library). Once that is done, any of the IBeeper interface methods can be called, which will result in the actual COM object's method being called:

```
m_Beeper = (IBeeper) new Beeper();   // m_Beeper is declared as an IBeeper ref.
m_Beeper.Beep();                     // calling IBeeper interface method.
```

Trapping COM Exceptions

A special exception class has been added by Microsoft in its JVM that specifically maps to problems that occur in COM objects. A com.ms.com.ComException is thrown by COM objects if there is any problem while performing a COM method.

In COM terms, a COM exception is thrown whenever an HRESULT is returned from a COM method that indicates the method failed. Maybe the COM server ran out of memory, or maybe it was not in a good state, or maybe the COM object decided to destroy itself for some reason. Whatever the case, you should surround calls to COM object methods that may fail with a try/catch block that catches com.ms.com.ComExceptions.

In the javabeep sample application, the call to the Beeper object's Beep( ) method is surrounded by a try/catch block that catches a com.ms.com.ComException.

COM Object Properties

The javacallingcom sample applet included in the Microsoft samples in the Visual J++ CD gives an example of a COM object that exposes properties. Through the magic of "dual-interfaces" (a COM term, which you don't really need to know to understand this section), COM objects can expose properties to other objects through interface methods. What this means, in effect, is that a COM object can enumerate its properties and methods for you at run time, so you don't have to know everything about the object at compile time in order to use it. These properties can be read-only or read-write. The javacallingcom sample includes a COM server that exposes two properties, one read-only and one read-write.

The COM server implements a COM coclass that is much like the Beeper class in the javabeep sample. The CCOMBeeper coclass can do more than the javabeep's Beeper class, however. It can play several different system sounds on demand. The javacallingcom sample applet presents a little user interface to this object, allowing you to play all sorts of system sounds from your Web browser.

After you copy the javacallingcom sample files to your local drive, you must first register the COM server and create its shim classes before you can run that sample applet. The COM server DLL in this sample is, appropriately enough, named comserver.dll. You must use the Windows system utility RegSvr32 to register this DLL as a COM server on your system. The RegSvr32 program is located in your \Windows\System directory; it is part of the operating system available on every Win32 platform. To register the comserver.dll server, from the javacallingcom directory type in this command-line:

```
\windows\system\regsvr32 comserver.dll
```

This will automatically register the DLL as the server for the CCOMBeeper coclass.

Step two is to create the shim classes for the server. As you read about in a previous section of this chapter, the Java Type Library Tool included under the Tools menu of Visual J++'s menu bar will generate the shim classes for you. After registering the server, an entry for COM Server 1.0 is available to select in the Java Type Library Wizard dialog. Select this item to generate the comserver.dll shim classes. After you do that, you just need to compile your project and run it.

Java and COM in Visual J++

Figure 7-6 is a screen shot of the OLE Object View's view on the COM Server 1.0 classes and interfaces. Notice that the ICOMServer interface (which is the interface to the CCOMBeeper class that this sample applet uses) has three methods: two overloaded versions of a Sound( ) method, and one SoundName( ) method. The Sound property of the CCOMBeeper class indicates to the CCOMBeeper which sound to play the next time its Play( ) method is called. One overloaded version of this method takes a sound value, and the other returns the sound value the CCOMServer is currently set at. The SoundName property is a human-readable string that describes the currently selected sound in the CCOMServer object. This property is read-only.

In Java, these three methods map to different names in the ICOMBeeper interface. In Java, all COM properties are represented by a getXXX( ) method and a setXXX( ) method that are used to access or modify the property's value. For example, the ICOMServer interface in Java code has a getSound( ) method, a setSound( ) method, and a getSoundName( ) method. (No setSoundName( ) method exists because the SoundName property is read-only.) If you take a look at the usecom applet that is in the javacallingcom sample, you can see that the getSound( ) and setSound( ) methods are used to get and set the Sound property of the CCOMServer object. The getSoundName( ) method is used to fill a listbox with human-readable strings representing the various system sounds.

Whenever you see an overloaded property method in the OLE Object View, that means the methods are property methods, and in Java you must use a get and a set method to access or modify the property's value. The name of

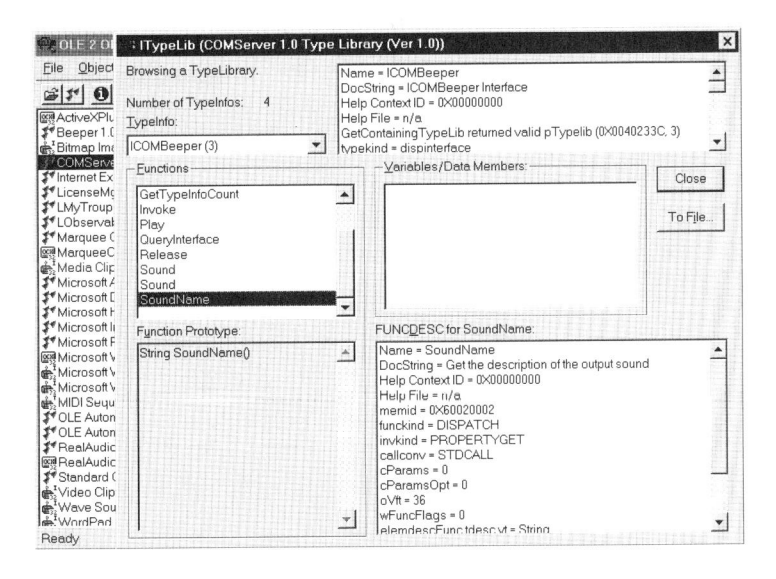

The OLE Object View tool examining the ICOMServer COM interface
Figure 7-6.

the method is either "get" or "set" plus the property name. So, in javacallingcom, to get the current sound number you would call getSound( ). To change the current sound, you would use setSound( ), and to get the sound string for the current sound, you would use a getSoundName( ) method in the ICOMBeeper interface.

COM Enumeration Types in Java

COM objects can expose a list of values as an enumeration type. These enumeration types are basically a list of numbers, similar to a C-language enum. Generally, these are used as a set of constants for use in COM method calls. For example, the javacallingcom example has an enumeration type that lists valid Sound property values for the CCOMBeeper class.

You can see the values of the javacallingcom example's enumeration in the OLE Object View tool. Figure 7-7 shows what the OLE Object View shows you about the COM Server 1.0's BeeperConstants interface. In the Variables/Data Members listbox to the right side of the OLE Object View's window, the various valid values for the Sound property of the CCOMBeeper class are listed. Each of these values is given a name that can be used instead of the value. That is, the value BeeperConstants.Asterisk is a constant with the value 64.

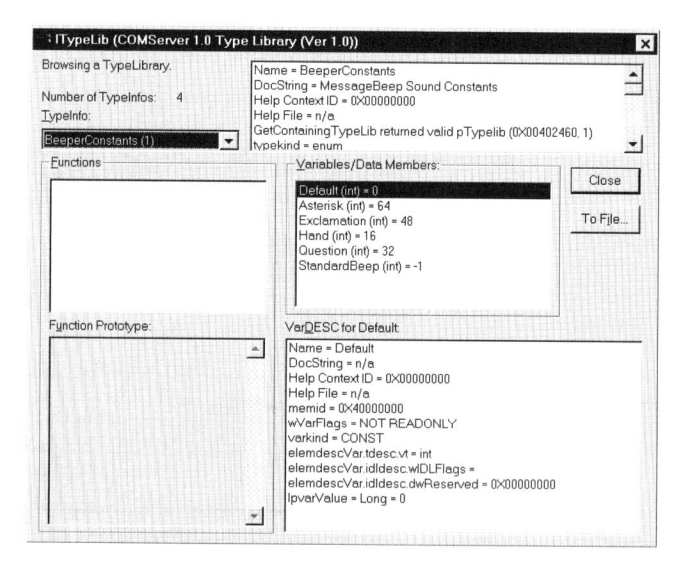

The Beeper-Constants COM interface in the OLE Object View tool
Figure 7-7.

Java and COM in Visual J++

In the javacallingcom sample, these constants are provided to make the CCOMBeeper easier to program, and to make program code more readable. This line taken from the usecom applet

```
m_beeper.putSound(BeeperConstants.Asterisk);
```

is a lot easier to understand than

```
m_beeper.putSound(64);
```

In Java, these constant interfaces are implemented as Java interfaces that only have a set of final numeric values. From the BeeperConstants enumeration type, the JVM creates a Java interface equivalent to the enumeration type. Code for the BeeperConstants interface might look like this:

```
public interface BeeperConstants {
    public final int Default = 0;
    public final int Asterisk = 64;
    public final int Exclamation = 48;
    public final int Hand = 16;
    public final int Question = 32;
    public final int StandardBeep = -1;
}
```

COM Using Java Objects

Not only can you use COM objects from your Java code, but you can also use Java objects from within COM. The Microsoft Java Virtual Machine for Windows comes with an inproc COM server called MSJAVA.DLL that acts as the translator between COM and Java. Figure 7-8 illustrates how COM calls Java objects' methods through the MSJAVA.DLL.

Through a similar mechanism, you can also make your Java objects callable remotely through DCOM. The JavaReg program (included with Visual J++) can act as a proxy DCOM server, allowing programs running on remote machines across the Internet to create and call your Java objects. (Chapter 12 also talks about a similar technology to DCOM, called Remote Method Invocation (RMI), that allows you to call remote Java objects' methods using a Java-based platform-independent technique. RMI is available in the Java 1.1 core libraries.)

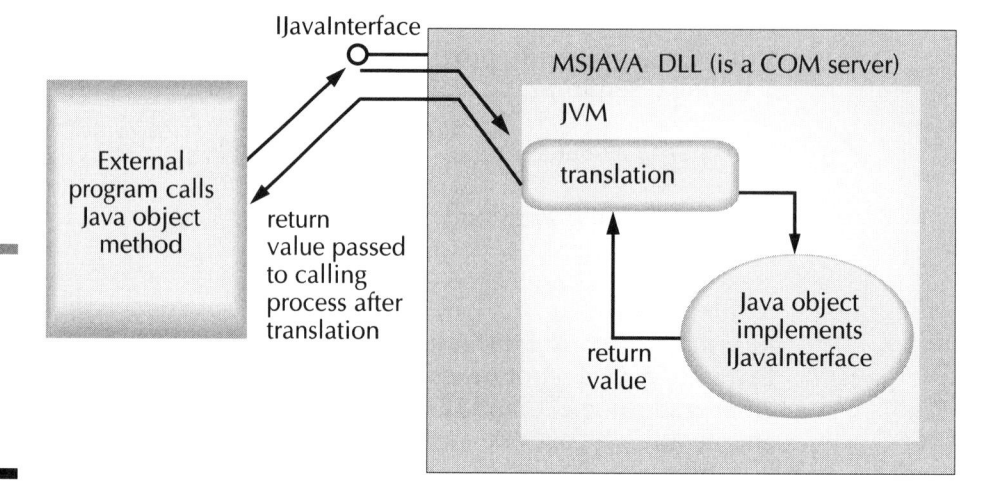

Figure 7-8.
COM calling Java methods through the MSJAVA.DLL server

There's not a lot of special coding you need to do to make your Java objects visible in COM. The trick to it is defining Java interfaces that COM can understand, and registering your Java objects in the Windows registry.

There are four steps to making your Java objects callable from COM and DCOM (each step is described next):

1. Describing your interfaces and classes using the Object Description Language (ODL) and creating a typelib of your classes and interfaces from the ODL description.
2. Writing your Java class.
3. (For COM-exposed objects only) Registering your Java class as a COM object in the Windows registry.
4. (For DCOM-exposed objects only) Registering your Java object as a DCOM object in the Windows Registry.

As an explanation of each of these steps is presented, you will read about an example set of Java classes and interfaces that is exposed as a COM and DCOM-callable class of objects. The Observable class and associated interfaces described herein are loosely based on the Observable/Observer framework in the java.util core package, which is described in Chapter 11.

Defining Java Interfaces So COM Understands Them

Calls to COM objects are done through COM interfaces. Just like in Java, a COM interface is just a collection of function signatures. A COM object implements an interface so that other COM code can call those functions.

To make your Java objects callable from COM, you must define Java interfaces in a way that COM objects can understand them. You do this using the ODL. ODL is an object description language that was developed for the purpose of defining objects and interfaces in a way that's not dependent on the actual implementation of the object. That is, using ODL you define your objects and interfaces, and then you implement the objects using whatever language you want: C++, Java, Visual Basic, Pascal, whatever.

In your case, you will first define your Java objects and interfaces in ODL, and then implement them in Java. Once the ODL description of the object is created, you use a special compiler to generate a typelib that describes your Java object and interfaces in COM. Remember that when creating the Java/COM shim classes using the Java Type Library Wizard, you need a typelib that describes the COM classes and interfaces for Java. This is the same thing in reverse: you need a typelib to describe the Java classes and interfaces to COM. The ODL is used to describe objects and interfaces, and the MkTypLib program, included in the \MSDEV\BIN directory of your Visual J++ installation, is used to compile your ODL files into typelibs (.TLB files).

Here is an example ODL file that describes the Observable class, which is a lot like the java.util package class Observable described in Chapter 11. (A complete explanation of the Object Description Language is included with the InfoViewer in your Visual J++ installation, and a further description of this language also follows in this chapter.)

```
// Observable.odl
[ uuid (27E955C0-13C6-11d0-AE38-444553540000) ]
library LObservable
{
    importlib("stdole32.tlb");

    [ odl, uuid(27E955C2-13C6-11d0-AE38-444553540000) ]
    interface IObserver
```

```
    {
        HRESULT update();
    }

    [ odl, uuid(27E955C1-13C6-11d0-AE38-444553540000) ]
    interface IObservable
    {
        HRESULT addObserver([in] IObserver* obs);
        HRESULT countObservers([out, retval] long* l);
        HRESULT deleteObserver([in] IObserver* obs);
        HRESULT deleteObservers();
        HRESULT hasChanged([out, retval] boolean *b);
        HRESULT notifyObservers();
    }

    [ uuid(27E955C3-13C6-11d0-AE38-444553540000) ]
    coclass Observable
    {
        interface IObservable;
    }
};
```

This file describes two interfaces and one class: IObserver and IObservable are the interfaces and Observable is the class. Yes, it is a little confusing. You will understand the syntax completely after reading this section. The Observable class is declared as implementing the IObservable interface. The IObservable interface has five methods in it: addObserver( ), countObservers( ), deleteObserver( ), deleteObservers( ), and hasChanged( ). The idea of the Observable object is an object that can notify "observers" about when it has some change in its state. For example, you could have an Observable that keeps track of the number of people that have signed on to a system. When the number of people changes, then the Observable object tells all its observers.

The IObserver interface describes the only method an observer must implement: update( ). This method is called by the Observable whenever a change in its state occurs. While the IObserver interface is described in this ODL file, no class actually implements it here. This interface, once it is available as a COM interface, can be used to communicate with an Observable object. The idea is that an Observable object is passed several objects that implement the IObserver interface. It doesn't matter if those objects are implemented in COM or in Java. As long as they implement the IObserver interface described in this ODL file, then the Observable object can call its update( ) method whenever the Observable's state changes.

Java and COM in Visual J++

Here's the equivalent Java description for the IObservable and IObserver interfaces. First, note that you will never actually write these definitions in Java. The ODL file is all you need to describe your Java interfaces. In a following section of this primer on ODL, you will learn that the JavaTLB utility included with Visual J++ will actually generate .CLASS files from your interface descriptions in ODL.

```
// The IObserver interface in Java as declared in Observable.odl
package observable;

import com.ms.com.IUnknown;

public interface IObserver extends IUnknown
{
    public abstract void update();
}


// The IObservable interface in Java as declared in Observable.odl
package observable;

import com.ms.com.IUnknown;

public interface IObservable extends Iunknown
{
    public abstract int countObservers();
    public abstract void deleteObservers();
    public abstract void notifyObservers();
    public abstract void addObserver(IObserver iObserver);
    public abstract boolean hasChanged();
    public abstract void deleteObserver(IObserver iObserver);
}
```

To make the Java/COM shim classes that the Observable.odl file describes, you start by using the MkTypLib program included in the \MSDEV\BIN directory of your Visual J++ installation. From the command prompt in the same directory as this ODL file, you would use this command-line:

```
C:>\msdev\bin\mktyplib /nocpp Observable.odl
```

When you run this program, a file named Observable.tlb is generated. The .TLB file is the typelib for the interfaces and classes described in the ODL file. Note that the /nocpp option is only required if you do not have Visual C++

installed on your machine. If you do have Visual C++ installed, don't include the /nocpp option.

The code below is an implementation in Java of the Observable class this ODL file describes. Note that the code includes the import statement import observable.*. The package this refers to (the *observable* package) is a package that is generated from the typelib, the same way that packages for Java/COM shim classes are generated from other typelibs. Well, actually, not in the same way, but the effect is the same.

Previously in this chapter, you used the Java Type Library Wizard tool from the Main menu of Visual J++ to generate the Java/COM classes for registered COM libraries. The typelib you've just created using the MkTypLib program actually describes classes and interfaces that are not yet registered in the Windows registry. So, the Java Type Library Wizard will not be able to create your Java/COM shim classes for the Observable class and associated interfaces. Instead, you use the JavaTLB program to generate these classes. (In fact, the Java Type Library Wizard is just a simple GUI for the JavaTLB utility program.) That is, the Java Type Library Wizard can only generate shim classes from libraries that are already registered in the Windows registry. The JavaTLB program has no such restriction.

To create the Java/COM shim classes using JavaTLB for the Observable typelib, use this command line from a command prompt in the directory of the .TLB file:

```
C:>\msdev\bin\javatlb Observable.tlb
```

This program should give you this output:

```
import observable.*;
```

which tells you that the JavaTLB program successfully generated the Java/COM shim classes for your typelib, and they are located in the \Windows\Java\Trustlib\Observable directory on your system. The .CLASS files created are Observable.class, IObservable.class, and IObserver.class.

This import statement also tells you that you need to import the Observable package classes and interfaces into your Java source code that use these interfaces. That is, in any Java source code file that refers to the interfaces of this package, include this same import statement at the top of the file.

The Object Description Language

As the Observable/Observer example shows, the ODL is a format designed specifically for defining classes and interfaces in a way that completely ignores any aspects of implementation. When defining components for use in COM, it really doesn't matter what language those components are created in. That's one of the great things about COM: different software components written in different languages, and even running on different platforms using disparate operating systems, can instantiate and use each other. A database server exposed as a COM object written in C++ can be used by, say, a Java application or applet running in a completely different address space, and maybe even on a different machine. The mechanics of how this communication takes place really don't matter. You don't have to think about it, it all just happens magically.

(Well, actually, you may have to worry about how this magic occurs. Specifically, if performance is an issue. That is, calling a COM object's method on a different machine across the Internet is obviously going to be a lot slower operation than calling another Java object's method within the same Java Virtual Machine. The difference can be on the order of thousands of times slower, or even more. This means you have to design the use of COM objects in your programs to be optimized when performance is an issue. For example, you're not going to be able to create a COM object that sorts strings by passing that COM object a letter of a string at a time; the communications between your Java process and the process that is running the sorting COM object are going to be way too slow to be useful.)

You describe your Java interfaces and classes in ODL. The only part of the Java interface you describe is the method signatures, and the only thing about the Java classes you describe is the interfaces that the class implements. That's the only job of ODL: to describe your classes and interfaces so that you can create a typelib. You can also define lists of constants and other elements that make using your Java interfaces and classes through COM easier. These more advanced elements are a little beyond the scope of this chapter, which is to provide a basic understanding of how to expose your Java classes to COM objects. The online documentation included with Visual J++ includes a complete description of the ODL syntax. If you are curious, you are encouraged to read that specification. Yes, it can be a little dry, but it is really worth it to gain full expertise in this area. Exposing your Java objects in COM makes them much more marketable to the software world in general.

Universal Identifiers

Unlike Java, COM has a very strict mechanism for "naming" unique interfaces, classes, libraries, enumerations, and so on. This is through the use of universally unique identifiers, or UUIDs. (Also commonly referred to using other acronyms according to what type of elements they represent: GUIDs, IIDs, and several other terms are all different types of UUIDs.)

A UUID is a very long binary number, 128 bits to be exact. Each UUID is a unique number that identifies an interface, a class, a library, etc. Once applied to an element, the element is never supposed to be changed. That is, once you publicly distribute an IObserver interface with a UUID *{27E955C2-13C6-11D0-AE38-444553540000}*, the method signatures of the interface should never change. The UUID represents a contract, a pledge by you that this UUID will always be used to represent the same interface, and that interface will never change.

The nearest equivalent you have to a UUID in Java is a fully qualified class name. The class name is used to refer to a specific Java class. Unlike UUIDs, however, a class can change over time. This can lead to some problems: imagine compiling a set of two classes like this:

```
// File Foo.java
package Moa;
public class Foo {
    public Foo() {}
}

// File Bar.java
package Moa;
public class Bar {
    private Foo foo;

    public Bar() {
        foo = new Foo();
    }
}
```

Now, at some time in the future you decide to change the Foo class by making the Foo class constructor private:

```
// File Foo.java (version 2)
package Moa;
public class Foo {
    private Foo() {}
}
```

You recompile Foo.java, but you keep around an old copy of Bar.class, compiled from Bar.java. Try to create a Bar object at that point, and you'll get a run-time exception (a SecurityException, to be exact). The Bar.class file defines a perfectly valid class, but it refers to an older version of the Foo class, one in which there is a public Foo class constructor. These types of incompatibilities are inevitable, and only through careful diligence can you avoid them within your own classes.

In COM, however, such problems will never occur. That's because a publicly distributed UUID is guaranteed to always represent the exact same interface. Maybe the implementation of the interface methods change, but the method signatures will always be the same. In order to change the interface, say to add a new method or change the parameters of an existing one, you must create a new interface and allocate a new UUID for it, though you can reuse the code that implemented the first interface, if the new interface is similar.

In ODL, you see a UUID line given before each element that is identified by one. For example, the IObserver interface in the Observer.odl file listed previously has this declaration header:

```
[ odl, uuid(27E955C2-13C6-11d0-AE38-444553540000) ]
interface IObserver
...
```

The UUID declares what the universal identifier for this interface will be.

Visual J++ includes a tool you can use to generate your own UUIDs. The algorithm used to generate these UUIDs is virtually guaranteed to provide you with a unique number every time you use it. That is, even if every person in the whole world did nothing but generate UUIDs using this tool on different machines around the world for a billion years straight, the chances against any two of them generating the same UUID are about as remote as the chances of you spontaneously sprouting a fourth eye. Generate as many of these as you wish, use them to serialize your socks and underwear, give them out to friends. There are plenty to go around.

The UUID-generating tool is located under the Tools menu of Visual J++'s Main menu bar. It is called Create GUID. Select this tool, and the Create GUID tool comes up, which will generate new UUIDs for you. The next illustration shows a screen shot of this dialog. Press the New GUID button to generate a new GUID, and the Copy button to copy the UUID into the Windows clipboard. The four radio buttons just format the UUID in different ways. The fourth option is the one you will use almost exclusively in ODL files, since the other three produce formats used in Visual C++ code only.

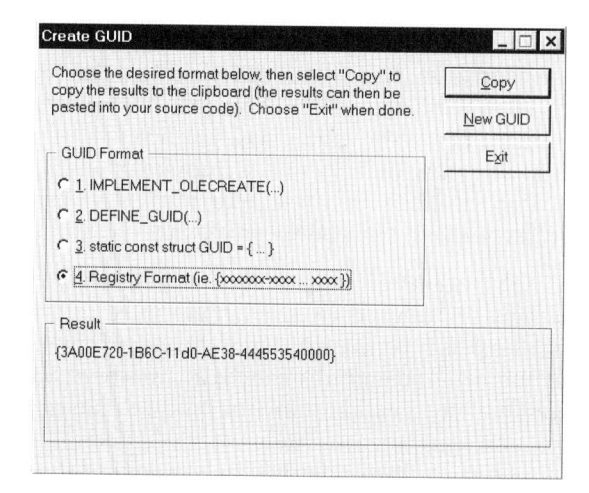

ODL Libraries

In ODL, objects and interfaces are described as belonging to a library. The line in the Observer ODL file given previously looks like this:

```
[ uuid (27E955C0-13C6-11d0-AE38-444553540000) ]
library LObservable {
...
}
```

The UUID is used to identify the library. The library name LObservable stands for Library Observable. You should prepend all your library names with an "L" like this.

The ODL library name corresponds to the Java package name your Java interfaces and classes will be located in. For example, when you create the Java/COM shim classes for the Observable ODL file, it will create shim classes in a package named observable.

The first line of this library definition reads

```
importlib("stdole32.tlb");
```

which indicates that all the interfaces and classes defined within the StdOLE32 typelib should be imported into this ODL file. For example, the IUnknown interface, IDispatch interface, and all the common predefined OLE interfaces are declared within this typelib. You should import it into all your libraries.

The rest of the library definition is made up of declared interfaces and classes contained in that library.

ODL Classes

Within a library definition, you can define one or more classes. Just like a library, the class is also assigned a UUID. Here is the full declaration of the Observable class from Observable.odl:

```
[ uuid(27E955C3-13C6-11d0-AE38-444553540000) ]
coclass Observable
{
    interface IObservable;
}
```

The ODL keyword *coclass* identifies the element as a class description. (In COM, the term "coclass" stands for "Component Object class".) Within the class declaration, you just identify the interfaces that the class implements. In the case of the Observable class, the file declares the class as implementing the IObservable interface declared within the same library. That's all you have in a class declaration: just implemented interfaces.

ODL Interfaces

You define the interfaces your COM-enabled Java classes will implement in the ODL file. This is very important, because the only way other COM objects can call your class' methods is through interfaces defined in the ODL file. Furthermore, while you still must provide the actual implementation of the Java classes in a .CLASS file, you never create any Java code for these interfaces. The JavaTLB program will create the .CLASS files for them instead.

An interface declaration is surrounded by a heading that looks like this declaration of the IObservable interface:

```
[ odl, uuid(27E955C1-13C6-11d0-AE38-444553540000) ]
interface IObservable
{
... // IObservable method signatures.
}
```

Like the class and library declarations, the interface declaration begins by listing the interface's UUID. Notice the extra keyword *odl* in the braces: "[odl, uuid(...)]." You must have both the "odl" and "uuid" entries listed within the braces.

Next you must give the name of the methods and list their parameters. The list of parameters has a particular format. Each parameter in the list has a type, a name, and a list of attributes. These attributes tell the COM object how to use the parameter.

In ODL, each interface method parameter is labeled as either an "in" parameter or an "out" parameter. An in-parameter is an argument to the method, while an out-parameter is a place for the method to return information. An example of an in parameter is shown in the declaration of the IObservable interface's addObserver( ) method declaration:

```
HRESULT addObserver([in] IObserver* obs);
```

The argument to this method is an IObserver. That is, an object, whether it be a COM object or a Java object, that implements the IObserver interface that is also declared in this ODL file. Note that when passing interfaces into a method, you use an asterisk after the interface name.

An out parameter is a parameter that your Java method can return data in. In C++, an out parameter would be a parameter for which you pass a pointer to memory ("call-by-reference") as opposed to an in parameter, which would just be passing a value on the stack ("call-by-value"). You have no pointers in Java. But you can have out parameters in your ODL methods. For example, let's say you want to implement a MinMax method in a COM interface. Given two input numbers, this method returns both the lowest and the highest one of the two. One way to declare such a method in ODL would be

```
HRESULT MinMax([in] int a, [in] int b, [out] int* lowest, [out] int* highest);
```

which would generate this method signature in your Java/COM shim class' .CLASS file:

```
public void MinMax(int a, int b, int ashLowest[], int ashHighest[])
        throws com.ms.com.ComException;
```

The point is, out parameters are translated to arrays of the same type in Java interfaces. These arrays will only have one element in them when your Java method is actually called. Change the zeroth element to this parameter, and the calling COM object's value will also be changed when the method returns. Here is an example implementation of the MinMax( ) method in Java:

```
import MinMax.*;    // or whatever the library's name is.
import com.ms.com.*;

public class Mathematics implements MinMaxInterface {
    public Mathematics() {}

    // The MinMax Interface method MinMax().
    public void MinMax(short a, short b, short ashLowest[], short ashHighest[])
            throws com.ms.com.ComException {
```

```
            if(a < b) {
                ashLowest[0] = a;
                ashHighest[0] = b;
            } else {
                ashLowest[0] = b;
                ashHighest[0] = a;
            }
        }
    }
}
```

When declaring parameters, either in or out parameters, using built-in types, there is a little conversion you must do. See, the Java built-in types are not exactly the same as the ODL types. The most important difference is the ODL type long, which corresponds to the Java type int (32 bit integer).

To define a return value, you use the combination of out-parameter attributes "out" and "retval" on one of the parameters. For example, here is the ODL declaration of the IObservable interface method countObservers( ), which returns the number of observers registered with the IObservable implementing object:

```
HRESULT countObservers([out, retval] long* l);
```

which corresponds to the Java declaration:

```
public int countObservers();
```

That is, the parameter that has the retval attribute defines the return value of your Java class method. Only one parameter can have the retval out-parameter property set, obviously, because your method can only return a single value. Of course, you can have as many out parameters as you wish, but only one of them can have the retval attribute set.

Writing the Java Class

Once you have the ODL definition of your Java interfaces and classes, the creation of the Java class is easy. That's what most of the rest of this book is about: how to write Java. Really, the only difference between normal, non-COM-itized Java code and Java code written for COM is how you throw exceptions.

The individual method signatures of ODL methods look pretty much like method signatures in Java, but with one very important difference. That is, all methods are declared as returning an *HRESULT*, as this declaration of the deleteObservers( ) method does:

```
HRESULT deleteObservers();
```

It's done this way because of how exceptions are passed between your Java objects and COM. When you throw an exception in a Java method called by a COM object, that exception must be either a com.ms.com.ComFailedException or a com.ms.com.ComSuccessException. When you throw either one, the Java/COM translator (the MSJAVA.DLL inproc server) actually translates the exception into a return value to the calling COM object. That return value is of type HRESULT. In fact, when you simply return from a Java method called by a COM object (i.e., without throwing an exception), the MSJAVA.DLL creates an HRESULT and returns that also.

(In COM terms, when you return from a Java method called by a COM object, the calling COM object gets an S_OK return value. To return any other value, you must throw either a com.mc.com.ComFailException or a com.ms.com.ComSuccessException. The ComFailedException returns one of the E_*XXXX* HRESULT values, and the ComSuccessException returns a S_*XXXX* HRESULT.)

That's why you need the funny retval out-parameter attribute. The HRESULT that is actually returned by COM interface methods is a success/failed indicator, which may or may not include additional information about why the method failed or succeeded. The actual return value of the method may not be as important as this information. For example, if you query a database COM object for the number of records in a particular table, and the database object encounters some sort of catastrophic error, then the method will return one of the E_*XXXX* HRESULT values (i.e., the top bit of the HRESULT value is set), indicating that the method could not be completed for one reason or another. In the event that a method does complete correctly, then one of the S_XXXX HRESULT values is returned (i.e., the top bit of the HRESULT value is not set), indicating that all went as planned and the out parameters contain the important information the method was supposed to return.

Here is an implementation of the Observable class described by the Observable.odl file. Note that the import statement "import observable.*;" actually imports the IObservable and IObserver interfaces created by the JavaTLB program:

```
import java.util.*;
import com.ms.com.*;
import observable.*;

public class Observable implements IObservable {
    private boolean m_fChanged = false;
```

Java and COM in Visual J++

```
        private Vector m_vectObservers;

    public synchronized void addObserver(IObserver obs) throws ComException {
        try {
            if (m_vectObservers == null)
                m_vectObservers = new Vector();

            if (!m_vectObservers.contains(obs))
                m_vectObservers.addElement(obs);
        } catch (OutOfMemoryError me) {
            throw new ComFailException(0x8007000E); // E_OUTOFMEMORY.
        }
    }

    public synchronized void deleteObserver(IObserver obs)
                throws ComException {
        m_vectObservers.removeElement(obs);
    }

    public void notifyObservers() throws ComException {
        if (!hasChanged() || (null == m_vectObservers))
            return;

        int ii = m_vectObservers.size();
        while (--ii >= 0) {
            IObserver obs = (IObserver)m_vectObservers.elementAt(ii);
            obs.update();
        }

        clearChanged();
    }

    public synchronized void deleteObservers() {
        m_vectObservers = null;
    }

    protected synchronized void setChanged() {
        m_fChanged = true;
    }

    protected synchronized void clearChanged() {
        m_fChanged = false;
    }

    public synchronized boolean hasChanged() throws ComException {
        return m_fChanged;
    }
```

```
    public synchronized int countObservers() throws ComException {
        if (m_vectObservers != null)
            return m_vectObservers.size();
        else
            return 0;
    }
}
```

Registering the Java Class as a COM Object

The last step to making instances of your Java class callable from other COM objects is to register the class in the Windows registry. You may know, all COM coclasses are registered in the Windows registry. This means that the registry contains entries, indexed by the coclass' UUID, that indicate what DLLs or EXEs can create and expose instances of the class. For all Java classes the same inproc server DLL is used: the MSJAVA.DLL server, which is distributed with the Visual J++ CD.

To register the Java class in the Windows registry by hand, you must create the following entries in the registry, typically by either using the RegEdit utility (available on all Win32 platforms), or by writing an installation program to create them for you. The registry must contain these entries:

```
HKEY_CLASSES_ROOT
    CLSID
        {uuid of your Java class, same as from the ODL file}
            InprocServer32 = msjava.dll
                JavaClass = coclass name from the ODL file
```

For example, the entry for the Observable Java class defined by the Observable.odl file in this chapter would be

```
HKEY_CLASSES_ROOT
    CLSID
        {27E955C3-13C6-11d0-AE38-444553540000}
            InprocServer32 = msjava.dll
                JavaClass = Observable
```

For convenience, Visual J++ comes with a utility program that can create these registry entries for you. The JavaReg program, located in the \MSDEV\BIN directory for your Visual J++ installation, will create the appropriate Windows registry entries for you.

Java and COM in Visual J++

The JavaReg program requires three command-line parameters in order to create the appropriate registry entries for you. For example, this command-line (if run from the directory where you compiled the Observable.java file) will register the Observable class taken from the Observable.odl file with the Windows registry:

```
\msdev\bin\javareg /register /class:Observable
                   /clsid:{27E955C3-13C6-11d0-AE38-444553540000}
```

Registering the Java Class as a DCOM Object

DCOM stands for Distributed COM. Promised for a long time, DCOM is finally available on Windows NT 4.0 platforms. Using DCOM objects, you can connect to and call methods of objects that live on platforms anywhere on the network, even across the Internet. As far as your Java programming is concerned, there is no difference between creating COM and DCOM Java objects.

The difference lies in the server program used to make the Java object callable from across the network. Basically, the problem is that you need a local server program to serve up your Java object on the server machine to make the Java object available through DCOM.

To make a Java object callable through plain old COM, you register an inproc server for the Java object. For all Java objects, the same inproc COM server is used: MSJAVA.DLL. Unfortunately, you cannot use an inproc server to serve up DCOM objects. You need a local server (an .EXE program). By the way, don't worry if all this makes little sense to you because you are unfamiliar with COM and DCOM. The solution to this problem is cookbook.

You can use the JavaReg program itself to act as the "surrogate" for the MSJAVA.DLL inproc server. That is, you can tell JavaReg to load the MSJAVA.DLL into its address space and pass all DCOM calls onto the MSJAVA.DLL inproc server. As far as the MSJAVA.DLL inproc server is concerned, it is being called just like any other COM inproc server. As far as the remote DCOM client is concerned, the JavaReg program is acting like the DCOM server. That way, everything's copacetic.

You can tell the JavaReg program to act as the Java object's DCOM server by adding a single command-line argument when registering the Java class as a COM object. Instead of the command line given above, you would give a command line that looks like this:

```
javareg /register /class:MyPerformer
         /clsid:{42E5AFC6-DBAA-11cf-BAFD-00AA0057B223} /surrogate
```

The addition of the command-line argument "surrogate" makes the JavaReg program create Windows registry entries that look like these entries for the Observable class:

```
HKEY_CLASSES_ROOT
    CLSID
        {27E955C3-13C6-11d0-AE38-444553540000}
            InprocServer32 = msjava.dll
              JavaClass = Observable
            LocalServer32 = javareg      // continued on next line
                /clsid:{42E5AFC6-DBAA-11cf-BAFD-00AA0057B223} /surrogate
```

CHAPTER 8

File I/O and Streams

A *stream* is a generic concept describing a sequence of bytes. There are several programming situations in which bytes are stored in a particular order, and read back in that same order. For example, the text of this book could be seen as a stream of characters. The author writes the characters from left to right continuously from the first page to the last. You read these same characters in the exact same order they were written.

Another real-world example that describes the stream concept is a magnetic tape of data. The tape is a long strip of material onto which single bytes of data can be stored serially. The tape, then, is essentially a one-dimensional string, or stream, of byte values. When you want to write a byte of data to this stream, you start at one end of the tape and record a single byte value. The tape then advances a little bit, and then is ready for the next byte of data. When you want to write the next byte of data, you write it to the next position on the tape, and the tape again advances. Follow this process over and over and you will eventually write all the data you want to the tape (stream).

That stream of bytes is now stored away and ready to be read back. To read it back, you first rewind the tape so that it's at the same position as the first byte of data you wrote. You would then read the first byte of data, and the tape would advance to the position of the second byte. You read the next byte, and the tape advances again. Eventually, you will read the whole stream of bytes in the exact same order they were written.

So you see, a stream is a sequence of bytes that is written and can be read back in a specific order. The concept does not encompass "random access," in which you can write or read back the bytes in any old order you please. The storage medium of the stream is such that the stream is written and read back in the exact same order, as in the magnetic tape example above.

The stream concept is very generic. The magnetic tape mentioned in the above example can be replaced by any number of different physical media, and the same concept still holds. A file on a disk is an obvious example of a data stream that has to do with computers. The stream is recorded as a sequence of bytes on sectors on the disk, and can be read back in the exact same order as it was written.

Another physical example is a network socket connection. On one end of the connection, you write individual bytes of data to the socket. On the other end, you read the bytes back in the exact same order they were written to the socket.

The InputStream and OutputStream Classes

You may have noticed in the examples given above that there was a definite differentiation between when you write to and when you read from a stream. You don't do both at the same time. The Java OutputStream class describes a stream that is being written to. The InputStream class, on the other hand, describes a stream that you are reading from.

The same physical storage media may be represented by an input stream and an output stream at different times. For example, when you write out files in Java, you write using a FileOutputStream object. That object is associated with a specific file on a local disk. Later, when you want to read

File I/O and Streams

the streamed data back, you can associated a FileInputStream object to the same file to read back the data you wrote out.

The InputStream and OutputStream classes are abstract classes. They describe and partially implement the functionality of a generic stream, as described previously. The InputStream class, for example, declares an abstract read() method. This method returns the next byte on the input stream. The OutputStream class declares an abstract write() method to which you pass the next byte you want to write out to the stream. The InputStream and OutputStream classes *declare* the methods that all stream classes actually implement.

But the InputStream and OutputStream classes are not actually wired up to any particular type of storage media. Remember, in the stream examples given previously that a stream is a sequence of bytes stored on some media, be that a disk, a network connection, or an array of bytes in memory. No matter what the different storage media, all streams have functionality described by the InputStream and OutputStream abstract classes.

Since the InputStream and OutputStream classes are abstract, you never actually create an instance of these classes. The java.io package declares several different stream classes derived from InputStream and OutputStream. These other classes provide actual implementation of the abstract InputStream and OutputStream class methods. These nonabstract stream classes can be broken up into two different categories. The first category is what you can call *physical stream classes*. The second category implements stream filters as streams that encapsulate other streams.

Physical InputStream Classes

A Physical Stream class implements the abstract methods of the InputStream or OutputStream class for a particular storage media. For example, the FileInputStream class implements the InputStream class' abstract read() method with calls to the native operating system that accesses files on the local disk. The FileOutputStream's write() method implementation also calls native operating system code that writes bytes to files on the local disk. The following table lists the different Java physical InputStream and OutputStream classes, and includes a description of each of them.

Class	Description
FileInputStream	InputStream that works on disk-based files
ByteArrayInputStream	InputStream providing access to the individual elements of an array of bytes

Class	Description
FileInputStream	InputStream that works on disk-based files
SocketInputStream	InputStream that can read bytes from a TCP/IP socket
PipedInputStream	InputStream built from bytes passed from a PipedOutputStream. Bytes written to the PipedOutputStream class are automatically buffered in the PipedInputStream class. Reading threads will be blocked until data is available from the PipedOutputStream class
StringBufferInputStream	Like a ByteArrayInputStream, only gets the sequence of bytes from a string

The InputStream Class Methods

The InputStream class declares several methods to make reading from streams easy. Note that all the nonabstract InputStream-derived classes implement or override the InputStream class implementation of all these methods.

The read( ) method of the InputStream class has three overloaded declarations, each of which reads one or more bytes from the stream. The no-parameter overloaded version of the read( ) method reads a single byte from the stream and returns it cast as an int in the range 0 to 255. If there are no more bytes left in the stream (i.e., if you have already read to the end of the stream position), then this method returns -1. This example code snippet demonstrates how to use an InputStream's read( ) method. This method will read from a passed input stream until a particular character is read, or until the end of the stream is reached.

```
public boolean readToChar(InputStream is, int ch) {
   for(int c = is.read() ; c != -1 && c != ch; c = is.read() );
   return(c != -1 ? true : false);
}
```

Two more overloaded versions of the read( ) method exist so that you can read multiple bytes at once into a byte array, instead of having to read a single character at a time using the no-parameter version of this method. The first overloaded version takes a single parameter: a byte array you want the method to fill with as much data from the stream as it can. The elements of the array will be overwritten. The method returns the number of bytes

File I/O and Streams

read from the stream, or -1 if no bytes can be read. No more bytes than can fit into the passed array object will be read from the input stream.

The second overloaded version also takes a byte array as its first parameter. The second parameter is the offset into the byte array where you want the method to start filling the array with bytes from the input stream. The third parameter is the number of characters you want read into the array from the stream. This example code demonstrates filling a byte array using this second overloaded version. This example method reads in as many bytes from the input stream as the next byte from the input stream says to read.

```
public void readSomeBytes(InputStream is, byte[] ab) {
    // Get number of bytes to read in from the stream.
    int n = is.read();

    // Read in the bytes to the byte buffer.
    is.read(ab, 0, n);
}
```

The InputStream class' skip( ) method will skip over a specified number of bytes of the input stream. These bytes will be lost, and you will not be able to read them later unless you close and reopen the stream. The skip( ) method takes one parameter, the number of bytes to skip.

The InputStream class declares nonabstract methods for creating *mark* functionalities in child classes. The mark( ) method, at least as a concept, should cause the InputStream class to start buffering changes to it so that you can rewind the tape to the position you marked it at. Not all InputStream-derived classes can actually achieve this mark-and-jump functionality. In fact, the InputStream class' implementation of this method does nothing! (The only Java InputStream method that does implement this mark-and-jump functionality is the BufferedInputStream, which you can read about in the following sections.)

To tell whether or not an InputStream can support the mark-and-jump functionality, the InputStream class method markSupported( ) was added to the InputStream class. This method returns true if the InputStream object can support the mark( ) and reset( ) methods. Otherwise, false is returned.

The reset( ) method is the companion to the mark( ) method. After you mark a position in the input stream using the mark( ) method, you can later use the reset( ) method to rewind the input stream to the marked position. For example, if you wanted to look ahead three of four characters in an input stream that supports the mark-and-jump functionality, you can write code like this:

```java
public byte[] lookAhead(InputStream is) {
    if(!is.markSupported())
        return null;

    is.mark();
    byte ab[] = new byte[4];
    is.read(ab);

    is.reset();
    return ab;
}
```

The InputStream class method available( ) returns the number of bytes of data available for immediate reading. This comes in especially useful for streams such as the socket input stream: streams that can block the thread calling read( ) until data becomes available. The available( ) method returns the number of bytes that can be read immediately without blocking the calling thread. It returns -1 if the file has been closed.

To close an input stream, use the object's close( ) method, which closes the stream and gets rid of any resources associated with opening the file.

FileInputStream

A FileInputStream is an InputStream that gets its data from a file on a local disk. When you create the FileInputStream, you hand a file name, a File, or a FileDescription object to the FileInputStream class constructor. The FileInputStream is created connected to the file indicated to the constructor. Here's an example of a program's initialization code that opens the file indicated by the first program argument for reading (i.e., as a FileInputStream):

```java
import java.io.*;

public class MyProgram {
    InputStream in;

    public void main(String[] astrArgs) {
        if(astrArgs.length < 1) {
            System.err.println("Usage Error: run MyProgram class through \
                                interpreter with arguments:\n\
                                <input-filename>");
            System.exit(-1);
        }

        try {
            in = new FileInputStream(astrArgs[1]);
```

File I/O and Streams

```
            } catch(FileNotFoundException e) {
                System.err.println("Error: file not found: " + astrArgs[1]);
                System.exit(-1);
            }

            // Do something with input stream...

            try {
                in.close();
            } catch (IOException e) {
                // handle exception here ...
            }
        }
    }
```

ByteArrayInputStream

You can turn any array of bytes into an input stream using the ByteArrayInputStream class. This class reads from the byte array as if it were a stream. The reset( ) method of the ByteArrayInputStream class is reimplemented to rewind the current position of the input stream to the first byte in the array.

When you create a ByteArrayInputStream object, pass the byte array you want associated with the stream to the object's constructor. Two constructors exist, so you can associate the stream with the entire array or just a range of bytes in the array:

```
byte ab[] = {0x00, 0x01, 0x02, 0x03, 0x04, 0x05};   // sample data.

InputStream is1 = new ByteArrayInputStream(ab);     // entire array as a stream
InputStream is2 = new ByteArrayInputStream(ab, 2, 3);
                                                    // array elements 2 through
                                                    //  (2+3) as a stream.
```

SocketInputStream

Given an opened network socket, you can expose the data on that socket as a stream of bytes by creating a SocketInputStream. The SocketInputStream class exists in the java.net package. Chapter 9 describes socket and networking in general in Java, so you can read more about this class in that chapter.

One quick note: it is precisely because the FileInputStream and SocketInputStream classes are derived from a class defining their common functionalities (the InputStream class) that applets can open files created from URLs. That's why if you open the applet from an HTML page on your local system, the applet will use the same code as if the applet is opened across the Internet: opened files in both cases are presented to the applet as input streams, which avoids ever having to worry or even think about the physical storage media of your data. If the data is stored on the local file system, then a FileInputStream is used to access the data in the file. If, on the other hand, the data is sent across the Internet through the HTTP or FTP protocols, then a version of the SocketInputStream is created. In either case, your applet looks at both classes as InputStreams, and thus does not have to code any differently according to where to data is located.

PipedInputStream

A piped input stream buffers bytes written to a piped output stream. A background thread is created for the piped output stream. When you write to the piped output stream, all connected piped input streams are passed the byte. The byte is then buffered by the piped input stream, and handed out whenever read( ) is called on the PipedInputStream object. Threads that read from a piped input stream while no data is buffered are blocked until data is written to the associated piped output stream. This sample applet uses a PipedInputStream/PipedOutputStream pair to pass bytes between different processing threads:

```
import java.applet.*;
import java.awt.*;
import java.io.*;

public class MyApplet extends Applet implements Runnable {
    PipedInputStream m_iskeys;
    PipedOutputStream m_oskeys;
    double m_dblAverageKey;
    int m_nKeyCount;
    Thread m_thread;

    public void init() {
        m_oskeys = new PipedOutputStream();
        try {
            m_iskeys = new PipedInputStream(m_oskeys);
        } catch (IOException e) {
            // handle exception...
        }
    }

    public void start() {
        m_dblAverageKey = 0.0;
        m_nKeyCount = 0;
        m_thread = new Thread(this);
        m_thread.start();
    }
```

File I/O and Streams

```java
    public void stop() {
        m_thread = null;
    }

    public boolean keyDown(Event evt, int key) {
        try {
            m_oskeys.write(key);
        } catch (IOException e) {
            // handle exception...
        }
      System.out.println("Key was hit: " + key);
       return true;
    }

    public void run() {

        int key;
         while(null != m_thread) {
            try {
               key = m_iskeys.read();
            } catch (IOException e) {
                // handle exception...
            }
            m_dblAverageKey *= m_nKeyCount;
            m_dblAverageKey += key;
            m_dblAverageKey /= ++m_nKeyCount;
            repaint();
        }
    }

    public void paint(Graphics g) {
        FontMetrics fm = g.getFontMetrics();
        g.drawString("Average key value: " + m_dblAverageKey,
                fm.getMaxAdvance(), fm.getHeight());
    }
}
```

StringBufferInputStream

The StringBufferInputStream is similar to a ByteArrayInputStream, but gets its bytes of data from a String object instead of an array of bytes. Since strings are generally easier to work with than byte arrays, because they can be concatenated, truncated, etc., StringBufferInputStreams might be easier for you to use than ByteArrayInputStreams. In either case, you use the ByteArrayInputStream and the StringBufferInputStream when you want to create a stream from bytes or characters that exist in memory.

Filter Input Stream Classes

The second type of InputStream-derived classes is different from the physical stream classes. Instead of having a physical storage media associated with the InputStream object, as is the case with all physical stream classes, filtered streams encapsulate other streams and use them as the storage media. That is, the filter object is a wrapper around an encapsulated stream. The FilteredInputStream has a protected member *in*, which is another InputStream of any derived class. When you read from the FilteredInputStream, the FilteredInputStream reads bytes from its *in* member.

The FilteredInputStream class itself does not actually alter the incoming streamed bytes from the *in* member InputStream. Thus, the FilteredInputStream itself is not very useful. There are several classes derived from FilteredInputStream that alter or in some way use the data from the InputStream member *in* as it passes through the FilteredInputStream's read( ) method. The following table lists all the FilteredInputStream classes included in the java.io package, and gives a brief description of each.

Class	Description
BufferedInputStream	Buffers input data. An internal buffer of arbitrary length is filled with data. Consolidates multiple disk reads by filling an internal buffer less frequently than multiple reads to normal InputStreams would.
DataInputStream	Has methods such as readBoolean( ) and readInt( ) that combine bytes into built-in data-type values.
LineNumberInputStream	Example of a simple odometer-type input filter. Keeps track of the number of new line characters that have been read or skipped over.
PushbackInputStream	Simple filter that allows you to push back a single character into the input stream. That is, you can read a character from the stream, push it back into to stream, then read it again. The maximum pushback depth of a PushbackInputStream is one character.
SequenceInputStream	Strings a sequence of input streams together as if they were all a single input stream.

File I/O and Streams

The FilteredInputStream class exposes all the methods of its parent class, the InputStream class, and no others. The classes in this table may or may not implement some additional public methods. For example, the LineNumberInputStream class has getLineNumber( ) and setLineNumber( ) methods in addition to the methods it inherits from the FilteredInputStream class.

BufferedInputStream

The BufferedInputStream class is an example of a functional stream buffer. That is, a buffered input stream does not in any way translate or change the bytes of the encapsulated *in* input stream. The BufferedInputStream class adds a little functionality to its InputStream instead.

A buffered input stream buffers input data by keeping it in an internal array of bytes. The first thing this does for an encapsulated input stream is to make it require less overall reads to the underlying storage media when individual bytes are read from it. See, instead of asking the encapsulated *in* stream for a single new byte whenever the BufferedInputStream's read( ) method is called, the internal buffer is filled up with many bytes from the input stream. This results in fewer overall calls to the underlying storage media. Many requests for a single byte are instead translated into one big request for many bytes.

Because the BufferedInputStream essentially "pre-fetches" as many bytes as its buffer can hold, it also implements the mark( ) and reset( ) methods of the InputStream class. When you call the mark( ) method, it's like setting a bookmark at that point in the byte stream. When you call the reset( ) method, the BufferedInputStream "rolls back" a pointer to your current read position in its internal buffer to the last marked position. The single int parameter to the mark( ) method tells the buffer the minimum number of lookahead bytes you want. That is, if you passed the number N into the mark( ) method, then you can read up to N bytes from the buffered input stream before the mark is erased.

LineNumberInputStream

The LineNumberInputStream is another example of a FilteredInputStream class that does not modify or translate the data coming from the encapsulated input stream. Just like the BufferedInputStream class, calls to a LineNumberInputStream class' read( ) method return pretty much the same data that a direct call to the encapsulated InputStream class' read( ) method would return.

Actually, there is a slight difference between the bytes of the encapsulated input stream and the bytes output by the LineNumberInputStream class. The LineNumberInputStream translates all possible line-terminating sequences into the same newline character. There are three possible line-termination sequences: a single line-feed character '\r', a single newline character '\n', or a newline character immediately followed by a linefeed character. Any one of these three sequences is automatically converted into a single newline character by the LineNumberInputStream as the bytes pass through it from the encapsulated input stream to your program code.

The value added by the LineNumberInputStream class is that it maintains a count of the number of new lines that it sends you. The getLineNumber( ) method returns the number of newline characters that have passed through so far. The method setLineNumber( ) allows you to change the current line number count, adjusting it to whatever value you want.

This is a simple line-counting program that uses the LineNumberInputStream to do the counting. In general, only the simplest of situations will call for using a LineNumberInputStream in your programs.

```java
import java.io.*;

public class LineCounter {
    static LineNumberInputStream m_istreamLineNum;

    public static void main(String astrArgs[]) {
        if(1 != astrArgs.length) {
            System.err.println("Usage error:\n LineCounter <input-file>");
            System.exit(-1);
        }

        try {
            FileInputStream is = new FileInputStream(astrArgs[0]);
            m_istreamLineNum = new LineNumberInputStream(is);
        } catch (Exception e) {
            System.err.println("Error:\n Opening input file " + astrArgs[0]);
            System.exit(-1);
        }

        try {
            while(-1 != m_istreamLineNum.read()) ;
        } catch (Exception e) {
            System.err.println("Error:\n Reading from the input file.");
```

File I/O and Streams

```
        }

        System.out.println("Line numbering complete. Number of lines is: " +
            m_istreamLineNum.getLineNumber());
    }
}
```

You can think of the LineNumberInputStream as a simple type of odometer attached to the encapsulated input stream. You can easily imagine other brands of odometer-type FilteredInputStreams: a ByteCounterInputStream to count the actually number of bytes that have passed through the read( ) method, a CharacterCounterInputStream could be created that counts any number of different specific characters as they pass through the read( ) method, etc. In a following section you will see how to create a speedometer-type FilteredInputStream that actually monitors the rate that bytes are read in from an encapsulated input stream, which could be used, for example, to monitor how quickly a download of a particular file is going.

PushbackInputStream

The PushbackInputStream does no translation or modification of the data stored in the encapsulated input stream, the same as the BufferedInputStream class. The added functionality of the PushbackInputStream class is that it allows you to "rewind" your stream by a single character. That is, you can perform a one-character lookahead on the encapsulated input stream. The PushbackInputStream method unread( ) (whose name was chosen because it essentially does the opposite thing as the read( ) method does) takes a character and stores it internally to the PushbackInputStream object. If immediately after calling the unread( ) method, you call the read( ) method, then the character you unread( ) will be returned to you.

DataInputStream

The DataInputStream class implements several different read methods, each one capable of reading in a built-in data type from the encapsulated input stream *in*. This can be of great help when you want to, for example, read in a long value or a string from an input stream. Without using the DataInputStream wrapper around another input stream, you would have to stick bytes together in the correct byte order to get this same functionality. This table lists all the different types of data that can be read in from a data input stream, and the method used to read in that type.

Built-In Type	DataInputStream Method and Description
boolean	readBoolean( ). Reads a single byte from the input stream. A zero byte means *false*, while any other value means *true*.
byte	readByte( ). No different than just plain read( ), except that a byte is returned instead of the same byte cast as an int. readUnsignedByte( ) returns exactly the same value that the read( ) method returns. The only difference is that you will not get a -1 value at the end of the input stream, which is what read( ) will return. As stated more fully below, you will instead get a EOFException thrown when the end of the input stream is reached.
char	readChar( ). A single Unicode (16-bit) character is returned. The first byte read becomes the high byte of the Unicode character sequence, and the second byte read becomes the low byte of the Unicode character sequence. This method blocks the calling thread (i.e., prevents it from executing further) until both bytes are read.
double	readDouble( ). Reads an eight-byte double-precision floating point number from the input stream. This method will block until all eight bytes are read.
float	readFloat( ). Reads in a 32-bit single-precision floating point number from the encapsulated input stream. This method will block until all four bytes are read from the input stream.
short	readShort( ). Reads in a 16-bit signed integer value from the encapsulated input stream. This method will block the calling thread until both of the bytes are read from the input stream. readUnsignedShort( ) will read in the same 16 bits from the input stream, but will load them into a 32-bit int variable.
int	readInt( ). Reads a signed 32-bit integer from the encapsulated input stream. This method will block until all four input bytes are read from the input stream.
long	readLong( ). Reads a signed 64-bit integer value from the encapsulated input stream. This method blocks until all eight bytes are read from the input stream.

File I/O and Streams

Built-In Type	DataInputStream Method and Description
boolean	readBoolean( ). Reads a single byte from the input stream. A zero byte means *false*, while any other value means *true*.
byte	readByte( ). No different than just plain read( ), except that a byte is returned instead of the same byte cast as an int. readUnsignedByte( ) returns exactly the same value that the read( ) method returns. The only difference is that you will not get a -1 value at the end of the input stream, which is what read( ) will return. As stated more fully below, you will instead get a EOFException thrown when the end of the input stream is reached.
String	readUTF( ). Reads a string in from the encapsulated input stream. Strings are stored in a format called UTF when they are written to streams (usually, you write them using DataOutputStream objects, the reciprocal class to the DataInputStream class).

Note that if you try to use any of the above methods when you have reached the end of the encapsulated input stream, then an EOFException is thrown to let you know that you are at the end of the file. The read( ) method, which the DataInputStream class inherits from its FilteredInputStream base class, still acts the same way it does in all other InputStream classes. It does not throw an EOFException if it is called when the encapsulated input stream is at the end of the stream. Instead, it returns a -1 value.

In Chapter 12, you will read about how to make a generic ObjectInputStream and a generic ObjectOutputStream, which will be based on the DataInputStream and DataOutputStream classes. The Object streams will be able to read and write almost any object you can implement.

SequenceInputStream
The SequenceInputStream class is something of a "fan-in" filter for input streams. Instead of being connected to a single input stream, it can be associated with multiple InputStreams. The SequenceInputStream class will serialize all those input streams through its own read( ) method. This means that if you, for example (as the code below demonstrates), associated a sequence input stream with two different input streams, when you called the SequenceInputStream's read( ) method multiple times you would get back first all the characters of the first input stream, and then all the

characters of the second input stream. In fact, you would not even be able to tell from which InputStream a particular byte came.

Here is a sample program, very similar to the LineCounter program given for the LineNumberInputStream class previously, that counts the number of lines in multiple files.

```java
import java.io.*;
import java.util.*;

public class MultiFileLineCounter {
    public static void main(String astrArgs[]) {
        SequenceInputStream sis;
        try {
            // arguments are the files to open and count lines.
            Vector vectFiles = new Vector();
            for(int ii=0 ; ii<astrArgs.length ; ii++)
                vectFiles.addElement(new FileInputStream(astrArgs[ii]));
            sis = new SequenceInputStream(vectFiles.elements());
        } catch (Exception e) {
            System.err.println("Problem opening input file(s).");
            System.exit(-1);
        }

        // Wrap line counter around the SequenceInputStream.
        LineNumberInputStream lis = new LineNumberInputStream(sis);

        try {
            while(-1 != lis.read()) ;
        } catch (Exception e) {
            System.err.println("Problem reading from input file(s).");
            System.exit(-1);
        }

        System.out.println("Total count of lines is " +
            lis.getLineNumber());
    }
}
```

There are two constructors for the sequence input stream. The first, demonstrated in the previous MultiFileLineCounter application, is passed an Enumeration of input streams. In that example application, the Enumeration is returned from the Vector.elements( ) method that creates an Enumeration listing all the elements in the Vector. The sequence input stream runs through each element in the Enumeration and appends all the input streams together.

File I/O and Streams

The second SequenceInputStream constructor takes just two input streams as its first and second arguments. This is a shorthand version of the first constructor that is easier to use when you only have two input streams to concatenate. It's easier just to pass the two to the SequenceInputStream constructor than it is to go through the trouble of generating an Enumeration with only two elements in it.

Chaining FilteredInputStreams

The MultiFileLineCounter example given in the previous section demonstrates one very useful thing you can do with filtered input streams: you can chain them together. In that example, a line number input stream is used to encapsulate another type of filtered input stream: a sequence input stream. The sequence input stream in turn encapsulates an input stream that is actually connected to a storage media, which is in this case a file input stream.

Since all filtered input streams ultimately are derived from the InputStream class, then a filtered input stream can be used to encapsulate another filtered input stream, which can in turn encapsulate another filtered input stream, and so on. Figure 8-1 illustrates this concept of FilteredInputStream objects encapsulating each other. You can imagine that with each level of encapsulation, you can gain more functionality, capabilities, and control of the content of a raw input stream of bytes. Again, the MultiFileLineCounter program demonstrates that fact. The SequenceInputStream is used to encapsulate several different FileInputStreams, essentially turning them all into a single concatenated input stream. The LineNumberInputStream in turn encapsulates the SequenceInputStream, allowing you to monitor a key metric of the bytes contained within the concatenated files (well, it may be a stretch to call a line number count a "key metric," but you can see how the concept can be extended to include more useful data metrics).

Custom FilterInputStreams

You can, of course, create your own filter input streams to add functionality or transform stream contents in other ways not done by the

Figure 8-1. Chained filterInputStreams

InputStream — Connected to a storage medium
Filter Input Stream — Encapsulates InputStream
Filter Input Stream — Encapsulates first FilterInputStream
Filter Input Stream — Encapsulates next most previous FilterInputStream

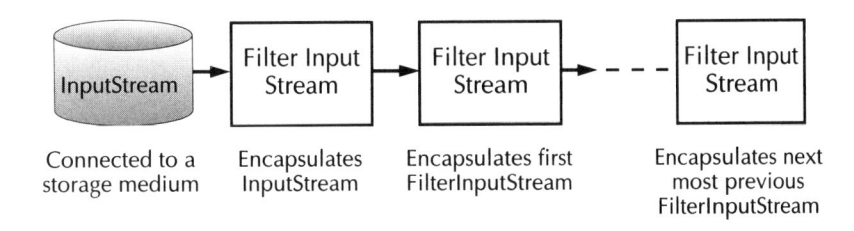

FilterInputStream classes included in the java.io package. Remember these three different basic operations that filter input streams perform on encapsulated input streams:

1. Measuring a metric of the input stream's data. For example, the line number input stream measures the number of lines that have passed through the encapsulated input stream so far.
2. Transforming the bytes of the input stream. That is, changing the individual bytes of data using some method. An example of this follows.
3. Translating the data of the input stream. As opposed to just transforming the individual bytes, a transforming FilterInputStream actually changes the form of the data. For example, the DataInputStream's multiple readXXX( ) methods, such as readBoolean( ) or readDouble( ), actually change the form of the data from a set of bytes into a greater structure.

The distinction between *transforming* and *translating* FilterInputStreams is not merely semantic; there is some import to the difference. See, when you merely transform the individual bytes of data into other bytes of data, then the output of your FilterInputStreams is still essentially a stream of bytes. However, when you translate the stream's bytes into some other form, such as multibyte integers, then the output of your filter cannot be passed on to other FilterInputStreams, since the data is no longer in the form of a stream of bytes.

Just a quick example can help solidify the difference. Let's say you have created a RatedInputStream that measures the rate bytes are being read from an encapsulated input stream (code for such a class is presented for you in a following section). If you tried to encapsulate a data input stream with a rated input stream, you would no longer have the functionality of the data input stream available! Since the RatedInputStream can only examine data that passes through its read( ) method, any data you read through the DataInputStream's readXXX( ) methods would not be counted by the RatedInputStream.

In general, you want the translating filter to be your outermost filter. Transforming and measuring filters, on the other hand, can be chained together in no particular order. So, in the example just given where you have a rated input stream and a DataInputStream, you would want the data input stream to encapsulate the rated input stream and not vice versa.

Back to making custom filter input streams. Here's code for creating the RatedInputStream mentioned just previously. This class just records the number of total bytes and the amount of elapsed time since the first time the read( ) method was called. A getRate( ) method is added to the classes public interface so you can get back the current rate of bytes/second passing

File I/O and Streams

through the rated input stream. A resetRate( ) method is also provided, which essentially clears the counters until the next byte is requested using the read( ) method.

```java
import java.io.*;

public class RatedInputStream extends FilterInputStream {
    // Constructor takes reference to encapsulated InputStream.
    public RatedInputStream(InputStream in) {
        super(in);
        m_dStartTime = -1.0;
        m_dByteCount = 0.0;
    }

    // read increments by one whenever it is called. If start
    // time hasn't been recorded yet, then it is recorded.
    public int read( ) {
        if(-1 == (int)m_dStartTime)
            m_dStartTime = System.currentTimeMillis();
        try {
            return in.read();
        } catch (IOException e) {
            return -1;
        }
    }

    // The getRate( ) method returns a double indicating rate
    // of bytes read/second.
    public double getRate() {
        if(m_dStartTime <= 0.0)
            return 0.0;

        return m_dByteCount / (m_dStartTime * 1000);
    }

    public void resetRate() {
        m_dStartTime = -1.0;
        m_dByteCount = 0.0;
    }

    // Private state variables.
    private double m_dStartTime;
    private double m_dByteCount;
}
```

The only method you need to override when implementing a custom filter input stream is the single-byte read( ) method. The implementation of the

FilterInputStream read( ) overloads for reading data into byte arrays (read(byte[]) and read(byte[], offset, length)) are already implemented to make multiple calls to the single-byte read( ) overloaded method. Of course, you could also implement the byte-array read( ) overloaded methods if you wanted to. This would be most efficacious when a multibyte read could be optimized.

OutputStreams

An output stream is a stream of bytes that you write to, as opposed to input streams that you read from. When you open a file for reading, you use a file input stream. When you open that file for writing, you use a file output stream. The InputStream and OutputStream classes are both abstract, not having any implementation of their respective read( ) and write( ) methods.

So, the most important method of the OutputStream class is the write( ) method. The OutputStream's write( ) method is symmetric to the InputStream's read( ) method. The write( ) method takes a single byte (cast as an int) as its only parameter. Conceptually, when you call this method the byte is added to the stream, and the "current pointer" of the stream is advanced by one position so that you may write another byte if you want to later.

Two overloaded versions of the write( ) method exist, just like two overloaded versions of the InputStream.read( ) method exist. These two overloaded versions allow you to write more than one byte at a time to the stream, where the bytes are all stored sequentially in a byte array. These are the signature of the two overloaded versions of the write( ) method, which you can see are symmetric with the two overloaded versions of the InputStream's read( ) method:

```
public void write(byte ab[]) throws IOException;
public void write(byte ab[], int offset, int length) throws IOException;
```

The only other OutputStream methods are flush( ) and close( ). You use flush( ) to ensure that data has been fully written to the underlying storage medium. For example, the BufferedOutputStream class' flush( ) implementation automatically writes the contents of the object's internal buffer to the encapsulated output stream, even if the buffer is not full yet. The flush( ) method has no parameters. All the different OutputStreams implement the various overloaded versions of the write( ) method, as well as a flush( ) method.

The close( ) method closes the encapsulated output stream. After closing an output stream, any call to write( ) or flush( ) will inevitably throw an IOException.

File I/O and Streams

The Types of OutputStreams

The table below lists the various types of output streams that exist and a short description of each. The output streams listed here are pretty much the symmetric equivalent of the input streams of the same type. So, the buffered output stream does the same thing as the buffered input stream, only in the opposite "direction." That is, the buffered output stream keeps an internal buffer of bytes that is filled as you write bytes to it using the object's overloaded write( ) methods. When the internal buffer is full, the data is written all at once to the encapsulated output stream. This is pretty much what the buffered input stream does, only in the opposite direction. You may notice that all input streams do not have an output stream matching them. The LineNumberInputStream, for example, does not have a matching LineNumberOutputStream in the java.io package. This does not preclude you from deriving your own LineNumberOutputStream from the FilteredOutputStream class. In most cases, that is what you will have to do if you want equivalent functionality in an output stream.

OutputStream	Description
OutputStream	Base abstract class for all output streams. Defines an overloaded write( ) method and a flush( ) method, although it provides no implementation for either.
ByteArrayOutputStream	When written to, it writes bytes to successive elements of an array of bytes.
FileOutputStream	When written to, it writes data out to a file on the local file system. Create one by passing the name of a file, a File object, or a FileDescriptor object.
SocketOutputStream	When written to, it writes bytes out to a network socket. A SocketInputStream connected to the other side of the network socket could then perform a read( ) and get back the same bytes that were just written, in the same order.
PipedOutputStream	PipedOutputStreams are connected directly with one or more PipedInputStreams within the same Java Virtual Machine. When you write to the PipedInputStream, the bytes are immediately handed over to any PipedInputStreams connected to the same PipedOutputStream.

OutputStream	Description
OutputStream	Base abstract class for all output streams. Defines an overloaded write( ) method and a flush( ) method, although it provides no implementation for either.
FilterOutputStream	Base class for any filtered output stream. When written to, writes bytes to an encapsulated OutputStream's write( ) method. A FilterOutputStream may either transform, translate, or measure a stream of bytes, in much the same way a FilterInputStream may to the same operations.
BufferedOutputStream	A simple type of FilterOutputStream. It keeps an internal buffer of bytes that have been written to it. When the buffer fills, all bytes in the buffer are transferred to the encapsulated OutputStream at once. This combines multiple smaller write( ) operations into a lower number of writes.
DataOutputStream	This translating FilterOutputStream is the symmetric equivalent to the DataInputStream. The methods such as writeBoolean( ), writeInt( ), and writeUTF( ) write out pieces of data as sets of bytes to the encapsulated OutputStream. Data written out with a DataOutputStream can be read back in with a DataInputStream at a later time.

Parsing an InputStream

Parsing an InputStream is a type of translation operation. The difference is that the contents of the input stream are unknown while you read from it. The data input stream does not parse its encapsulated input stream. That's because you must tell the data input stream what type of data to read in. You tell the DataInputStream to readBoolean( ), readInt( ), or readUTF( ), meaning that you know what type of data you want to read from the stream before even looking at it. This is useful if you already know, for example, the layout of the bytes in the InputStream.

A specific example of using the data input stream is if you have a byte stream that you know starts with an integer, whose value tells you how

File I/O and Streams

many strings to read in next. The code for using a data input stream to read such a structure might look like this:

```
public String[] readStrings(InputStream is) throws IOException {
    DataInputStream dis = new DataInputStream(is);
    int nStrings = dis.readInt();
    String[] astr = new String[nStrings];
    for(int ii=0 ; ii<nStrings ; ii++)
        astr[ii] = dis.readUTF();
    return astr;
}
```

But what if you didn't already "know" the format of your input stream? For example, what if you were trying to parse a Java source code file? You know beforehand the syntax of the Java input, but you don't necessarily know exactly what to read in. Furthermore, a Java source code file is written in ASCII characters, so that even if you know you want to read in some series of strings, those strings are not laid out in the UTF format. The data input stream can only read UTF-format string data (the same format written out by the DataOutputString.writeUTF( ) method).

The StreamTokenizer class was created and added to the java.io package to handle just such a situation. A stream tokenizer takes an input stream and parses it into *tokens*. A token is a quanta of data of some type. The string tokenizer can read in and recognize strings and numbers from ASCII character-based input streams. Furthermore, the stream tokenizer can recognize what type of token it is reading in, so you don't have to know the exact structure of a stream to parse it using a stream tokenizer.

So, the difference between translating and parsing is that when you parse, you do not know necessarily beforehand the exact structure of your input stream. When you translate, you do know the layout beforehand and can tell the translating filter, such as a data input stream, exactly what type of data to read in next.

The StreamTokenizer is not derived from the FilterInputStream class. That's because there is no read( ) method in the StreamTokenizer class. Instead, you read in the input stream's data as a series of tokens of either string or numeric type. The StreamTokenizer class method nextToken( ) returns a constant telling you the type of the next token read in from an associated InputStream.

There are four different types of tokens defined by the StreamTokenizer class. The following table lists the StreamTokenizer public constants that define each of those types and gives a description of each.

Token Type Constant	Description
TT_NUMBER	Indicates a number token was read in. The *nval* member of the StreamTokenizer holds the value of the token.
TT_WORD	Indicates a string token was read in. The *sval* member of the StreamTokenizer holds the string value of the token.
TT_EOL	Indicates an end-of-line was reached.
TT_EOF	Indicates the end of the input file was reached.
<value>	Any other value returned is the actual ASCII value of an *ordinary character*. An ordinary character has no significance as part of a word or a number.

So, to read in a file that is a series of words and numbers separated by white space, you would use code similar to this:

```
public void parseInputStream(InputStream is) {
    StreamTokenizer st = new StreamTokenizer(is);
    int nTokenType;
    while((nTokenType = st.nextToken()) != StreamTokenizer.TT_EOF) {
        switch(nTokenType) {
            case StreamTokenizer.TT_EOL:
                doSomethingWithEOL();
                break;

            case StreamTokenizer.TT_WORD:
                doSomethingWithString(st.sval);
                break;

            case StreamTokenizer.TT_NUMBER:
                doSomethingWithDouble(st.nval);
                break;
        }
    }
}
```

StreamTokenizers are very configurable objects. Through the StreamTokenizer class' many methods, you can specify what characters to include in a TT_WORD token, what characters constitute white space,

File I/O and Streams

whether or not the StreamTokenizer should tell you about TT_EOL tokens at all, etc.

In addition, the StreamTokenizer class can automatically parse out and ignore different types of delimited comments. You can tell the StreamTokenizer whether or not to ignore C-language-type comments, which are delimited by the /* */ delimiting symbols. You can also tell it whether or not to ignore C++ single-line-type comments, which are defined as everything from a "//" symbol to the end of the line.

First, all tokens are separated by white space. Whitespace characters are considered as totally insignificant by stream tokenizers. They are simply tossed away by the stream tokenizer, and they never are included as part of a token. The only thing whitespace characters are used for is to delimit where TT_WORD and TT_NUMBER tokens start and stop. By default, when a string tokenizer is created, all characters from 0 to 32 are considered whitespace characters. You can add new whitespace characters to this list using the StreamTokenizer class method whitespaceChars( ). You specify the first character and the last character in a range of ASCII values as the first and second parameters to this method, respectively. All characters between the low and high characters are then considered whitespace characters by the stream tokenizer. If you were parsing a file that contained a comma-delimited set of numbers, you could add the comma character to a stream tokenizer's list of whitespace characters so that it could use the command to delimit individual numbers, as in this code sample:

```java
public int[] parseCommaDelimitedNumbers(InputStream is) {
    int anRet[] = new int[10];
    int nNumbers = 0;
    StreamTokenizer st = new StreamTokenizer(is);
    is.whitespaceChars(',', ',');
    while(StreamTokenizer.TT_NUMBER == st.nextToken()) {
        if(nNumbers == anRet.length) {
            int an[] = new int[anRet.length*2];
            System.arraycopy(anRet, 0, an, 0, anRet.length);
            anRet = an;
        }
        anRet[nNumbers++] = (int)st.nval;
    }

    int an[] = new int[nNumbers];
    System.arraycopy(anRet, 0, an, 0, nNumbers);
    return an;
}
```

By default, when you create a string tokenizer, it automatically is set up to parse numbers. That's because the StreamTokenizer constructor includes a call to the StreamTokenizer class method parseNumbers( ), telling the object to parse double-precision floating point numbers. The only way to tell the StreamTokenizer *not* to parse numbers is to call the clearSyntax( ) method, which causes all ASCII characters to be ordinary characters. After calling this method, you must remake the syntax with calls to the wordChar( ), ordinaryChar( ), whitespaceChar( ), commentChar( ), and quoteChar( ) methods. Actually, that is the same method you use to change the syntax parsed by the stream tokenizer in general. You cannot remove a character for the list of word characters without calling the clearSyntax( ) method and recreating the state of the StreamTokenizer with several calls to these methods.

Similarly to how you specify whitespace characters using the whitespaceChars( ) method, you specify ordinary characters using the ordinaryChar( ) and ordinaryChars( ) methods. The ordinaryChar( ) method takes a single character to add to the list of ordinary characters in the syntax, while ordinaryChars( ) adds a whole range of character values to this list.

You can also specify the word characters using the wordChar( ) and wordChars( ) methods similarly. Use wordChar( ) to add a single character to the list of recognized word characters, and use wordChars( ) to add a range of ASCII character values to the same list.

All text appearing between sets of *quote* characters is read in to the stream tokenizer as a single TT_WORD token, even if the text between a pair of quoted characters includes whitespace or numeric characters. Use the StreamTokenizer class method quoteChar( ) to add a character to the list of quoting characters the stream tokenizer knows about. All text appearing between two quote characters is treated as a single TT_WORD token. By default, when a stream tokenizer is created, its list of quote characters includes the single-quote character '\'', and the double-quote character '\"'.

A comment character, like a quote character, defines a comment as all characters appearing between two comment characters. You add a comment character to the list of known comment characters for a StreamTokenizer using the commentChar( ) method, passing in the character you want to add to the list. In addition, the stream tokenizer can be configured to recognize the C-comment delimiters /* */ and the C++ comment delimiter //. Use slashStarComments( ), passing in a boolean that is true if you want everything between the /* */ in an InputStream to be ignored. Pass in false if you want the /* */ delimiters to be parsed like any other characters. The slashSlashComments( ) method, similarly, is handed a true value if you want all characters appearing after a // delimiter and up to an end-of-line to be ignored by the stream tokenizer. If you pass false to this method, then it will parse these comments like any other characters.

A StreamTokenizer Example

The Sun samples included with Visual J++ include an example of using a stream tokenizer to parse a file. This example is part of the WireFrame sample applet. The WireFrame applet displays a 3D wire-frame model, and actually lets the user rotate the model in three dimensions by dragging the mouse around within the applet.

One of the parameters to the WireFrame applet is called "model." This parameter specifies the URL to a file describing a 3D wire-frame model. The format of that wire-frame model file is made up of a series of single-line descriptors. There are two different types of descriptor lines. The first type describes a vertex in the 3D model. Those lines look like this:

```
v   X   Y   Z
```

where the *X*, *Y*, and *Z* variables define a point in 3D space. Between the 'v' character and the three numbers is some amount of white space, and the whole line ends with an end-of-line character (a newline). Internally, the WireFrame applet assigns a one-based index to these vertexes. So, the first vertex defined in the file is assigned the number 1, and the second gets the number 2, and so on.

The second type of descriptor defines an actual connection between two or more vertexes in the wire frame. Those lines look like this:

```
(f or fo or l)  v1 v2 [v3 [v4 [...]]]
```

where the variables *v1*, *v2*, etc. are vertex identifying numbers. The line leads with one of three different character strings "f", "fo", and "l". There is no difference between what these three strings mean or how they are parsed by the WireFrame program. (The author can only assume that when this sample was developed, the three different strings were used to indicate different types of descriptors, but that these three descriptor types were combined into one for simplicity.) The meaning of the series of vertex identifiers *v1*, *v2*, etc. is that a connecting line is to be drawn in the wire-frame model starting at vertex *v1*, going to vertex *v2*, and then to vertex *v3*, etc. Like the vertex descriptor lines, these connector lines also end with an end-of-line character. Figure 8-2 is a screen shot of the WireFrame sample applet displaying a simple cube. The cube is defined by this model file:

```
v 0 0 0
v 1 0 0
v 1 1 0
v 0 1 0
v 0 0 1
v 1 0 1
v 1 1 1
v 0 1 1
f 1 2 3 4
f 5 6 7 8
1 1 5
1 2 6
1 3 7
1 4 8
```

So, now that you know the layout and definition of the model files used by the WireFrame sample program, you can probably see why a filter input stream cannot be used to simply transform these files into useful data within the WireFrame applet. The reason is that the file needs to be *parsed*, not

The WireFrame sample displaying a cube model
Figure 8-2.

File I/O and Streams

translated or transformed, which means you need to use a stream tokenizer (or some parsing object of your own creation).

The WireFrame example stored wire-frame models within an instance of a Model3D object. The Model3D class has a constructor that takes as its only parameter an input stream. The Model3D object being created actually parses the input stream using a stream tokenizer, and the data from the input stream is used to initialize the internal variables of the Model3D object. Here is a copy of the Model3D constructor that parses model files:

```
Model3D (InputStream is) throws IOException, FileFormatException {
    this();
    StreamTokenizer st = new StreamTokenizer(is);
    st.eolIsSignificant(true);
    st.commentChar('#');
scan:
    while (true) {
        switch (st.nextToken()) {
            default:
                break scan;
            case StreamTokenizer.TT_EOL:
                break;
            case StreamTokenizer.TT_WORD:
                if ("v".equals(st.sval)) {
                    double x = 0, y = 0, z = 0;
                    if (st.nextToken() == StreamTokenizer.TT_NUMBER) {
                        x = st.nval;
                        if (st.nextToken() == StreamTokenizer.TT_NUMBER) {
                            y = st.nval;
                            if (st.nextToken() == StreamTokenizer.TT_NUMBER)
                                z = st.nval;
                        }
                    }
                    addVert((float) x, (float) y, (float) z);
                    while (st.ttype != StreamTokenizer.TT_EOL &&
                            st.ttype != StreamTokenizer.TT_EOF)
                        st.nextToken();
                } else if ("f".equals(st.sval) || "fo".equals(st.sval) ||
                        "l".equals(st.sval)) {
                    int start = -1;
                    int prev = -1;
                    int n = -1;
                    while (true)
                        if (st.nextToken() == StreamTokenizer.TT_NUMBER) {
                            n = (int) st.nval;
                            if (prev >= 0)
                                add(prev - 1, n - 1);
                            if (start < 0)
                                start = n;
```

```
                        prev = n;
                } else if (st.ttype == '/')
                    st.nextToken();
                else
                    break;
                if (start >= 0)
                    add(start - 1, prev - 1);
                if (st.ttype != StreamTokenizer.TT_EOL)
                    break scan;
            } else {
                while (st.nextToken() != StreamTokenizer.TT_EOL
                        && st.ttype != StreamTokenizer.TT_EOF);
            }
        }
    }
    is.close();
    if (st.ttype != StreamTokenizer.TT_EOF)
        throw new FileFormatException(st.toString());
}
```

Summary

A stream is an abstract concept that describes a sequence of bytes. A stream of bytes can only be read in order, and can only be written in order. The java.io package's InputStream and OutputStream classes are abstract classes that describe a generic stream. When the stream is opened for reading, the input stream is an adequate description of the stream object. When the stream is opened for writing, then the output stream is an adequate description. The InputStream and OutputStream classes are symmetric descriptions of different capabilities of a stream. Specific classes derived from the InputStream and OutputStream classes are used to attach the stream concept to different physical storage media. For example, the FileInputStream class lets you *read* bytes from a file in the local file system. The FileOutputStream class lets you *write* bytes to a file on the local file system. A filter input stream encapsulates another input stream, and may measure, translate, or transform the bytes read from the encapsulated input stream. Similarly, a filter output stream has an encapsulated output stream whose bytes it may measure, translate, or transform.

When parsing an ASCII text file, you use a stream tokenizer instead of any type of filtered stream. Parsing is a fundamentally different task than translating or transforming, and so requires a different type of object to be performed. When parsing, an input stream is cut up into a series of tokens. The stream tokenizer performs the task for cutting a stream into tokens. The stream tokenizer tells you both the type and the value of a token that it parses, using its nextToken( ) method.

CHAPTER 9

Networking in Java

Undoubtedly, one of the most time-reducing capabilities of Java is its built-in Internet programming facilities. In Java's early stages, this capability contributed greatly to its popularity, both because of the ability it gave programmers to program interactive content on the World Wide Web using embedded applets, and because of the java.net package's networking classes.

Java was designed with the Internet and intranets in mind. The underlying system of networking communications, or *protocols*, of the Internet is called TCP/IP. The TCP/IP protocol is built into every platform that can connect to the Internet and associated intranets. Following Java's platform-independent model, a whole package of integrated classes called java.net is built into the set of Java core packages. What this means is that no matter what platform your applet or Java application is running on, it can communicate throughout the Internet using these platform-independent networking classes.

TCP/IP programming can be a little difficult on many platforms. The asynchronous nature of networking in general, in which there can be time delays and network interruption at any point during network communications, has been mitigated to a great extent in the java.net classes. The programming difficulty has been reduced, or you could even say made easy.

For example, Internet communications happens through virtual circuits of data, called *sockets*. A socket is basically a data communications pipeline that is set up between exactly two programs. Each program "owns" one endpoint of the pipeline. Data pushed into one end of the pipeline by one program is read out of the pipeline by the other program at the other end. The Java abstraction of sockets is the Socket class of the java.net package. Furthermore, when you communicate through a socket, Java uses its InputStream and OutputStream streaming classes as the basis for socket communication classes. (You can read about Java's streaming classes and how to use them in Chapter 8.) That means you use the same methods for writing to and reading from a socket that you do when writing to or reading from a file on the local file system. If you know how to do one, then you automatically know how to do the other!

This chapter starts by describing a little bit about the Internet, explaining basically how machines are addressed on the Internet using what's called *IP addresses*. You will then read about the Java classes that allow you to set up communication sockets between two different programs using the Java networking classes. You will read about server sockets, which allow you to write your own Internet information servers, like an HTTP server, completely in Java. Then you will read about the URL class, which has fabulous capabilities for getting content from HTTP and FTP servers.

The Internet Language: TCP/IP

All machines that are connected to the Internet "speak" the same network language. TCP/IP (transmission control protocol/Internet protocol) is the name of this Internetworking language. TCP/IP is a suite of communications protocols that allow different computers hooked up to different areas of the Internet to communicate with each other across a vast and complex web of interconnections. The connections can be of many different types: local 10-base T lines, satellite links, ISDN telephone lines, and even the telephone

Networking in Java

lines commonly used by home users, form the communications network that is the Internet.

TCP/IP is a complex set of serialized data packet formats and handshaking protocols that describe how computers can reliably (or, if you want them to, unreliably) exchange streams of data. Wait a second: was that *streams* of data? Yes! The same basic idea of streams described in Chapter 8 that are used to describe file input and file output mechanisms is also used to describe networking communications on the Internet. More on that later. The ins and outs of the TCP/IP protocol, which has a pretty complex specification, will not be described in this book. If you want to learn a lot more about TCP/IP, you can read about it from various sources on the World Wide Web. Most notably, the InterNIC source at *http://ds.internic.net* holds a vast array of information describing the Internet protocols in existence today and proposed for the future.

IP Addresses

The most basic thing you need to know about the Internet is that every machine hooked up to the Internet has at least one Internet address. This Internet address is how different computers hook up to each other. Given one machine's Internet address, or *IP address*, you can send and receive streams of data to and from that machine.

Actually, that's not entirely true. Only computers that have software set up to "listen" for your data on the network will talk to you. Furthermore, some machines can be shielded from contact altogether by *firewalls*. A firewall is something like a network bottleneck that may or may not allow your machine access to other machines on the other side of the firewall, according to whether or not the security policies of the firewall allow public access. Firewalls are set up to maintain security within a subset of the Internet. For example, you cannot reach most of the computers within the U.S. Department of Defense. Understandably, the maintainers of the U.S. military's computer system don't want just anyone to be able to reach their computers, especially if the computers trying to contact them are controlled by someone perceived as hostile to the military's interests. Many corporations also maintain firewalls so that people outside the corporation can't access their computers and get sensitive information out of them.

Rest assured that there are many, many computers out on the Internet that actually do want your computer to connect to them so that you can find information, update data stored on those systems, or interact with some software like a chat network. When you contact these systems using your Java applications or applets, you do it using one of the remote machine's IP addresses.

An IP address is a 32-bit number. That's pretty simple. When they are passed around within Java programs, IP addresses are stored in an array of four bytes. The most significant byte is stored at array index zero, and the least significant in array index three. By convention, when you write out an IP address as a string, you also split up the number into four separate bytes, writing the most significant byte first and ending with the least significant byte. Each byte is separated from the others by a period, like this:

```
192.176.7.45
```

which is read as, "one ninety-two dot one seventy-six dot seven dot forty-five." Boy, that's a real mouthful! Imagine what a pain it was and what problems were often caused by the early users of the Internet who tried to tell each other the IP addresses of their machines.

"Hi, Bob! Why don't you connect to my machine and download my proposal for us to get rich? The IP address is two seventy-seven dot seven dot six twenty-seven dot two—no wait...that's dot seven."

"Seven twenty-seven dot what?"

"No, two seventy-seven"

"What?"

"Huh?"

No kidding, trying to remember all those numbers was a real problem for those Internet users. So, the Internet wizards convened and came up with a scheme whereby you could name individual machines (or, more specifically individual IP addresses) using more human-readable strings. And those are the machine names you see commonly in URLs, such as

```
http://www.microsoft.com/visualj
```

The part that reads "www.microsoft.com" is the *machine name* of a machine somewhere within Microsoft's benevolent empire. You could also use this URL, which would get you the same thing:

```
http://198.105.232.30/visualj
```

See, the machine name "www.microsoft.com" is a synonym within the Internet for the actual IP address "198.105.232.30."

The InetAddress Class

Within Java, objects of the InetAddress class of the java.net package represent individual IP addresses on the Internet. In order to connect to

Networking in Java

another computer on the Internet, you must first create an InetAddress object that refers to that computer.

The InetAddress class' static method getByName( ) creates a new InetAddress object for a given Internet machine name or a valid IP address, as these examples demonstrate:

```
InetAddress inetaddr = InetAddress.getByName("www.microsoft.com");
```

and

```
InetAddress inetaddr = InetAddress.getByName("198.105.232.30");
```

(Note that in the second example the IP address was passed in as a string, using the same byte ordering and dot separation described earlier.) If the machine name cannot be looked up, for example, if it is not a valid name on the Internet, then an UnknownHostException is thrown by this method.

The getAllByName( ) method is similar to the getByName( ) method. The difference is that the getAllByName( ) returns all the IP addresses associated with a given machine name. Remember, a single IP address can have multiple machine names registered with it on the Internet, and a single machine can (and often does) have multiple IP addresses. Thus, it is often the case that a single machine may have multiple IP addresses on the Internet. The getAllByName( ) method returns an array of IP addresses, each of which refers to the same machine that a given machine name refers to. Here's a simple sample application that, given a machine name, prints out all the InetAddresses associated with that machine:

```
import java.net.*;

public class ShowAddresses {
    public static void main(String[] astrArgs) {
        // Each command-line argument is the machine name of a machine
        // to look up on the Internet.
        for(int ii=0 ; ii< astrArgs.length; ii++) {
            try {
                InetAddress[] inetaddrs =
                    InetAddress.getAllByName(astrArgs[ii]);
                System.out.println(astrArgs[ii] + ":");
                for(int jj=0 ; jj<inetaddrs.length ; jj++)
                    System.out.println(inetaddrs[jj]);
            } catch (UnknownHostException e) {
                System.out.println("Error connecting to " + astrArgs[ii]);
            }
        }
```

        }
}

which produces this output when run with the command-line "jview ShowAddresses www.microsoft.com java.sun.com www.javasoft.com":

```
www.microsoft.com:
www.microsoft.com/198.105.232.6
www.microsoft.com/198.105.232.7
www.microsoft.com/198.105.232.30
www.microsoft.com/198.105.232.10
www.microsoft.com/207.68.137.7
www.microsoft.com/207.68.137.8
www.microsoft.com/207.68.137.9
www.microsoft.com/207.68.137.34
www.microsoft.com/207.68.137.35
www.microsoft.com/207.68.137.36
www.microsoft.com/207.68.137.40
www.microsoft.com/207.68.137.41
www.microsoft.com/207.68.137.42
www.microsoft.com/207.68.137.43
www.microsoft.com/198.105.232.4
www.microsoft.com/198.105.232.5
java.sun.com:
java.sun.com/206.26.48.100
www.javasoft.com:
www.javasoft.com/206.26.48.100
```

which demonstrates that the machine name "www.microsoft.com" has several IP addresses associated with it on the Internet, while the two machine names java.sun.com and www.javasoft.com each have only one IP address associated with them.

Once you have a valid InetAddress object in hand, there's a few things you can do with it. The getAddress( ) method returns an array of four bytes that is the IP address being referred to by the InetAddress object. As mentioned previously, the most significant byte of the 32-bit IP address is stored in the zero-th element of this array, and the least significant byte of the IP address is stored in the third element of this array.

The getHostName( ) method returns one of the machine names associated with the IP address in a string. If the InetAddress was created using an actual machine name, then that machine name will be returned by this method. If the InetAddress was created in some other manner, then the machine name returned will be one of the valid machine names associated with the IP address referred to by the InetAddress object.

Networking in Java

One other very useful method of the InetAddress class is the static getLocalHost( ) method. This method returns an InetAddress referring to the IP address of the machine the application or applet is currently running on. For example, if you are running a Java application from a machine with the name "cyrano.supercorp.com" (a made-up name), then this code

```
InetAddress inetlocal = InetAddress.getLocalHost();
String strLocalHostName = inetlocal.getHostName();
System.out.println(strLocalHostName);
```

will, predictably, produce this output

```
cyrano.supercorp.com
```

Ports in Cyberspace

An IP address is, conceptually, a switchboard in cyberspace. That is, an IP address refers to an array of connection points, called *ports*, that other computers on the Internet can connect to. Figure 9-1 illustrates this concept.

When you communicate between two machines on the Internet, you set up a virtual communication line between any two ports on the Internet. You can connect a port on one machine to a port on another machine, or a port on your machine to another port on the same machine. In fact, the only way to perform interprocess communications in Java, other than using

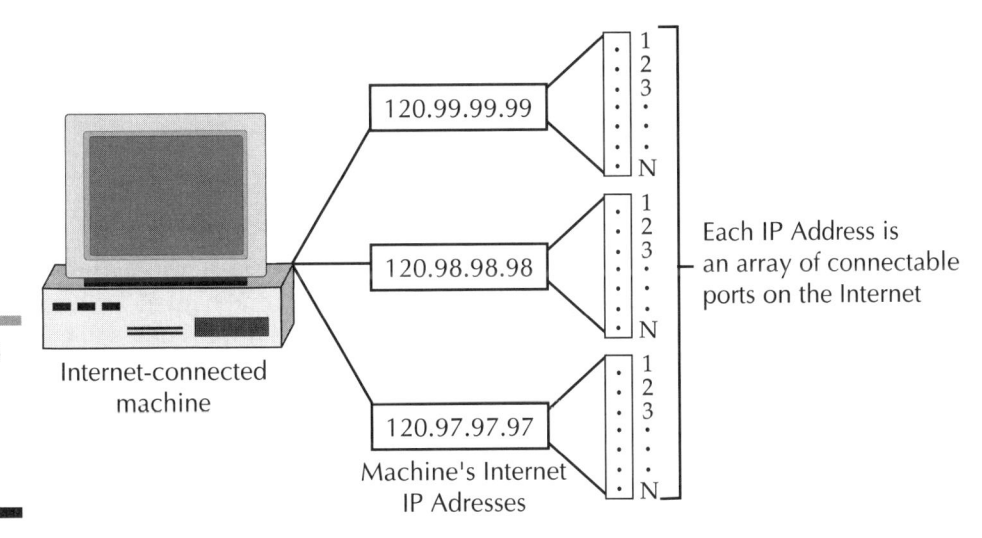

An IP address is an array of ports in cyberspace
Figure 9-1.

native methods or COM/DCOM objects, is through sockets on the same machine. It is intriguing to realize that as far as programming goes, the programming techniques you use to communicate between two processes on the same machine are the same techniques (and usually the same exact code) that you use to communicate between two processes running on computers in different hemispheres of the globe!

The term *socket connection* is used to describe the virtual circuit set up between any two ports on the Internet. The word "socket" is used because individual ports can be seen as sockets that you can string a data wire between. Perhaps a better analogy than sockets and wires is that of telephone lines. Each port on the Internet can be seen as a single telephone. When you "call" from one port to another, you set up a communication line between the two telephones. Anything you say into one receiver can be heard on the other end. The connection terminates when one side or the other "hangs up." The term *socket* is used to refer to any port on the Internet.

Creating Socket Connections

So, to set up a socket connection between your machine and another machine on the Internet, you need an InetAddress object that refers to the remote IP address. The previous section describes how to create InetAddress objects. Once you have an InetAddress you want to connect to in your hot little hands, you have only to create a Socket object from it to achieve a socket connection in Java.

Objects of the Socket class represent socket connections over the Internet in Java. To create a socket, you use the new operator to generate it. Pass the InetAddress and the port number of the address you want to connect to, and the Socket class constructor will set up the socket connection. Note that you need to pass in the port number you want to connect to on the remote machine. Here's an example:

```
InetAddress inetaddr = InetAddress.getByName("www.microsoft.com");
Socket sock = new Socket(inetaddr, 80);
```

This example creates a socket connection between some port on your local machine and port number 80 on the machine named "www.microsoft.com" somewhere in cyberspace. Actually, this example code will connect you to Microsoft's central World Wide Web server. If you wrote a program that could "speak" the HTTP protocol, then at this point you could download HTML documents or whatever else was stored up on Microsoft's Web server.

Remember that a socket connection on the Internet exists between two ports: one on your local machine and one on the remote machine. The Socket class constructor only requires the port number of a port to connect to on the remote machine. The Socket class assumes that you don't care which port number you use on the local machine, and so chooses some unused one on the local machine when it sets up the socket connection. Indeed, there is almost no situation that would require you to know which local port was being used when setting up socket connections.

Socket Communications

Once you have a Socket object, you can start passing data from your application and receiving data from whatever application is connected to the remote port on the other end of the socket connection. When you pass data through the socket connection, you use an output stream that is handed to you by the Socket object. The Socket class method getOutputStream( ) returns an output stream. When you write bytes to that output stream, those bytes are transferred over the Internet to the program connected to the other end of your socket connection.

Note that all communications are through streams. These streams are, as far as your programming is concerned, no different than file output streams. That is, you use the same code to write data out to a file that you would to write that same data out to a socket connection. This is one of the most time-saving and convenient aspects of the Java classes. You don't have to learn a new API or any new classes to actually send data over the Internet.

The Echo Example

A few of the port numbers on the Internet are reserved for specific uses. They don't have to be set up to actually perform all those specific functions, but most do. For example, port number seven is reserved for *echoing*. Whenever you connect up to another machine's port number seven, on any IP address, any data you send through the socket connection will be *echoed* back to you. This is a testing mechanism that is built into the Internet so that you can make sure you have valid network connections and your Internet software is working correctly.

The example Java application below is a simple echo client. Given a machine name or IP address (in dotted format) on the command line, this program connects to that machine's port number seven. Anything you type into the keyboard is copied onto the socket connection, and then the program waits for some response. Of course, since you're hooked up to an echoing port on the remote machine, the bytes you get back should be the same characters you just typed into the keyboard. Using just the InetAddress and Socket classes described previously, this echo client is very easy to create.

Note that not all machines on the Internet actually have an echo server hooked up to the machine's port number seven. If you're using the Windows 95 operating system, you may notice through experimentation with this program that you cannot connect this echo client program up to your computer. That's OK. Most Internet machines actually do implement the echo port. Try this program connecting to "www.microsoft.com" or "www.javasoft.com", and you'll see the expected results: anything you type into the keyboard will be repeated back to you on the screen.

Here's the echo client Java application:

```java
import java.io.*;    // needed for the stream classes.
import java.net.*;   // needed for the Internetworking classes.

public class EchoClient {
    public static final int ECHO_PORT = 7;

    public static void main(String[] astrArgs) {
        // The first (and only) command-line argument is the machine name
        // or IP address (in dotted-format) of the machine to connect to.
        if(0 == astrArgs.length) {
            System.err.println("Usage Error: \n EchoClient <machine-name>");
            System.exit(-1);
        }

        PrintStream out = null;
        DataInputStream socket_in = null;
        DataInputStream user_in = new DataInputStream(System.in);
        try {
            InetAddress addr = InetAddress.getByName(astrArgs[0]);
            Socket sock = new Socket(addr, ECHO_PORT);
            out = new PrintStream(sock.getOutputStream());
            socket_in = new DataInputStream(sock.getInputStream());
        } catch (Exception e) {
            System.err.println("Error:\n Connecting to remote port: " + e);
            e.printStackTrace(System.err);
            System.exit(-1);
        }

        // For each input line, write it out to the socket, then read the
        // socket's response. If user types "QUIT", then quit.
        try {
            boolean fDone = false;
            while(!fDone) {
                String str = user_in.readLine();
                if("QUIT".equals(str)) {
                    fDone = true;
                    break;
                }
```

```
                    out.println(str);
                    String strResponse = socket_in.readLine();
                    System.out.println("From the socket: " + strResponse);
            }
        } catch (Exception e) {
            System.err.println("Error:\n Problem with communications: " + e);
            e.printStackTrace(System.err);
            System.exit(-1);
        }

        try {
            if(null != out)
                out.close();
            if(null != socket_in)
                socket_in.close();
            user_in.close();
        } catch (Exception e) {
            System.err.println("Error:\n Problem closing the socket: " + e);
            e.printStackTrace(System.err);
            System.exit(-1);
        }
    }
}
```

Blocking Sockets

The echo client program uses an input stream and an output stream that are attached to the echo socket connection. Now, you are most probably aquainted with the fact that network connections are not always very speedy. If you are connected to the Internet, for example, through a 28.8 modem like most home users of the Internet, then you know that Internet communications can sometimes be downright slow. Of course, they are much slower for accessing data than the average file system would be.

When you read data from an input stream attached to a socket connection, then any read( ) operations you perform on that input stream will *block* until data is fully read over the socket. This means that the thread that called read( ) will wait until the requested data is transferred over the Internet to your machine. Sometimes, that can be an appreciable wait. For example, if you tried to read 10,000 bytes from a socket in one call to read( ), the read( ) call will not return until all 10,000 bytes are downloaded to your machine (several seconds if using a 28.8 modem), or until the socket connection is broken from the other side.

If the socket connection is broken from the other side, then the call to read( ) will throw an EOFException, indicating that the socket has closed. The code from the EchoClient application class could be rewritten to handle this situation like this (the bold lines are lines that have been added to the program:

```
...
        // For each input line, write it out to the socket, then read the
        // socket's response. If user types "QUIT", then quit.
        try {
            boolean fDone = false;
            while(!fDone) {
                String str = user_in.readLine();
                if("QUIT".equals(str)) {
                    fDone = true;
                    break;
                }

                out.println(str);
                String strResponse = socket_in.readLine();
                System.out.println("From the socket: " + strResponse);
            }
        } catch (EOFException eEOF) {
            System.out.println("Socket has been closed from the other side");
            fDone = true;
        } catch (Exception e) {
            System.err.println("Error:\n Problem with communications: " + e);
            e.printStackTrace(System.err);
            System.exit(-1);
        }
...
```

Similarly, when writing data to a socket connection through the attached output stream, then the call will block until all data is written out to the socket. If the socket is closed from the other side of the connection during a call to write( ), then an IOException will be thrown. To handle this situation in the echo client application, this catch block is added to the try/catch block surrounding the socket_out.println( ) call after the catch of the EOFException:

```
...
} catch (IOException eWrite) {
    System.out.println("Socket was closed from other side during write( )");
    fDone = true;
...
```

Sending and Receiving Nonguaranteed Data

All the information about socket connections and Internet communications given thus far is only partly true. That's because it all presents socket communications as guaranteed streams of bytes. Well, that's only partly true. It is true that if you follow the code presented thus far, it will act as described: any data you send to a remote port will be received on the other side, in order. There are circumstances where you don't need to send data like that, however. There are situations where you don't need to guarantee your data gets to the other side, or where you don't need to guarantee your data gets to the other side in order.

Consider, for example, that you made a simple program that transmitted the exact atomic time to the other end of a socket connection, assuming you had that kind of information available. You are going to send out the time in some format of packed bytes across the output stream attached to your socket connection. Every second, you send out a bunch of bytes representing a clock tick. In this case, you don't really need your individual packets of data arriving at the other side of the socket connection in the exact order you sent them. That is, if you send out the clock tick for 12:00:01, and then a second later you send out 12:00:02, you don't really care if the other side gets 12:00:01 before 12:00:02. By the time 12:00:02 goes out, 12:00:01 is obsolete, so you don't really care if the other side receives it at all.

In cases like these, you don't have to use guaranteed socket connections (called *TCP* connections). The other type of socket connection you can create is a *datagram socket connection*. In a datagram socket connection, each packet of data is individually addressed and sent out. The same packets are received on the other end without regard to whether or not the other packets have arrived, or if copies of the same packet arrive multiple times at the other end.

Part of the definition of how the Internet works includes the fact that a single packet of data is not guaranteed to arrive at its destination, and that multiple copies of a single packet may end up at the destination. TCP socket connections are designed so that each packet of data is individually numbered. When the destination port receives a packet out of order, it waits until preceding packets arrive before handing the received packets to your program. When a packet never arrives, the socket connection asks the sending port to send it again. When duplicates arrive, they are ignored. Datagram sockets, however, don't number individual packets, and don't check to make sure they arrive, nor do they detect when a duplicate arrives at the destination. Again, for some applications on the Internet, it's OK for these situations to occur.

The "cost," in terms of time and network traffic, for TCP (guaranteed) socket connections is higher than that for datagram socket connections. So you can see that, when possible, it is sometimes advantageous to use datagram instead of TCP socket connections. The clock example described above is one example of when using a datagram socket is preferable to using a TCP socket connection.

One overloaded version of the Socket class constructor exists so that you can create datagram sockets. This constructor has the signature

```
public Socket(InetAddress addr, int port, boolean stream);
```

If the stream parameter is true, then a TCP socket connection is created. If it is false, then a datagram socket connection is created.

Creating Internet Servers

The previous example, the echo client Java application, works by connecting up to the seventh port of another Internet machine. This program will only work, however, if there is an echo *server* program attached to the seventh port on the remote machine. A server is a program that listens to a socket, waiting for an incoming connection. Using the telephone analogy to sockets given previously, a server program is like the person waiting by the phone for you to call. If there's no such server program present, its like trying to make a call to a phone that no one answers.

If, for example, you try to make a connection to a port on a machine that has no server program waiting for your connection, you will get an IOException thrown. A printout of such an IOException would look something like this, which was generated by trying to connect the EchoClient program to a port where no server program was waiting for connections:

```
Error:
 Connecting to remote port: java.net.SocketException: connect
```

The ServerSocket Class

A special class, the ServerSocket class, is used to create *listening* sockets in Java. A server socket is attached to a local Internet port. The server socket sits on the local port, waiting for remote connections. When a remote connection is received, the server socket transfers the connection to a different local port, and can be set up to wait for yet another remote connection.

Networking in Java

Transferring the connection to another local port is critical for server sockets to work correctly. It is like when you call into some office on your telephone, say your dentist's office. Generally, you'll receive the receptionist. Rather than asking the receptionist all your important dental questions, you ask to talk to the dentist. At that point, the receptionist transfers you to another line so that he can answer other incoming calls.

The server socket is analogous to the receptionist in this case. Rather than connect up to a single incoming socket connection on the port, the server socket transfers the connection to a different port so that other connections can be received on the same port. This is why some port numbers can be reserved for specific protocols on the Internet. The echo port, port seven, generally has a server program listening for connections. When a remote connection is made, the server transfers it to another port and starts listening for other connections, still on port number seven.

Server Programs in Java

Generally, most server programs in Java look pretty much the same. The main server program thread controls a server socket in some loop, repeatedly listening for and connecting to incoming connections. For each incoming connection, the server program spawns an additional thread to actually handle the communication with the individual client. For the most part, the main application is one class, and an additional class is created to handle individual connections.

Here, for example, is one possible implementation of an echo server. If you run this Java application on your local machine, the EchoServer class will create a server socket that waits for incoming connections on port number seven, using the ServerSocket class method accept( ). When a connection is received, then the EchoServer class creates an echo client handler to handle that individual connection. Note that the echo server creates a main window that displays the current number of connections and the local server's machine name.

```
import java.net.*;
import java.awt.*;
import EchoClientHandler;

public class EchoServer extends Frame {
    private static int ECHO_PORT = 7;
    private static String m_strServerName;
    private static int m_cClients;
    private static EchoServer m_f = null;
    private static ServerSocket sock;
```

```java
// main program creates an EchoServer that handles display
// of the server's machine name and the number of connected clients.
public static void main(String[] astrArgs) {
    try {
        sock = new ServerSocket(ECHO_PORT);
        m_cClients = 0;
        m_strServerName = InetAddress.getLocalHost().getHostName();
    } catch (Exception e) {
        System.err.println("Error:\n Problem creating the ServerSocket: " +
            e);
        e.printStackTrace(System.err);
        System.exit(-1);
    }

    // Create frame that will display local server and number
    // of connections.
    m_f = new EchoServer();
    m_f.resize(300, 200);
    m_f.repaint();

    while(true) {
        try {
            Socket s = sock.accept();
            new EchoClientHandler(s);   // class to handle connection.
            m_cClients++;
            m_f.repaint();
        } catch (Exception e) {
            System.err.println("Error:\n Problem listening for clients: " +
                e);
            e.printStackTrace(System.err);
            System.exit(-1);
        }
    }
}

public static void decrementClientCount() {
    m_cClients--;
    m_f.repaint();
}

public static void shutdown() {
    System.out.println("Shutting down...");
    System.exit(-1);
}

public EchoServer() {
    super("EchoServer Application");
}
```

Networking in Java

```java
        public void paint(Graphics g) {
            FontMetrics fm = g.getFontMetrics();
            g.drawString("Server: " + m_strServerName + "\n" +
                    "Clients: " + m_cClients, 10, 10);
        }

        // Handle WINDOW_DESTROY events by calling shutdown().
        public boolean handleEvent(Event evt) {
            if(evt.id == Event.WINDOW_DESTROY) {
                shutdown();
                return true; // never gets here, but need this line to compile.
            }
            return false;
        }
    }
```

The EchoClientHandler class maintains a daemon thread whose job it is to constantly read from the input stream attached to a socket connection, and repeat back the same bytes to the output stream attached to the same socket connection. The background thread is a daemon thread so that it will be destroyed automatically when the Server program shuts down.

```java
import java.net.*;
import java.io.*;

public class EchoClientHandler implements Runnable {
    // State is a Socket, handed to constructor.
    private Socket m_sock = null;

    // Constructor just stores away Socket reference and creates
    // a background thread that runs on this method's run( ) method.
    public EchoClientHandler(Socket s) {
        m_sock = s;

        Thread t = new Thread(this);
        t.setDaemon(true);
        t.start();
    }

    public void run() {
        try {
            DataInputStream is = new DataInputStream(m_sock.getInputStream());
            PrintStream os = new PrintStream(m_sock.getOutputStream());
            while(true) {
                String str = is.readLine();
                os.println(str);
```

```
            }
        } catch (Exception e) {
            System.err.println("Error:\n Problem in client, killing: " + e);
            e.printStackTrace(System.err);
        }
        EchoServer.decrementClientCount();
    }
}
```

URLs and Protocols

When getting most data from servers on the Internet, the vast majority of transactions follow the same basic model:

1. Client connects to a specific server through a socket connection.
2. Client and server programs engage in some handshaking exchange that establishes exactly what information the client wants from the server.
3. Server hands the requested information to the client.
4. If client wants further information (and the protocol allows it), go to 2.
5. When client has all the information it wants from the server, the client and server socket connection is closed down by the client.

These five steps describe how most client/server transactions happen on the Internet, especially when looking at information on the World Wide Web. Take a look at a specific transaction. Say you want to get the HTML page served up by Microsoft's World Wide Web server about Visual J++. This information is available through Microsoft's WWW server, with the special unique identifier "visualj." Following the five steps given above, specifically as they apply to the HTTP protocol (the protocol of the World Wide Web), here's the transaction that would occur:

1. Your client program would create a socket connection to the Internet computer with the machine name "www.microsoft.com." You would connect to port 80, which is the port commonly reserved for the HTTP protocol. You've already read about how to do this. Here's a method that would make this connection as described:

```
public Socket makeHTTPConnection(String strServerName) {
    try {
        InetAddress addrServer = InetAddress.getByName(strServerName);
        return new Socket(addrServer, 80);   // 80 is the commonly reserved HTTP
                                             // port on the Internet.
    } catch (Exception e) {
        return null;
```

Networking in Java

```
        }
    }
```

2. After sending and receiving some identifying information indicating which server program and which client program are running, your client programs would issue this command:

    ```
    GET /visualj/ HTTP/1.0
    ```

    which tells the HTTP server that you want the resource identified by "/visualj." Note that the information exchanged about the server and client programs is mostly for bookkeeping, so that web administrators at Microsoft can have some idea of who is connecting to their servers.

3. Microsoft's WWW server at this point sends the "/visualj" HTML file to your client program over the socket connection. Preceding the actual content of the resource, the server will send some data specifying what type of data is included in this resource, its encoding (if any), the date the resource was created, etc. Your client program might use this data to properly decode the "/visualj" data.

4. Actually, step 4 from the list of client/server steps is always a no-op when using the HTTP protocol. That's because currently this protocol does not allow a client to request multiple data resources within the same connection. To get additional resources from the same server, your client program would have to establish yet another HTTP connection to Microsoft's Web server, which would follow steps one through five in pretty much the same way. So, on your program goes to step 5...

5. The client, after receiving all the "/visualj" data (which is actually an HTML file), would close the socket connection.

Many other information-receiving protocols also follow the same basic five steps. For example, the FTP protocol (file transfer protocol), follows the same basic steps. The connection made in step 1 is made pretty much the same way, although a different port number is used. The Internet port commonly reserved for FTP servers is port number 21. Steps 3 through 5 are also very similar when getting data from an FTP server.

Of course, step 2 is going to be quite a bit different when doing HTTP versus FTP. The handshaking that goes on is really the "meat" of the different protocols. In HTTP, this handshaking consists of exchanging some basic client and server program information (version numbers, program names, user's e-mail address if your client program chooses to share that information with the server, etc.), and the client issuing a "GET," "POST," or "HEAD" command to specify what information it wants from the server. In FTP, on the other hand, the protocol consists of very different looking commands. For example, to get the resource named "/some/cool/resource.zip" from an FTP server, the client program could issue this set of commands:

```
CD some
CD cool
GET resource.zip
```

which looks quite a bit different than the commands you issue to an HTTP server. Note that the two protocols have similar *functionality*, but the specifics of the two protocols are actually quite different.

URLs

As you probably know, the standard for identifying resources on the World Wide Web is called a URL: a uniform resource locator. Here's an example URL for the Visual J++ information title page on the Internet:

```
http://www.microsoft.com/visualj
```

In general, URL's are composed of three separate parts. First is the protocol used to actually access the information. In this example, the protocol is "http," and is always separated from the rest of the URL by a colon. The second part of the URL is the name of the machine where the server program that will give this information is running. The machine name is preceded by a set of two forward slashes and ends with another forward slash. In this example, the server name is "www.microsoft.com." Third is a resource identifier, which in this example would be "/visualj." The identifier part of a URL is technically referred to as a URI, or uniform resource identifier. URIs look like paths or file pathnames, using forward slashes between directory/subdirectory splits. Actually, URIs are generally interpreted as actual file pathnames or directory paths by the server program. That is, individual resources are stored somewhere on the local file system on the server machine, and the URI is a file pathname for the file a client program wants to download.

URLs provide a generic system for referring to resources on the World Wide Web. Using URLs, you can refer to resource files accessed through an HTTP server ("http://www.microsoft.com/visualj"), through an FTP server, a Gopher server, or any other type of common Internet server. Since URLs all take on the same basic form, they are easier to use and remember than by using a different syntax based on different protocol types.

In Java, URL class objects represent individual URLs. Given a valid URL object, you can use its public methods to actually download the data that

Networking in Java

the URL refers to. That is, if you created a URL for the Visual J++ title page on Microsoft's Web server, you can use that URL to download the Visual J++ HTML page. You don't have to open a socket connection by hand, or deal with input streams or output streams, or any of that technical stuff. Methods within the URL class exist that completely perform all five steps of the data access process described above.

This is an important time-saver: you never need program-specific code to deal with communicating using common protocols. Opening socket connections, reading from socket input streams, sending specific commands to the server—all these steps are completed for you automatically. Here's all the code you need to download Microsoft's Visual J++ title page from the Internet in Java:

```
URL urlVJ = new URL("http://www.microsoft.com/visualj");
Object obj = urlVJ.getContent();
```

Content Types

All resources identified by a URL have a *content type*. A content type describes what the resource is and the format of the data. For example, the "image/gif" content type says that a resource is an image, and its image data is encoded using the .GIF file format.

For example, this example program creates a URL using the "file:" protocol identifier. The server name in the URL is left blank, indicating that the local machine should be used. The URI part of the URL is the first command-line argument to the program. Note that the "file:" protocol identifier is not a standard protocol. It is an indication that the resource being referred to is a file on the local file system. This program uses the URL.getContent( ) method to actually open the file indicated on the command line, and the program writes the contents of this file to the System.out PrintStream. Here's the program code:

```
import java.io.*;
import java.net.*;

public class PrintOutText {
    // Only command-line parameter is a filename to open. Note that you must
    // leave off a drive letter. The program will assume it should use the
    // currently selected drive.
    public static void main(String astrArgs[]) {
        if(0 == astrArgs.length) {
            System.err.println("Usage Error:\n PrintOutFile <file path>");
```

```
                System.exit(-1);
            }

            Object obj = null;
            try {
                URL url = new URL("file://" + astrArgs[0]);
                obj = url.getContent();
                if((null == obj) || (!(obj instanceof InputStream))) {
                    System.out.println("Content could not be read: " + obj);
                    System.exit(-1);
                }
            } catch (Exception e) {
                System.err.println("Error:\n Unable to open file: " + e);
                e.printStackTrace(System.err);
                System.exit(-1);
            }

            // Read each line of the input file and write them out to
            // System.out
            DataInputStream is = new DataInputStream((InputStream)obj);
            try {
                String str = "";
                do {
                    System.out.println(str);
                    str = is.readLine();
                } while((null != str) && (str.length() != 0));
                is.close();
            } catch(IOException ioe) {
                System.err.println("Error:\n Reading from file: " + ioe);
                ioe.printStackTrace(System.err);
                System.exit(-1);
            }
        }
    }
}
```

With just slight modifications, this program can be made to read and print out any resource identified by a URL. Similar to how the PrintOutText program works, this program will connect to any URL and try to print out the contents. If the object returned by getContent( ) is not an output stream, then the object itself is returned, since the program doesn't know what to do with it. This could happen, for example, if the URL passed as the first command-line argument referred to a .GIF image file or an .AU audio file. In either case, the getContent( ) method actually reads in all the data in an Image or AudioClip object, as appropriate given the resource's content type.

```
import java.io.*;
import java.net.*;
```

Networking in Java

```java
public class PrintOutURL {
    // Only command-line parameter is a URL to open.
    public static void main(String astrArgs[]) {
        if(0 == astrArgs.length) {
            System.err.println("Usage Error:\n PrintOutURL <URL>");
            System.exit(-1);
        }

        Object obj = null;
        try {
            URL url = new URL(astrArgs[0]);
            obj = url.getContent();
            if((null == obj) || (!(obj instanceof InputStream))) {
                System.out.println("Content could not be read as text: " + obj);
                System.exit(-1);
            }
        } catch (Exception e) {
            System.err.println("Error:\n Unable to open file: " + e);
            e.printStackTrace(System.err);
            System.exit(-1);
        }

        // Read each line of the input file and write them out to
        // System.out
        DataInputStream is = new DataInputStream((InputStream)obj);
        try {
            String str = "";
            do {
                System.out.println(str);
                str = is.readLine();
            } while((null != str) && (str.length() != 0));
            is.close();
        } catch(IOException ioe) {
            System.err.println("Error:\n Reading from file: " + ioe);
            ioe.printStackTrace(System.err);
            System.exit(-1);
        }
    }
}
```

Getting the URL Contents by Hand

Instead of relying on the URL class' getContent( ) method to get and interpret the contents of a URL resource, what if you wanted to do that yourself? The URL class provides methods so that you can get access to the resource referred to by the URL object as an input stream of bytes.

The URL class method getURLConnection( ) will return a URLConnection object for the resource file identified by the URL object. A URL connection is pretty similar to a socket connection, at least conceptually. That is, given a URL connection, you can get an input stream and an output stream associated with that Internet resource. The difference is that, by the time you get the URLConnection object back from the call to getURLConnection( ), all the protocol handshaking and socket connecting has been completed for you. This is like getting the raw bytes of an Internet resource file without having to deal with all the protocol details.

You might want to get a URL connection if the resource data was in a format unknown to Java. For example, maybe you defined a new file format that describes a game of chess using raw bytes and numbers. When you download one of these files, whose content type is unknown to the java.net classes, you could open a URL connection and read the bytes into your internal data structures directly.

Here's how you create a URL connection and read in the bytes from the Internet resource in example code:

```
URL url = new URL(strResource);
URLConnection conn = url.getURLConnection();
conn.connect();
InputStream is = conn.getInputStream();
...
// read in resource contents.
...
is.close();
```

Note that the connection was opened in two steps. First, the URL connection was created from the URL. Second, the connection was opened using URLConnection.connect( ). In between these two calls, you can set various specifics for the URL connection that can be used by the connection while it is handshaking with and requesting the resource from the server. For example, some Internet protocols require user interaction. FTP is one such protocol, especially if the user must type in a password. For such situations, you would call the URLConnection object's allowUserInteraction( ) method.

Other protocols require you to send additional information to the server through the URL connection's output stream (returned by URLConnection.getOutputStream). For example, an HTTP "POST" request requires HTML form data, or some other type of data, to be sent to the server along with the request for the URL resource. You probably have filled out forms on the World Wide Web before. If you have ever wondered how the data you fill in the form gets to the HTTP server, this is how. The form itself is associated with a program running or ready to run on the HTTP server.

When the form is completed in your Web browser, the browser connects to the server and makes a "POST" request, and the URI passed to the server is an identifier associated with the form-processing program on the server machine. In addition, after the URI is sent, then the contents of the form are also sent.

So you can see that some protocols may require any number of bytes of *additional information* to be sent to the server. To send these extra bytes to a server using a URLConnection object, you open up an output stream using URLConnection.getOutputStream( ). However, before you can do this you must call the URLConnection method setDoOutput( ), which tells the URL connection whether or not you want to send additional information to the server over an output stream. Here's an example method code that sends some array of bytes to a server and returns the resulting input stream from a URL connection.

```
public InputStream getPostedDataInputStream(URL url, byte[] ab, int offset,
        int length) throws IOException {     // IOExceptions not caught for
                                             // code clarity.
    // Open connection and post data in ab array to it.
    URLConnection conn = url.openConnection();
    conn.setDoOutput(true);
    OutputStream os = conn.getOutputStream();
    os.write(ab, offset, length);
    os.close();

    // Note, unless allowUserInteraction( ) is called, you must
    /// close OutputStream before attempting to open InputStream
    // for URLConnections.
    return conn.getInputStream();
}
```

Resource Content Types
As indicated earlier, an Internet resource has a content type that tells what type of information it is, and what format it's in. In general, the content type is described using a string of the form "<type>/<subtype>." For example, .GIF images have the content type "image/gif." .AU audio files have the content type "audio/au." HTML file have the content type "text/html." And plain old text files have the content type "text/plain." Oh yes, you should also know that, by convention, any resource that is not any of the predefined content types uses the content type "application/octet-stream," and is read as a simple stream of bytes.

Once you connect a URLConnection object to the associated server, you can get the content type of the resource using the URLConnection method getContentType( ). In fact, there are several other general properties of resources you can get from the URL connection. These properties, along with the content type property, are generally sent across a socket connection from a server to a client before the actual resource data is sent. Each property is sent in text form, one per line. The format generally looks like this:

```
property-type: property value
```

The following table lists what properties are available through methods of the URLConnection class, and describes the methods that you use to get those properties.

Method	Description of Information Returned
getURL( )	Returns the URL from which this URL connection was created. Available at any time during the URLConnection object's lifetime.
getContentLength( )	Returns the length, in bytes, of the resource content. This is available after the connection has been made using URLConnection.connect( ). This information is only available for some resources. For example, most HTTP resource do have this information, while many FTP resources do not.
getContentType( )	Returns a string of the form "<type>/<subtype>" describing the type and format of the resource. All HTTP and FTP resources have this information available. Unknown binary data is given the type "application/octet-stream." Resources with unknown text data are given the content type "text/plain."
getContentEncoding( )	Returns a string describing any secondary content encoding that has been applied to the resource data. For example, the resource data may have been zipped. The string returned by this method describes the type of secondary encoding and can be used to decode the resource data.
Method	Description of Information Returned

Networking in Java

getExpiration( )	Many Internet resources have a "freshness date" applied to them, so you can know for how long they are valid. For example, a stock market quote may expire within 24 hours. A beta version of a technical specification may expire after six months.
getDate( )	Gets the date the resource was originally created.
getLastModified( )	Some servers and resources also maintain information about when the resource was last modified. Generally, this information is not very reliable, and is often not present.
getHeaderField( )	Returns any other protocol-specific property. Pass in the property name, and the string value of the property is returned. Alternatively, pass a zero-based integer *n*, and the value of the *n*th header property will be returned.
getHeaderFieldInt( )	Assumes that a property's value is an integer. That is, the header line will look like "property name: number." Gets any header line identified by the property name passed as the only parameter to this method, and returns the value as an integer.
getHeaderFieldDate( )	Gets a header property by name, assuming the value is a date. Pass the property name as the only property to this method, and the value will be parsed into a date, and an equivalent Date object will be returned.
getHeaderFieldKey( )	Returns the *n*th property name associated with the resource. Pass the integer *n* as the only parameter to this method.

Summary

The native "language" of the Internet is called *TCP/IP*. All machines hooked up to the Internet speak TCP/IP to each other. Each machine connected to the Internet also has one or more addresses, which identify an array of virtual *ports* where data packets can be sent from and received. The InetAddress class represents IP addresses within Java. A socket is a connection between two Internet ports. These ports can be on the same or on different machines.

To connect a socket to a remote Internet port, there needs to be a server program listening for new connections on that remote port. Examples of such servers are HTTP and FTP servers. You can make your own Internet servers using a ServerSocket object. This object listens for new connections on a given port, and returns sockets from its accept( ) method whenever a new connection is made.

A URL is a generically formatted "address" of a specific data resource on the Internet. This resource can be a file stored on a remote machine or a dynamically generated piece of information. For example, it could be a static HTML file, or the exact atomic time at the instance the URL was requested. A URL includes a protocol, a machine name (or IP address), and a URI that specifies which resource you want for the server. A URI looks like a file pathname, using forward slashes (/) instead of the backslash typically used in Windows machine pathnames.

The URL class represents individual URLs in Java. Using a URL, you can request the contents of the resource the URL refers to through the getContents( ) method. Alternatively, you can open a stream connection and download the data *by hand*, using the getInputStream( ) method. To give additional information to the protocol server (some protocols, such as HTTP, allow this), write the extra information to the output stream returned by the URL method getOutputStream.

CHAPTER 10

Database Programming in Java

The depth of tools for doing database programming you get by using Visual J++ presents something of an embarrassment of riches. There are no less than three separate and completely functional APIs available in Visual J++ for using relational database management systems (RDBMSs).

The easiest to use is Microsoft's Data Access Object (DAO) API. The Data Access Objects are a collection of COM objects you can use through the Java/COM bridge provided in Microsoft's Java Virtual Machine for Windows.

The DAO API is a programming interface for Microsoft's Jet database engine, which can query and edit Microsoft Access databases, common ISAM file-based databases, and ODBC data sources. And the API classes are very object-oriented, very easy to use.

The Remote Data Object (RDO) API, not to be confused with the DAO API, is yet another completely functional COM interface to ODBC databases. RDO is not quite as easy to use as DAO, but it is more powerful. The RDO objects provide you with a more direct interface to your ODBC database drivers and data sources. Applications and applets written using the RDO classes are also easier to distribute than the DAO objects, since they don't require the use of Microsoft's Jet database engine.

Both DAO and RDO are platform-specific solutions. DAO uses a Microsoft database engine, which must be licensed separately. Both DAO and RDO use the ODBC (Open Database Connectivity) DLL system, which is a Microsoft solution available almost exclusively on Microsoft Windows machines. Both of these APIs also use the Java/COM bridge, which is, as of the time of this book's printing, only available on Microsoft platforms.

The good people of JavaSoft have also developed a set of standard API classes for doing generic RDBMS programming in Java. Based on the ODBC API, the Java Database Connectivity (JDBC) API is a platform-independent standard Java API, able to be used on any machine that implements a Java Virtual Machine (JVM). Like in ODBC, database developers use RDBMS-specific JDBC database drivers written in Java (with a healthy amount of native code thrown in usually), that are exposed to a central driver manager. The JDBC solution is the most distributable and open standard for your Java applications and applets. Unfortunately, it is also much more difficult to learn than DAO.

So, you have three different APIs to choose from. The Visual J++ development environment allows you to program in all three. Unfortunately, the vast amount of online documentation that comes with Visual J++ does not include any documentation on the DAO and RDO APIs. There is not a lot of freely available information about these APIs available on the Internet, either. If you are a subscriber to the Microsoft Developer Network (MSDN), as many professional Visual C++ and Visual Basic programmers are, then you get the entire DAO and RDO software development kit (SDK) documentation included with your MSDN CDs. The DAO and RDO descriptions are, in their current form, written using Visual Basic as the target language, since DAO and RDO were originally developed for Visual Basic. In this chapter, you will be taking a close look at these two APIs from the Java point of view.

As for the JDBC API, the entire documentation and downloadable classes are available on the World Wide Web from JavaSoft. The JDBC API will be discussed briefly in this chapter so that you can compare it conceptually

Database Programming in Java

with DAO and RDO to see which of the three APIs you should be using for your projects. To find out all there is to know about JDBC, however, you'll have to visit JavaSoft's Web site at *http://splash.javasoft.com*.

Data Access Objects

The Data Access Objects are a collection of COM objects, arranged in a single COM library, that allow applications and applets to interact with Microsoft's Jet database engine. The Jet engine is a fine piece of componentry. It is the backbone of Microsoft's Access database product. It not only creates and manages databases using Access' own proprietary format files (*.MDB files), but it can also access and manage ISAM files and ODBC databases.

An ISAM file is a simple formatted database file, storing one database table per file, with possibly more files added for table indexes. Examples of ISAM-formatted database systems are dBase, Paradox, FoxPro, or even tabbed text files. The Jet engine is able to read, query, and modify these files just like its own proprietary format .MDB files. This allows you to create larger databases made up of many differently formatted database tables. The idea being that the database format shouldn't get in the way of your programming, since it's the data stored within the database that's really important.

ODBC database sources can be any sort of database at all. ODBC is an API developed by Microsoft to make database programming in Windows easier and more standardized. The same database API is used to access and modify databases of very disparate types. Local proprietary format database files, or remote network server systems like Oracle or Sybase all can be accessed through the ODBC API. The Jet engine is aware of and can "speak" to any type of ODBC database driver, and so through the Jet engine you can query and modify databases of almost any brand out there. In Java, the DAO API is your control panel, allowing you to programmatically interact with Microsoft's very powerful Jet database engine.

The DAO API is by far the easiest to use, the most object-oriented, and the most intuitive of the three database APIs available in Java. The DAO's simple set of Database, DBEngine, Table, Query, etc. classes are simple to understand, and will make your programming task a whole lot easier.

Redistribution of the Jet Engine

One word of caution about the Jet database engine: it's not free. Well, that is it is not free for you to distribute. In fact, your Visual J++ development system comes with a copy of the Jet database engine DLLs, COM objects, etc. So you can develop your DAO applications and applets that use the Jet database engine.

You will not be able to distribute the Jet engine DLLs to your users, however. Microsoft's requirements for distribution of solutions that use the Jet database engine and DAO objects are available on the Web at *http://www.microsoft.com/accessdev/accwhite/qalicen.htm*. What this requirements document states is that in order for a user to use a DAO solution you developed in Visual J++, that user must have installed one of Microsoft's products that comes with a run-time version of the engine. The Microsoft applications that are listed in that document are Microsoft Access, Microsoft Excel, Microsoft Office, Visual Basic, or Visual C++ (though this list is not necessarily inclusive of all Microsoft products that include such a run-time license). Once the user has installed one of these applications on their Windows system, then the Jet engine included in that product can also be used by your application. It stinks, but it's true.

Note that both the RDO and JDBC APIs do not have this kind of restriction. So, if you find that the restrictions on use of the Jet engine are too heavy for your project's distribution targets, then DAO is not the solution for you. If, on the other hand, you are developing a standalone or intranet solution whose target system(s) you know will have one of the Microsoft applications listed above installed on them, then DAO is probably what you will want to go with.

Creating the DAO Java/COM Classes

The Data Access Objects are a set of COM objects that implement an interface to Microsoft's Jet database engine. Chapter 7 explains in detail how to use COM objects from within Java using Microsoft's Java Virtual Machine for Windows. As that chapter tries to explain, use of COM objects is very easy in Visual J++. One thing you have to do when using COM in Java is to generate the "shim" classes that translate between the Java world and the COM world.

You must generate the Java/COM shim classes for the DAOs before you can use them in Java. To generate these classes, you must use the Java Type Library Wizard in Visual J++. This tool is located under the Tools menu, in Visual J++'s Main menu, by hitting the Java Type Library Wizard menu option. When you do this, the Type Library Wizard appears and asks you which COM library you'd like to generate Java/COM shim classes for. The Type Library Wizard dialog appears when you choose this option. Select the Microsoft DAO Object Library item from this dialog, making sure to click on the checkbox to create the Java/COM shim classes.

The .CLASS files for these classes are then automatically created, by the mechanism described in Chapter 7. These classes are now located in a package called *dao3032*. Note that the actual .CLASS files are created in your Windows directory, under the Java\TrustLib\dao3032 directory on your system by the

Database Programming in Java

Type Library Wizard. When distributing your Java application or applet that uses the DAO objects, you must make sure to distribute these .CLASS files in the appropriate directory structure (i.e., in a directory for a *dao3032* package).

Once you have generated these .CLASS files, you are ready to create Data Access Objects in Java.

The DBEngine Object

The DAO class that represents the Jet engine itself is the DBEngine class. Only one instance of this class exists in a JVM at a time. It is through this object that you get all the other database manipulation objects.

The DBEngine manages a collection of workspaces, and has a set of properties associated with it. These properties are the OLE Automation type of properties, which means they each have get and set methods in Java, as described in Chapter 7. A workspace is essentially a user session in the Jet database engine. Each user can have zero or more concurrent sessions, or workspaces, open in a Jet database engine at the same time.

This example program instantiates the Jet database engine's DBEngine object and interrogates its list of properties, which are returned by a DBEngine class method getProperties( ). Note that the DAO classes have their own definition of a Properties class, completely unrelated to the java.util.Properties class described in Chapter 11.

First, here's a class that can create a DBEngine object. This class is taken from the DAOSample, from the Microsoft samples in Visual J++'s InfoViewer. The DBEngine class can only be created by a License Manager object, because the Jet engine is a licensed piece of software. The License Manager is Microsoft's way of ensuring only those who are supposed to be using the engine are being allowed to use it. Here's the code for the dao_dbengine class:

```
// Create a DAO DBEngine object with the license
import dao3032._DBEngine;
import com.ms.com.*;

public class dao_dbengine
{
    // The static public method creates the DBEngine object
    static public _DBEngine create()
    {
        // The return value
        _DBEngine result;

        // Create the License Manager object
        ILicenseMgr mgr = new LicenseMgr();
```

```
            // Use the License Manager to create the DBEngine
            result = (_DBEngine) mgr.createWithLic(

                // The license key for the DAO DBEngine
                "mjgcqcejfchcijecpdhckcdjqigdejfccjri",

                // The CLSID for the DAO DBEngine
                "{00025E15-0000-0000-C000-000000000046}",

                // The aggregation IUnknown* punkOuter
                null,

                // The ctxFlag to create in inproc server
                ComContext.INPROC_SERVER
            );

            return result;
      }
}
```

This same code is available on your Visual J++ CD, under the InfoViewer's DAOSample sample applet. You should use this same class in all your DAO Java applications and applets to create an initial DBEngine object for you.

Now, to the program. This program lists an engine's currently running sessions, or workspaces, and the DBEngine's properties. Three of the properties have API methods for them: the .INI path, LoginTimeout, and Version properties:

```
import dao3032.*;

public class DBEngineProperties {
    public static void main(String[] astrArgs) {
        // Get the DBEngine object.
        _DBEngine engine = dao_dbengine.create();

        // Enumerate all workspaces.
        System.out.println( "Workspaces: Name, UserName" );
        Workspaces workspaces = DBEngine.getWorkspaces();
        for(int ii=0 ; ii<Workspaces.getCount() - 1 ; ii++) {
            Variant var = new Variant();
            var.putInt(ii);
            Workspace wrksp = Workspaces.getItem(var)
            System.out.println("   " + wrksp.getName() + ", " +
                    wrksp.getUserName());
        }
```

Database Programming in Java

```
        // Enumerate built-in properties.
        System.out.println("DBEngine.Version: " + engine.getVersion());
        System.out.println("DBEngine.Timeout: " + engine.getLoginTimeout());

        // Enumerate other properties.
        Properties props = engine.getProperties();
        for(int ii=0 ; ii<props.getCount() ; ii++) {
            Variant var = new Variant();
            var.putInt(ii);
            Property prop = Properties.getItem(var);
            System.out.println("DBEngine." + prop.getName() + ": " +
                prop.getValue());
        }
    }
}
```

This example demonstrates an important DAO programming truism: that there are a lot of collections objects in DAO. The Workspaces object and the Properties object are just two that you can see in this example. In fact, there are a lot more, as the Samples.txt file shows if you take a peek into it. There are collections calls for Tables, Queries, TableDefs, QueryDefs, Fields, Users, Groups, and on and on. The two for loops in the previous example demonstrated one way to use these collection objects, all of which have pretty much the same fingerprint. You can pass in an integer value, as a Variant object, into the collection's getItem( ) method. This will return the *n*th member of the collection.

Usually, in DAO, objects also have names. You can see that in the previous example the getName( ) method of the Workspace and Property classes were both called. You can also pass an object's name to a Collection object's getItem( ) method. The return variant will hold a reference to the object in the collection that matches the name you passed.

Default Workspace, User, and Password
There is always at least one workspace open whenever you create a DBEngine object. That workspace is called the *default workspace*. The default workspace is a workspace opened up using a default user name and default password. (As you can read in a following section, DAO has facilities for access protection by user accounts. Users' names and group names are stored with each individual database in DAO.)

To set the default user name and default password to use in the DBEngine object, use the DBEngine object's setDefaultUser( ) and setDefaultPassword( ) methods. You can see the signatures for these two methods in the Summary.txt file generated by the Type Library Wizard when the DAO Java/COM shim classes were created. This file is located in the same directory as the DAO shim class files. Usually, that's in WINDOWS\JAVA\TRUSTLIB\DAO3032.

The DBEngine object has a method called openDatabase( ), which is essentially the same thing as the Workspace class' openDatabase( ) method. The DBEngine's version of this method opens the database and creates a Database object in the default workspace. No user name or password is required since the default user and default password are used.

Workspaces

A workspace represents one user's session with the Jet engine. It is through a workspace that you open or create databases. So, to open a database using DAO objects, you first create a DBEngine, then you create a workspace, then you open or create the database within the workspace.

Creating a Workspace

By creating a workspace, you are essentially signing on as a new user (or re-signing on) with the DBEngine. The Workspace object is your session with the DBEngine. Note that a single user may have multiple different workspaces open at the same time. (As you can read about in this section, database transacting is on the workspace level, so if the same user wants to open and do transactions with databases that are independent of each other, that user must have two different workspaces, one for each independent transaction.)

The DBEngine's method CreateWorkspace( ) is used to create new workspaces. The method takes three string parameters: the name to use for the new workspace, the name of the user whose workspace is being created, and the password of that user. (The user and password must have been previously created using the Workspace method CreateUser( ).) This sample code creates a new workspace for a particular user:

```
public Workspace makeUserWorkspace(String strWorkspaceName) {
    // m_strUsername and m_strPassword are class variables that have been
    // previously filled in with the user's name and password.
    return m_dbengine.CreateWorkspace(strWorkspaceName, m_strUsername,
        m_strPassword);
}
```

Opening and Creating Databases

It is through a workspace that you open and create databases in the DAO API. To open an existing database, use the Workspace class method OpenDatabase( ). This method takes a string name for the database, a couple

Database Programming in Java

of boolean flags, and some additional information used for opening ODBC database sources. Here's the signature of this method:

```
public Database OpenDatabase(String strDBName, Variant varFExclusive,
        Variant varFReadOnly, Variant varStrODBCSource);
```

The strDBName is either a filename for an ISAM or MS Access database file to open, or the name of an ODBC data source that has already been set up with the ODBC administration program in the Windows control panel. This parameter can also be blank ("") if the varStrODBCSource parameter is a simple string "ODBC". In that case, the ODBC administrator will automatically pop up, letting the user choose from a list of available ODBC data sources. This example code demonstrates how to do this:

```
Workspace wspace = m_dbengine.CreateWorkspace("UserSpace", m_strUsername,
        m_strPassword);

Variant varFExclusive = new Variant();
varFExclusive.putBoolean(false);

Variant varFReadOnly = new Variant();
varFReadOnly.putBoolean(false);

Variant varStrODBCSource = new Variant();
varStrODBCSource.putString("ODBC");

Database myDB = wspace.OpenDatabase("", varFExclusive, varFReadOnly,
        varStrODBCSource);
```

The varFExclusive parameter is true if the database is to be opened in exclusive mode. Note that the OpenDatabase( ) method call will fail if another user has already opened up the indicated database in exclusive mode, or if you are trying to open up a database in exclusive mode that another user has opened in either exclusive or nonexclusive mode.

The varFReadOnly parameter is true if you only want the database to be opened for reading. If you want the database opened for reading or writing, make this parameter false.

The varStrODBCSource is the ODBC connection string to use when opening ODBC data source. For example, you may need to specify a remote user name and password in this string when connecting to remote ODBC data sources. This parameter should be blank if the database name you supplied in the *strDBName* parameter is a database filename.

The DAO library of classes will only allow you to create new MS Access database files using the DAO objects. To do this, use the Workspace class' CreateDatabase method. This method takes three string parameters. The first parameter is the filename for the file to create. The second is an integer that describes the sorting order for text and strings within the database. The third parameter is a collection of options, each of which is indicated by a constant. The constants are logically OR-ed together. Here is a simple example:

```
Variant varStrDBFilename = new Variant();
Variant varNCollatingOrder();
Variant varOptions = new Variant();

varStrDBFilename.putString(C:\\MyDB");
varNCollatingOrder.putInt(Constants.dbSortGeneral);
varOptions.setInt(Constants.dbEncrypt | Constants.dbVersion30);

 Database myDB = m_workspace.CreateDatabase(varStrDBFilename,
varNCollatingOrder, varOptions);
```

Only MS Access .MDB files can be created by the Jet database engine. Specifying a different file extension in the name parameter of this method will not change the fact that the file is still an Access file.

The various possible values of the collating order (called *locale*) parameter are defined in the Constants DAO interface. There are many different possible collating orders. For normal English, you use the *Constants.dbSortGeneral* value. Look at all the possible *dbSortXXX* constant values for this parameter in the summary.txt file. Other possible values let you sort based on the Dutch alphabet, Greek alphabet, Hebrew alphabet, Cyrillic alphabet, etc.

The varOptions parameter bears a little more explaining. There is a class in the DAO classes that only contains static final integer constant values. That class is the Constants class of the dao3032 package. All the various specific constants you need for different method calls are located in this class. In the last example, two options were specified in the varOptions parameter. These two options told the Jet engine to create an encrypted MS Access v3.0 format file. This table lists all the possible values that could be used with this method:

Constant	Description
dbEncrypt	Creates an encrypted form of the database, which can help if security is needed
dbVersion10	Creates an MS Access v1.0 format new database file
dbVersion11	Creates an MS Access v1.1 format new database file

Database Programming in Java

Constant	Description
dbVersion20	Creates an MS Access v2.0format new database file
dbVersion30	Creates an MS Access v3.0format new database file

If the encryption option is not present, the database will not be encrypted. All the dbVersionXX constants tell which MS Access format to use. Only one of these four can be used at the same time. If none is specified, the Jet engine will create a database file in MS Access 3.0 format.

Listing Open Databases

Each workspace has a list of opened databases, which is given in a Databases property. As with all OLE Automation properties, when accessing this property in Java, you use the getXXX( ) method of the Workspace COM object. The actual value of this property is another COM object that implements a Databases interface:

```
dao3032.Databases dbs = myWorkspace.getDatabases();
```

The Databases interface is functionally similar to the Enumeration interface of the java.util standard core Java package. That is, it allows you to enumerate a list of other objects. In the case of the Databases interface, it allows you to enumerate a list of databases that are open in the workspace. The Count property of the Databases object returns the number of databases listed in the Databases object. The getItem( ) method of this object takes a zero-based index parameter in a variant and returns the index-th Database object opened in the workspace. Here is a quick example of how to enumerate all the open databases in a workspace:

```
// Assume myWorkspace has been initialized to a valid Workspace object
dao3032.Databases dbs = myWorkspace.getDatabases();

for(int ii=0 ; ii<dbs.getCount() ; ii++) {
    Variant varIndex = new Variant();varIndex.putInt(ii);
    dao3032.Database db = dbs.getItem(varIndex);

    // Do something with the Database...
}
```

The Various Collections

There are several collections within the DAO objects that are used the same way as the Databases object in the previous section. That is, each of these collections has a Count property that returns the number of items in the collection, and a getItem( ) method that you use to retrieve a reference to one of the items in the collection. So, each collection implements a getCount( ) method with this signature:

```
public int getCount();
```

And it also implements a getItem( ) method, although the return value type of this method is different for each collections type. In general, the signature will look like this:

```
public <type> getItem(Variant varIndex);
```

Each of these various collections only holds a particular type of object. For example, Databases objects hold a list of Database objects. Similarly, a TableDefs collection object holds only TableDef objects. A RecordSets collection object holds only RecordSet objects. You still use the same getCount( )/getItem( ) methods to retrieve any of the items in any one of these collections, but just remember that the types of items that are returned from the getItem( ) method are different for each different type of collection.

In later sections of this chapter, you will run across references to collections that will not have been mentioned previously. You can assume the interface to these collections is the same as the Databases interfaces, which are the same as the interfaces of all the collection types. The name of the collections object will also tell you the type of objects the collection holds. The Databases collection holds Database objects, and the RecordSets collection holds RecordSet objects, etc.

Databases and TableDefs

A relational database is made up by a set of *tables*. Each table is made of several *fields*. You can picture a table in your head as a columnated table of rows. Each column is one field in the database table, and each row is a single *record* in the table.

In DAO, each table in an opened database is described by a TableDef object. The TableDef describes the name and type of each field in the table. That is, it describes the type of data and the identifying name of each column in the table of records.

All the TableDef objects that describe the tables in a database are stored in a collection object, named TableDefs, that is a property of the Database object. You use this TableDefs object to enumerate all the TableDef objects in a database in the same way you use the Workspace object's Databases collection. That is, you use the getCount( ) and getItem( ) methods.

Database Programming in Java

The Fields of a TableDef

The TableDef object's getFields( ) method returns a collection object filled with Field objects. Each Field object describes one of the fields (columns) defined in the table. Not only TableDef objects have fields. In the Jet database engine, there is also such a thing as a QueryDef, which defines a Jet engine query. QueryDef objects have fields in the same way that TableDef objects do. When you perform a query or look at the individual records of a table in DAO, the records are presented in a RecordSet object. RecordSets also have Field objects, one for each field in the resultant record set.

The getName( ) method of the Field object returns the string name for the field. Note that you can refer to a Field object in its Fields collection either by an ordinal number or by the field's name:

```
// Assume myTableDef TableDef object was created correctly.
Fields flds = myTableDef.getFields();

// Find the first field in the Fields collection.
Variant var1 = new Variant();
var1.putInt(0);
Field f1 = flds.getField(0);

// Get the first field's name.
String strName = f1.getName();

// Find the field named "DOB".
var2 = new Variant();
var2.putString("DOB");
Field f2 = flds.getField(var2);
```

In the following section on record sets, you will see how to access the individual record field values using Field objects.

A field is described by its attributes. The various attributes a field can have are enumerated as part of the Constants interface in the DAO library. The getAttributes( ) method of the Field class returns an int that is an OR-ing of the various attribute values. The following table describes all the Field attribute values in the DAO Constants interface:

Attribute Value	Description
dbFixedField	The field size is fixed (default for Numeric fields).
dbVariableField	The field size is variable (Text fields only).

Attribute Value	Description
dbAutoIncrField	The field value for new records is automatically incremented to a unique integer that can't be changed (supported only for Microsoft Jet database tables). Convenient for use as an identifying number (key field) for each record in the table.
dbUpdatableField	The field value can be changed.
dbDescending	The field is sorted in descending (Z–A or 100–0) order (applies only to a Field object in a Fields collection of an Index object). If you omit this constant, the field is sorted in ascending (A–Z or 0–100) order (default).
dbSystemField	The field is a replication field (on a TableDef object) used on replicable databases and cannot be deleted.

The use and meaning of some of these attribute values have not yet been discussed. For example, the dbDescending attribute value only applies to fields in an index.

Here's an example use of a field's attributes: this sample application opens a DAO database, given a filename on the local file system, and reads in all the TableDefs and fields in that database. Note that, in the interest of more readable code, exception handling has been omitted.

```
import dao3032.*;

public class DatabaseFieldAttributes {
    public static void main(String[] astrArgs)
            throws com.ms.com.ComException {
        // First and only arg is a Jet database filename.
        if(astrArgs.length != 1) {
            System.err.println(
            "Usage Error:\n jview DatabaseFieldAttributes <database-filename>");
            System.exit(-1);
        }

        // Create the DAO DB engine using the license manager.
        ILicenseMgr mgr = new LicenseMgr();
        _DBEngine dbeng = (_DBEngine) mgr.createWithLic(
                "mjgcqcejfchcijecpdhckcdjqigdejfccjri",
```

Database Programming in Java

```java
            "{00025E15-0000-0000-C000-000000000046}",
            null, ComContext.INPROC_SERVER);

// Open the database indicated by the command-line filename for
// non-exclusive access.
Variant v1 = new Variant();
Variant v2 = new Variant();
Variant v3 = new Variant();

v1.putBoolean(false);
v2.putBoolean(false);
v3.putString("");

Database db = dbeng.OpenDatabase(astrArgs[0], v1, v2, v3);

// Get the list of TableDefs, for each one list all the
// fields and field attributes.
TableDefs tds = db.getTableDefs()
for(int iTable=0 ; iTable<tds.getCount() ; iTable++) {
    TableDef td = tds.getItem(iTable);
    System.out.println("Definition for table: " + td.getName());

    Fields fds = td.getFields();
    for(int iField=0 ; iField<fds.getCount() ; iField++) {
        Field f = fds.getItem(iField);
        System.out.print("\tField '" + f.getName() + "': ");

        int attribs = f.getAttributes();
        boolean fFirstAttribPrinted = false;
        if(0 != (attribs & Constants.dbFixedField))
            System.out.print( "dbFixedField   ");
        if(0 != (attribs & Constants.dbVariableField))
            System.out.print( "dbVariableField   ");
        if(0 != (attribs & Constants.dbAutoIncrField))
            System.out.print( "dbAutoIncrField   ");
        if(0 != (attribs & Constants.dbUpdatableField))
            System.out.print( "dbUpdatableField   ");
        if(0 != (attribs & Constants.dbDescending))
            System.out.print( "dbDescending   ");
        if(0 != (attribs & Constants.dbSystem))
            System.out.print( "dbFixedField   ");
    }
    System.out.println("\n");
}

db.Close();
        }
    }
```

Adding New Fields to a Table

Use the TableDef method CreateField( ) to add a new field to a DAO database table. When you create a new field in a table, you must specify the new field's name, type, and size. For some of the valid field types, the size is implicit, so your specified size is ignored. The signature of the TableDef method CreateField( ) looks like this:

```
public Field CreateField(Variant varStrName, Variant varIntType,
       Variant varIntSize);
```

The valid field types are defined in the Constants interface of the dao3032 package. The following table lists each of these constants, and describes each of them.

Field Type	Description
dbBoolean	Variant boolean type. The size parameter is ignored if you use this field type.
dbByte	Variant byte type. The size parameter is ignored.
dbInteger	16-bit integer type. The size parameter is ignored.
dbLong	32-bit integer type. The size parameter is ignored.
dbCurrency	A currency value is a type of value sufficient to store up to 11 digits before the decimal point, and four digits after the decimal point. In Java, the Variant.currencyVal( ) method returns a 64-bit integer value.
dbSingle	A single-precision floating point number. The size parameter is ignored.
dbDouble	A double-precision floating point number. The size parameter is ignored.
dbDate	A double-precision floating point value, which indicates the number of days since midnight, Dec. 30, 1899 (e.g., value of 1.5 would be noon, Jan. 1, 1900).
dbText	A String value field. The size parameter indicates the maximum length of the string value.

There are also dbLongBinary, dbMemo, and dbGUID field types.

Database Programming in Java

This example method creates a new field in the given TableDef. The new field has the name "DOB" and is of type *dbDate*. Once the new field is created in the TableDef, all the records of the table will have an empty value for this field.

```
public void addDOBField(TableDef td) throws com.ms.com.ComException {
    Variant varStrName = new Variant();
    Variant varIntType = new Variant();
    Variant varIntSize = new Variant();

    varStrName.putString("DOB");
    varIntType.putInt(Constants.dbDate);
    varIntSize.putInt(0);

    td.CreateField(varStrName, varIntType, varIntSize);
}
```

Record Sets: Looking at a Table's Records

To look at a table's records, you must create a record set from the table's TableDef method OpenRecordSet( ). There are also several different ways of creating record sets in DAOs. Following sections will describe the other types. This type of record set, created from a TableDef, can only be created from Jet engine (.MDB) databases or ISAM file databases.

The TableDef class' OpenRecordset( ) method takes two parameters. Both of the parameters are variants. The first parameter always has the same integer-variant value: *Constants.dbOpenTable*. (As following sections describe, other objects' implementation of the OpenRecordset( ) method accept different values for this parameter also. For the TableDef OpenRecordset( ) method, however, only the dbOpenTable value is accepted.)

The second Variant parameter describes the access rights you want placed on the table's records. There are three possible values when opening a TableDef record set. These values can be OR-ed together. The following table lists the values and describes each of them.

Option Value	Description
dbDenyWrite	Other simultaneous users of the same database may not update any of the record field values in this table while you have your record set open.
dbDenyRead	Other simultaneous users of the same database may not read any of the field values in this table while you have your record set open.

Option Value	Description
dbReadOnly	You may only examine the values of each record's fields in the record set. You may not update any of the field values.

Here's the signature of the TableDef method OpenRecordset:

```
public Recordset OpenRecordset(Variant varIntType, Variant varIntOptions);
```

Running Through a Record Set's Records

A record set represents a set of records in a table. While it exists, the record set is "positioned" at a particular record in the table. When the record set is first created, for example, the record set is positioned at the first record in the table. Use the Recordset methods MoveFirst( ), MovePrev( ), MoveNext( ), and MoveLast( ) to change the current record in the record set.

The Microsoft DAO sample included with Visual J++ demonstrates the use of these Recordset methods to navigate through a record set's various constituent records. You are encouraged to copy the DAO sample from the InfoViewer and look through its code. Here is a quick explanation of the sample.

When the DAOSample applet is started, the applet opens a Jet engine database named Sample Database.mdb. The applet creates a record set from the Employees table in this database. (Note that the Microsoft sample does not use the TableDef.OpenRecordset( ) method. It uses a similar method in the Database object to create a record set from the Employees table. The effect is exactly the same as using the TableDef class method OpenRecordset( ).)

Here is a copy of the action( ) method from this sample applet. The four interface buttons (First, Next, Prev, and Last) indicate which way the user wants to move through the record set. The action( ) method handles each one of these button actions.

```
public boolean action(Event  evt, Object  what)
{
    // Handle click on the First button
    if (evt.target == m_first)
    {
        // Move to the requested record
        recordset.MoveFirst();

        // Show that record
        m_form.showData();
```

Database Programming in Java

```
        // Event handled
        return true;
    }

    // Handle click on the Prev button
    if (evt.target == m_prev)
    {
        // Move to the requested record
        recordset.MovePrevious();

        // Show that record
        m_form.showData();

        // Event handled
        return true;
    }

    // Handle click on the Next button
    if (evt.target == m_next)
    {
        // Move to the requested record
        recordset.MoveNext();

        // Show that record
        m_form.showData();

        // Event handled
        return true;
    }

    // Handle click on the Last button
    if (evt.target == m_last)
    {
        // Move to the requested record
        recordset.MoveLast();

        // Show that record
        m_form.showData();

        // Event handled
        return true;
    }

    // Event not handled
    return false;
}
```

Using Fields to Examine Recordset Values

Like a TableDef object, a Recordset object has a Fields property. You get a reference to the Fields property using the Recordset object's getFields( ) method. The values of each Field object in the Fields collection are the field's values for the Recordset's current record.

For example, this sample code examines and prints out the values of a field named DOB in a Persons table in a database. Note that the variant date values must be converted to Java date values before being displayed.

```
public void showDOBField(Database db) throws com.ms.com.ComException {
    // Open a table named "Persons" from the database.
    Variant varStrPersons = new Variant();
    varStrPersons.putString("Persons");
    TableDef td = db.getTableDefs().getItem(varStrPersons);

    // Create a Recordset from the TableDef.
    Variant varIntType = new Variant();
    Variant varStrOptions = new Variant();

    varIntType.putInt(Constants.dbOpenTable);
    varIntOptions.putInt(0);

    Recordset rs = td.OpenRecordset(varIntType, varIntOptions);

    // For each record in the database...
    while(!rs.getEOF()) {
        Variant varStrDOB = new Variant();
        varStrDOB.putString("DOB");
        double dCOMDate = rs.getFields().getItem(varStrDOB).getValue();

        // Convert COM date to Java date.
        dCOMDate -= (365 * 70) // days difference b/t 1970 and 1900
            + 17 // Taking leap days into account
            + 1 // COM dates start on 12/30, Java dates on 1/1 => 1 diff
        dCOMDate *= MILLIS_PER_DAY;

        Date date = new Date(dCOMDate);

        // Print out the date.
        System.out.println("Next record's date: " + date);

        // Advance to next Recordset record.
        rs.MoveNext();
    }
}
```

Database Programming in Java

Updating Records

You can use a record set's Field objects to change individual record values in the database. The Field method setValue( ) will change the value of the field in the database. Before you can use this method, however, you must let the Recordset object know you are going to modify a field's value. So, use the Recordset Edit( ) method to indicate you are about to modify the field values of the current record.

Once you are done modifying individual field values, use the Recordset method Update( ) to commit all the field changes to the table in the database. If you don't call Update( ), all the changes you make in the field values for the current record will be lost. The three steps for modifying a record's field values in the database are

1. Call the Recordset's Edit( ) method once the current position of the record set is on the record you want to modify.
2. Modify each field's values using the setValue( ) method of the appropriate Field object. The Field objects are all located in the Recordset's Fields collection (returned from the getFields( ) method).
3. Commit the changes to the database by calling the Recordset method Update( ).

Creating Record Sets from Queries

More interesting than creating record sets from the full contents of a particular table, you can create record sets from the results of an SQL query statement, or from a stored Jet database query. The record sets created by these queries will only hold the records you want them to hold.

A QueryDef object represents an SQL database query in DAO. QueryDefs can either be saved with an opened database, or temporary QueryDef objects can also be created. Saved QueryDef objects are nice because you can reuse the same query in different database sessions. Queries that you plan on using often should be saved with the database. Queries that you only plan on using once or only plan on using during a single open session can be created dynamically. These are temporary QueryDef objects that are destroyed after the session ends.

The Database method CreateQueryDef( ) is used to create a new QueryDef. This method takes two parameters. Both parameters are passed as Variant objects. The first parameter is the name the query is saved under. Only queries that you plan on saving with the database should be given a name. For temporary queries, pass an empty Variant object. The second parameter is an SQL string that defines the query.

If you are not familiar with SQL (Structured Query Language), which is a standard database querying language in common use, you should familiarize yourself with it. All the Microsoft products that come packaged with the Jet database engine (except Visual J++ and the Office products) are bundled with some amount of documentation on SQL. Otherwise, you might want to pick up a book from your local technical book store or join the Microsoft Developer Network to learn more about SQL.

Here is an example code snippet that creates a named QueryDef with a simple SQL query in it:

```
String strSQL = "SELECT DOB from Persons";

// Assume Database variable db has been created correctly
Variant varStrName = new Variant();
Variant varStrSQL = new Variant();

varStrName.putString("SimpleSelectQuery");
varStrSQL.putString(strSQL);
QueryDef qd = db.CreateQueryDef(varStrName, varStrSQL);
```

Valid SQL query types include select queries, delete queries, append queries, update queries and table create queries. The only type of query that you can create a usable record set through, however, is a select query. In a following section devoted to the different types of QueryDefs, you can read about all the other types of DAO queries.

Once you have created your QueryDef object (using an SQL select statement), you can create a record set, which will be comprised of the records and fields defined by the SQL statement. For example, the SimpleSelectQuery example above will create a record set comprised of the DOB field from the Persons table. Only the fields explicitly named (or implicitly named using a wildcard "*" character) in the select statement will be included in the resultant record set:

```
// Create Recordset from the "SimpleSelectQuery" QueryDef defined in previous
// example.
Variant varIntType = new Variant();
Variant varIntOptions = new Variant();

varIntType.putInt(Constants.dbOpenSnapshot);
varIntOptions.putInt(0);
Recordset rs = qd.OpenRecordset(varIntType, varIntOptions);
```

Snapshot and Dynaset Recordset Types

Note that, in this code, the type parameter to the OpenDatabase( ) method has the value *Constant.dbOpenSnapshot*. When using a TableDef to open the records of a table in a record set, you may only use the *Constants.dbOpenTable* Recordset type parameter. But when opening a record set that is the result of an SQL query, there are two different possible types of record sets you may create.

A *dynaset* is a set of records that is updated dynamically. You may modify the field values of your dynaset records using the same mechanism that you use to modify the values of a record set generated from a TableDef. In addition, any changes to records in your dynaset made by other users are simultaneously updated in your dynaset records. For example, if you submit a query that finds all the DOB fields in the Persons table of your database, while at the same time another user is modifying values of the same field in the same table, then the records of your record set reflect those changes made by the other user as soon as they are made.

A *snapshot* is also a set of records. You can examine the field values of records in your snapshot record set; however, you cannot update those values. In addition, changes made by other users while you have your snapshot record set open will not be reflected in your snapshot's field values. As the name suggests, the snapshot is a static *view* of the records in your database at one moment in time, and those values cannot be changed.

To create a dynaset or a snapshot, you pass the appropriate Recordset type value to the QueryDef.OpenRecordset( ) method when opening the record set. In the previous example, in which the SimpleSelectQuery SQL statement was used to generate a record set, a snapshot of the database records was created by these lines of code:

```
varIntType.putInt(Constants.dbOpenSnapshot);
varIntOptions.putInt(0);
Recordset rs = qd.OpenRecordset(varIntType, varIntOptions);
```

Alternatively, you can create a dynaset from the same QueryDef by using the *Constants.dbOpenDynaset* value as the first parameter to the QueryDef.OpenRecordset( ) method, as this code demonstrates:

```
varIntType.putInt(Constants.dbOpenDynaset);
varIntOptions.putInt(0);
Recordset rs = qd.OpenRecordset(varIntType, varIntOptions);
```

In this example dynaset, you can update the values of the individual fields in the dynaset Recordset using the same Edit( ), modify, Update( ) mechanism that was demonstrated previously:

```
// Change the current "DOB" field's value by making it exactly one year later.
Field f = rs.getFields().getField("DOB");
Variant varVal = f.getValue();
varVal.putDoubleValue(varVal.getDouble() + 365.0);
f.setValue(varVal);
```

Saving QueryDefs in the Database

As stated earlier, you can store commonly used queries with the database using the DAO API. To do this, start by naming your QueryDef when you create it. If you do not pass a non-null name for the QueryDef object when you first create it, then the QueryDef will automatically be temporary, and it will be destroyed when the program ends.

In the previous SimpleSelectQuery example, the QueryDef was created with a string name:

```
varStrName.putString("SimpleSelectQuery");
varStrSQL.putString("SELECT DOB FROM Persons");
QueryDef qd = db.CreateQueryDef(varStrName, varStrSQL);
```

To store the QueryDef permanently in the database, you only need to append the newly created QueryDef to the database's QueryDefs collection:

```
QueryDefs qds = db.getQueryDefs();
qds.Append(qd);
```

And that's it. The QueryDef is permanently stored in the database. In a later session, you can generate the same QueryDef object again simply by looking it up in the QueryDefs collection:

```
// Get the saved QueryDef.
QueryDefs qds = db.getQueryDefs();
Variant varQueryName = new Variant();
varQueryName.putString("SimpleSelectQuery");
QueryDef qdSimpleSQL = qds.getItem(varQueryName);

// Generate a Snapshot of the query results at this time.
Variant varIntType = new Variant();
Variant varIntOptions = new Variant();

varIntType.putInt(Constants.dbOpenSnapshot);
varIntOptions.putInt(0);
Recordset rs = qd.OpenRecordset(varIntType, varIntOptions);
```

Executable Queries

The previous section dealt only with select queries. That is, it dealt only with queries made from SQL statements that began with "SELECT <fields>...". These types of queries only look data up in the database. There are several other types of SQL queries that actually perform actions on the database. However, these *executable queries* cannot be used to create a record set, since they never actually create one. That is, append queries and delete queries do not return a set of records. Nor do any of the other types of executable queries.

For example, this SQL statement deletes every record in a Persons table whose DOB field has a value less than 36,500 (roughly the beginning of the year 1910):

```
DELETE FROM Persons WHERE (DOB < 36,500)
```

You create a QueryDef object from this SQL statement in the same way you would create a select statement QueryDef:

```
// Assume Database db variable has been created correctly already.
Variant varStrName = new Variant();
Variant varIntOptions = new Variant();

varStrName.Empty();   // unnamed query, temporary.
varIntOptions.putInt(0);
QueryDef qdDeleteQuery = db.CreateQueryDef(varStrName, varStrOptions);
```

To run this executable query, which will cause all the indicated records to be deleted from the database, you use the QueryDef method Execute( ). This method takes an options parameter that describes how you want the query to be executed. The following table lists out the possible option values and describes each of them. Note that, like all other constant values in the DAO API, the value is defined in the Constants interface in the dao3032 package.

Option Value	Description
dbDenyWrite	Denies write permission to other users.
dbInconsistent	Allows inconsistent updates. For example, when joining two tables in a one-to-many relationship, it allows you to update the many-side key field to a value that does not occur in the one-side key field. This is the default action.
dbConsistent	Only permits consistent updates. For example, when joining two tables in a one-to-many relationship, does not allow you to update the many-side key field to a value that does not occur in the one-side key field.

Option Value	Description
dbSQLPassThrough	Passes the SQL statement straight through to the ODBC data source driver. Note that by default the DAO library will modify SQL statements before passing them through to underlying ODBC drivers, which can sometimes cut down on efficiency. This options tells the DAO engine not to do that.
dbFailOnError	Automatically rolls back all changes to the database if any error is encountered while executing the query. This is not the default action.
dbSeeChanges	Generates a run-time error if another user is editing data that you are modifying or deleting as a result of your executable query.

Other than a delete query, the other types of executable queries are update queries and append queries.

DAO Summary

The previous sections have briefly outlined the basic database capabilities of the DAO COM objects when using them from Java. The DAO API is a complete API, with many more functionalities and capabilities than can be handled within the scope of this book. After reading this section, you should have a good overview of the types of things that DAO gives you. Specifically, you should be aware that the Jet database engine can join tables across different database types. That is, you can create a single database made from FoxPro ISAM tables, native Jet database .MDB files, and tables from other ODBC data sources. The Jet database engine can handle all these different table types consistently, allowing you to perform join queries with tables from different databases.

You should also be aware that with the added DAO functionalities and abstraction comes a little inefficiency. You will find that queries run through the DAO API will be a little slower than those run through the ODBC database driver directly, or through the RDO API.

Remote Data Objects

The Remote Data Objects (RDO) are a library of OLE Automation objects. Through the miracle of the Java/COM bridge, which is built into the Microsoft Java Virtual Machine, you can use RDO to control ODBC sessions. RDO

Database Programming in Java

represent another database API that is completely separate from the Jet database engine's DAO API.

The biggest differences between DAO and RDO are

- DAO is an automation interface to the Jet database engine. RDO is a thin wrapper of COM classes and APIs around the ODBC (Open Database Connectivity) library in Windows. This means that the additional functionalities DAO brings you are not present in RDO. It also means that using RDO provides faster access, in general, to the database data.

- RDO is a more complex API than DAO, since it mimics much of the ODBC API functions. One of the main reasons for the complexity is that ODBC was not designed to be an object-oriented API. A little bit of shoe-horning had to occur to "fit" a set of RDO classes around the ODBC API.

- When using RDO, you don't necessarily have to license anything else to make your Java programs work. When using DAO, you must license the Jet database engine for each system your software is deployed on (or at least make sure your user has such a license). This is really a major difference. Basically, it means your RDO-employing applications or applets will work on any Win32 platform. But your DAO-employing applications or applets will have to have some extra DLLs deployed on the target system to work.

Building the RDO Java/COM Shim Classes

Since RDO is a set of COM classes, you must make a set of RDO Java/COM shim classes to create and use the RDO objects from within Java. (Chapter 7 describes the Java/COM bridge built into the Microsoft Java Virtual Machine for Windows.) You use the Visual J++ Java Type Library Wizard tool to create these shim classes.

To build the classes, start the Java Type Library tool from within Visual J++. One of the libraries in the list of registered COM libraries will be "Microsoft Remote Data Object 1.0." Select this item in the list, make sure its checkbox is checked, and press the OK button on the Java Type Library Wizard dialog.

When you do this, you will see this output in the Java Type Library Wizard output window:

```
import msrdo32.*;
C:\WIN95\SYSTEM\MSRDO32.DLL(0,0) : warning J5008: method ... (error message)
C:\WIN95\SYSTEM\MSRDO32.DLL(0,0) : warning J5008: method ... (error message)
C:\WIN95\java\trustlib\msrdo32\summary.txt(1): Class summary information created
```

Note that you can ignore the two error messages. They basically indicate that there are two methods within the RDO API that have parameter types that cannot be converted to Java (such as data pointers or some such type that has been banished from Java). These two methods aren't completely necessary in RDO, anyway.

The first line in this output is the import statement you must include at the top of each Java source code file that refers to any of the RDO objects. The msrdo32 Java package of classes is created in the <windows>\Java\TrustLib\msrdo32 directory. Once you have completed the generation of the RDO Java/COM shim classes, you can use RDO at will in your Java applications and applets.

The rdoEngine Object

The rdoEngine object represents the RDO engine in your Java applications and applets. You should only create one of these objects in your application. Note that the COM interface you cast this rdoEngine object to is called *_rdoEngine* (same name, but with a preceding underscore). This code demonstrates creation of your rdoEngine object:

```
import msrdo32.*;    // you must always include this statement!

...

// Within the code of some method, either an Applet's start() method,
// or an application's main() method...
_rdoEngine eng = (_rdoEngine)new rdoEngine();
```

RDO Environments

Within DAO, you have a Workspace object that represents each individual session with the Jet database engine. In RDO, you have an equivalent type of object called the Environment object. Multiple connections to multiple databases can all be opened and used within the context of a single Environment object.

Note that database transactions are all grouped together under the Environment context in RDO. That is, if you make six different connections to six different ODBC data sources under the same environment in RDO, all of the transactions you make in these six database connections will be handled as a single transaction. If you started transacting on two of the database connections, wrote five new records in one database, and then deleted five

Database Programming in Java

in the other before rolling back the transaction on the first database, all ten record modifications in both databases would be rolled back.

This also means that you can use multiple different Environment objects to differentiate your database transactions in RDO. In the previous example, if the two databases were opened under two different environments, the rolling back of a transaction in one database would not affect the proceeding of the other transaction at all.

The Default Environment and the Environments Collection

Just like DAO, RDO has a set of collection properties peppered throughout the API classes. The rdoEnvironments property of the rdoEngine object holds a list of all the open environments in your program. When the rdoEngine object is first created, in fact, a default rdoEnvironment object is created automatically. To get a reference to this default rdoEnvironment, get the zero-th item in the rdoEnvironments collection, which also has the name Default_Environment. This code demonstrates how to create an rdoEngine and get a reference to its default rdoEnvironment object:

```
import msrdo32.*;

...

// At some point later in your application or applet:
_rdoEngine eng = (_rdoEngine)new rdoEngine();
rdoEnvironments envs = eng.getrdoEnvironments();

Variant varIndex = new Variant();
varIndex.putInt(0);
rdoEnvironment env = envs.getItem(varIndex);

// Alternatively, you can look up the default Environment by name
// by replacing the previous three lines with this code:
Variant varStrEnvName = new Variant();
varStrEnvName.putString("Default_Environment");
rdoEnvironment env = envs.getItem(varStrEnvName);
```

Environment Properties

The rdoEnvironment object has six different properties. These Automation properties can be accessed and modified using the getXXX() and setXXX() methods built into the rdoEnvironment Java/COM shim class. The following table lists the six rdoEnvironment properties, their default values, and a description of what each means:

Property	Default Value	Description
rdoDefaultCursor Driver	rdUseIfNeeded	ODBC cursor to use.
rdoDefaultPassword	""	Password to use when connecting to new ODBC data sources, if a password is needed and none is specified at time of connection.
rdoDefaultName	""	User name to use when connecting to new ODBC data sources, if a password is needed and none is specified at time of connection.
rdoDefaultError Threshhold	-1	Error level above which errors are considered to be fatal. The default value of -1 indicates that no level is high enough to shut down the environment.
rdoDefaultLogin Timeout	15 (seconds)	Duration to wait to log into remote data sources.

Note that the default rdoEnvironment has all its properties set to the default values. For the remainder of this chapter, the samples will assume use of the default rdoEnvironment object.

Creating Your Own rdoEnvironment Objects

The _rdoEngine interface method CreateEnvironment( ) is used to create new RDO environments. The three string parameters to this method are, in order, the name to use for the environment (can be used to look up the rdoEnvironment in the rdoEnvironments collection), the default user name, and the default password.

Even if you drop a reference to the rdoEnvironment returned by the CreateEnvironment( ) method, you can look up the rdoEnvironment in the rdoEnvironments collection at a later time. To get rid of an rdoEnvironment altogether, call the Environment object's Close( ) method. This will close the rdoEnvironment, as well as any opened database connections within that Environment context.

Database Connections

It is within the context of an rdoEnvironment object that you create connections to ODBC data sources. An ODBC data source connection is

Database Programming in Java

represented by an rdoConnection object in RDO. You connect to a registered ODBC data source, and that connection is completely controlled through the rdoConnection object.

Creating New Database Connections

In order for you to connect to an ODBC data source, the source must be registered with the ODBC Administration program in the Windows Control Pad. This registration defines both the network location of the ODBC server (or the local file system location of the database file, as the case may be) and the ODBC driver type.

The rdoEnvironment object's OpenConnection( ) method is used to create new database connections under the rdoEnvironment context. There are four parameters to the OpenConnection( ) method. The first parameter is a String object, and it is the name that will be used to refer to the database connection within RDO. (You can use this name to look up the rdoConnection object in the rdoConnections( ) collection of the rdoEnvironment.)

The second parameter, a Variant object, indicates whether or not you want the user to be able to fill in extra information using the ODBC connect dialog. To disallow this, set the parameter integer value to *rdDriverNoPrompt*. The PromptConstants interface in the msrdo32 package defines this constant. The *rdDriverPrompt* value allows the user to enter connection information into the ODBC connect dialog.

The third parameter is another variant whose boolean value indicates whether or not the connection is read-only. Set this to false if the connection should allow reads and writes. The fourth parameter is an ODBC connection string, which is also passed as a Variant object.

The following code is taken from the RDO Sample applet, which is included with the Visual J++ Microsoft samples, and it demonstrates how to connect to a ODBC data source named Sample Database in read-write mode, disallowing the user to fill in the ODBC connect dialog:

```
Variant v1, v2, v3;
          .
          .
          .
// Set optional parameter values
v1.putInt(PromptConstants.rdDriverNoPrompt);
v2.putBoolean(false);
v3.putString("DSN=Sample Database;UID=;PWD=;DATABASE=Sample Database");
```

```
// Open a connection to the data source
m_IConnection = m_IEnvironment.OpenConnection("",v1,v2,v3);
```

Looking Up Existing Connections

As each rdoConnection object is created, it is automatically appended to the rdoConnections collection, which is a property of the rdoEnvironment object. So, even if you drop all references to an extant rdoConnection object, the object will still exist within the rdoConnections collection. The getItem( ) method of the rdoConnections collection is used to find existing connections. To destroy a connection, you must call its Close( ) method. Once that method is called, then the connection is removed from the rdoConnections collection.

RDO Result Sets

Just like in DAO, your submitted queries are returned in a result set in RDO. The rdoResultset object returned from rdoConnection.OpenResultset( ) is used to read and modify values in a particular result set.

Note that you can also create prepared statements in RDO. A prepared statement is like a saved QueryDef in DAO. That is, it defines a query that you plan on using over and over within the same rdoEnvironment. Once you create a prepared statement, you can also use it to generate result sets. Prepared statements will be discussed in a following section, but the section is relevant because the resulting record sets are used the same way as the record sets generated by a rdoConnection object's OpenResultset( ) method.

There are four parameters to the OpenResultset( ) method. The first parameter is a String object that is an SQL statement to be used to generate the rdoResultset. Alternatively, you can pass the name of an rdoPreparedStatement object, or an rdoTable object. For an rdoPreparedStatement name or an rdoTable name, the same result set will be returned as would be returned by the OpenResultset( ) method of the rdoPreparedStatement or rdoTable object. A third option for this parameter is to pass the name of a stored procedure name, prepended with the string "EXEC." Stored procedure names will only work, of course, if the ODBC data source supports stored procedures.

The second parameter defines what type of cursor you want to use. The four different types of cursors define how you can access the various records of the result set, and how the result set is updated. There are four constants in the ResultsetTypeConstants interface of the msrdo32 package. The following table lists the four type constants and describes how the various cursor types work.

Type Value	Description
rdOpenForwardOnly	The records of the rdoResultset can only be accessed sequentially, from first record to last. This is the fastest type of cursor, but it has the restriction of only allowing you to read the records in order.
rdOpenStatic	Static cursors are similar to the DAO snapshot-type record sets. That is, the records in the record set are not updated until the cursor is closed and reopened. The records can be accessed in random order.
rdOpenKeyset	A keyset-type recordset is similar to the DAO dynaset type. A unique key is stored for each record in the record set. When a particular record is accessed, the values of the record are retrieved from the server. This means that any updates to the records made since the record set was created will be reflected in the field values of the record. Records that are deleted from the record set, or whose updated values make them no longer a valid solution to the current query, are not removed from the result set.
rdOpenDynamic	Identical to the keyset-type rdoResultsets, except that the cursor constantly re-evaluates record set members so that deleted records are removed from the record set, and records that are modified so that they are no longer valid solutions to the query are also removed. Note that records that were not originally in the record set will not be added to the dynamic record set, even if they are modified by other users so that they become valid solutions to the query.

The third parameter to the OpenResultset( ) method is a Variant object whose integer value indicates the type of concurrency policy you want to use while viewing members of the record set. The different possible concurrency policies are available in the LockTypeConstants interface of the msrdo32 package. The rdConcurReadOnly value indicates that the records of the rdoResultset are read-only. The rdConcurLock value will lock the table(s) of the record set so that other users cannot modify the values at the same time.

The fourth and final parameter to the OpenResultset( ) method is another Variant object. This value indicates whether the query should be performed asynchronously or synchronously. The OptionConstants interface value *rdAsynchEnable* can be used to enabled asynchronous processing of the query. The default action of the OpenResultset( ) method executes the query synchronously.

Creating Result Sets from Tables

Just like in DAO, you can create a record set just from the contents of a single database table. The rdoTables collection that is returned from the rdoConnection method getrdoTables( ) holds a reference to all the tables defined in the database. The rdoTable object's OpenResultset( ) method returns a result set made up of all the records in the table.

The OpenResultset( ) method of the rdoTable object takes three arguments, which have the same definition as the final three parameters to the rdoConnection object's OpenResultset( ) method. That is, the first parameter defines the cursor type, the second describes the concurrency policy you want used, and the final parameter tells whether you want synchronous or asynchronous query execution.

Working with Record Sets

Just like in DAO Recordset objects, only a single record is available for looking at or modifying field values in rdoResultset objects. The rdoResultset MoveXXX( ) methods can be used to sequentially navigate through the records in the result set. The MoveFirst( ), MovePrev( ), Move Next( ), and MoveLast( ) methods do what you would expect them to in terms of letting you navigate through the records in the record set. The getBOF( ) and getEOF( ) methods do the same thing as the DAO Recordset object's methods of the same names. That is, they return a boolean true value if you are at the first record (getBOF( ), that is), or at the last record in the Resultset (getEOF( )).

To examine the field values of the current record, use the rdoResultset( ) method getrdoColumns( ) to get the various rdoColumn objects that describe the fields of the result set. The rdoColumns object is a collection object that holds all the rdoColumn objects for the result set. The rdoColumn getValue( ) method is used to get the value of the field.

To modify the values of a particular field, you go through a similar mechanism that you go through in DAO. You first call the rdoResultset method Edit( ). This prepares the current record for modification by copying the various field values to a temporary buffer. Change the various field values using the rdoColumn.setValue( ) method, using the rdoColumn object for the field you want to change. When you are ready to commit the record changes to the database, use the Resultset method Update( ).

Quick JDBC Description

The third database API available to you in Java is the Java database connectivity API, brought to you by JavaSoft. The JDBC API differs from DAO and RDO because JDBC was built from the ground up in Java. This means it preserves platform independence. DAO and RDO, on the other hand, can only be used on Win32 machines.

What JDBC gives you that DAO and RDO don't is real platform independence. All of the JDBC code has been written in Java, and thus can be used on any machine with a JVM. The JDBC classes have been added to the Java 1.1 list of core APIs, so they will be available on every Java 1.1 JVM, including any available Web browser.

The JDBC API is based largely on ODBC, with some minor modifications to make it either easier to use in an object-oriented atmosphere, or to make it easier to use in the Java language. The API is so similar to ODBC that if you have familiarity with ODBC, then you can start programming using JDBC almost right away.

Also, the design of JDBC is similar enough to ODBC that one of the first JDBC drivers available was a JDBC/ODBC bridge. This bridge makes it possible to program for ODBC data sources straight from Java without using COM objects. This may or may not be faster than using natively coded COM objects to access your database from within Java.

The full JDBC API has been published by JavaSoft, and you can read about it today on the Web at *http://splash.javasoft.com*.

Summary

There are three separate APIs available for programming databases in Java. This chapter serves as an overview of each of them for the purposes of evaluating which one you want to use on your projects. In addition, using this chapter you should have gleaned enough information to feel comfortable making simple database applications or applets.

The DAO (Data Access Objects) API is a COM interface to the Jet database engine. This is the easiest API to use, having the most consistent and well-designed set of object classes. The Jet database engine can be a drawback, since you must have licensed it for every system you want your database to work on. Several of the Microsoft office and productivity software packages come with a run-time version of the Jet database engine, but on systems without these office products, you can get burned trying to run your DAO applications or applets.

The RDO (Remote Data Objects) API is a wrapper around the ODBC API. Queries run through RDO will always be at least as fast as those queries run on DAO systems. Since RDO is so tightly linked to ODBC, and the ODBC API is not an object-oriented API, the RDO objects can be a little cumbersome to use. But if efficiency and having no need for run-time licenses fits within your design goals, then this is probably the API for you to use.

The JDBC API is a completely Java API. This means that the JDBC API is platform-independent, and is available on every Java 1.1 (and up) JVM. The JDBC API is based pretty closely on Microsoft's ODBC API. So, if you are familiar with ODBC, then JDBC should not be hard for you to learn at all.

CHAPTER 11

Utility and Language Class Reference

Two packages of the Java core packages set have not really been touched on yet in this book, or at least only touched on peripherally. The classes of the java.util package and the java.lang package will probably be some of the most used by you in your Java programs, however. The reason they haven't been directly dealt with yet is that the classes of those chapters are so basic to Java programming, so ground-level to Java's form of object-oriented programming, that they are hard to envision without first having a firmer grasp of the "way of Java."

Try to imagine how hard it would have been to learn mathematics in grade school not from examples and application, but rather from first principals. If instead of learning that if you had one apple in a bag and then added another apple to the bag that you would have two apples, you learned first the concept of number sets, the concept of number operators, and the concept of mathematical equations in general. More than likely, you would have been completely lost before you learned that one plus one equals two!

The same sort of situation exists for many of the classes in the java.util and java.lang packages. For example, the Runtime class of the java.lang package represents the run-time environment of the Java Virtual Machine. But if you hadn't first learned that JVM is the run-time interpreter of Java byte codes, then the Runtime class would be a complete mystery: a concept floating without anchor in a vague sea of "Java-ness." Assuming you have read the previous chapters of this book, or at least a smattering of them sufficient to give you a decent grasp of what Java is, then you should be comfortable being introduced to these java.lang and java.util classes.

The java.util package includes utility classes, such as storage devices and miscellaneous other "helper" classes, that you will find you use in almost every one of your Java applets and applications. The storage classes of this package include these data storage devices: a simple object stack; an expandable array class called a *Vector*; an associative array class called a *Hashtable*; a version of the Hashtable class used specifically to store string-based key/value pairs that is called the *Properties* class; and a *BitSet* class to store and manipulate large arrays of binary values much more efficiently than any array of boolean elements can. You might have noticed that a great number of the example code presented in this book used one or more of these storage devices. As any basic library of prefab C++ classes would include stacks, variable-length arrays, associative arrays, etc., so the Java core packages have included analogous classes as part of Java. These classes are equivalent to the MFC CStack, CMap*XToY* classes, and other MFC storage classes. Because all JVMs have these storage classes included already in the core Java package java.util, you don't have to reimplement them ever, nor distribute the associated .CLASS files.

There are also a few miscellaneous utility classes included with the java.util package. Date objects, which are instances of the java.util.Date class, can store any date/time from the beginning of the 20th century until many eons in the future with a resolution down to the second. To generate random numbers, a system-dependent task in many C/C++ compilers, the java.util.Random class is included. A Random object generates a pseudorandom sequence of numbers from random number generator seeds, much like the rnd( ) and random( ) functions present in many C implementations.

Finally, the StreamTokenizer class, which is described in detail in Chapter 9, is also included as a utility class in this package. Since that class is used very often to parse input streams, the description of that class has been placed with the chapter describing streams and stream filtering/parsing, even though technically it is a utility class of the java.util package and not a streaming class of the java.io package.

The java.lang package includes classes that can be divided into five functional groups. The first group includes classes to represent simple built-in variable types. For example, the Boolean class is a simple object to represent boolean values. Why would you need a class to represent boolean values when you already have a built-in boolean variable type in Java? Specifically for those instances when you need to pass around an object that represents a boolean value. Like when you want to fill a vector with several boolean values. Since the vector can only store objects (derived ultimately from the Object class), you need an object that represents boolean values. Hence, the java.lang package includes a Boolean class for just such applications. Similarly, the package also includes classes for representing all the built-in types like characters, integers, floats, and doubles.

The second group of classes in the java.lang package are meta-class classes. That is, elements that give information about or let you create Java classes at runtime. The Class class represents a specific Java class in the run-time environment. A ClassLoader, which is another class in the java.lang package, allows you to dynamically load classes in Java applications. That is, a ClassLoader class is able to make new Class object instances from .CLASS data your program supplies. Dynamic class loading and creation are powerful techniques with different uses in Java applications and applets. Those uses and the techniques for doing them are described in this chapter.

The Math class is a single-instance class whose static member methods include many basic mathematical operations you would expect to be present in any programming language. Trigonometric functions, min/max comparison functions, rounding functions, and many others are all implemented as static methods of this class.

A collection of classes in the java.lang package exist to give you some amount of control over the JVM and the Java run-time environment. The Runtime class and System class give you access to the JVM's run-time process. For example, through these classes you can access environment variables and execute external programs from within your Java applications or applets. A SecurityManager object controls access to potentially sensitive system resources. The security manager either approves or disapproves of allowing certain operations to take place, like creating new sockets or server sockets, opening or creating files on the local file system, etc.

Finally, the fifth group of java.lang classes are covered in this book as part of other Java concepts. The Object class, which is the ultimate base class of all other Java classes, is part of the java.lang package, as are the String and StringBuffer classes. These three classes are all described in Chapter 1. The Thread and ThreadGroup classes as well as the Runnable interface are the basis for multithreading in Java. A large number of Exception classes, as well as the Exception class itself, are also defined in the java.lang package.

The java.util Storage Classes

A basic requirement for almost all nontrivial applications and Java applets is the need for usable data storage devices. Stacks, expandable arrays, hashtables, and other different types of storage classes are defined in the java.util package to make these programming requirements minimal. No doubt you will eventually have to implement your own storage classes, whether for optimization of speed, or because the java.util storage classes just don't have the functionality you need. But the java.util storage classes are a good 90-percent solution. That is, ninety percent of your storage needs are solvable using these classes.

Note that, perhaps more than most other core Java classes and packages, you may want to look at the actual implementations of the storage classes. This is for two reasons. The first is that when you are creating your own custom storage classes, you may want to look at these classes as reference implementations. The second reason is that you might want to derive classes from these storage classes in order to extend them with additional methods. While you may not see yourself doing this now, the more you use these classes, the more you will want to do this.

The Enumeration Interface

The Enumeration interface is a very simple interface to present a sequence of objects in some standard way. In many programming situations, you will need to pass around sequences of objects. The Enumeration interface can be declared by any class that implements two simple methods: hasMoreElements( ) and nextElement( ).

An enumeration defines an interface through which a sequence of objects can be given out. The sequence is assumed to be forward only, much like the stream of bytes concept described at the beginning of Chapter 9. When you get an enumeration, you can do two things: query whether or not you have enumerated all the objects in the enumeration using the Enumeration.hasMoreElements( ) method, and get the next object in

Utility and Language Class Reference

the enumeration using the nextElement( ) method. Most code that uses enumerations uses them in while loops that look like this:

```
Enumeration enum;
...
// The Enumeration variable enum is given some object reference...

while(enum.hasMoreElements()) {
    Object o = enum.nextElement();

    // Do something with the Object o.
}
...
```

The two Enumeration class methods make it perfect to use in this type of while loop. Alternatively, if the index of the various items in the enumeration is needed by your code for some reason, you can use a for loop that looks like this:

```
Enumeration enum;
...
// The Enumeration variable enum is given some object reference...

for(int index=0 ; enum.hasMoreElements() ; index++) {
    Object o = enum.nextElement();

    // Do something with the Object o.
}
...
```

The storage classes of the java.util package all use enumerations to pass around "snapshots" of their contents. For example, the Vector class, which is an expandable array of objects, has a method called elements( ) that returns an enumeration of the objects currently stored in the vector, as demonstrated by this code:

```
Vector vect = new Vector();

// Vector is filled with various Objects...
...

// Sometime later, get Enumeration of the contents of the Vector:
Enumeration enum = vect.elements( );

// Run through Vector contents, doing whatever operation with
// each Object:
```

```
while(enum.hasMoreElements()) {
    Object o = =vect.nextElement();

    // Do something with the Object...
}
...
```

The Stack Class

A stack is a LIFO storage device: last in, first out. You place a series of objects in the stack using the push( ) method. Each push( ) of an object is like placing the object on top of a stack (hence the device's name). To get an object off the top of the stack, use the Stack object's pop( ) method. Figure 11-1 illustrates the stack storage device concept.

Both push( ) and pop( ) change the state of the stack. That is, the contents of the stack change with every call to push( ) and pop( ). The peek( ) method,

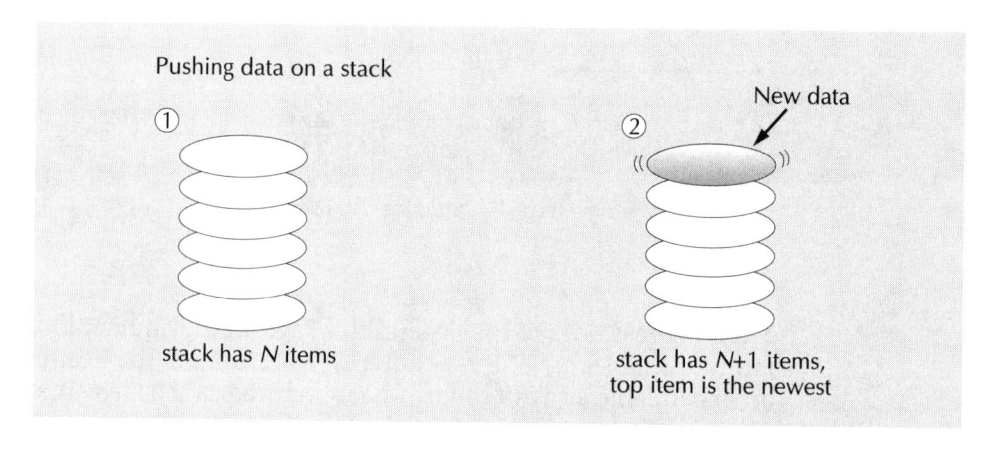

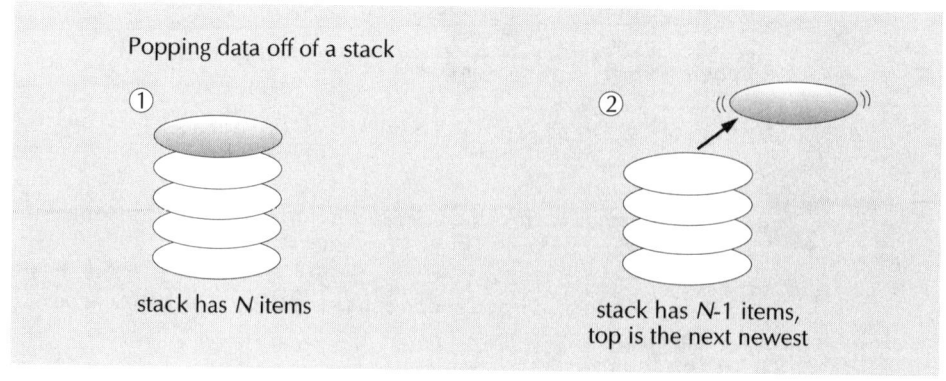

Figure 11-1. The Stack

on the other hand, returns the object that is at the top of the stack but does not remove it from the stack, so that the next call to pop( ) or peek( ) will return the exact same Object reference.

The only Stack class constructor takes no parameters:

```
public Stack(); // signature of only Stack class constructor.
```

In the following section that describes the java.lang numeric classes, an example Calculator program that uses a stack to store intermediate calculation results is presented. That program uses a stack as its only internal data structure to store numbers and operands to create a fully functional (though quite simple) calculator applet.

The Vector Class

A vector is an expandable array of objects. That is, it is like an array in that elements stored in the vector are identified by their zero-based index in the vector. And, in addition, a vector is expandable so that you can never run over a preset bounding number of elements like you can with a normal array. When you add one more element to the vector than the vector has room to store, the vector just allocates more storage to accommodate you. Obviously, you have the practical limit of available memory that may prevent the vector from being able to allocate more space. Also since an int index is used to identify objects stored in the vector, then you can't have more than about two billion elements stored in a vector at a time.

The Stack class is actually derived from the Vector class. So, in addition to the push( ), pop( ), and peek( ) methods implemented in that class, you also can use any of the methods publicly defined as part of the Vector class. The Vector class allows you to inspect and change any of the Object references stored at the various indexes within the vector. So, you're not restricted to just using push( ) and pop( ) to get values into and remove values from a stack.

Adding and Removing Elements

Each object added to the vector is stored at a particular index in the vector. You can assign an object to a particular index using one of the two Vector class methods setElementAt( ) or insertElementAt( ). Both methods take two parameters: the object to store and the index to store it at. The method setElementAt( ) will replace whatever object is stored at the given index with the new object. The method insertElementAt( ) will shift all elements in the vector up by one index value starting at the given index to make room for the new object. Figure 11-2 shows the difference between a setElementAt( ) and an insertElementAt( ) operation.

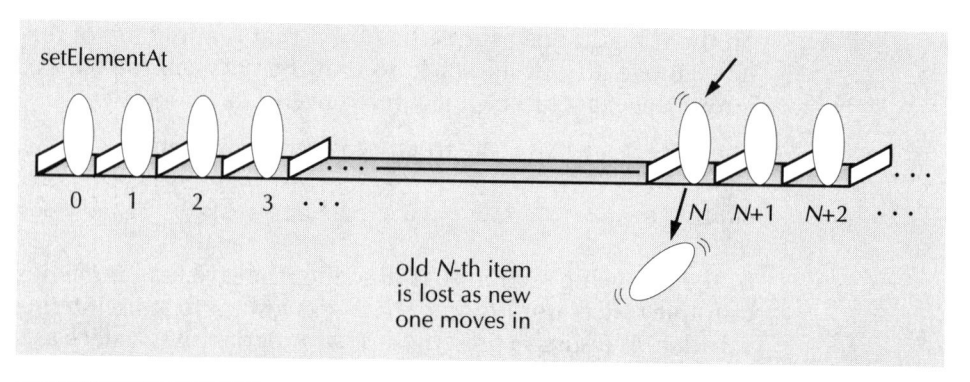

Figure 11-2.
The setElementAt( ) and insertElementAt( ) Vector class operations

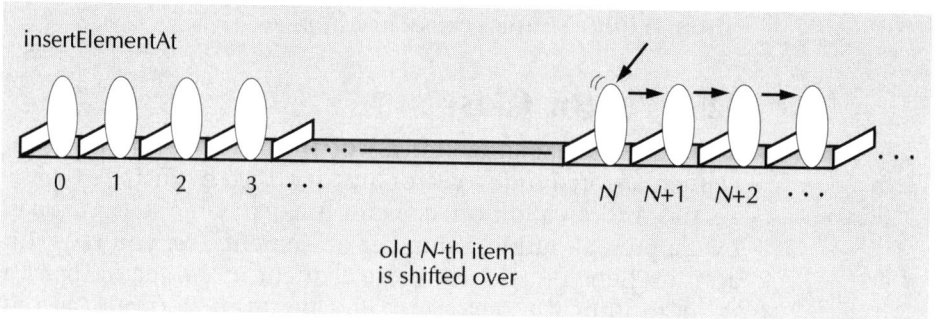

The addElement( ) method appends the given object to the vector. It adds the element to the next available index, which is the same number returned by the size( ) method. The setSize( ) method takes a single parameter, which is the maximum valid index of elements after the method is called. That is, the setSize( ) method deletes all objects from the vector whose indexes are greater than the given value.

So, in summary, there are three methods for adding elements to a vector: addElement( ) appends objects to the vector, insertElementAt( ) inserts an object at a particular index in the vector, and setElementAt( ) replaces whatever object is at the given index with a new object.

There are also three methods for deleting specific objects from a vector: removeElement( ) removes a specific element from a vector, the removeElementAt( ) method deletes whatever element is stored at a particular index, and the removeAllElements( ) method deletes all elements from the vector. Calling removeAllElements( ) does the same thing as calling setSize( ) with a value of zero.

Utility and Language Class Reference

A Vector's Capacity

A vector works by internally allocating an array of Object references. The protected Vector class member *elementData[]* is this array. When you create a vector, you can specify the initial size of this array. You can also specify the increment by which this array grows whenever the vector needs to allocate new space to store more elements. There are three Vector class constructors, whose signatures look like this:

```
public Vector();
public Vector(int initialCapacity);
public Vector(int initialCapacity, int capacityIncrement);
```

The no-argument constructor uses default values for the initial internal element array size and capacity increment. The single-argument constructor uses the default value for the capacity increment.

The Vector method capacity( ) returns the current capacity of the vector. That is, the current number of objects the vector *could* store without having to allocate a large elementData[ ] array. The ensureCapacity( ) method is used to increase the current capacity of a vector.

The trimToSize( ) method of the Vector class will deallocate any excess *elementData[]* elements that are not being used. That is, it will reallocate the array to have only as many elements in it as the value returned by the size( ) method.

Getting Elements from a Vector

The contains( ) method returns a boolean value indicating whether or not a particular object is contained within the vector. Pass an Object reference, and this method will return true if the object is included in the vector, and false if it is not.

This sample program uses a vector as a simple database of names. The command-line argument to this program is the name of a file that contains a list of strings. Type in a string, and the program will return the index of that string in the vector.

```
import  java.util.Vector;
import  java.io.*;

public class SimpleStringDB {
    public static void main(String[] astrArgs) {
        Vector vect = new Vector();
```

```java
        // Get command-line arg, which is name of file of strings.
        if(1 > astrArgs.length) {
            System.err.println("Usage Error:\n SimpleStringDB <filename>");
            System.exit(-1);
        }

        // Read in input file of Strings into the Vector.
        DataInputStream in;
        try {
            in = new DataInputStream(
                    new FileInputStream(astrArgs[0]));
            for(String str ; (str=in.readLine()).length() > 0 ; )
                vect.addElement(str);
            in.close();
        } catch (EOFException eof) {
        } catch (IOException ioe) {
            System.err.print("Error:\n error reading from input file ");
            System.err.println(astrArgs[0] + ioe);
            System.exit(-1);
        }

        // Read in the user's input, printing out the index number of the
        // String that the user types in.
        try {
            String user_in;
            DataInputStream in2 = new DataInputStream(System.in);

            while((user_in = in2.readLine()).length() > 0) {
                int index;

                if("QUIT".equals(user_in))
                    System.exit(0);

                if(-1 != (index = vect.indexOf(user_in)))
                    System.out.println("\tIndex is : " + index);
                else
                    System.out.println("\t\"" + user_in +
                            "\" is not in the list");
            }
        } catch (EOFException eof) {
        } catch (IOException ioe) {
            System.err.println("Error:\n Reading from user: " + ioe);
            System.exit(-1);
        }
    }
}
```

Utility and Language Class Reference

The indexOf( ) method returns the index of a given Object, if the object exists in the Vector. If it doesn't exist in the Vector, then a -1 value is returned. Note that the test in the previous program

```
-1 != (index = vect.indexOf(str))
```

is just a shorthand for writing

```
if(vect.contains(str)) {
    int index = vect.indexOf(str);
```

The second overloaded version of indexOf( ) takes a second argument, which is the index to start searching from. Using a loop that looks like the following code, you can run through all occurrences of a given object in a vector. Note that you can add the same element more than once to a vector at different indexes.

```
public int indexesOf(int[] an, Vector vect, Object o) {
    int count = 0;

    for(int nIndex=0 ; -1 != an[count] = vect.indexOf(o, nIndex)
            ; nIndex=an[count++]) ;

    return count;
}
```

So, the indexOf( ) method allows you to run through a vector, getting all the references to an object starting at index zero and going to the end of the vector. The lastIndexOf( ) method allows you to do the opposite. That is, it finds the highest index of a given object in the vector. The second overloaded version of the lastIndexOfMethod( ) takes two parameters, an object to look up and the last index to start searching from. So, this reimplementation of the indexesOf( ) method will do the same thing as the last one just given, although the values written to the *an* array will be in the reverse order:

```
public int indexesOf(int an[], Vector vect, Object o) {
    int count = 0;

    for(int nIndex=vect.size() ; -1 != an[count] = vect.lastindexOf(o, nIn-
dex)
            ; nIndex=an[count++]) ;

    return count;
}
```

Other Vector Class Features

The Vector class implements the Cloneable interface. This means that the method clone( ) is implemented for this class. (Note that only classes that implement the Cloneable interface actually have a valid clone( ) implementation.) So, if you want a vector that is an exact copy of a given vector, just use the clone( ) method:

```
Vector vectCopy = vect.clone();
```

The copyInto( ) method will copy the objects contained by the vector into an array of objects that you provide. This method makes an exact copy of the vector's *elementData[]* array, copying only up to size( ) elements. You must make sure the array you pass to this method is sufficiently long to hold all the elements of the vector, or else the method will throw an ArrayIndexOutOfBoundsException. Use code that looks like this:

```
Object[] aobj = new Object[vect.size()];
vect.copyInto(aobj);
```

The Hashtable Class

A hashtable is a storage device for storing key/value pairs. The key is an object that identifies the value object. Where a vector uses index values to identify individual elements in the vector, the hashtable uses key objects to identify value objects stored in the hashtable.

The name of the class, "Hashtable," indicates that the keys are stored internally by a hash value. This is a very efficient method for storing objects because it makes it very easy to look them up by their hash value. You may remember that the Object class has a method called hashCode( ). This method is in turn inherited by all other Java classes. The sole purpose of this method is to provide a hash value for all Objects used as keys in hashtables. (Of course, you can also use the value returned from hashCode( ) to do your own hashing calculations in Java. The core Java packages only use this method to facilitate the Hashtable class, however.)

To make your hashtables as efficient as possible, you may want to create your own implementation of the hashCode( ) method for your custom classes. Your implementation should create a semiunique 32-bit int value for each class instance. The more unique values your hashCode( ) method hands out, the more efficiently a hashtable that uses key objects of that class will be when looking up values.

Adding and Removing Objects from a Hashtable

The Hashtable class' put( ) method is used to add an object to the hashtable. Pass the put( ) method a key object and a value object. The get( ) method returns whatever value object is associated with the key object passed as its only parameter.

The remove( ) method of the Hashtable class takes a key object as its only parameter. When called, the method gets rid of any value object associated with the given key object. The clear( ) method clears all key/value pairs from the hashtable. Note that the Hashtable class provides no methods for looking up a key given a value object; you can only look up value objects from a key object.

The Hashtable class' contains( ) method is very similar to the Vector class' contains( ) method. It returns true if the object passed as its only parameter is a value object stored within the hashtable. Similarly, the containsKey( ) method returns true if the single object parameter it is passed is a key object in the hashtable.

The size( ) method of the Hashtable class does the same thing as the method of the same name in the Vector class. It returns the number of key/value pairs stored in the hashtable.

The elements( ) method of the Hashtable class returns an enumeration that contains a snapshot of the value objects currently stored in the hashtable. Note that these values are in no particular order as they are returned from the enumeration. Presence of a value object in the enumeration only means that there was—at the time the elements( ) method was called that created the enumeration—a value object stored under some key object in the hashtable.

The keys( ) method of the Hashtable class is similar to the elements( ) method. The keys( ) method returns an enumeration that lists all the valid key objects in the hashtable at the time the keys( ) method was called. This sample code will return all the key objects a particular value object is stored under in a hashtable. Note that while a single key object can only have a single value object associated with it in a Hashtable, a single value object can have any number of key objects. (Conceivably, you could easily create a hashtable, all of whose key/value pairs had the exact same value object, though different key objects.)

```
public int getKeysForValue(Object aobj[], Hashtable h, Object val) {
    Enumeration enum = h.keys();
    int count = 0;
```

```
        while(enum.hasMoreElements()) {
            Object objKey = enum.nextElement();
            if(val == h.get(objKey))
                aobj[count++] = objKey;
        }

        return count;
    }
```

The Properties Class

Most obviously, hashtables are used to store string key/value pairs. Since this is such a common and useful thing to do with a hashtable, the java.util class also includes a Hashtable-derived class with methods especially for storing and retrieving string-based key/value pairs (i.e., where both the key and the value objects are in fact strings). This class is called the Properties class.

Properties are used in several different places in Java. For example, the single-instance System class, which represents some aspects of the run-time environment of a Java application or applet, stores all the Java environment variables as properties in a Properties object. When you call the System class method getProperties( ), a Properties object filled with string-based property name/property values pairs is returned. This simple sample program prints out all the current system properties to the System.out PrintStream. The output shown after the code listing is output from one sample running of this program on the author's machine.

```
import java.util.Properties;

public class ShowSystemProps {
    public static void main(String astrArgs[]) {
        // Ignore command-line arguments.

        Properties props = System.getProperties();
        props.list(System.out);
    }
}
```

Listing of a sample run of the ShowSystemProps Java application:

```
-- listing properties --
java.home=c:\java\bin\..
awt.toolkit=sun.awt.win32.MToolkit
java.version=1.0.2
file.separator=\
line.separator=
```

Utility and Language Class Reference

```
java.vendor=Sun Microsystems Inc.
user.name=Wizard
os.arch=x86
os.name=Windows NT
java.vendor.url=http://www.sun.com/
user.dir=C:\doc\brian\jakarta\chap12\projects\...
java.class.path=.;C:\java\lib\classes.zip;c:\java\cla...
java.class.version=45.3
os.version=3.50
path.separator=;
user.home=C:\users\default
```

More will be discussed about the System class, and about its Properties class, in a following section of this chapter. The important thing here is to show that the Properties class, in addition to all the methods it inherits from the Hashtable class, also has a crude serialization method called list( ). The list( ) method writes out the string-based key/values pairs in such a manner that they can be read back in again using the load( ) method. Pass an input stream to load( ), and it will fill the Properties object with the key/value pairs that were previously written out.

Like the Hashtable class, the Properties class implements the Cloneable interface. So you can create an exact duplicate of a Properties object using the clone( ) method.

Unlike the Hashtable class, however, a Properties object has the concept of *default properties* built into it. One constructor of the Properties class takes as its only argument another Properties object to use for default values. That is, if you use this constructor to create a Properties object, and then at a later time ask the created Properties object for the value associated with a key that does not exist, then the properties will query the default Properties object passed to the constructor for a value to return. Thus, when looking up values to return, a Properties object returns value objects by looking for them in this order:

1. If the key string exists in this Properties object, return the associated value String, otherwise go to step 2.
2. Ask the default Properties object passed to the constructor for a value string associated with the given key string. If the no-parameter constructor was used, just return null.
3. If the default Properties object doesn't have a value for the associated key object, then have the default Properties object recursively ask its own default Properties object for a value string associated with the given key string.

Note that step 3 here is recursive, so you could create a long chain of Properties objects to default Properties objects if you wanted.

The Properties class method getProperty( ) is the same thing as the Hashtable class method get( ). The only difference is that you must pass a key string to getProperty( ), while the Hashtable class get( ) method takes any key object. An overloaded version of the getProperty( ) method exists that takes a second argument: a default value to return if there is no value string associated with the given key string in the Properties object.

The BitSet Class

The final storage class included with the java.util package is the BitSet class. A BitSet is a large array of single bits, each bit having a boolean true of false value. The implementation of the BitSet class is to allocate an array of 32-bit ints, each int holding 32 bits in the BitSet. You don't have to know this at all. You just refer to each bit in the BitSet by a zero-based index.

The BitSet class is implemented to present your array of bit values as an infinite array. That is, if you ask for the value of bit number 10 billion, the BitSet will return a value. If you ask for the value of a bit that is clearly past the end of the array, then the class returns a simple false, protecting you from having to do too much exception handling.

The BitSet class is an expandable array, much like the Vector class. When you set a particular bit's value, the BitSet makes sure it has allocated space to store that bit. For bits whose values have not yet been set, the BitSet just remembers that it doesn't have storage for those bits currently and returns a false value whenever asked for their values.

The get( ), set( ), and clear( ) methods of this class each take a zero-based index to a particular bit in the BitSet. The get( ) method returns the currently stored value of that bit (which is false when the BitSet is created, and stays that value until you explicitly use the set( ) method to change it). The set( ) method sets a particular bit to true, and the clear( ) method sets a particular bit to false.

The BitSet class includes convenient methods for combining large BitSets. The implementations of these methods are also much more optimized and efficient than you could achieve using long loops of clear( ) and set( ) calls. The and( ) method performs a bitwise AND operation on two BitSets. That is, this code will AND the BitSet bs2 with bs1, and the results will be stored in bs1.

```
BitSet bs1 = new BitSet();
BitSet bs2 = new BitSet();
```

Utility and Language Class Reference

```
// BitSets bs1 and bs2 get filled with values at some point...

// AND the two BitSets together, putting the result in BitSet bs1.
bs1.and(bs2);
```

Used similarly, the or( ) and xor( ) methods perform large bitwise OR and XOR operations on two BitSets, respectively. To clear a BitSet of all values (i.e., to set all bits to false), XOR the BitSet with itself:

```
bs1.xor(bs1);
```

Like the other storage classes of the java.util package, the BitSet class implements the Cloneable interface. So, you can create an exact copy of a BitSet using the BitSet's clone( ) method.

The Observer/Observable Framework

The java.util package defines a framework for generic notification, similar to the java.awt package's Event notification framework, using observers and observables. An *Observable* object is a source of asynchronous updates. The *Observer* is the receiver of those asynchronous updates.

For example, let's say you want to have an observer notified whenever an item is popped from or pushed onto a stack. The Observer/Observable framework implements much of the code for you in a thread-safe manner. Using this framework you would save a lot of time and debugging effort compared to reimplementing this functionality yourself. This specific example will be explored in this section as a demonstration of how to program this type of functionality in general into your programs.

Observable Objects

You may have noticed that, in general, the names of Java interfaces end with the suffix "*-able*", indicating that the capability connoted by the interface is implemented in the specific class. The Vector, Stack, and Hashtable classes all are declared as implementing the Cloneable interface, indicating that objects of these classes can be cloned using their inherited clone( ) methods. Objects that can be the targets for background threads to run on are declared as implementing the Runnable interface.

The opposite is true of Observer/Observable objects. In the Observer/Observable framework, all observable objects are derived, ultimately, from an Observable base class. Within this base class, which is defined and implemented as part of the java.util package, is included a great portion of code for making thread-safe observable objects. As you soon shall see, it is the Observer interface that must be implemented for all objects that can be a sink for update notifications sent by Observable objects.

By the way, the ImageObserver interface also loosely follows the same pattern: Objects that want to receive update notifications about the construction of images in memory are declared as implementing the ImageObserver interface. The Component class of the java.awt. package, which is a base class for all classes in the Component/Container hierarchy, is declared as implementing the ImageObserver interface. Thus, any component or container can receive update notifications about the progress of image construction.

Why this deviation of nomenclature? Basically, this is because the onus for delivering update notifications and for maintaining lists of observers lies with the Observable object. Therefore, the code that maintains the internal list of observers, and that delivers the update notifications to those observers, is defined within the update source. That is, within the Observable object. The designers of the Observable/Observer framework probably could have avoided this slight name ambiguity by using the terms "Notifier" and "Notifiable" instead of "Observer" and "Observable". However, the Observable/Observer framework was obviously based on the common observer-observable design pattern that is used quite often in object-oriented programming in general.

All Observable objects maintain an internal list of all observers it should send update notifications to. This list is already implemented for you in the Observable class. Conversely, it is also possible for a single Observer interface-implementing object to have multiple observables that send it simultaneous update notifications. Remember that any Component object, which all automatically inherit implementation of the ImageObserver interface, may get update notifications of the construction progress of multiple images. Similarly, any observer may receive update notifications from multiple observables. (In general, however, you may find it easier to implement Observer-implementing classes that assume only a single observable will send it messages at a time.) Figure 11-3 shows how observables can supply update notifications to multiple observers, and how observers can receive update notifications from several different observables.

Adding and Removing Observers from an Observable

To add an observer to the list of objects an observable is to send update notifications to, use the Observable class method addObserver( ). This method takes a single argument that is the observer to add to the internal list of objects to send notifications to. To remove an observer from the update notification list, use the Observable class method deleteObserver( ),

Utility and Language Class Reference

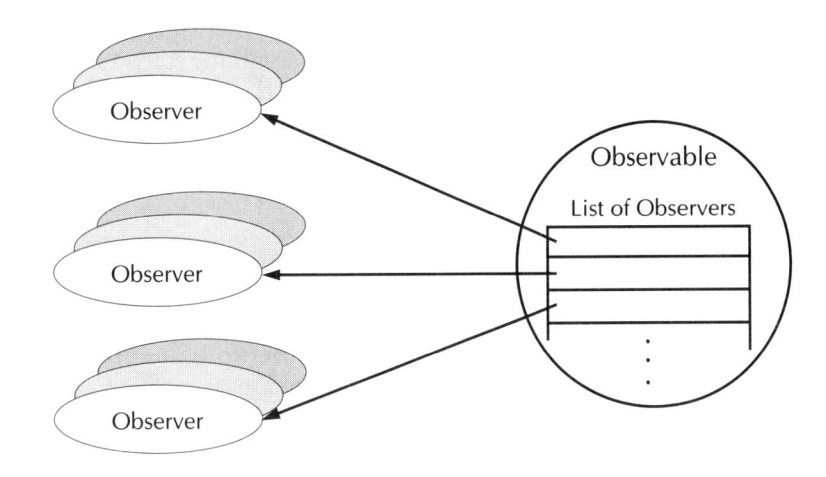

The Observable/Observer framework
Figure 11-3.

again passing in a single parameter that is the observer to remove from the list.

Remember, these methods are already implemented for you. The default implementations of the addObserver( ) and deleteObserver( ) methods update the internal list of observers such that each unique observer will only appear in the list once. That is, if you try to call addObserver( ) twice with the same observer passed as the argument, the second invocation will be ignored and simply return benignly.

The deleteObservers( ) method will completely clear the internal list of observers. No update notifications will be sent to any Observer object after this method is called.

"Dirty" Observables

Observable objects maintain one additional piece of state information in addition to the internal list of Observable objects to notify of change. This is a "dirty" bit, indicating whether or not the Observable object has changed, or, to say it another way, whether or not the observable is "dirty."

The setChanged( ) method of the Observable class sets the dirty bit to true. The hasChanged( ) method can be called by any external object to tell whether or not the observable is currently dirty or not. The clearChanged( ) method clears the dirty bit, so that any subsequent call to hasChanged( ) will return false.

The dirty bit is used internally by Observable objects. In order for the observable to send any notifications out to the observable's list of observers, its dirty bit must be set. To test whether or not the dirty bit is set, the Observable object uses its own hasChanged( ) method, so if you have some complex method for determining that your observable is dirty or not (that is, some method not based solely on the dirty bit), then reimplement the hasChanged( ) method to return true only at the appropriate times.

Notifying Observers

The notifyObservers( ) method is all you have to call in order to get an Observable object to send update notification messages to all its observers. When you call this method, the Observer's update( ) method is invoked. That is, the Observer's update( ) methods are only invoked if the observable's dirty bit is set, as indicated by the Observable's hasChanged( ) method.

An overloaded version of the notifyObservers( ) method also exists that you pass a single object parameter. That object is passed on to the Observers' update( ) method. You can use this version of the notifyObservers( ) method to pass extra information on to your observers, instead of just sending them an update( ) invocation indicating only that the observable has changed in some unknown way. For example, as you will see in the code following this section, an observable stack might send its observers an argument indicating what type of change has happened: whether a push or a pop operation was just performed on the observable stack.

Here is a simpler example of an ObservableInteger class. Note that within the setInt( ) method of this class a setChange( ), notifyObservers( ), clearChanged( ) sequence of calls occurs. This is the common sequence for notifying observers that a change has occurred in the Observable object. That is, you always want to proceed your call to notifyObservers( ) with a setChanged( ) call to set the observable's dirty bit. Without this invocation, the call to notifyObservers( ) would be ignored since the internal dirty bit is set to false.

```
import java.util.Observable;

class ObservableInteger extends Observable {
    // Private state is just an integer value.
    private int m_nVal = -1;

    public ObservableInteger() {
    }

    public ObservableInteger(int n) {
        m_nVal = n;
    }

    public synchronized void setVal(int n) {
```

```
        m_nVal = n;

        setChanged();
        notifyObservers();
        clearChanged();
    }

    public int getVal() {
        return m_nVal;
    }
}
```

The Observer Interface

Any object that implements the Observer interface can receive update notifications from any Observable object. To add the object to the list of observers that an observable sends update notifications to, pass the observer to the Observable object's addObserver( ) method. Thereafter, whenever the Observable's notifyObservers( ) method is called (and the observable's internal dirty bit is set), then the observer will receive the notification of any changes in the observable.

The Observer interface has only a single method declared in it, the update( ) method:

```
public abstract void update(Observable o, Object arg);
```

Whenever the observable sends update notifications to its list of observers, it does so by calling each Observer's update( ) method. The observable parameter is a reference to the observable that is sending the update notification. The *arg* object parameter is the same object given to the overloaded version of the Observable's notifyObservers( ) method that takes a single object parameter. That is, the same object passed to this overloaded version of notifyObservers( ) is passed on the Observer's update( ) method as the *arg* parameter.

An Observable/Observer Applet Example

Here is a client/server applet that utilizes the Observable/Observer interface. The applet connects up with a server program running on the server where the applet came from through an Internet socket connection. This server sends user input that it reads in through to whichever client programs are hooked up to it. Within the applet, an Observable object maintains a recording of the last 10 strings sent from the server application through the socket. (The DataInputStream/DataOutputStream UTF methods are used to read and write String objects through to socket connection.) A background thread within the applet periodically wakes up and calls the Observable's notifyObservers( ) method and clears the observable's dirty bit. The interface of the applet is set up as an observer. Whenever an update to the observable occurs, the applet updates a listbox displaying the 10 strings stored in the observable. Thus, no matter how many strings are sent across the socket connection, the applet only updates itself every 5 seconds.

First, here's the server program. This program accepts clients and writes out to each client socket whatever the user types in. An Observable/Observer setup is used here, too, to notify each client object about when the user has typed in a new string.

```java
import java.net.*;
import java.io.*;
import java.util.Observable;
import java.util.Observer;

public class UserInputServer extends Observable implements Runnable {
    // Private state consists of the ServerSocket, and the
    // port number for the server socket to connect to.
    private ServerSocket m_sock;
    private int m_nPort;

    // Main method expects one command-line arg, which is the
    // port to listen for connections.
    public static void main(String[] astrArgs) {
        if(1 > astrArgs.length) {
            System.err.println("Usage Error:\n UserInputServer <port>");
            System.exit(-1);
        }

        int nPort = 0;
        try {
            nPort = Integer.parseInt(astrArgs[0]);
        } catch (NumberFormatException nfe) {
            System.err.println("Usage Error:\n UserInputServer <port>");
            System.exit(-1);
        }

        new UserInputServer(nPort);
    }

    public UserInputServer(int nPort) {
        // Create thread that will wait for user input.
        m_nPort = nPort;
        Thread t = new Thread(this);
```

Utility and Language Class Reference

```
            t.start();

          // wait until server socket created.
        try
        {
            while(null == m_sock)
                Thread.currentThread().sleep(500);
        } catch (InterruptedException e) {
           // This shouldn't happen.
        }

          // Given user input, send it to the various Observers.
        try {
            DataInputStream in = new DataInputStream(System.in);
            for(String s; !("quit".equals(s = in.readLine())) ; ) {
setChanged();
                notifyObservers(new String(s));
                clearChanged();
            }
            m_sock.close();
        } catch (EOFException eof) {
        } catch (Exception e) {
            System.err.println("Error:\n reading user input.");
            System.exit(-1);
        }
    }

      // The run method is run by a background thread that is to
      // wait for socket connections and create Client objects from them.
    public void run() {
        try {
            m_sock = new ServerSocket(m_nPort);
            for(Socket s = m_sock.accept(); true ; s = m_sock.accept() )
                new ClientHandler(this, s);
        } catch(IOException ioe) {
            System.err.println("Error:\n Opening server or listening: " + ioe);
            System.exit(-1);
        }
    }
}

  // Client class instance created for each individual connection.
  // Client implements the Observer interface, and waits for
  // String objects to be sent to update(). Those are to be sent over
  // the Socket connection handed to the constructor.
class ClientHandler implements Observer {
      // Private state consists of a DataOutputStream to is connected
      // to the socket (where to write strings).
```

```java
        private DataOutputStream m_out;

        // Constructor passed an Observable, and a socket to connect to.
        public ClientHandler(Observable o, Socket s) {
            // Create DataOutputStream from the Socket.
            try {
                m_out = new DataOutputStream(s.getOutputStream());
            } catch(IOException ioe) {
                System.err.println("Error:\n trying to create new socket stream.");
            }

            // Register as Observer for the Observable to send update
            // notifications.
            o.addObserver(this);
        }

        // The update() method is called by the UserInputServer object
        // whenever user types in a new line of text. This text is to
        // be sent across the socket.
        public void update(Observable o, Object objText) {
            try {
                String strText = (String)objText;
                m_out.writeUTF(strText);
            } catch (ClassCastException cce) {
                // arg must not be a string. ignore.
            } catch (IOException ioe) {
                System.err.println("Error:\n writing out to a socket: " + ioe);
                o.deleteObserver(this);
            }
        }
    }
}
```

The client end of this client/server framework is an applet. The applet connects up with the server port on the machine it was served from. The port that it will be connected to is indicated by the "port" parameter to the applet. An internal observable keeps track of the last 10 strings sent over the socket connection from the server. The applet is an observer of this observable. Every half-second, a background thread calls the Observable's notifyObservers( ), which will only cause the applet to update its display if the observable's dirty bit is set.

```java
import java.applet.Applet;
import java.awt.*;
import java.net.*;
import java.io.*;
import java.util.*;
```

Utility and Language Class Reference

```java
public class UserInputClient extends Applet implements Observer, Runnable {
    // Private state consists only of the listbox used for the Applet's
    // interface, and the thread that is used to periodically ask the
    // UserInputClientObservable to send out update notifications, and
    // the UserInputClientObservable itself.
    private List m_list;
    private Thread m_threadTimer;
    private UserInputClientObservable m_observable;
    private int m_nPort = -1;

    // Init just creates the user interface, including the display list. It
    // also gets the server port to connect to on start().
    public void init() {
        setLayout(new BorderLayout());

        try {
            m_nPort = Integer.parseInt(getParameter("port"));
        } catch(NumberFormatException nfe) {
            add("Center", new Label("Need a valid 'port' parameter"));
            return;
        }

        m_list = new List();
        add("Center", m_list);
        add("North", new Label("Last 10 from the server."));
    }

    // start kick-starts a new timer thread, and creates a new
    // UserInputClientObservable, adding this Applet as an
    // Observer.
    public void start() {
        try {
            m_observable = new UserInputClientObservable(
                    InetAddress.getByName(getDocumentBase().getHost()),
                    m_nPort);
            m_observable.addObserver(this);
        } catch (UnknownHostException uhe) {
            m_observable = null;
            return;
        }

        m_threadTimer = new Thread(this);
        m_threadTimer.start();
    }

    // Stop method must stop both the UserInputClientObservable,
    // and the timer thread.
    public void stop() {
```

```java
            m_observable.stop();
            m_threadTimer = null;
        }

        // The run() method is what the timer thread runs on. Every
        // half-second it asks the UserInputClientObservable to send
        // out update notifications.
        public void run() {
            try {
                while(m_threadTimer == Thread.currentThread()) {
                    Thread.currentThread().sleep(500);
                    if(null != m_observable)
                        m_observable.notifyObservers();
                }
            } catch (InterruptedException ie) {
                return;
            }
        }

        // update() method called by UserInputClientObserver whenever
        // new input comes from the server. Applet updates display
        // by getting rid of contents of m_list and re-filling with
        // Strings the observer has stored up.
        public void update(Observable o, Object arg) {
            if(o != m_observable)
                return;

            String[] astr = m_observable.getLatestStrings();
            m_list.clear();
            for(int ii=0 ; ii<astr.length && null != astr[ii] ; ii++)
                m_list.addItem(astr[ii]);
        }
    }

    // UserInputClientObservable keeps a background thread running
    // that listens for incoming strings from a server. Connects to server
    // and sets up background thread in constructor. Just sets dirty bit
    // when new string comes in.
    class UserInputClientObservable extends Observable implements Runnable {
        // Private state is list of latest 10 strings (not necessarily
        // in order), background thread, and port to connect to.
        private String[] m_astr = new String[10];
        private Socket m_sock;
        private Thread m_thread;

        // Constructor takes port to connect to, creates background thread.
        public UserInputClientObservable(InetAddress addrHost, int nPort) {
            try {
```

Utility and Language Class Reference

```
            m_sock = new Socket(addrHost, nPort);
        } catch(IOException ioe) {
            System.err.println("Error:\n connecting to server");
            m_sock = null;
            return;
        }

        m_thread = new Thread(this);
        m_thread.start();
    }

    // stop() method called by Applet whenever Applet's stop method
    // is called.
    public void stop() {
        m_thread = null;
        if(null != m_sock)
            try {
                m_sock.close();
            } catch (IOException ioe) {}
    }

    // getLatestStrings() called by Applet to get the latest 10 strings.
    public String[] getLatestStrings() {
        clearChanged();
        return m_astr;
    }

    // run method is run by the background thread. It creates DataInputStream
    // and reads strings from server, placing them in m_astr.
    public void run() {
        int m_nStr = 0;

        try {
            DataInputStream in = new DataInputStream(m_sock.getInputStream());
            while(m_thread == Thread.currentThread()) {
                String s = in.readUTF();
                m_astr[m_nStr] = s;
                m_nStr = (m_nStr + 1) % m_astr.length;
                setChanged();
            }
            m_sock.close();
        } catch (Exception e) {
            System.err.println("Error:\n reading from server.");
        }


    }
} (1) The Miscellaneous java.util Classes
```

There are three miscellaneous java.util classes. These classes are nonetheless quite useful. Even though they are hard to categorize with other Java core classes, they are relatively simple to explain. One of these classes, the StreamTokenizer, is explained in detail in Chapter 9 because objects of that class are used to parse streams of data.

The Date Class

A Date object is able to represent any date and time from the very beginning of the 20th century until eons in the future. The resolution of the Date object is down to the second.

The Date class is aware of year, month, date or day, hour, minute, and second of the time it represents. There are six constructors for the Date class, each one allowing you to specify more or less resolution in a particular Date object, or able to use different time/date formats for creating Date objects. Here are the signatures of the six constructors:

```
public Date();
public Date(int year, int month, int date);
public Date(int year, int month, int date, int hours, int mins);
public Date(int year, int month, int date, int hours, int mins, int secs);
public Date(long time);
public Date(String strTimeDate);
```

The first, no-argument constructor creates a Date object representing the current day and time. The second will create a Date object representing midnight at the beginning of the specified date, month, and year. The third allows you to create a Date object specifying down to the minute. And the fourth lets you specify the exact time down to the second. The fifth take a long integer value that is the number of milliseconds past midnight, 1/1/1900. (Note that the System.currentTimeMillis( ) method will return a number in this exact format.) And the sixth takes a UNIX time-date formatted string. Those strings look something like this:

```
Sat, 12 Aug 1995 13:30:00 GMT
```

It also understands the U.S. timezone abbreviations, as well as an offset abbreviation from GMT:

```
Sat, 12 Aug 1995 13:30:00 GMT+0500
```

Note that this is the same syntax as the string that is returned from the toGMTString( ) method of this class, and is also the Internet standard used, for example, in e-mail Date headers.

The Date class includes get/set methods for each one of the parameters' year (getYear( ), setYear( )), month (getMonth( ), setMonth( )), date, hour, minute, and second. It also has get/set methods for setting the day, where zero means Sunday and 6 means Saturday.

The getGMTString( ) and getLocaleString( ) methods of this class return string representations of the time. The before( ) and after( ) methods are boolean comparison methods. The before( ) method returns true if the Date object passed as the only parameter is earlier in time than the given Date object. The after( ) method then obviously returns true if the Date object passed as its only parameter is after the given Date object. The equals( ) implementation of this class returns true for two different Date objects as long as they represent the exact same time.

Finally, the UTC( ) method of this class returns a long value that is the exact number of milliseconds since midnight on 1/1/1900 that is represented by the Date object.

The Random Class

In order to generate a pseudorandom series of numbers automatically, the designers of Java included the Random class in the java.util package. Given a random number seed, which is a long value, a Random object will generate a pseudorandom series of ints, longs, doubles, and floats.

One constructor, the no-argument constructor, is initialized using the long value returned by System.currentTimeMillis( ). The second constructor takes a single long parameter that is the random number seed it should use to generate new numbers. At any time, you can change a Random object's seed using the Random class' setSeed( ) method, which takes a new long integer value for it to use as its new seed.

The nextInt( ), nextLong( ), nextFloat( ), and nextDouble( ) methods return the next pseudorandom value in the sequence. The int and long values may have any value from the lowest possible to the highest possible represented by the integer type. The nextFloat( ) and nextDouble( ) methods will return values between 0.0 and 1.0.

The java.lang Numeric Classes

During the course of programming in Java, you may find it necessary to store a simple numeric value away for later use. However, if you wanted to store that value away into one of the java.util storage classes, you wouldn't be able to. That's because you have to store objects in those storage devices, and the built-in numeric data types of Java are not objects, so you can't store them. That could be a real problem, causing silly workarounds where a simple solution should exist.

To accomplish this task, you have two options: First, to create an array of the numeric type with only one element in it, and store that array in the storage device, as this code demonstrates:

```
public void storeVal(Vector vect, int n) {
    int[] an = new int[1];
    an[0] = n;
    vect.addElement(an);
```

This works because arrays are actually objects in Java, and as objects they are ultimately derived from the Object class.

The second way to accomplish this task is to create an instance of one of the numeric classes included in the java.lang package, as this example code demonstrates:

```
public void storeVal(Vector vect, int n) {
    vect.addElement(new Integer(n));
}
```

Both techniques have advantages and disadvantages. The advantage of using an array is that the value is changeable after the array has been created. This is not true of Integer objects which, once created, cannot change the values of the int they represent.

In any event, the java.lang numeric and built-in-type classes were created so that you could pass around objects that represented simple built-in-type values. The following table lists all the built-in-type classes included in the java.lang package.

Class	Represents
Boolean	Built-in boolean-type values
Character	Built-in char-type values
Double	Built-in double-type values
Float	Built-in float-type values
Integer	Built-in int-type values
Long	Built-in long-type values

The numeric-type values (i.e., Float, Double, Integer, and Long) are all based on the Number base class. This base class defines four abstract methods:

Utility and Language Class Reference

```
public double doubleValue();
public float floatValue();
public int intValue();
public void longValue();
```

These are essentially casting methods, allowing you to convert from any number to one of these four basic forms. (Note also the Java 1.1 specification also includes a java.lang class for the short type. This book is here mostly to describe the Java 1.0 specification that Visual J++ is based on. The final chapter, Chapter 12, describes some of the advances that will be added to Java in upcoming versions and enhancements to be added to Visual J++ in the future.)

In addition to these conversion methods, the number-based numeric classes also include a bevy of methods for converting to and from string representations of numbers. For example, the Integer class includes a getInteger( ) method for parsing a string into a new Integer object. The parseInt( ) method of this class will parse a string into a simple int value in much the same way.

To convert an integer into its string form, the toBinaryString( ), toOctalString( ), toHexString( ), and toString( ) methods all will convert an integer into an appropriate format for the given radix.

Note that all these parseXXX( ) and toXXXString( ) methods are static members of the various numeric classes. That means you must pass in an int (or an Integer, according to the overloaded version of the method) or a string. The static method will parse the passed-on string to an int or Integer value. The toXXXString( ) will generate and return a new string given an int or Integer value. (There is also a nonstatic toString( ) method, which will convert the Integer to its decimal form.)

So, you use these numeric class objects to use numeric values where methods call for any object. Here's an example program that utilizes these numeric types to store numeric objects in a java.util.Stack object. You may be familiar with the semipopular "reverse Polish" mathematics notation. In this notation, instead of writing operations like

```
<operand> <operator> <operand>
```

as in

```
5 + 2,
```

you write operations like

```
<operand> [<operand> [<operatand> ...] ] <operator>
```

as in

```
5 2 +
```

This notation makes it easier to evaluate equations. For example, the complex equation

```
((5 * 4) + 10 + 20 / (2 + 1)) % 7
```

would look like

```
5
4
*                       // (5 * 4)
10
+                       // (5 * 4) + 10
20
2
1
+
/                       // 20 / (2 + 1)
+                       // (5 * 4) + 10 + 20 / (2 + 1)
7
%                       // ((5 * 4) + 10 + 20 / (2 + 1)) % 7
```

Obviously, this equation doesn't make it easier to *write* equations, just evaluate them. Using just a single stack, the following program implements a reverse-Polish notation calculator. The way it works is to push successive numeric elements onto an internal stack using Double objects to represent the numbers. Every time an operator is entered, such as '*' or '+', then the most recent operands are popped off the stack, evaluated using the operator, and the answer is pushed back onto the stack. You may recognize this program as a common Computer Science 101-type programming problem. Here is how to implement this program in Java:

```java
import java.util.Stack;
import java.io.*;

public class RPCalculator {
    public static void main(String astrArgs[]) {
        // Ignore command-line arguments.

        // Each line read in from System.in is either an
        // operand (number) or operator. If operand, push onto
```

Utility and Language Class Reference

```java
            // stack. If operator, evaluate using operands that are
            // on the stack.
            Stack stack = new Stack();

            try {
                String str;
                    DataInputStream in = new DataInputStream(System.in);
                while(true) {
                        str = in.readLine();

                    // If is operand, call appropriate handler
                    // method.
                    if("+".equals(str))
                        doAdd(stack);
                    else if("-".equals(str))
                        doSub(stack);
                    else if("*".equals(str))
                        doMult(stack);
                    else if("/".equals(str))
                        doDiv(stack);
                    else if("%".equals(str))
                        doMod(stack);
                      else if("quit".equals(str))
                            break;
                    else try {       // push operand onto stack.
                        Double d = Double.valueOf(str);
                        stack.push(d);
                    } catch (NumberFormatException nfe) {
                        System.err.println("\tWhat?");
                    }

                    // Show current state of the stack
                    doShowResult(stack);
                }
            } catch (EOFException eof) {
                // End of the program, print out the result.
                doShowResult(stack);
            } catch (IOException ioe) {
                    System.err.println("IO error: " + ioe);
                    System.exit(-1);
            }
        }

        public static void doAdd(Stack s) {
            Double op1, op2;
            try {
                op1 = (Double)s.pop( );
                op2 = (Double)s.pop( );
```

```java
                s.push(new Double(op1.doubleValue() + op2.doubleValue()));
        } catch (ClassCastException cce) {
            System.err.println("Error:\n improper args on the stack.");
            System.exit(-1);
        }
    }

    public static void doSub(Stack s) {
        Double op1, op2;
        try {
            op1 = (Double)s.pop( );
            op2 = (Double)s.pop( );
            s.push(new Double(op2.doubleValue() - op1.doubleValue()));
        } catch (ClassCastException cce) {
            System.err.println("Error:\n improper args on the stack.");
            System.exit(-1);
        }
    }

    public static void doMult(Stack s) {
        Double op1, op2;
        try {
            op1 = (Double)s.pop( );
            op2 = (Double)s.pop( );
            s.push(new Double(op1.doubleValue() * op2.doubleValue()));
        } catch (ClassCastException cce) {
            System.err.println("Error:\n improper args on the stack.");
            System.exit(-1);
        }
    }

    public static void doDiv(Stack s) {
        Double op1, op2;
        try {
            op1 = (Double)s.pop( );
            op2 = (Double)s.pop( );
            Double d = new Double(op2.doubleValue() / op1.doubleValue());
              if(d.isNaN() || d.isInfinite()) {
                    System.err.println("Illegal arithmetic operation.");
                     System.exit(-1);
                }
               s.push(d);
        } catch (ClassCastException cce) {
            System.err.println("Error:\n improper args on the stack.");
            System.exit(-1);
        }
    }
```

Utility and Language Class Reference

```
public static void doMod(Stack s) {
    Double op1, op2;
    try {
        op1 = (Double)s.pop( );
        op2 = (Double)s.pop( );
        Double d = new Double(op2.doubleValue() % op1.doubleValue());
          if(d.isNaN() || d.isInfinite()) {
                System.err.println("Illegal arithmetic operation.");
                System.exit(-1);
          }
          s.push(d);
    } catch (ClassCastException cce) {
        System.err.println("Error:\n improper args on the stack.");
        System.exit(-1);
    }
}

// doShowResult() prints the state of the stack on the screen.
// Uses the Stack methods inherited from the Vector class.
public static void doShowResult(Stack s) {
    System.out.println("\tStack's current state:");
    for(int ii=0 ; ii<s.size() ; ii++)
        System.out.println("\t" + s.elementAt(ii));
    }
}
```

Class Objects and Class Loaders

As is explained in Chapter 1, each Java class is stored in a single .CLASS file. Only after that class is loaded in the Java run-time environment can you create an instance of that class. For example, when your browser loads a Java applet into a remote HTML file, the first thing the JVM does is load the applet's .CLASS file from a remote URL. Similarly, when loading that applet into the JVM, all other classes that your Applet class refers to are also loaded either from the local file system (using the CLASSPATH environment variable to tell the JVM where to look for .CLASS files) or from a remote URL.

Each class loaded into the JVM has a run-time representation that is an object of the Class class. Using this Class object directly, you can get the name of the class, create a new instance of the class, and even enumerate the interfaces that the class implements. All these operations can be done through the Class class methods.

This section first describes the Class class: its methods and how to get Class objects from the run-time environment, and even how to load class objects into the run-time environment in your applications or applets. In addition, this section also describes how to create class loaders to add classes to your run-time environment yourself. While class loaders are powerful, allowing you to essentially augment your list of available classes with almost any new class, they are also restricted in that an applet cannot create new classes using a class loader.

The Class Class

Given any Java object, the Object class method getClass( ) that it inherits will return a reference to the Class object representing the class of that object. For example if you created a Vector object, you can get a reference to the Class object representing the Vector class using the Vector's getClass( ) method. Here's an example of how this is done:

```
Vector vect = new Vector();

Class classVector = vect.getClass();
```

Remember, *any* object will return the Class object representing its class. Just use the getClass( ) method.

There's also another way to get a Class object given just the name of the class. The static Class class method forName( ) will return the Class object for any class given a string holding the class' name. For example, this code will give you the Class object of the "Object" class:

```
Class classObject = Class.forName("Object");
```

The forName( ) method will work even if the specified class has not yet been loaded into your run-time environment! The forName( ) method works by directly telling the JVM's class loader to find the specified class. If the class hasn't been loaded yet, the class loader will attempt to load it into the run-time environment. If the associated .CLASS file is present in one of the CLASSPATH directories on the local file system, then the JVM's class loader will load the .CLASS file from the local file and then return the associated Class object from your call to forName( ). Note that this way of loading classes into the run-time environment works in either Java applications or even in Java applets.

So, once you have a reference to a Class object, what can you do with it? Well, first of all you can create a new instance of the class. The Class class method newInstance( ) will return a new instance of the class. This is just like using the new operator and a no-argument constructor to create a new object. In fact, it is almost exactly the same thing. The only difference is that you don't have to know the name of the class at compile time. Instead,

Utility and Language Class Reference

using the forName( ) method of the Class class, you can create instances of objects whose classes did not even exist when your application or applet was created!

This sample application takes as a command-line argument any number of class names. The application will attempt to load the named class into the run-time environment and create a new instance of it using the Class class method newInstance( ). Following that listing is a listing for a simple HelloWorldFrame, which is a frame that displays the text "Hello, World!" By running the InstantiateClass application with the command-line argument "HelloWorldFrame," the application will actually load the HelloWorldFrame class and create an instance of it. If you run the InstantiateClass program like this, you will see a frame appear that looks like Figure 11-4.

```
public class InstantiateClass {
    public static void main(String[] astrArgs) {
        // For each command-line argument, attempt to load the class and
        // create an instance of it.
        for(int ii=0 ; ii<astrArgs.length ; ii++) {
            try {
                Class cls = Class.forName(astrArgs[ii]);
                Object o = cls.newInstance();
            } catch (ClassNotFoundException cnfe) {
                System.err.println("Class not found: " + astrArgs[ii]);
            } catch (InstantiationException ie) {
                System.err.println("Instantiation error with class " +
                        astrArgs[ii]);
                System.err.println("\texception is: " + ie);
            } catch (IllegalAccessException iae) {
                System.err.println("No rights to constructor for class " +
                        astrArgs[ii]);
            } catch (NoSuchMethodException nsme) {
                System.err.println("Class doesn't have no-arg constructor" +
                        astrArgs[ii]);
            }
        }
    }
}
```

Note that to use the InstantiateClass program, you must pass the fully qualified class name of the class to instantiate. That is, you must pass both the class name and the package name. To create a Label object from the java.awt.package, you would have to pass the command-line argument "java.awt.Label."

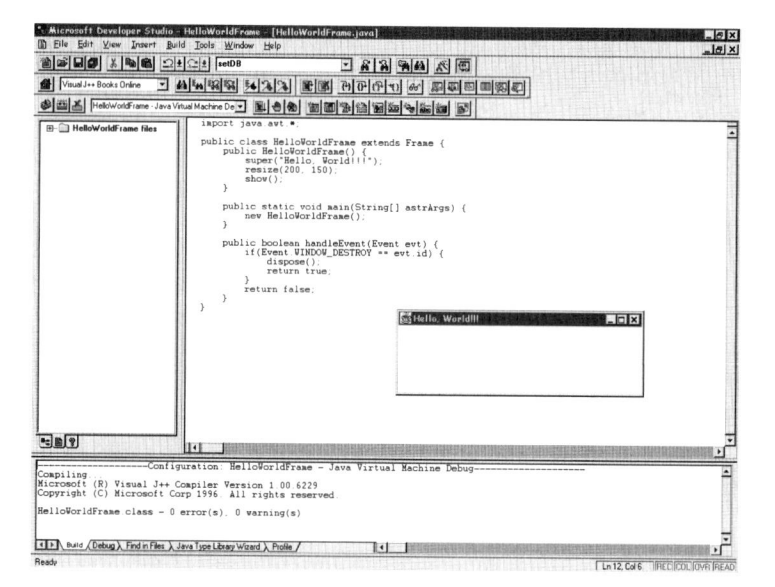

The HelloWorld-Frame created from the InstantiateClass application
Figure 11-4.

Here is the listing for the HelloWorldFrame class. Figure 11-4 is a screen shot of an instance of this class created using the InstantiateClass application:

```java
import java.awt.*;

public class HelloWorldFrame extends Frame {
    public HelloWorldFrame() {
        super("Hello, World!!!");
        resize(200, 150);
        show();
    }

    public boolean handleEvent(Event evt) {
        if(Event.WINDOW_DESTROY == evt.id) {
            dispose();
            return true;
        }
        return false;
    }
}
```

The first thing to note about the InstantiateClass application is how many catch blocks there are surrounding the calls to Class.forName( ) and Class.newInstance( ). Each one of those catch blocks catches a different type of error that can occur while either trying to load a class into the run-time environment, or while trying to create a new instance of the class. Here's an explanation of each of them, one by one.

If the JVM's class loader cannot find the .CLASS file to load, then the call to Class.forName( ) will cause a ClassNotFoundException to be thrown. Note that if the class is already loaded into the run-time environment, then this exception will never be thrown. In fact, the JVM's class loader will never be asked to load the class, since the class has already been loaded. The only time this exception will be thrown is if the JVM cannot find the .CLASS file for the class. This touches on the subject of class loaders, which is discussed following this section on Class objects, so hold off any questions about ClassNotFoundExceptions until you read that description.

The next exception being caught in the InstantiateClass application is an InstantiationException. An InstantiationException is thrown if you try to create a new object of an abstract class, or of an interface. For example, if you used the InstantiateClass application and passed it the command-line argument "java.lang.Observer," then the application would report that an instantiation error had happened. That's because the class name "java.lang.Observer" is actually a name for an interface: the Observer interface of the java.lang package. You can't instantiate interfaces or abstract classes. Anytime you try using the newInstance( ) method of the Class class, then an InstantiationException will be thrown.

An IllegalAccessException will be thrown by the newInstance( ) method if the class that was loaded has a nonpublic no-argument constructor. See, by definition the newInstance( ) method creates a new instance of the class by calling the class' no-argument constructor. If the no-argument constructor is not a public method of the class, however, then you are essentially trying to call a method you do not have access to. Whenever you try to do this and it is caught by the run-time system, then an IllegalAccessException is thrown.

Finally, the NoSuchMethodException is thrown by the newInstance( ) method if the class does not have any no-argument constructors at all. This is very important, because the newInstance( ) method can only create new objects by using their no-argument constructors. If there are no such constructors of the class, then a NoSuchMethodException is thrown by the run-time environment.

Thus, while the combination of the newInstance( ) and forName( ) methods of the Class class are powerful in that they allow you to augment your run-time environment at run time, there are several pitfalls that must be detected and avoided when using this technique. Specifically, the four are ClassNotFoundExceptions, InstantiationExceptions, IllegalAccessExceptions, and NoSuchMethodExceptions.

Other Class Class Methods

The isInterface( ) method of the Class class returns true if the Class object represents an interface only, and not a class. Otherwise, this method returns a false value. You can use this method to avoid some amount of InstantiationExceptions from being thrown, but remember that an InstantiateException will also be thrown if the class is an abstract class.

The Class class method getName( ) returns the string name of the class, as demonstrated by the next example program.

The getInterfaces( ) method returns an array of Class objects, each one representing one of the interfaces implemented by the class. As an example of its use, this sample application takes a command-line argument that is a class name to load. The program then will enumerate all the interfaces that the class implements.

```
public class ListInterfaces {
    public static void main(String[] astrArgs) {
        for(int ii=0 ; ii<astrArgs.length ; ii++) {
            try {
                Class cls = Class.forName(astrArgs[ii]);
                Class[] aclsInterfaces = cls.getInterfaces();
                System.out.println("Class " + cls.getName() + ":");
                for(int jj=0 ; jj<aclsInterfaces.length ; jj++)
                    System.out.println("\t" + aclsInterfaces[jj].getName());
            } catch (ClassNotFoundException cnfe) {
                System.err.println("Error:\n class not found " + astrArgs[ii]);
            }
        }
    }
}
```

The getSuperclass( ) method returns a reference to the Class object representing the given class' superclass. For example, if you got a reference to the class representing the java.awt.Container class and called its getSuperclass( ) method, it would return a reference to the Class object representing the Component class in Java. That's because the Container class inherits directly from the Component class.

Finally, the Class class method getClassLoader( ) returns a reference to the class loader used to load the class into the run-time environment. You haven't read anything yet about actual ClassLoader objects, so read about those first, and then you can read about how Class objects and ClassLoader objects relate to one another.

Class Loaders

So, how *does* the JVM load new classes? How does it "know" how to read .CLASS files from the local file system, or across the Internet (in the case of applets). And how does it know how to interpret those files into usable executable byte codes? All this magic is achieved using *class loaders*. The ClassLoader class includes implementation for converting an array of bytes that matches the format of a .CLASS file into executable code in the Java Virtual Machine. By implementing your own class loader, you can augment your run-time environment by loading classes from files, from URLs, or from any other storage medium.

When asked to load a class with the name "Foo," the Java Virtual Machine's default class loader is built to search through the directories (and zip files) listed in the CLASSPATH environment variable for a file by the name "Foo.class." When it finds a file by this name, the class loader will read the entire file into a local byte array and call its protected method defineClass( ), passing it the byte array. The defineClass( ) method will inject the class into the run-time environment, and return a Class object for the newly loaded class.

All nonsystem classes have a class loader that was used to load the class into the run-time system. The Class class method getClassLoader( ) returns a reference to this class loader. To demonstrate this fact, the following program, which loads the Vector class and prints out its ClassLoader's toString( ) return value, uses the getClassLoader( ) method to retrieve a reference to a class' class loader:

```
public class GetThisClassLoader {
    public static void main(String[] astrArgs) {
        new GetThisClassLoader();
    }

    public GetThisClassLoader() {
        Class cls = this.getClass();
        ClassLoader cl = cls.getClassLoader();
        System.out.println("The " + cls.getName() + " class ClassLoader: " +
            cl);
    }
}
```

When run, this simple application will produce this output:

```
The GetThisClassLoader class ClassLoader: null
```

Whoops! How come the class loader is null? Well, basically it's because you cannot get a reference to the JVM's default class loader. That class loader is protected from you using it or getting a reference to it directly. Classes loaded by the JVM directly from the local file system are, by default, loaded by the JVM's class loader, which you cannot get a reference to.

There is a method that allows you to load a class using this class loader, however. The ClassLoader class' getSystemClass( ) method will load a class using the default class loader.

So, when is the JVM's default class loader *not* used to load a class? The default class loader is not used when the class trying to load another class into the run-time system was itself loaded by a class loader other than the JVM's default class loader. That is, once you load a class by hand using a custom class loader, that class loader is used by the Java system to load any other classes required by that class. Otherwise, the JVM's default class loader is used to inject classes into the run-time system.

Making a Custom Class Loader

Say you wanted to make an application that is capable of loading classes from across the Internet. Obviously, an applet running in a browser has this capability. The JVM that is programmed into the browser has a class loader that can do just that: it can look not only on the local file system for a .CLASS file, but it can also look in a URL based on the applet's .CLASS file's URL. For example, if your applet's .CLASS file was loaded from a URL "http://www.whatever.com/MyApplet.class," and your applet explicitly refers to a class named "MyHelperClass," then the browser's class loader will look for a URL named "http://www.whatever.com/MyHelperClass.class."

But that, of course, is a browser with a built-in JVM. How do you get your Java application to load new classes across the Internet using URLs? The only way to do it is by creating a custom class loader.

To make a custom class loader, derive your new class loader from the java.lang.ClassLoader class, and provide an implementation for the loadClass( ) method. All this method needs to do is retrieve a .CLASS file from somewhere (in this case, from the Internet) and call the ClassLoader protected method defineClass( ) with the data from the URL. That's it. Here's an implementation of a URLClassLoader class:

```java
import java.net.*;
import java.io.*;

class URLClassLoader extends ClassLoader {
    private URL m_urlBase;
```

Utility and Language Class Reference

```java
    public URLClassLoader(URL urlBase) {
        m_urlBase = urlBase;
    }

    public Class loadClass(String strClassName, boolean resolve)
            throws ClassNotFoundException {
        Class cls;
        try {
            URL urlClassFile = new URL(m_urlBase, strClassName + ".class");
            InputStream is = urlClassFile.openStream();

            ByteArrayOutputStream out = new ByteArrayOutputStream();
            int n;
            while(-1 != (n = is.read()))
                out.write(n);

            cls = defineClass(out.toByteArray(), 0, out.size());
        } catch (IOException ioe) {
            throw new ClassNotFoundException(strClassName);
        }

        if(resolve)
            resolveClass(cls);

        return cls;
    }
}
```

Now, using this URL class loader, you can create a program similar to the InstantiateClass application previously listed that can load a class from a URL. This application, called InstantiateURLClass, takes at least two command-line arguments. The first command-line argument is a URL base to use when creating the URL class loader. Each command-line argument after that is the name of a class for the program to load and create an instance of. Here's the code for the InstantiateURLClass application that uses the URL class loader given previously:

```java
import java.net.*;

public class InstantiateURLClass {
    public static void main(String[] astrArgs) {
        // First command-line argument is URL base to use when creating
        // a URLClassLoader.
        URLClassLoader url_cl;
        try {
            URL urlBase = new URL(astrArgs[0]);
            url_cl = new URLClassLoader(urlBase);
```

```
        } catch (MalformedURLException mue) {
            System.err.print("Usage Error:\n InstantiateURLClass ");
            System.err.println("<url-base> <classname> [<classname> ...]");
            System.exit(-1);
        }

        // For each command-line argument, attempt to load the class and
        // create an instance of it.
        for(int ii=1 ; ii<astrArgs.length ; ii++) {
            try {
                Class cls = url_cl.loadClass(astrArgs[ii], false);
                Object o = cls.newInstance();
            } catch (ClassNotFoundException cnfe) {
                System.err.println("Class not found: " + astrArgs[ii]);
            } catch (InstantiationException ie) {
                System.err.println("Instantiation error with class " +
                    astrArgs[ii]);
                System.err.println("\texcpetion is: " + ie);
            } catch (IllegalAccessException iae) {
                System.err.println("No rights to constructor for class " +
                    astrArgs[ii]);
            } catch (NoSuchMethodException nsme) {
                System.err.println("Class doesn't have no-arg constructor" +
                    astrArgs[ii]);
            }
        }
    }
}
```

The Math Class

All of the trigonometric and mathematical functions you might want to use for complex computations are included within a single-instance class called the java.lang.Math class. The Math class is a class that only has public static methods, so that you access all the mathematical methods using the "Math" class name, like this:

```
int nMin = Math.min(10, 20);
```

The trigonometric methods of the Math class all take angles measured in radians. In case you don't remember what radians are, here's a quick review. A radian is an angle measure, such that there are 2π radians in a full circle. To make working with radians easier, the Math class includes a static double value called PI, which is a very close approximation of the value of π. Since most engineers think in degrees, not radians, here are some quick conversion functions:

```
public double degreesToRads(double dDegrees) {
    return (Math.PI * dDegrees / 180.0);
}

public double radsToDegrees(double dRads) {
    return (180.0 * dRads / Math.PI);
}
```

Note that the Math class includes a random( ) method, which returns successive double values in a pseudorandom sequence when called multiple times. Rather than using this method, your programs will be easier to test and control if you use Random objects from the java.util package. This is because, for debugging purposes, you can control the random number seed used by the Random object(s), while the random number seed used by the Math class' random( ) method is not controllable, and thus the random number sequence it produces is not reproducible.

All the methods of the Math class are well-known trigonometric, rounding, min/max, exponential, or other types of methods. The online documentation of the Math class is available in the Visual J++ InfoViewer. In the interest of keeping you awake while reading this text, a full listing of those mathematical methods is excluded. Again, please refer to the Math class documentation for specifics about the mathematical methods of the Math class.

The Run-Time System Classes

The run-time environment of your Java applications and applets is presented through a group of four java.lang classes. The Runtime class and the System class, which have some amount of overlapping functionality, expose the run-time environment. Through these classes you can control the run-time environment and get information about the environment your Java executables are running in.

Java exposes the ability to secure certain local resources to prevent access by unauthorized classes. The SecurityManager is a single-instance class through which pass all requests to access local file system, make Internet connections, execute new processes, link to native libraries, etc. Any potentially sensitive operation possible in Java is first checked against the security manager. If the operation is not to be allowed, then the security manager can stop it, and is responsible for canceling the operation.

As just mentioned, you can execute external programs from within the Java context. The Process class represents processes that have been spawned by your Java application. (Note that applets are generally not allowed to execute external applications from within the browser. Although, if you make your own browser you could of course allow such execution to take place.)

The Runtime and System Classes

The Runtime and System classes of the java.lang package provide access to the run-time environment your Java applications and applets are running in. Both of these classes are single-instance classes, and they have some amount of overlapping functionality, so it is easier to think of them as a pair of complementary classes, providing different views on what is essentially the same realm of capabilities.

The Runtime class is used to control processes and manage the free memory of the system. It is through this single-instance class that you execute external processes and find out more about the memory allocation currently being used by the JVM.

Spawning External Processes

To spawn an external process from within your Java program, use the Runtime class method exec( ). There are four overloaded versions of this method, whose method signatures are

```
public Process exec(String   command);
public Process exec(String   command, String  envp[]);
public Process exec(String   cmdarray[]);
public Process exec(String   cmdarray[], String  envp[]);
```

The first overloaded version of this method simply takes a command line to be executed. The command line obviously is going to have a system-dependent format, so that on a Windows machine the command-line string would look different than on a UNIX machine, which would also be different than command lines executed on a Macintosh system.

The second overloaded version of this method allows you to define the run-time environment variables and values used by the externally executed program. The command-line string looks the same as it would in the first overloaded version of this method. The envp[] array of strings is an array of variable/value environment variable definitions. The format of each string in this line is "variablename=value."

The third overloaded version of this method allows you to define your command line as an array of string tokens. The first token is the name of the program to execute, and each additional token is a separate command-line

Utility and Language Class Reference

argument that will be passed to the executed program. For example, this line of code that uses the first overloaded version of the exec( ) method

```
Process proc = Runtime.exec("java AnotherClass arg1 arg2");
```

can also be executed using this code, which uses the third overloaded version of the exec( ) method:

```
String[] astr_cmndline = { "java",
        "AnotherClass", "arg1", "arg2" };
Process proc = Runtime.exec(astr_cmdline);
```

And the fourth overloaded version of this method is just like the third, but it also allows you to pass a set of environment variables to be used by the executed process. The format of the variable/value strings that make up the members of the *envp[]* array is the same as the format for the *envp[]* parameter to the second overloaded version of this method.

The Process Class

As you may have noticed, the various versions of the Runtime class' exec( ) method return Process objects. A Process object represents an external run-time process within your Java run-time environment. Using the Process object, you can control the coordinated execution of your Java program with the externally executed process.

The Process class has methods that allow you to access and use the input, output, and error streams of the externally executed process. The getInputStream( ) method returns an input stream. The data you read from this input stream is the data written to the subprocess' output stream.

Conversely, the getOutputStream( ) method of the Process class returns an output stream. The data you write to this output stream is piped through to the subprocess as the subprocess' input stream.

The input stream returned by the getErrorStream( ) returns an input stream. The data you read from this input stream is the data written to the subprocess' error stream.

For example, if you execute an external Java program (that is, start a Java process in a new JVM instance), then data written to that subprocess' System.out PrintStream can be read in by your program from the input stream returned by the Process' getInputStream( ) method. If the java subprocess tries to read from System.in, then it will read the data that you write to the output stream returned from the Process.getOuputStream( ) method.

The exitValue( ) method of the Process class returns the exit code the external process terminates with. If the external process is another Java process, then the exit value is the value passed to the System.exit( ) method. If the external process has not yet terminated when you call this method, then an IllegalThreadStateException will be thrown.

In order to suspend your parent Java process until the spawned subprocess is started by a call to Runtime.exec( ), use the Process class method waitFor( ). This method will suspend the calling thread until the spawned subprocess terminates. Note that if the subprocess has already terminated when this method is called, then the call to waitFor( ) returns immediately.

The destroy( ) method of the Process class terminates the spawned process immediately.

Using the Process and Runtime classes together, you could easily create a shell or launcher application completely in Java.

Memory, Garbage Collection, and Finalization Control

The freeMemory( ) and totalMemory( ) methods of the Runtime class both tell something about the memory condition on the local system. The method freeMemory( ) indicates how much memory is free, and totalMemory( ) indicates the total amount of memory on the local system. The long integer values that are returned indicate the number of bytes of addressable memory that are on the local system. Given that the Java Virtual Machine does not allow allocation of simple blocks of memory (but rather constricts you to allocating objects only), the usefulness of these methods is limited. Of course, you can determine if you are completely out of memory when you receive a MemoryException by checking the return value from Runtime.freeMemory( ).

If you suspect that memory is low, or you just want to make sure as much memory is as free as possible at some point while your program is running, use the Runtime.gc( ) and Runtime.runFinalization( ) methods. The gc( ) method kick-starts a session of the garbage collector immediately. The runFinalization( ) method completes memory deallocation by finalizing (destroying) any garbage-collected objects that have not yet been destroyed.

The System Class

The System class is a single-instance class that exposes the system variables of the run-time environment your Java applications and applets are running in. Through the System object, you have access to the environment variables, input and output streams, as well as the error output stream, and current system time. In addition, some of the Runtime class methods are also

Utility and Language Class Reference

exposed as part of the System class (for example, the exit( ) method, which is also a method of the Runtime class that is reimplemented in the System class).

Accessing Environment Properties

The environment properties tell you information about the platform your executable (application or applet) is running on and about the JVM. The properties are exposed as a Properties object, which is a hashtable specifically filled with string-based keys and values. The online documentation available in the InfoViewer lists specifically which properties are available and what they are for.

For example, there is a system property called "user.dir" whose value is the path of the current working directory when the JVM was started. The user.home property lists the user's home directory. The user.name property gives the account name for the currently logged-in user. See the InfoViewer topic for the getProperties( ) method of the System class for a full description of all system properties available through the Properties object returned by the System object's getProperties( ) method.

The Input, Output, and Error Streams

Undoubtedly you have noticed in the various example applications and applets in this book that extensive use is made of the streams System.in, System.out, and System.err. These streams are the main input, output, and error streams for all Java processes.

For applets specifically, the System.in and System.out streams are not functional. That is, the user does not type input in to a command-line-like teletype interface. Instead, the user interacts with the applet solely through AWT input and display controls. The System.err stream goes to different places, which is completely browser-specific. In the Netscape Navigator, an applet's System.err output is written to the Java Console windows, which can be displayed used the Options|Java Console Main menu option.

Java applications can read input from the System.in stream and write output to the System.out stream. The input will come from the user's typewriter, or from a redirected input file. The output will go to the screen, or to a file if the program's output was redirected on the command line.

The arraycopy( ) Method

The System.arraycopy( ) method will copy whole arrays or subarrays from source to destination arrays. This method is highly optimized using native code to make copying arrays in Java quite fast. Without using this method, you would have to copy array elements individually to duplicate arrays.

For example, to reallocate an array and make it larger, you would use code that looks like this:

```
public int[] doubleIntArraySize(int[] an) {
    int[] anRet = new int[an.length * 2];

    System.arraycopy(an, 0, anRet, 0, an.length);
}
```

The arraycopy( ) method's signature looks like this:

```
public void arraycopy(Object src, int srcOffset, Object dst, int dstOffset,
        int length);
```

The arraycopy( ) method will throw an ArrayStoreException if the types of source and destination arrays are not exactly the same. If the destination array is not large enough to be copied to, then this method will throw an ArrayOutOfBoundsException, which it will also do if the offset integers are negative or too large for the sizes of the source or destination arrays.

Finally, the currentTimeMillis( ) method of the System class returns a long integer with the current system time when the method was called. The return value from this method is the number of milliseconds since midnight, 1/1/1900. You can use the return value to instantiate Date( ) objects to indicate the current date and time.

The SecurityManager

Sensitive system resources are protected within Java by the security manager. Whenever one of the server operations occurs that could potentially compromise the system, the security manager is queried to ask whether or not the operation is allowed.

For example, whenever your applications of applets try to open a file on the local file system, the security manager is queried to find out whether or not the process is allowed to open the file. Similarly, if you try to open a socket to a remote system, the security manager must sign off in order for you to do this.

The most prominent place where the security manager is used is within browsers when applets are run. As you know, Applet objects have a lot of restrictions with respect to sensitive system resources. Applets may not open files on the local file system, create server sockets, load classes using their

Utility and Language Class Reference

own class loaders, or instantiate COM objects. All of these restrictions are controlled by the security manager.

The SecurityManager's public interface is a series of checkXXX( ) methods. These methods all have pretty much the same signature:

```
public void checkXXX(<args>);
```

If the operation is to be allowed by the security manager, then the security manager simply returns from the appropriate checkXXX( ) method. If the operation is not to be allowed, however, then the SecurityManager throws a SecurityException.

Here's an example: Whenever an applet tries to open a file for reading, the Java system calls the SecurityManager's checkRead( ) method. For applets, this method always throws a SecurityException, which prevents the applet from being able to open the file for reading. Similarly, if an applet attempts to establish a socket connection, the SecurityManager's checkConnect( ) method is invoked. If the remote server is the same server that the applet was served from, the SecurityManager just returns from this method. Otherwise, its method throws a SecurityException, preventing the applet from setting up the socket connection.

See the Visual J++ online documentation for a complete listing of all the checkXXX( ) methods included in the SecurityManager class. Keep in mind that each of these methods is declared as a returning void. Instead of returning a true or false value, the SecurityManager throws a SecurityException when a particular operation is not to be allowed.

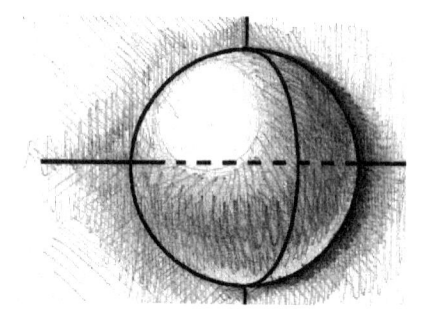

CHAPTER 12

Other Java APIs

When Visual J++ was released, the Java core packages had a version number of 1.0.2. The Java core packages are being augmented to include a lot of capabilities and functionalities even Visual J++ cannot handle. These new core packages and additional classes add a lot of whiz-bang to Java, and the next version of Visual J++ will not only give you full access to those capabilities, but with its wizards and intuitive interface, Visual J++ will remain the best Java development environment you can buy.

In this chapter, you will read a brief overview of the new Java APIs, packages, and classes. The purpose of this chapter is to keep you looking forward, towards the leading edge of Java technologies. It is also to keep you from "reinventing the wheel." For example, the 2D animation section of this chapter describes the 2D animation engine that is included in Java 1.1. If you are a particularly active developer, you might have been inclined to create just such an engine with Visual J++ to make creating animations even easier and more flexible than what Visual J++'s AppletWizard gives you. You might be wasting your time, somewhat, since Java 1.1 includes an animation engine to make arbitrary 2D animations simple to perform.

To read about these newer APIs, and even newer ones as soon as they are developed, visit JavaSoft's homepage on the Web. JavaSoft is the company that controls the growth of the Java language and its core APIs. Their WWW homepage address is *http://splash.javasoft.com*.

Remote Technologies APIs

Java was built to be a programming tool for the Internet. That means Java is supposed to be distributable, remotable, and networkable. Four of the Java 1.1 APIs add an incredible level of networkablility to Java. The object serialization APIs are built right into the Java 1.1 JVM. The object serialization capabilities allow you to write your Java objects, any objects, out to a stream. So, for example, you can deliver an object clear across the Internet to be recreated and allowed to run on a faraway server machine. You can also store objects persistently in JAR archives, CAB files, or any arbitrary file you wish.

Object serialization is a basic technology that, once you have it, allows you to use a lot of other remote programming techniques. The remote method invocation (RMI) API is Java's answer to Windows DCOM, for one example. Using RMI, you can "server up" an interface to a local object across the Internet. That is, a remote application or applet can get an interface to your local object and call its methods from across the globe. An RMI interface could serve as the gateway to your information server or supercomputing application.

What DCOM is to RMI, ActiveX is to the new *Java Beans* API. Despite its unfortunate name, the Beans API is a great new addition to Java. A *Java Bean* is an embeddable component, much like an applet. The difference is that Beans will be able to interact with other system-dependent component technologies. Using Java in Windows, you can already expose a Java applet as an ActiveX component in any ActiveX container application. For example, you can embed an applet in a Visual Basic program or in any of the Microsoft Office 97 applications.

Other Java APIs

However, you cannot send or receive ActiveX events in your embedded Java applet. You could not create even a simple push-button that could interact with its container using embedded Java applets as ActiveX components. With the Java Beans API, you can send and receive events, expose properties, create property sheets, or have a special editing dialog to make using your Bean easier for other developers. Basically, a Bean will be the equivalent of an ActiveX component.

Unlike ActiveX components, however, Java Beans will also be able to be plugged into other component technology frameworks. Java Beans will be able to be embedded in CORBA interfaces, Macintosh OpenDoc applications, and Netscape LiveConnect frameworks. The same Java Bean, without any change in source code and without even having to be recompiled, will be able to be dropped into any or all of these frameworks.

Java Database Connectivity (JDBC) is the name of the Java 1.1 technology that allows your Java applications or applets to work with any relational database management system (RDBMS). Using the same basic design pattern that Windows' ODBC uses, the JDBC classes work by using a database driver class object. This object is responsible for communicating with the specific RDBMS, using whatever communication and protocol it is programmed to. Individual drivers are all Java objects that expose the same set of public functions to your program. Using the same API, you can query or add data to any RDBMS for which you have a driver object.

Similar to applets, there is a symmetric server-side technology in Java 1.1 called a *servlet*. A servlet is an executable Java object that lives on a Web server machine. It is pretty much the same thing as a CGI-BIN program, or a Microsoft Internet Information Server ISAPI DLL, or a Netscape NSAPI loadable library. It is an executable program that creates Web-content "on the fly," and leaves the job of delivering the content to a user's Web browser up to the Web server itself. Until the servlet API was available, you had to create CGI-BIN server-side programs—written is some language such as Perl or C—and use them with Java applets to create distributed computing solutions on the Web. Using the servlet API included in the Java 1.1 core technology packages, you can now create both sides of the client/server system in Java.

Media APIs

Java 1.1 includes a bunch of technologies for making Java a more robust, more multimedia-aware development system than the 1.0 libraries had. These API extensions include extending the Graphics class with all sorts of additional capabilities: "bitblting" (bit block transferring), robust text rendering, and just more capabilities all around have been added. A 2D animation engine, a 3D graphics package, a telephony package, a distributed sharable application framework, and an arbitrary multimedia framework have all been added to the Java 1.1 API.

Object Serialization

If you are familiar with the common COM interfaces, then you are probably familiar with the IPersist interface. Through this interface, or interfaces derived from it, you can transcribe your COM objects to arbitrary streams. For example, you can commit an ActiveX object's state along with a containing document in a single file. You can also send the object's state through an asynchronous stream, such as an Internet socket.

Even with the Java 1.0 libraries, you can effectively stream your objects to files and socket streams. This section details how you can do that with Visual J++ today. This section also describes the object serialization API added to Java 1.1, which requires absolutely no additional programming to allow you to serialize your objects in Java. Not even COM can do that. That is, you must implement your own IPersist interface in COM to get the persistent serialized object capabilities of OLE in COM. In Java 1.1, every object automatically becomes serializable. You will be able to write *any* object to any output stream.

Adding Serialization to Visual J++

The purpose of this section is to show you how to add object serialization capabilities to your Java application and applet using Visual J++, right now. In the course of learning how to do this, you will become aware of the technological hurdles that need to be overcome to add object serialization to all objects in Java, which is what the object serialization APIs do in Java 1.1. The classes developed in these pages are to be used in your Java 1.0 (and 1.0.2) applets and applications. When Java 1.1 is available with Visual J++, you will be able to use the object serialization API automatically without having to use these classes at all.

Object Streams and Serializable Objects

The idea of object serialization is that your serializable objects "know how" to read or write themselves to special stream objects, called object input streams and object output streams. These object streams are actually implemented as something like a stream filter (though, as you'll see, they are not in fact derived from the FilterInputStream or FilterOutputStream classes).

For example, an object output stream can encapsulate any other type of output stream, such as a file output stream or a socket output stream. Thus, using the same object output interface, you can write any serializable object to the encapsulated output stream. When reading the object back from the

Other Java APIs

stream, you would use an object input stream. This object input stream would encapsulate an input stream that had been previously written to through an ObjectOutput object. That is, if you serialized an object to a file through an object output stream that encapsulated the file output stream connected to the file, then you would later (perhaps even years later in another program on another machine) create an object input encapsulating a file input stream connected to the same file. You could then read the object in from the stream. Figure 12-1 illustrates the process of writing an object to, and then later reading the object back from, an object stream.

In both cases, when writing an object to a stream or reading the object from a stream, the object itself must "know how" to read or write itself to an object input or object output stream. The way to implement this is to have your object's class implement the Serializable interface. The Serializable interface, reproduced in the following code, describes two methods that an object uses to write itself or read itself from an object stream. The serializeTo( ) method is passed an object output that the serializable object is to write itself to. The serializeTo( ) method is implemented by having your object write any of its persistent data to the object output. In the serializeFrom( ) method of the Serializable interface, your object's implementation would read the

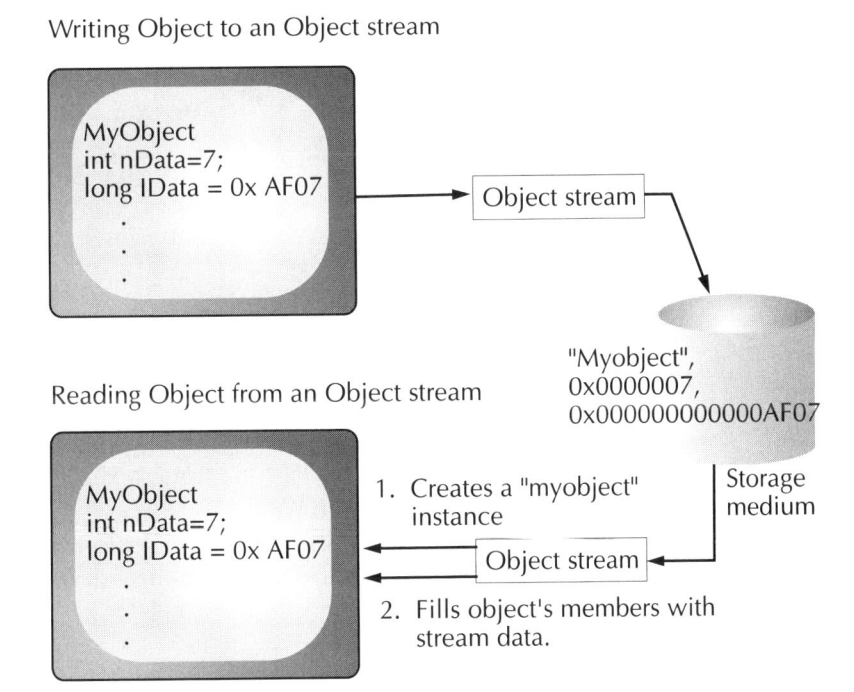

Writing and reading objects from object streams
Figure 12-1.

exact same data back from an object input. Here is the declaration of the Serializable interface:

```
public interface Serializable {
    // The serializeTo( ) method is responsible for writing the  object's
    // persistent state to an ObjectOutput object. The same order and data
    // written to the ObjectOutput must be read back from the ObjectInput
    // in your implementation of the serializeFrom( ) method.
    public void serializeTo(ObjectOutput oo) throws IOException;

    // The serializeFrom( ) method is called to have your object re-initialize
    // itself from persistent data written to an ObjectOutput stream in an
    // earlier call to serializeTo( ).
    public void serializeFrom(ObjectInput oi) throws IOException;
}
```

Any object that can serialize itself to an object output or recreate itself from an object input implements this interface.

ObjectOutput is an interface that describes all the methods a serializable object can use to serialize itself. This interface includes methods for writing any one of the built-in Java types, such as boolean, int, etc. This is pretty much the same method that the DataOutput interface of the java.io package has. Therefore, the ObjectOutput interface is derived from the DataOutput interface, adding only one method to that interface: writeSerializable( ), which passes a serializable object. Here's the declaration of the ObjectOutput interface:

```
import java.io.DataOutput;

public interface ObjectOutput extends DataOutput {
    // In addition to all the DataOutput methods (writeBoolean( ), writeInt( ),
    // etc.), the ObjectOutput allows you to write Serializable objects also.
    public void writeSerializable(Serializable ser) throws IOException;
}
```

Now, this interface must be implemented by an object that not only implements the writeSerializable( ) method declared in the ObjectOutput interface, but must also implement all the methods of the DataOutput interface. Luckily, the java.io package includes a DataOutputStream class that implements the DataOutput interface. You can create an ObjectOutputStream class, derived from DataOutputStream, that only includes an implementation of the writeSerializable( ) method. Here's an implementation of the ObjectOutputStream class:

Other Java APIs

```java
import java.io.*;

class ObjectOutputStream extends DataOutputStream implements ObjectOutput {
    public ObjectOutputStream(OutputStream out) {
        super( (out instanceof DataOutput) ? out :
            new DataOutputStream(out));
    }

    public void writeSerializable(Serializable ser) throws IOException {
        DataOutput outLocal = (DataOutput)out;
        if(null == ser) {
            outLocal.writeUTF("<null>");
            return;
        }

        Class cls = ((Object)ser).getClass();
        outLocal.writeUTF(cls.getName());
        ser.serializeTo(this);
    }
}
```

The writeSerializable( ) implementation here tries to first write out the passed object's class name, then tells the Serializable object to write itself out to the stream. The class name is important. Without it, the object input stream could never recreate the object, because it wouldn't know what *type* of object to create. It would be able to read the data that the Serializable object wrote out to the object output stream, but it would not know how to actually create the object so that it could call its serializeFrom( ) method.

The ObjectInput interface is symmetric to the ObjectOutput interface. That is, it is derived from the DataInput interface and inherits that interface's various methods for reading in built-in data variables such as boolean values and integers. Here is the declaration of the ObjectInput interface:

```java
import java.io.DataOutput;

public interface ObjectInput extends DataInput {
    // In addition to all the DataInput methods (readBoolean( ), readInt( ),
    // etc.), the ObjectInput allows you to write Serializable objects also.
    public Serializable readSerializable() throws IOException;
}
```

The implementation of this interface is as easy as the implementation of the ObjectOutputStream class. ObjectInputStream is a class based on the

DataInputStream class. It inherits all that base class' methods for reading built-in types from encapsulated InputStream objects. These methods include readBoolean( ), readInt( ), etc. The implementation of the readSerializable( ) method must perform these steps:

- Read in the class name from the encapsulated input stream.
- If the class name is just "<null>," then return null.
- Instantiate an object of the class indicated by the string that was read in. Tell that object to serialize itself from the object input stream using its serializeFrom( ) method.

Here's an implementation of the ObjectInputStream class:

```java
import java.io.*;

class ObjectInputStream extends DataInputStream implements ObjectInput {
    public ObjectInputStream(InputStream in) {
        super((in instanceof DataInput) ? in :
            new DataInputStream(in));
    }

    public Serializable readSerializable( ) throws IOException {
        DataInput localIn = (DataInput)in;

        String strClassname = localIn.readUTF();
        if("<null>".equals(strClassname))
            return null;

        Object o;
        try {
            Class cls = Class.forName(strClassname);
            o = cls.newInstance();
        } catch (ClassNotFoundException cnfe) {
            return null;
        } catch (InstantiationException ie) {
            return null;
        } catch (IllegalAccessException iae) {
            return null;
        }

        if(!(o instanceof Serializable))
            throw new ClassCastException("Serialized class not Serializable");

        ((Serializable)o).serializeFrom(this);
        return (Serializable)o;
    }
}
```

Other Java APIs

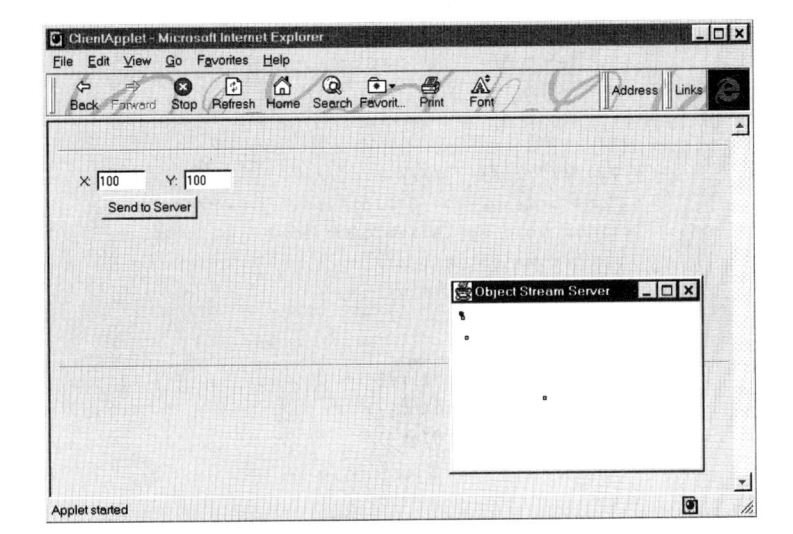

Figure 12-2.
The Serializable-Point Client-Applet/Server system

That's it. These interfaces and streaming classes are the basis of a simple form of object serialization that you can use with Visual J++ today. Here, for example, is a simple applet/server program pair that allows the applet user to write SerializablePoint objects to the server. The server takes those SerializablePoint objects and draws a small box around the corresponding point in its main window. This simple client/server system requires three classes in total: SerializablePoint, Server, and ClientApplet. Following is an implementation of those classes. Figure 12-2 is a screen shot of the client and server programs running on the same system.

```
import java.net.*;
import java.io.*;
import java.awt.*;
import java.applet.Applet;
import Serializable;
import ObjectInputStream;
import ObjectOutputStream;
import java.util.*;

class SerializablePoint implements Serializable {
    // Private state is an X and a Y axis coordinate.
    public int m_x;
    public int m_y;

    public SerializablePoint() {
        this(0, 0);
    }
```

```java
    public SerializablePoint(int x, int y) {
        m_x = x;
        m_y = y;
    }

    /////////////////////////////////////
    // Methods of the Serializable interface.
    public void serializeTo(ObjectOutput out) throws IOException {
        out.writeInt(m_x);
        out.writeInt(m_y);
    }

    public void serializeFrom(ObjectInput in) throws IOException {
        m_x = in.readInt();
        m_y = in.readInt();
    }
}

// The Applet client's job is to read new points from the user interface, make
// SerializablePoints from them and transfer those points to the server.
// This requires a socket connection to a server application to be created
// during the Applet's init( ) method.
public class ClientApplet extends Applet {
    // Part of applet's state is a permanent connection to a server
    // application. This is stored as an ObjectOutputStream that encapsulates
    // a SocketOutputStream.
    private ObjectOutputStream m_out;
    private TextField m_textX;
    private TextField m_textY;

    // init() must make connection with server, and set up user interface.
    public void init() {
        // Open up connection with server, encapsulated with an
        // ObjectOutputStream object.
        try {
            Socket sock = new Socket(InetAddress.getByName(
                    getDocumentBase().getHost()), 1001); // assume server port
            OutputStream out = sock.getOutputStream();
            m_out = new ObjectOutputStream(out);
        } catch (IOException ioe) {
            System.err.println("Unable to lookup or connect to server:"+ioe);
            return;
        }

        // Create the User interface.
        setLayout(new FlowLayout());
        add(new Label("X: "));
        add(m_textX = new TextField(5)); // 5 cols.
```

Other Java APIs

```java
        add(new Label("Y: "));
        add(m_textY = new TextField(5)); // 5 cols

        add(new Button("Send to Server"));
    }

    // When "Send to Server" button is pressed, create a new SerializablePoint
    // object from the contents of the X and Y edit boxes, and send that object
    // to the server.
    public boolean action(Event evt, Object what) {
        if(!(what instanceof String))
            return false;
        if(!"Send to Server".equals((String)what))
            return false;

        try {
            int x = Integer.parseInt(m_textX.getText());
            int y = Integer.parseInt(m_textY.getText());
            SerializablePoint ser = new SerializablePoint(x, y);
            m_out.writeSerializable(ser);
        } catch (NumberFormatException nfe) {
            System.err.println("Must have numbers in X and Y edit boxes.");
        } catch (IOException ioe) {
            System.err.println("Error writing point to the server: " + ioe);
        } finally {
            return true;
        }
    }
}

// Server application must set up a server socket and maintain a list of
// SerializablePoints that have been passed to it. When repainted, draws
// little boxes around all the points. Multiple connections are not allowed;
// this makes implementation easier. You can easily add multiple connections
// to this code.
public class Server extends Frame implements Runnable {
    // The server socket, and the list of points describe the state of this
    // server object. Thread waiting to service connections is also
    // stored in a private member variable.
    private ServerSocket m_socketServer;
    private Vector m_vectPoints;
    Thread m_thread;

    // Main method just creates a new instance of this class and shows it as
    // a Frame.
    public static void main(String[] astrArgs) {
        Server s = new Server();
        s.resize( 500, 300);
```

```java
        s.show();
    }

    // Constructor creates a server socket, and a vector to store received
    // points in.
    public Server() {
        super("Object Stream Server");
        m_vectPoints = new Vector();

        try {
            m_socketServer = new ServerSocket(1001);
        } catch (IOException ioe) {
            System.err.println("Error setting up server socket.");
            return;
        }

        // Kick-start thread that waits for server connections.
        m_thread = new Thread(this);
        m_thread.start();
    }

    // Paint method paints little boxes around each Point in the
    // m_vectPoint vector.
    public void paint(Graphics g) {
        Enumeration enum = m_vectPoints.elements();
        while(enum.hasMoreElements()) {
            Point p = (Point)enum.nextElement();
            g.drawRect(p.x-1, p.y-1, 3, 3);
        }
    }

    // The run() method is what the background thread executes.
    // It waits for new server connections, and reads SerializablePoint
    // objects from the connection until the other end breaks it.
    public void run() {
        while(m_thread == Thread.currentThread()) {
            ObjectInputStream ois;
            try {
                Socket sock = m_socketServer.accept();
                ois = new ObjectInputStream(sock.getInputStream());
            } catch (IOException ioe) {
                System.err.println("Error waiting for new connection: " +ioe);
                return;
            }

            try {
                while(true) {
                    SerializablePoint p =
```

Other Java APIs

```
                    (SerializablePoint)ois.readSerializable();
                m_vectPoints.addElement(new Point(p.m_x, p.m_y));
                repaint();
            }
        } catch  (EOFException eof) {
            // closed from the other side.
        } catch (IOException ioe) {
            System.err.println("Problem reading new Point: " + ioe);
            break;
        }
    }
  }
}
```

Object Serialization in Java 1.1

The previous section outlined a method for you to serialize objects in Java to files or to socket-based streams. The object classes that were able to perform object serialization implemented an interface called Serializable. There are at least a couple of problems with this method of serialization, however.

The first problem is that it is not secure. Any object that serializes itself exposes all of its data to any encapsulating input stream or output stream that the object input or object output uses. For example, if you have a CreditCardTransaction object that you are serializing to a server program, an underlying, encapsulated InputStream class could record the credit card number from your Transaction class. Of course, the class could implement its serializeTo( ) and serializeFrom( ) methods to encrypt the object's private data, but it's still not the most secure system.

In addition to the security problem, there's also the problem of class identification within the object input and object output streams. As the classes are designed, just the class name is written to the object stream to identify the type of object being written. No mention is made of the class' version number, or even package name. This could lead to all sorts of versioning problems in the future. You could write an object of class "MyDataClass," which has two member integers. And then you store 50 of these important data objects in some secure file on your system. At a time much later in the future, you realize that your class needs another integer member to be *really* useful, so you add it to the class definition. Then you try reading in the object stream with the 50 saved MyDataClass objects serialized to it. That won't work at all! The new class definition can't handle the way the old data was written.

And the final big problem is that of reusability. The Serializable interface must be reimplemented for each class that wants to be able to serialize itself. What a lot of coding! Not to mention the fact the Hashtables, Vectors, and other useful data storage objects don't implement this interface, and so wouldn't be able to be serialized. What you want is a solution that allows you to serialize arbitrary objects to an object stream.

The object serialization API for Java 1.1 solves some of these problems. The problem of data security still exists, but the problems of class identification and arbitrary object serialization are solved. Since the object serialization API is being added to the Java 1.1 core package, the capabilities of this package will be inherited automatically on all systems that have a Java 1.1 JVM, and will be available to you in Visual J++ as soon as you either upgrade to Java 1.1 or download the object serialization package from the JavaSoft download site (and install the package on your machine).

The object serialization API uses some rather powerful new capabilities of the Java 1.0.2 JVM that allow it to serialize any object to an object output stream or recreate the object from an object input stream. As in the simple implementation of object serialization given previously, the objects that you write objects to or read them from are still called ObjectInputStreams and ObjectOutputStreams. These classes have methods called readObject( ) and writeObject( ) that will read or write arbitrary objects. The object serialization libraries and documentation are available at the JavaSoft Web site today, so check them out.

Remote Method Invocation

With object serialization, you can send a copy of any Java object to a file, or to another running JVM, through socket connections. This allows you to have multiple running copies of the same object in several different JVMs at the same time. Those objects, once instantiated in the various different JVMs or files, are essentially "cut off" from each other. While each one would have originally been a copy of the same original object (or a copy of a copy of that object), each individual copy could easily diverge from the others.

For example, let's say you create a picture object of some sort, and then distribute that picture to a file and to three other JVMs running somewhere on the Internet. Each copy that got distributed across the Internet is then separately modified by different users. Now you have basically four different and disparate picture objects. The original that was saved to the file holds the picture as it was sent to each location on the Internet, and the three distributed versions have different data added or removed by three different users. There's no way to coordinate the activities of these various objects easily without creating in each of them some complex distributed notification and updating mechanism. Figure 12-3 illustrates a single serialized object being distributed around the Internet.

Other Java APIs

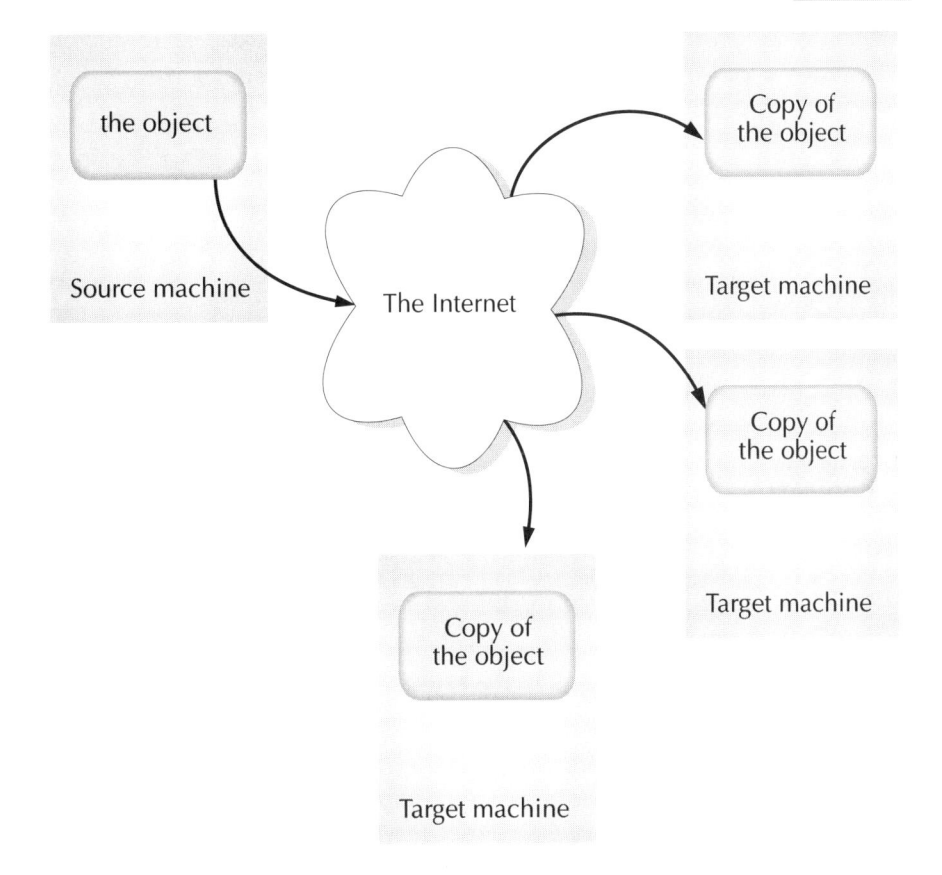

Figure 12-3.
An object serialized to locations across the Internet

Almost the exact opposite of the objects distributed using object serialization are single objects exposed across the Internet using a Java 1.1 technology known as *remote method invocation* (RMI). In RMI, a single object can inject itself into various other JVMs across the Internet in such a way that only a single copy of the object exists at a time. Using RMI, different programs on different JVMs can effectively use the methods and capabilities of a single object running on a server JVM. Figure 12-4 is an illustration of the RMI concept.

Getting RMI Libraries

RMI is a part of the core libraries in Java 1.1. If you are using the Java libraries sent with Visual J++, you will not have RMI, since these libraries are Java 1.0.X libraries. A beta runnable version of the RMI packages can be downloaded today from JavaSoft's Web site. These libraries only work with

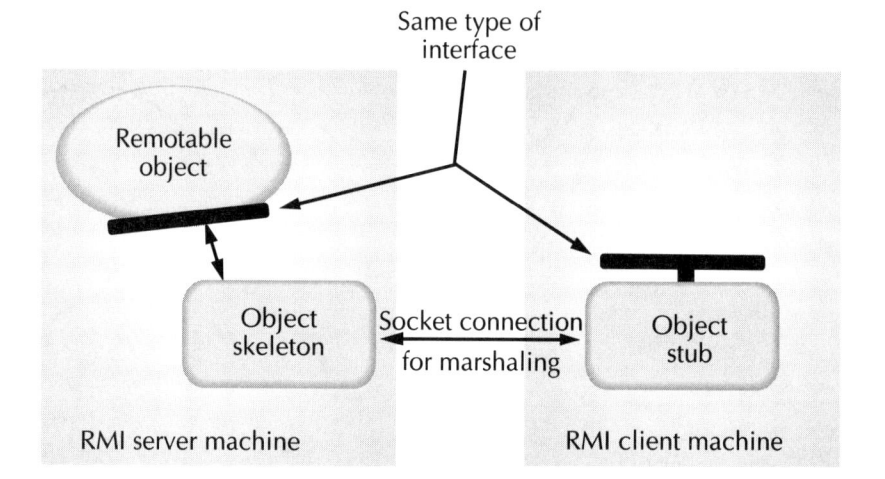

An RMI object distributing interfaces across the Internet
Figure 12-4.

Java 1.0.2 or later. You can go to the JavaSoft site and download the RMI libraries and load them on to your local machine today.

Stubs and Skeletons

What Figure 12-4 shows is a single Java object, located in a single JVM, passing out *proxy stubs* of itself across the Internet. The proxy stubs are objects that implement the same interface(s) as the remote object. In the user's environment, a method call to one of the proxy stub's methods causes the stub to send the method parameters to the RMI server machine. The server machine then calls the object's method and sends the result back to the user's machine. Both the communications to and from the server machine are done through socket connections on the Internet. Figure 12-5 illustrates this remote method calling (or "remote method invocation") protocol.

In this way, the user's program doesn't actually "know" that the object whose methods it's calling is not actually located in the local JVM. Only a proxy of the remote object is located in the user's JVM. It really doesn't matter, though. As far as the user's program is concerned, the proxy stub acts *just like* the remote object. That is, you call the proxy's method and you get a result back. The result you get back is exactly the same result you would have gotten back had the remote object actually been located in your local JVM.

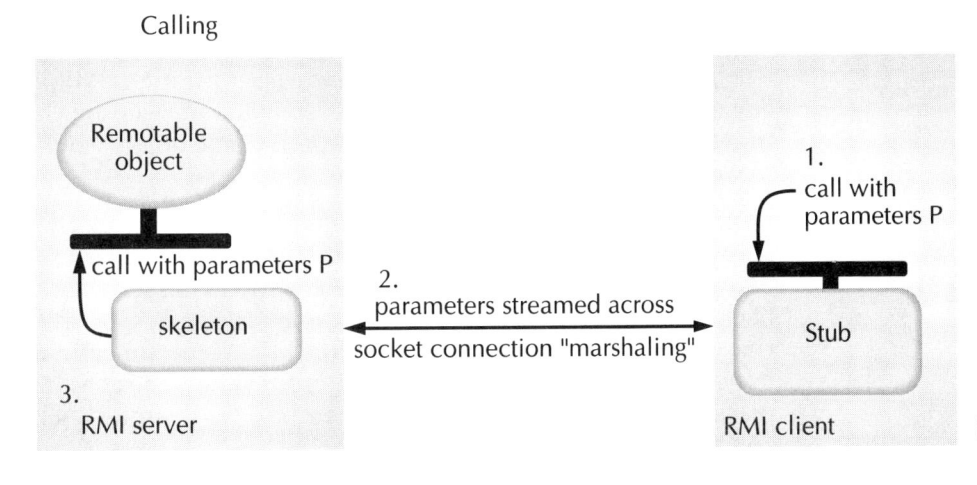

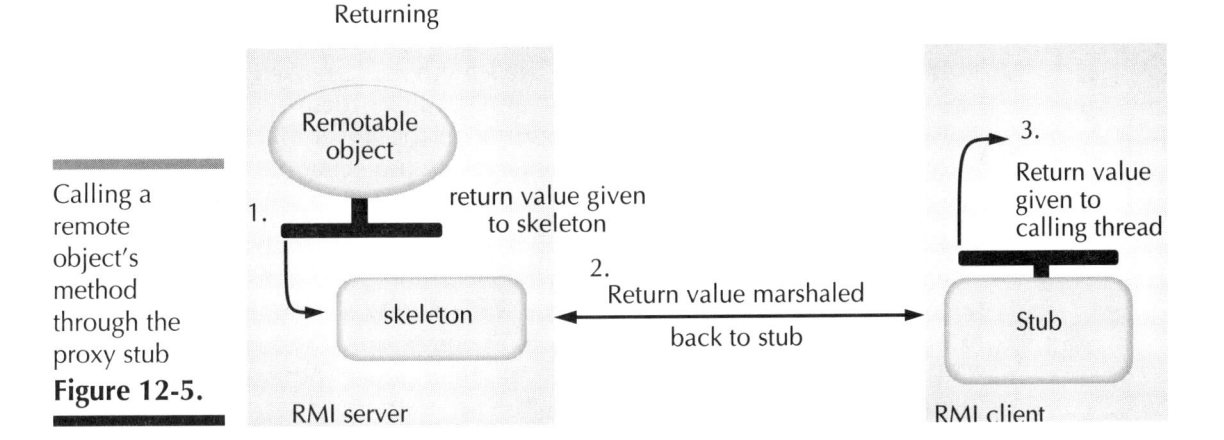

Other Java APIs

Calling

- Remotable object
- call with parameters P
- skeleton
- 3. RMI server
- 2. parameters streamed across socket connection "marshaling"
- 1. call with parameters P
- Stub
- RMI client

Returning

- Remotable object
- 1. return value given to skeleton
- skeleton
- 2. Return value marshaled back to stub
- 3. Return value given to calling thread
- Stub
- RMI server
- RMI client

Calling a remote object's method through the proxy stub
Figure 12-5.

That's pretty cool! You can have a single Java object running in your local JVM, and multiple other users across the Internet can call your object's methods. For example, you could have a simple Counter object with only two methods: increment( ) and getCount( ). Ten different applets running on 10 different user's machine could each be individually incrementing the counter and getting its value. The value each client user gets back would be the *total* number of increments. That is, the total number of times all 10 users' applets have incremented the counter.

A slightly more useful example would be that of a Game object. You have a single Game object running on your local server, with two different users (the game players) accessing the Game object through RMI proxy stubs across the Internet. Each player could individually call the Game object's movePiece( ) method, and the centralized Game object would reflect the player's move to the other player.

Of course, you could implement a similar system yourself by opening socket connections from the player's applets back to a centralized server and defining some communications protocol involving serializing Move objects back and forth between the various game players. You definitely could do it this way. But with Java 1.1's RMI API, all the communications stuff is handled for you! You need only write your Game object as if the various players are local objects calling its methods. No complex socket-based communications are necessary!

As Figure 12-5 illustrates, there are two objects that actually handle the communications in RMI. On the client side, there is a proxy stub object. On the server side, there is an object called a *skeleton*. The stub and the skeleton work together like this: whenever a stub's method is invoked, the stub packages the method's parameters up and serializes them across the RMI connection to the skeleton object running on the server machine. The skeleton then unpacks the method parameters and other information needed to perform the remote method invocation.

The skeleton, which holds a reference to the remote object in the local JVM, actually calls that object's method. The result from the method call is then serialized across the Internet, the same way the method parameters were sent to the skeleton, back to the proxy stub. The proxy stub, which has been waiting for the results of the method call, then unpacks the result sent from the skeleton. The result is returned to the program that made the call in the first place.

The act of packaging up the method parameter and the result is called *marshaling*. Marshaling is basically a fancy form of object serialization. And, in fact, Java's RMI system relies heavily on Java 1.1's object serialization APIs.

Remoting an Object

There's a little bootstrap problem not addressed so far: How do you load a proxy stub for a remote object into your program's local JVM? For example, let's say you know there is a Game Server object running on a server at

Other Java APIs

address "game.mycompany.com" somewhere on the Internet. How do you get a stub for that game server into your local program so that the user can start playing a game remotely?

You do it by using the remote system's RMI Registry. An RMI Registry is a directory of all the remotable objects that can be served up from a particular machine. In the gaming example, the server's game program would create a Game object and hand it to the local machine's Registry. Remote applications or applets could then ask the Registry for a particular remotable object. What the Registry sends is a proxy stub for that object. At the same time, the Registry creates a skeleton in the remote server system. That's it. The communications channels are set. Your user's game client application or applet will have a proxy stub for the remote Game object. Any calls to the Stub object's methods are marshaled to the remote server's skeleton and the normal RMI way of communicating continues as described earlier. Figure 12-6 shows how the Registry is used to get a proxy stub for a remotable object into your program's JVM.

Remote Interfaces

The way that the remotable object and its stub "look" the same in both the remote server's JVM and any client application's JVM is the same way you get any two object's to "look" the same: using Java interfaces. That is, your remotable object has one or more public methods that you want your client application to be able to call. For example, a simple remote CounterObject

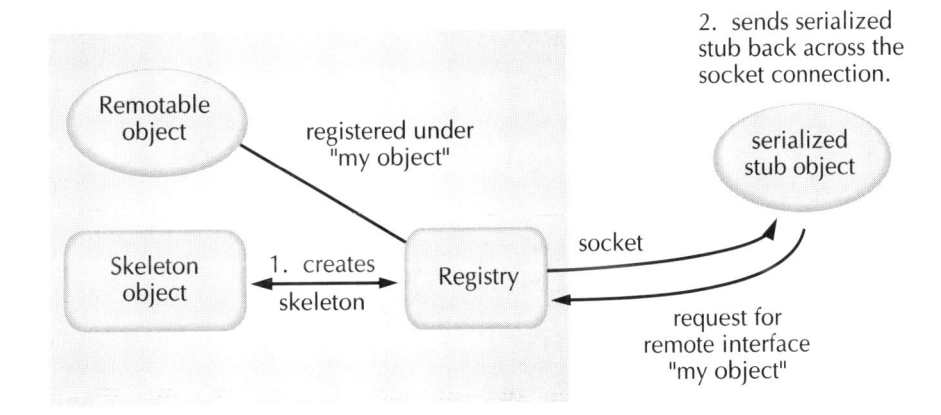

The RMI Registry Passing as Proxy Stub
Figure 12-6.

class might have a fingerprint that looks like this (note that a *fingerprint* is the collection of a class' method signatures):

```
class CounterObject {
    public void increment(){
        ...
    }

    public int getCount() {
        ...
    }
}
```

To make the Counter object remotable, you start by declaring an interface composed of the methods you want remote methods to be able to call. For example, this is a Counter interface:

```
public interface Counter extends Remote {
    public void increment() throws RemoteException;
    public int getCount() throws RemoteException;
}
```

and this is a Counter interface implementing class calls CounterImpl that implements this interface:

```
public class CounterImpl implements Remote {
    private int m_nCount;

    public CounterImpl() {
        m_nCount = 0;
    }

    public synchronized void increment() {
        m_nCount++;
    }

    public synchronized int getCount(){
        return m_nCount;
    }
}
```

These two files are all you need to make a very simple, remotable object using RMI.

Other Java APIs

Now, when your client program gets a proxy stub for a remote CounterImpl object, what it gets is an object that implements the Counter interface. That is, the stub's class is unknown, but it is known that the stub's class implements the Counter interface. So, you know the increment( ) and getCount( ) methods can be called by your client application or applet. (In fact, the name of the proxy stub's class in this case would be CounterImpl_Stub, and the name of the skeleton would be CounterImpl_Skeleton.)

A couple of notes about the code in the previous example. First, you'll note that the Counter interface is declared as extending the interface named "Remote." All remotable interfaces in RMI must be derived from the Remote interface. One of the reasons for this is so the RMI compiler knows which methods to make available in the proxy stub for client applications to use. Here's an example of when this would be necessary: You may declare a class that happens to implement two interfaces, one of which you want to be a remote interface and the other you don't. In order for the RMI compiler to know which interfaces to implement marshaling for in the Skeleton and Stub classes, you must declare the remotable interfaces as being derived from the Remote interface. Note that the Remote interface itself has a pretty simple declaration:

```
public interface Remote {}
```

It's really just a placeholder.

The second thing to note is that all the methods of the Counter interface from the previous example were declared as "throws RemoteException." A RemoteException is a remotable exception. That is, if in your server object's implementation of one of its remotable methods you end up throwing an exception, then as long as the exception you throw is derived from the RemoteException class, the exception will be marshaled to the client application. That's something that object serialization could never get you: remote exception throwing. In your client application or applet, you may have a remote exception thrown if, for example, there is a communication problem between the server and the client, or if the server suddenly shuts down while your client application is running.

The third thing to note is that in the declarations of the Counter interface function in the CounterImpl class, there is no "throws RemoteException" clause. That's because the method never actually does throw a remote exception. If you look at the implementations, all they do are increment a counter and return an int value. No exceptions are going to be thrown with that code.

RMI Summary

This section should have given you a quick overview of the RMI technologies included in Java 1.1. You may have noted quite a few similarities between RMI and Windows DCOM. That's because there are. What DCOM is to COM, RMI is to Java. In DCOM, you can make a COM object remotable by exposing some of its implemented interfaces into other process spaces or across the network on other computers. In RMI, there is no way to join two process' address spaces, so all remotable objects are remoted across a network connection. Specifically, they are marshaled across a TCP/IP socket connection the Internet. The big difference between them is that RMI is platform-independent, just like Java in general is. COM and DCOM are Microsoft's brainchildren. And while they are being deployed on other platforms, the deployment is not universal to say the least.

Of course, if you were following along in this section, you probably have more questions than answers at this point. How do you make an RMI application, or server, and where are the code samples? Again, this section is only intended to give you an introduction to the new technologies that RMI will bring to every Java Virtual Machine. To find out everything you need to know to get started developing with RMI, see JavaSoft's main Web page. From there, you can follow the latest developments in RMI and other Java 1.1 technologies.

Java Beans

Java Beans is the name used for Java's upcoming component technology. Java Beans is an attempt to apply the platform-independent philosophy of Java to the various different component technology frameworks out there (for example, ActiveX and COM, OpenDoc and CORBA, to name just a few).

The Java Beans API is part of Java 1.1, so you will not be able to develop Java beans using Visual J++ alone. You will have to download the Beans libraries from JavaSoft's Web download sight. Once you have all the binaries and classes installed, Java Beans will be as usable as any library from your Visual J++ development environment.

What a Java bean allows you to do is to place an object as a component in an ActiveX container, or an OpenDoc container, etc. A bean is really a whole lot like an applet, conceptually. The difference is that beans are made for generic distribute objects, not just executable content for the Web. A bean will have the ability to send and receive events from its container, no matter what type of platform it is being run on. The bean will also be able to

Other Java APIs

serialize itself, or be serialized from, coded and signed Java archives (JAR files, which are described in Chapter 6). A Java bean will be able to meld its preferred menu with its container's menu, much like OLE objects create hybridized menus from a combination of the container's and the component's preferred menu.

The Java Beans API relies quite heavily on several different new Java 1.1 technologies. It relies on object serialization to send bean property sheets across the Internet, and to serialize the bean along with its container document when that is appropriate. It relies on RMI to do some of its communications, and it relies on some of the new Java 1.1 technologies that have not even been mentioned in this book (such as the Reflection API, which will allow you to get arbitrary information about the members and methods exposed by an object's class).

Think of Java beans as superapplets: applets that can sit in arbitrary container applications, on different platforms, can migrate around the network to do mobile computing, and can contain other Java Bean objects. This is a very exciting technology that may even be the subject of another whole book. Please feel free to check out JavaSoft's online 90-page description of the Java Beans API, and get ready for Beans support to be added to later versions of the Visual J++.

Other New APIs

There are so many new Java APIs added to version 1.1 that were not present in version 1.0.2 that this chapter cannot hope to cover them all sufficiently. In the previous sections, there were descriptions of the technologies added to Java 1.1 that are expected to be most influential and useful in Java programming in general. In addition to these APIs, there are several other, smaller APIs that will prove to be very useful in some of your Java applications or applets. Up to the minute information about each of these APIs is available at JavaSoft's Web site. Here is a description of the new graphics APIs being added in Java 1.1.

2D Animation

As Chapter 6 describes, the AppletWizard can automatically generate for you a simple animation applet. This applet displays an animated sequence of downloaded images. But for all but the simplest applet, this functionality is not enough. You want overlaid images, moving sprites, and interactive animations that "come to life," not just static looping animation displays.

The 2D animation API gives you this functionality. Using it, you can create timed, interactive animation displays. You can define paths along which individual sprites move, and define a z-order to overlay them on top of each other. Place this on an image background, and add mouse click handlers for the individual sprites, and you can create all sorts of powerful displays from your applets.

Creating such a framework is possible in Visual J++ without using the Java 1.1 2D animation APIs, but it would take not a little bit of work. Included on the Visual J++ CD is a trial distribution of the Liquid Reality animation creator from DimensionX. You can load the Liquid Reality animation applet builder, which allows you to build animated applets using a visual development environment. Load the DimensionX Liquid Reality applet builder from your Visual J++ CD by selecting the Explore the CD option of the Visual J++ autostart screen. Open up the COOL TOOLS folder from the CD, and then open the DIMENSIONX folder. Open up the Default.htm file in this folder, and follow the links to find out more or to install Liquid Reality on your system.

3D Graphics

3D graphics capabilities are something that is sorely lacking in the Java 1.0.X libraries. Almost every major operating system that Java runs on has some sort of 3D graphics drawing capabilities. With Windows 95 and Windows NT, a 3D rendering engine was added to the Windows operating system. X-Windows also has a similar system.

The 3D graphics APIs being added to the Java 1.1 API extend Java by adding the ability to render 3D scenes from program code. You will be able to render VRML-like scenes from your Java application and applets using this new Java capability.

Multimedia Framework

Using just interpreted Java bytecodes, some of the more computationally intensive multimedia capabilities you may want for Internet programming are just out of reach. For example, Java is just not efficient enough to use to make a real-time high-compression audio or video codec (*codec* is a concatenation of the words *coder* and *decoder*). But audio and video are what people are clamoring for on the Internet. How to provide these capabilities in Java?

The Java Media Framework is a generic set of interfaces that describe media players and timer synchronizers you can use to provide the kind of video and audio that your Internet applications and applets demand. The framework defines a set of base classes for media-playing components. The interfaces to these classes include time-synching methods to make synchronized multimedia a reality.

Summary

The additions and updates being made to the Java 1.1 APIs are too numerous to even cover tersely in this one chapter. Rest assured that what Java 1.0 was to Internet programming, Java 1.1 will be to Java programming. A whole new level of capabilities will be available to you.

The remote programming capabilities allow you to distribute objects across the Internet using two different methods. Using the object serialization APIs, you can send Java objects to remote machines or stream them to and read them back from any arbitrary stream, such as a file on the local file system or a socket connection. Object serialization is also one of the bases of the new Java Beans APIs. Java Beans are distributed Java components, which are essentially superapplets. A Java Bean will be able to be embedded in many different types of containers that use different component technologies. For example, beans will be able to be loaded directly into ActiveX containers like Visual Basic applications and Office 97 applications.

Using remote method invocation (RMI), you can send Proxy Stub objects across the Internet. A proxy object method works by packaging parameters into a streams, connected to an Internet socket, and sending parameters back to the remote object server using a technique called marshaling. On the server side, an object called a Skeleton unpackages method call parameters and repackages the call's return value back to the Proxy object. Using RMI, you can easily create, for example, a remote Game object that can be accessed from multiple different players from different points on the Internet. These remote capabilities come without you having to write any networking code: the RMI classes take care of all networking and marshaling for you.

The numerous other APIs being added to Java 1.1 include Java database connectivity (JDBC) for connecting to RDBMSs, expanded graphics capabilities, a 2D animation engine, and a 3D graphics library. And there are still several other APIs that have not even been covered at all in this chapter: Telephony API, sharing API, and on and on. The central location for finding out and downloading the Java 1.1 APIs piecemeal so that you can incorporate them into your Visual J++ application and applets is JavaSoft's main Web page. JavaSoft's main Web page is located at *http://splash.javasoft.com* on the World Wide Web.

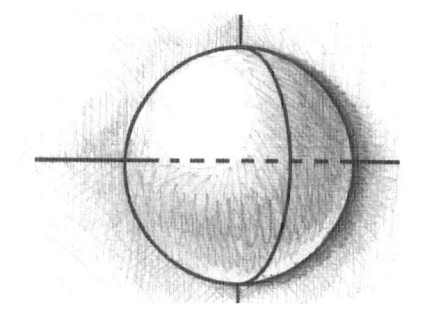

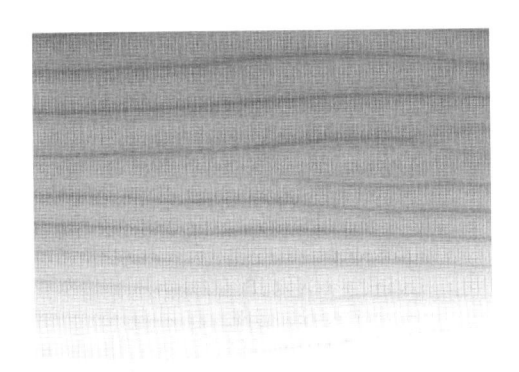

Index

2D animation APIs, 419-420
3D graphics APIs, 420
+ (plus operator), in Java, 22

A

Abstract methods in Java, 29-30
Abstract Windows Toolkit (AWT) classes, 74, 106-126
    Button class, 109-111
    Checkbox class, 111-113
    Choice class, 124-126
    Label class, 107-109
    List class, 120-124
    overview of, 74, 106-107
    TextArea class, 116-117, 119
    TextField class, 116-119
Accessing environment variables for Java System class, 393
Access privileges for Java packages, 37
Access specifiers
    for Java methods, 13-14
    for Java variables, 9-12
ActiveX components, 398-399
Adding
    elements to vectors, 351-352
    fields to tables in DAO record sets, 324-326
    object serialization APIs to Visual J++, 400-409
    objects to hashtables, 357-358
    Observer objects to Observable objects, 362-363
Anchor layout manager, 92-93
Animation, 171-179
    avoiding "flicker," 176
    defined, 171
    double buffering and, 176-179
    frame time-sequencing, 173-176
    with Graphics objects attached to in-memory images, 178-179
    overview of, 171-173
    See also Graphics
APIs, 397-421
    2D animation APIs, 419-420
    3D graphics APIs, 420

ActiveX components and, 398-399
Java Beans API, 398-399, 418-419
Java Database Connectivity (JDBC) API, 310-311, 343, 399
Java Media Framework, 420
media APIs, 399-400, 420
object serialization APIs, 398, 400-410
    adding to Visual J++, 400-409
    in Java, 409-410
    overview of, 398
overview of, 397-398, 421
remote method invocation (RMI), 410-418
    overview of, 410-411, 418
    proxy stubs and skeletons, 412-414
    remote interfaces, 415-418
    remoting objects, 414-415
    retrieving RMI libraries, 411-412
    RMI Registries, 415
remote technology APIs, 398-399
servlets and, 399
See also Data Access Objects (DAO) API; Remote Data Objects (RDO) API
Applets, 181-217
    applet-aware Web browsers, 184-185
    applet parameters, 191-192
    class hierarchy of Applet class, 183
    creating with Applet Wizard, 196-203
    defined, 183
    embedding in Web pages, 185-190
        applet archive files and, 188-190
        .CAB files and, 189-190, 217
        how applets are loaded by browsers, 186-188
        .JAR files and, 189-190
        overview of, 185-186
    methods, 192-195, 203-208
        AppletContext methods, 206-207
        applet information methods, 203-204
        for browser/applet communications, 205-208
        for communicating with other applets, 207-208
        for downloading images and audio files, 205-206
        getCodeBase(), 206
        getDocumentBase(), 206
        init(), start(), stop(), and destroy(), 192-195
        lifetime methods, 192-195
        for retrieving parameters from browsers, 206
    Observer/Observable applet example, 365-372
    overview of, 181-182
    security restrictions, 208-217
        .CAB files and, 217
        COM restrictions, 217
        digital signatures and, 217
        Java SecurityManager and, 210
        overview of, 209
        and performing file-based operations in Java, 210-216
        socket connection restrictions, 216-217
        viruses and, 208-209
    servlets and, 399
    See also Programs
Archive files for applets, 188-190
Arcs, drawing, 169-170
Arrays in Java, 23-26
    arraycopy() method for System class, 393-394
    declaring, 23-24, 25-26
    initializing, 25
    multidimensional arrays, 25
    of objects, 24-25
Attaching Graphics objects to in-memory images, 178-179
Audio files, applet methods for downloading, 205-206
Available() InputStream class method, 256
AWT. *See* Abstract Windows Toolkit

B

BitSet class, 360-361
Blocking sockets, 291-292
Boolean class, 373-379
BorderLayout layout manager, 90-91
Breakpoints, 66-67
Browsers
    applet-aware browsers, 184-185
    how applets are loaded by, 186-188
    methods for browser/applet communications, 205-208
Browse toolbar, 48

Index

BufferedInputStream class, 260, 261
BufferedOutputStream class, 272
Built-in variable types in Java
 casting between, 31-32
 overview of, 8
Button class, 109-111
ByteArrayInputStream class, 253, 257
ByteArrayOutputStream class, 271

C

.CAB files, 189-190, 217
Calling object methods in Java, 19-20
Call Stack window in Visual J++, 71
C and C++ languages
 Java and, 1-2
 Microsoft Visual C++, 312
CardLayout layout manager, 92
Casting Java variables, 30-32
CD-ROM installation option, 43
Chaining FilteredInputStream classes, 267
Changing field values in RDO result sets, 342-343
Character class, 373-379
Checkbox class, 111-113
Choice class, 124-126
Class class in Java, 347, 380-384
Class constructor method, in Java, 14-17
Classes
 Abstract Windows Toolkit (AWT) classes, 74, 106-126
  Button class, 109-111
  Checkbox class, 111-113
  Choice class, 124-126
  Label class, 107-109
  List class, 120-124
  overview of, 74, 106-107
  TextArea class, 116-117, 119
  TextField class, 116-119
 in Java
  class inheritance, 4-7
  declaring classes as part of a package, 35-36
  implements keyword and, 33
  Object class, 6-7
  overview of, 3-4
  String class, 22-23

ODL classes, 243
packages of classes in Java, 35-37
 .CLASS file locations and, 36
 copackage access privileges, 37
 overview of, 35-36
 private to package access privilege, 37
shim classes
 creating DAO Java/COM shim classes, 312-313
 creating Java/COM shim classes, 224-226
 creating RDO Java/COM shim classes, 335-336
See also Java language classes; Java utility classes; Methods; Objects
.CLASS files in Java
 bytecode and, 3
 packages and location of, 36
ClassLoader class in Java
 creating custom ClassLoader objects, 386-388
 overview of, 347, 385-386
ClassView tab in project window, 55-58
Clipping rectangle variable for Graphics objects, 152-155
Close() InputStream class method, 256
Collection properties
 for rdoEnvironment object, 337, 340
 Workspace objects and, 319-320
Color variable for Graphics objects, 150-152
Component Object Model (COM), 217, 219-250
 COM interfaces, 226-227
 COM objects in Java, 228-233
  creating COM objects, 228-229
  enumeration types, 232-233
  properties of, 230-232
  trapping COM exceptions, 229-230
 COM restrictions on applets, 217
 creating DAO Java/COM shim classes, 312-313
 creating Java/COM shim classes, 224-226
 creating RDO Java/COM shim classes, 335-336
 versus Java model, 220-223
 Java objects in COM, 233-250
  creating Java classes, 245-248

defining Java interfaces for COM, 235-238
object description language (ODL) and, 235-245
ODL classes and, 243
ODL interfaces and, 243-245
ODL libraries and, 242
overview of, 233-234
registering Java classes as COM objects, 248-249
registering Java classes as DCOM objects, 249-250
universally unique identifiers (UUIDs) and, 240-242
overview of, 219-221
typelibs, 223-224, 225, 226
Components in HelloX GUI example
Component class, 76-77
component/container hierarchy, 77-78
size and position of, 78-80
Containers, 87-88
Content types of URL class objects, 301-303
Copackage access privileges, in Java, 37
Creating
applets with Applet Wizard, 196-203
COM objects in Java, 228-229
custom ClassLoader objects, 386-388
custom component classes, 85-87
DAO Java/COM shim classes, 312-313
DAO record sets from queries, 329-330
database connections, 339-340
databases, 316-319
executable QueryDef objects, 333-334
fonts for Graphics objects, 160-162
graphical user interfaces with ResourceWizard, 126-133
HelloX GUI example, 75-76
Internet servers, 294-298
overview of, 294
server programs in Java, 295-298
ServerSocket class, 294-295
Java classes in COM, 245-248
Java/COM shim classes, 224-226
Java interfaces for COM, 235-238
LayoutManagers, 94-96
Menu classes with ResourceWizard, 141-144
objects in Java, 17-19

projects, 53-55, 59-60
rdoEnvironment objects, 338
RDO Java/COM shim classes, 335-336
RDO result sets from tables, 342
socket connections, 288-289
toolbars, 49
Workspace objects, 316
See also Declaring
Current color variable for Graphics objects, 150-152
Current font variable for Graphics objects, 155-162
creating fonts, 160-162
font size, 155-159
font styles, 159
typefaces, 159-160
See also Graphics
Custom FilteredInputStream classes, 267-270
Custom installation option, 44
Customizing toolbars, 49

D

Data Access Objects (DAO) API, 309-334, 343-344
creating DAO Java/COM shim classes, 312-313
DBEngine object, 313-316
Jet database engine and, 311-312
overview of, 309-311, 334, 343-344
QueryDef objects
creating executable queries, 333-334
saving in databases, 332
record sets, 325-332
adding fields to tables, 324-326
creating from queries, 329-330
navigating records, 326-327
parameters, 325
saving QueryDef objects in databases, 332
snapshot and dynaset record set types, 331-332
updating records, 329
viewing record set values with fields, 328
versus Remote Data Objects (RDO) API, 335

Index

TableDef objects, 320-325
    fields of, 321-325
    overview of, 320
Workspace objects, 315-320
    collection properties and, 319-320
    creating, 316
    DBEngine object and, 315-316
    listing open databases, 319
    opening and creating databases, 316-319
See also Remote Data Objects (RDO) API
Database connections, 338-340
    creating, 339-340
    looking up existing connections, 340
    overview of, 338-339
See also Remote Data Objects (RDO) API
Database programming. *See* Data Access Objects (DAO) API; JDBC; Remote Data Objects (RDO) API
Datagram socket connections, 293-294
DataInputStream class, 260, 263-265
DataOutputStream class, 272
Date class in Java, 346, 372-373
DBEngine object, 313-316
DCOM objects, 249-250
Debugging in Visual J++, 48, 60-67
    breakpoints, 66-67
    Debug toolbar, 48
    overview of, 60-61
    starting debugging sessions, 62
    stepping through programs, 63-66
    stopping debugging sessions, 62
Declaring
    arrays in Java, 23-24, 25-26
    classes as part of a package in Java, 35-36
Deleting
    elements from vectors, 351-352
    objects from hashtables, 357-358
    Observer objects from Observable objects, 362-363
Destroy() applet method, 192-195
Destroying objects in Java, 17-19
Destructor method in Java, 19
Dialog editor, 127-128
DialogLayout class, 133-134
DialogLayout layout manager, 93-94
Dialog resources, 127-130
Digital signatures, 217
"Dirty" Observable objects, 363-364

Display surfaces, 146-149
    overview of, 146-147
    retrieving surfaces' Graphics objects, 147-149
See also Graphics
Docking
    InfoViewer window, 51
    toolbars, 47
Documentation. *See* InfoViewer window
Dot operator in Java, 19-20
Double buffering for animations, 176-179
Double class, 373-379
Downloading images and audio files, applet methods for, 205-206
Drawing graphics, 165-171
    arcs, 169-170
    images, 170-171
    lines, 165
    ovals, 169
    polygons, 166-168
    rectangles, 166
See also Graphics
Dynaset DAO record set types, 331-332

E

Echo client program example, 289-291
Edit toolbar, 48
Embedding applets in Web pages, 185-190
    applet archive files and, 188-190
    .CAB files and, 189-190, 217
    how applets are loaded by browsers, 186-188
    .JAR files and, 189-190
    overview of, 185-186
See also Applets
Enumeration interface, 348-350
Enumeration types for COM objects in Java, 232-233
Environment objects in RDO API, 336-338
    collection properties, 337, 340
    creating, 338
    environment properties, 337-338
    overview of, 336-337
Equals() method in Java, 23
Error streams for Java System class, 393

Event handling in HelloX GUI example, 80-85
Executable queries in DAO API, 333-334
Explore the CD option, 45
Extends keyword in Java, 13
Extensions
 .CAB, 189-190, 217
 .MDB, 311, 318, 325
External processes in Java, 390-391

F

Fields
 adding to tables in DAO record sets, 324-326
 changing field values in RDO result sets, 342-343
 of TableDef objects, 321-325
 viewing DAO record set values with fields, 328
 viewing field values in RDO result sets, 342
 See also Variables
File-based operations, performing in Java, 210-216
FileInputStream class, 253, 256-257
Filename extensions
 .CAB, 189-190, 217
 .MDB, 311, 318, 325
FileOutputStream class, 271
FileView tab in project window, 58-59
FilteredInputStream classes, 260-270
 BufferedInputStream class, 260, 261
 chaining, 267
 custom FilteredInputStream classes, 267-270
 DataInputStream class, 260, 263-265
 LineNumberInputStream class, 260, 261-263
 overview of, 260-261
 PushbackInputStream class, 260, 263
 SequenceInputStream class, 260, 265-267
 transforming versus translating, 268
 See also Streams
FilterOutputStream class, 272
Finalization control, Java Runtime class and, 392
Finalize() method, in Java, 19

"Flicker" in animations, 176
Float class, 373-379
FlowLayout layout manager, 90
Font variable for Graphics objects, 155-162
 creating fonts, 160-162
 font size, 155-159
 font styles, 159
 typefaces, 159-160
 See also Graphics
Frame time-sequencing for animations, 173-176

G

Garbage collection in Java, 18-19, 392
GetCodeBase() applet method, 206
GetDocumentBase() applet method, 206
Graphical user interfaces (GUIs), 73-103, 105-106
 Abstract Windows Toolkit (AWT) classes, 74, 106-126
  Button class, 109-111
  Checkbox class, 111-113
  Choice class, 124-126
  Label class, 107-109
  List class, 120-124
  overview of, 74, 106-107
  Scrollbar class, 113-116
  TextArea class, 116-117, 119
  TextField class, 116-119
 containers, 87-88
 creating with ResourceWizard, 126-133
 HelloX example, 74-87
  Component class, 76-77
  component/container hierarchy, 77-78
  component size and position, 78-80
  creating, 75-76
  creating custom component classes, 85-87
  event handling, 80-85
  overview of, 74-75
 LayoutManagers, 88-98
  Anchor, 92-93
  BorderLayout, 90-91
  CardLayout, 92
  creating custom LayoutManagers, 94-96
  DialogLayout, 93-94

Index

FlowLayout, 90
GridBagLayout, 92
GridLayout, 91
overview of, 88-90
setting to null, 97-98
menus, 135-144
    code example, 137-138
    creating Menu classes with
        ResourceWizard, 141-144
    Menubar class, 136
    Menu class, 140
    Menu class object hierarchy, 135-138
    MenuItem class, 138-139
    overview of, 135
overview of, 73-74, 103, 105-106, 144
ResourceWizard, 40, 126-134, 141-144
    creating graphical user interfaces, 126-133
    creating Menu classes with, 141-144
    dialog code example, 130-133
    DialogLayout class, 133-134
    overview of, 40
    Visual J++ dialog editor and, 127-128
TabbedPanel example, 98-102
See also Menus
Graphics, 145-179
    animation, 171-179
        avoiding "flicker," 176
        defined, 171
        double buffering and, 176-179
        frame time-sequencing, 173-176
        with Graphics objects attached to
            in-memory images, 178-179
        overview of, 171-173
    applet methods for downloading, 205-206
    display surfaces, 146-149
        overview of, 146-147
        retrieving surfaces' Graphics objects, 147-149
    drawing, 165-171
        arcs, 169-170
        images, 170-171
        lines, 165
        ovals, 169
        polygons, 166-168
        rectangles, 166
    Graphics objects, 147-165, 178-179
        attaching to in-memory images, 178-179

        clipping rectangle variable, 152-155
        creating fonts, 160-162
        current color variable, 150-152
        defined, 149
        font size, 155-159
        font styles, 159
        font variable, 155-162
        overview of, 149-150
        paint and XOR painting modes, 162-165
        retrieving display surfaces' Graphics objects, 147-149
        typefaces, 159-160
    overview of, 145-146
GridBagLayout layout manager, 92
GridLayout layout manager, 91
GUIs. *See* Graphical user interfaces

H

Hashtable class, 346, 356-358
HelloX GUI example, 74-87
    Component class, 76-77
    component/container hierarchy, 77-78
    component size and position, 78-80
    creating, 75-76
    creating custom component classes, 85-87
    event handling, 80-85
    overview of, 74-75
    See also Graphical user interfaces
Hierarchy
    of Applet class, 183
    of Menu class objects, 135-138

I

IDE (integrated development environment)
    of Visual J++, 39-41
Images. *See* Graphics
Implements keyword in Java, 33
InetAddresss class, 284-287
Information methods for applets, 203-204
InfoViewer window, 46, 49-52
    docking, 51
    InfoViewer toolbar, 46
    navigating, 51-52
    overview of, 49-51
    See also Visual J++

Inheritance in Java classes, 4-7
Init() applet method, 192-195
Initializing arrays in Java, 25
In-memory images, attaching Graphics objects to, 178-179
InputStream classes, 252-270, 272-280
　ByteArrayInputStream class, 253, 257
　FileInputStream class, 253, 256-257
　FilteredInputStream classes, 260-270
　　BufferedInputStream class, 260, 261
　　chaining, 267
　　custom FilteredInputStream classes, 267-270
　　DataInputStream class, 260, 263-265
　　LineNumberInputStream class, 260, 261-263
　　overview of, 260-261
　　PushbackInputStream class, 260, 263
　　SequenceInputStream class, 260, 265-267
　　transforming versus translating, 268
　methods, 254-259
　　available(), 256
　　close(), 256
　　mark(), 255
　　read(), 254-255
　　reset(), 255-256
　　skip(), 255
　overview of, 252-253, 254-256
　parsing into tokens, 272-280
　physical InputStream classes, 253-254
　PipedInputStream class, 254, 258-259
　SocketInputStream class, 254, 257-258
　StreamTokenizer class, 273-277, 347
　StreamTokenizer example, 277-280
　StringBufferInputStream class, 254, 259
　See also Streams
Input streams for Java System class, 393
Installing
　Internet Explorer, 45
　Visual J++, 41-44
　　CD-ROM installation option, 43
　　Custom installation option, 44
　　Minimum installation option, 43
　　overview of, 41-42
　　Typical installation option, 42-43
Instance data in Java, 9
Instanceof operator in Java, 32

Integer class, 373-379
Integrated development environment (IDE) of Visual J++, 39-41
Interfaces
　COM interfaces, 226-227
　Enumeration interface, 348-350
　IPersist interface, 400
　Java interfaces
　　defining for COM, 235-238
　　overview of, 33-35
　ObjectInput interface, 403-405
　ObjectOutput interface, 402-403
　Observer interface, 365
　ODL interfaces, 243-245
　remote interfaces, 415-418
　Serializable interface, 401-402, 409-410
　See also Graphical user interfaces
Internet Explorer, installing, 45
Internet programming, 281-308
　creating Internet servers, 294-298
　　overview of, 294
　　server programs in Java, 295-298
　　ServerSocket class, 294-295
　IP addresses, 283-288
　　InetAddresss class, 284-287
　　machine names and, 284
　　overview of, 283-284
　　ports and, 287-288
　overview of, 281-282, 307-308
　socket connections, 288-294
　　blocking sockets, 291-292
　　communications through, 289
　　creating, 288-289
　　datagram socket connections, 293-294
　　defined, 288
　　echo client program example, 289-291
　　sending and receiving nonguaranteed data, 293-294
　TCP/IP protocol and, 281-283
　URLs (uniform resource locators), 298-307
　　content types, 301-303
　　overview of, 300-301
　　protocols and, 298-300
　　resource content types, 305-307
　　retrieving URL contents manually, 303-305
　　URL class methods, 301-307
　See also URLs; World Wide Web

Index

Introducing Visual J++ option on Visual J++ CD, 45
IPersist interface, 400

J

J++. *See* Visual J++
.JAR files, 189-190
Java Beans API, 398-399, 418-419
Java Database Connectivity (JDBC) API, 310-311, 343, 399
Java language, 1-38
   arrays, 23-26
      declaring, 23-24, 25-26
      initializing, 25
      multidimensional arrays, 25
      of objects, 24-25
   classes
      class inheritance, 4-7
      declaring classes as part of a package, 35-36
      implements keyword and, 33
      Object class, 6-7
      overview of, 3-4
      String class, 22-23
   .CLASS files
      bytecode and, 3
      packages and location of, 36
   COM objects in Java, 228-233
      creating COM objects, 228-229
      creating Java/COM shim classes, 224-226
      enumeration types, 232-233
      properties of, 230-232
      trapping COM exceptions, 229-230
   Component Object Model versus Java model, 220-223
   InetAddresss class, 284-287
   instanceof operator, 32
   interfaces
      defining Java interfaces for COM, 235-238
      overview of, 33-35
   Java Media Framework, 420
   Java objects in COM, 233-250
      creating Java classes, 245-248
      defining Java interfaces for COM, 235-238
      object description language (ODL) and, 235-245
      ODL classes and, 243
      ODL interfaces and, 243-245
      ODL libraries and, 242
      overview of, 233-234
      registering Java classes as COM objects, 248-249
      registering Java classes as DCOM objects, 249-250
      universally unique identifiers (UUIDs) and, 240-242
   Java Virtual Machine (JVM), 3
   methods, 6-7, 12-22, 26-30
      abstract methods, 29-30
      access specifiers, 13-14
      calling object methods, 19-20
      class constructor method, 14-17
      creating and destroying objects, 17-19
      destructor method, 19
      dot operator, 19-20
      equals() method, 23
      extends keyword and, 13
      finalize() method, 19
      garbage collection and, 18-19
      Object class methods, 6-7
      overloading, 26-27
      overriding, 28
      overview of, 12
      references and, 18-19, 21-22
      static class initializer methods, 20-21
      super keyword and, 16-17
      syntax of, 13
      this variable, 21-22
   object serialization APIs, 409-410
   overview of, 1-2
   packages of classes, 35-37
      .CLASS file locations and, 36
      copackage access privileges, 37
      overview of, 35-36
      private to package access privilege, 37
   performing file-based operations, 210-216
   plus (+) operator, 22
   program code, 37-38
   run-time type identification, 32
   SecurityManager, 210

ServerSocket class, 294-295
variables, 7-12, 30-32
    access specifiers, 9-12
    built-in variable types, 8
    casting, 30-32
    casting between built-in types, 31-32
    instance data and, 9
    overview of, 7-9
    private access specifier, 10-12
    private protected access specifier, 12
    protected access specifier, 12
    public access specifier, 10-12
    references and, 9
    static class data and, 9
    this variable, 21-22
See also APIs; Internet programming
Java language classes, 345-348, 373-395
    class objects and class loaders, 379-388
        Class class, 347, 380-384
        ClassLoader class, 347, 385-386
        creating custom ClassLoader objects, 386-388
        overview of, 379-380
    Math class, 347, 388-389
    numeric classes, 373-379
    overview of, 345-348
    Runtime class, 346, 347, 389-392
        memory, garbage collection, and finalization control, 392
        overview of, 346, 347, 389-390
        Process class, 389-390, 391-392
        spawning external processes, 390-391
    SecurityManager, 210, 394-395
    System class, 347, 389-390, 392-394
        accessing environment variables, 393
        arraycopy() method, 393-394
        input, output, and error streams, 393
        overview of, 347, 389-390, 392-393
Java utility classes, 345-373
    Date class, 346, 372-373
    Observer/Observable framework, 361-372
        adding and deleting Observer objects to/from Observable objects, 362-363
        applet example, 365-372
        "dirty" Observable objects, 363-364
        notifying Observer objects, 364-365
        Observable objects overview, 361-362
        Observer interface, 365
    overview of, 345-348
    Random class, 373
    storage classes, 348-361
        BitSet class, 360-361
        Enumeration interface, 348-350
        Hashtable class, 346, 356-358
        overview of, 348
        Properties class, 358-360
        Stack class, 350-351
        Vector class, 351-356
    StreamTokenizer class, 273-280, 347
JDBC (Java Database Connectivity) API, 310-311, 343, 399
Jet database engine, 311-312
JVM (Java Virtual Machine), 3

L

Label class, 107-109
Language classes. *See* Java language classes
LayoutManagers, 88-98
    Anchor, 92-93
    BorderLayout, 90-91
    CardLayout, 92
    creating custom LayoutManagers, 94-96
    DialogLayout, 93-94
    FlowLayout, 90
    GridBagLayout, 92
    GridLayout, 91
    overview of, 88-90
    setting to null, 97-98
    See also Graphical user interfaces
Libraries
    object description language (ODL) libraries, 242
    remote method invocation (RMI) libraries, 411-412
    typelibs in Component Object Model, 223-224, 225, 226
Lifetime methods for applets, 192-195
LineNumberInputStream class, 260, 261-263
Lines, drawing, 165
List class, 120-124
Listing open databases in Workspace objects, 319
Long class, 373-379
Looking up existing database connections, 340

Index

M

Machine names, 284
Mark() InputStream class method, 255
Marshalling, 414
Math class in Java, 347, 388-389
.MDB files, 311, 318, 325
Media APIs, 399-400, 420
Memory
 attaching Graphics objects to in-memory images, 178-179
 Java garbage collection and, 18-19
 Java Runtime class and, 392
Menus, 135-144
 code example, 137-138
 creating Menu classes with ResourceWizard, 141-144
 Menubar class, 136
 Menu class, 140
 Menu class object hierarchy, 135-138
 MenuItem class, 138-139
 overview of, 135
 See also Graphical user interfaces
Methods
 Applet class methods, 192-195, 203-208
  AppletContext methods, 206-207
  applet information methods, 203-204
  for browser/applet communications, 205-208
  for communicating with other applets, 207-208
  for downloading images and audio files, 205-206
  getCodeBase(), 206
  getDocumentBase(), 206
  init(), start(), stop(), and destroy(), 192-195
  lifetime methods, 192-195
  for retrieving parameters from browsers, 206
 InputStream class methods, 254-259
  available(), 256
  close(), 256
  mark(), 255
  read(), 254-255
  reset(), 255-256
  skip(), 255
 in Java, 6-7, 12-22, 26-30
  abstract methods, 29-30
  access specifiers, 13-14
  arraycopy() method, 393-394
  calling object methods, 19-20
  class constructor method, 14-17
  creating and destroying objects, 17-19
  destructor method, 19
  dot operator, 19-20
  equals() method, 23
  extends keyword, 13
  finalize() method, 19
  garbage collection and, 18-19
  Object class methods, 6-7
  overloading, 26-27
  overriding, 28
  overview of, 12
  references and, 18-19, 21-22
  static class initializer methods, 20-21
  super keyword, 16-17
  syntax of, 13
  this variable, 21-22
 OutputStream class methods, 270
 URL class methods, 301-307
 See also Classes; Objects
Microsoft Access, 311, 312, 318
Microsoft Excel, 312
Microsoft Internet Explorer, installing, 45
Microsoft Visual Basic, 312
Microsoft Visual C++, 312
Minimum installation option, 43
Multidimensional arrays in Java, 25
Multimedia APIs, 399-400, 420

N

Navigating
 InfoViewer window, 51-52
 RDO result sets, 342
 records in DAO record sets, 326-327
Networking in Java. *See* Internet programming
Notifying Observer objects, 364-365
Null setting for LayoutManagers, 97-98
Numeric classes in Java, 373-379

O

Object class in Java, 6-7
Object description language (ODL), 235-245
   ODL classes, 243
   ODL interfaces, 243-245
   ODL libraries, 242
   See also Component Object Model
ObjectInput interface, 403-405
Object methods in Java, 19-20
ObjectOutput interface, 402-403
Objects
   class objects and class loaders in Java, 379-388
      Class class, 347, 380-384
      ClassLoader class, 347, 385-386
      creating custom ClassLoader objects, 386-388
      overview of, 379-380
   COM objects in Java, 228-233
      creating COM objects, 228-229
      enumeration types, 232-233
      properties of, 230-232
      trapping COM exceptions, 229-230
   DBEngine object, 313-316
   DCOM objects, 249-250
   environment objects in RDO API, 336-338
      collection properties, 337, 340
      creating, 338
      environment properties, 337-338
      overview of, 336-337
   Graphics objects, 147-165, 178-179
      attaching to in-memory images, 178-179
      clipping rectangle variable, 152-155
      creating fonts, 160-162
      current color variable, 150-152
      defined, 149
      font size, 155-159
      font styles, 159
      font variable, 155-162
      overview of, 149-150
      paint and XOR painting modes, 162-165
      retrieving display surfaces' Graphics objects, 147-149
      typefaces, 159-160
   in Java
      arrays of objects, 24-25
      calling object methods, 19-20
      creating and destroying, 17-19
      Object class, 6-7
   Java objects in COM, 233-250
      creating Java classes, 245-248
      defining Java interfaces for COM, 235-238
      object description language (ODL) and, 235-245
      ODL classes and, 243
      ODL interfaces and, 243-245
      ODL libraries and, 242
      overview of, 233-234
      registering Java classes as COM objects, 248-249
      registering Java classes as DCOM objects, 249-250
      universally unique identifiers (UUIDs) and, 240-242
   Observer/Observable framework in Java, 361-372
      adding and deleting Observer objects to/from Observable objects, 362-363
      applet example, 365-372
      "dirty" Observable objects, 363-364
      notifying Observer objects, 364-365
      Observable objects overview, 361-362
      Observer interface, 365
   QueryDef objects
      creating executable queries, 333-334
      saving in databases, 332
   TableDef objects, 320-325
      fields of, 321-325
      overview of, 320
   Workspace objects, 315-320
      collection properties and, 319-320
      creating, 316
      DBEngine object and, 315-316
      listing open databases, 319
      opening and creating databases, 316-319
   See also Classes; Methods
Object serialization APIs, 398, 400-410
   adding to Visual J++, 400-409
   in Java, 409-410
   overview of, 398
   See also APIs

Index

Observer/Observable framework in Java, 361-372
   adding and deleting Observer objects to/from Observable objects, 362-363
   applet example, 365-372
   "dirty" Observable objects, 363-364
   notifying Observer objects, 364-365
   Observable objects overview, 361-362
   Observer interface, 365
ODL. *See* Object description language
Online documentation. *See* InfoViewer window
Opening databases, 316-319
Output pane, 46
OutputStream classes, 252-253, 270-272
   defined, 270
   methods, 270
   overview of, 252-253
   types of, 271-272
   See also Streams
Output streams for Java System class, 393
Ovals, drawing, 169
Overloading methods in Java, 26-27
Overriding methods in Java, 28

P

Packages of classes in Java, 35-37
   .CLASS file locations and, 36
   copackage access privileges, 37
   overview of, 35-36
   private to package access privilege, 37
Painting mode variable for Graphics objects, 162-165
Parameters
   applet methods for retrieving parameters from browsers, 206
   applet parameters, 191-192
   DAO record set parameters, 325
   RDO result set parameters, 340-342
Parsing InputStream classes into tokens, 272-280
Performing file-based operations in Java, 210-216
Physical InputStream classes, 253-254
PipedInputStream class, 254, 258-259
PipedOutputStream class, 271

Plus (+) operator in Java, 22
Polygons, drawing, 166-168
Ports, IP addresses and, 287-288
Private access specifier
   for Java methods, 13-14
   for Java variables, 10-12
Private protected access specifier for Java variables, 12
Private to package access privilege in Java, 37
Process class in Java, 389-390, 391-392
Programs
   program code in Java, 37-38
   stepping through Visual J++ programs, 63-66
   See also Applets
Projects, 46, 52-60
   creating, 53-55, 59-60
   defined, 52-53
   Project toolbar, 46
   See also Visual J++
Project window
   ClassView tab, 55-58
   FileView tab, 58-59
   overview of, 53
   See also Visual J++
Properties
   collection properties
      for rdoEnvironment object, 337, 340
      Workspace objects and, 319-320
   of Java COM objects, 230-232
   Properties class, 358-360
   rdoEnvironment object collection properties, 337, 340
   rdoEnvironment object environment properties, 337-338
Protected access specifier
   for Java methods, 13-14
   for Java variables, 12
Protocols
   TCP/IP protocol, 281-283
   URLs (uniform resource locators) and, 298-300
Proxy stubs, 412-414
Public access specifier
   for Java methods, 13-14
   for Java variables, 10-12
PushbackInputStream class, 260, 263

Q

QueryDef objects
   creating executable queries, 333-334
   saving in databases, 332
   See also Data Access Objects (DAO) API
QuickWatch feature, 67-71
   Call Stack window, 71
   overview of, 67-69
   Variables window, 70
   Watch window, 69-70
   See also Visual J++

R

Random class in Java, 373
RDO. *See* Remote Data Objects (RDO) API
Read() InputStream class method, 254-255
Receiving nonguaranteed data, 293-294
Record sets, 325-332
   adding fields to tables, 324-326
   creating from queries, 329-330
   navigating records, 326-327
   parameters, 325
   saving QueryDef objects in databases, 332
   snapshot and dynaset record set types, 331-332
   updating records, 329
   viewing record set values with fields, 328
   See also Data Access Objects (DAO) API
Rectangles, drawing, 166
References in Java, 9, 18-19, 21-22
Registering Java classes
   as COM objects, 248-249
   as DCOM objects, 249-250
Relational database programming. *See* Data Access Objects (DAO) API; JDBC; Remote Data Objects (RDO) API
Remote Data Objects (RDO) API, 310-311, 334-344
   creating RDO Java/COM shim classes, 335-336
   versus Data Access Objects (DAO) API, 335
   database connections, 338-340
      creating, 339-340
      looking up existing connections, 340
      overview of, 338-339
   overview of, 310-311, 334-335, 343-344
   rdoEngine object, 336
   rdoEnvironment objects, 336-338
      collection properties, 337, 340
      creating, 338
      environment properties, 337-338
      overview of, 336-337
   result sets, 340-343
      changing field values, 342-343
      creating from tables, 342
      navigating, 342
      parameters, 340-342
      viewing field values, 342
   See also Data Access Objects (DAO) API
Remote method invocation (RMI), 410-418
   overview of, 410-411, 418
   proxy stubs and skeletons, 412-414
   remote interfaces, 415-418
   remoting objects, 414-415
   retrieving RMI libraries, 411-412
   RMI Registries, 415
   See also APIs
Remote technology APIs, 398-399
Reset() InputStream class method, 255-256
Resource content types for URL class objects, 305-307
Resource toolbar, 47-48
ResourceWizard, 40, 126-134, 141-144
   creating graphical user interfaces, 126-133
   creating Menu classes with, 141-144
   dialog code example, 130-133
   DialogLayout class, 133-134
   overview of, 40
   Visual J++ dialog editor and, 127-128
   See also Graphical user interfaces
Result sets, 340-343
   changing field values, 342-343
   creating from tables, 342
   navigating, 342
   parameters, 340-342
   viewing field values, 342
   See also Remote Data Objects (RDO) API
Retrieving
   display surfaces' Graphics objects, 147-149
   elements from vectors, 353-355
   remote method invocation (RMI) libraries, 411-412
   URL contents manually, 303-305

Index

RMI. *See* Remote method invocation
Runtime class in Java, 346, 347, 389-392
    memory, garbage collection, and finalization control, 392
    overview of, 346, 347, 389-390
    Process class, 389-390, 391-392
    spawning external processes, 390-391
    See also Java language classes
Run-time type identification in Java, 32

S

Saving QueryDef objects in databases, 332
SecurityManager in Java, 210, 394-395
Security restrictions for applets, 208-217
    .CAB files and, 217
    COM restrictions, 217
    digital signatures and, 217
    Java SecurityManager and, 210
    overview of, 209
    and performing file-based operations in Java, 210-216
    socket connection restrictions, 216-217
    viruses and, 208-209
Sending nonguaranteed data, 293-294
SequenceInputStream class, 260, 265-267
Serializable interface, 401-402, 409-410
Server programs in Java, 295-298
ServerSocket class, 294-295
Servlets, 399
Setting LayoutManagers to null, 97-98
Shim classes
    creating DAO Java/COM shim classes, 312-313
    creating Java/COM shim classes, 224-226
    creating RDO Java/COM shim classes, 335-336
Skeletons, 412-414
Skip() InputStream class method, 255
Snapshot DAO record set types, 331-332
Socket connections, 216-217, 288-294
    blocking sockets, 291-292
    communications through, 289
    creating, 288-289
    datagram socket connections, 293-294
    defined, 288
    echo client program example, 289-291

    sending and receiving nonguaranteed data, 293-294
    socket connection restrictions for applets, 216-217
SocketInputStream class, 254, 257-258
SocketOutputStream class, 271
Spawning external processes in Java, 390-391
Stack class, 350-351
Standard toolbar, 46
Start() applet method, 192-195
Starting debugging sessions, 62
Static class data in Java, 9
Static class initializer methods in Java, 20-21
Stepping through Visual J++ programs, 63-66
Stop() applet method, 192-195
Stopping debugging sessions, 62
Storage classes in Java, 348-361
    BitSet class, 360-361
    Enumeration interface, 348-350
    Hashtable class, 346, 356-358
    overview of, 348
    Properties class, 358-360
    Stack class, 350-351
    Vector class, 351-356
    See also Java utility classes
Streams, 251-280
    defined, 251
    FilteredInputStream classes, 260-270
        BufferedInputStream class, 260, 261
        chaining, 267
        custom FilteredInputStream classes, 267-270
        DataInputStream class, 260, 263-265
        LineNumberInputStream class, 260, 261-263
        overview of, 260-261
        PushbackInputStream class, 260, 263
        SequenceInputStream class, 260, 265-267
        transforming versus translating, 268
    input, output, and error streams in Java System class, 393
    InputStream classes, 252-270, 272-280
        available() method, 256
        ByteArrayInputStream class, 253, 257
        close() method, 256
        FileInputStream class, 253, 256-257
        mark() method, 255

methods, 254-259
  overview of, 252-253, 254-256
  parsing into tokens, 272-280
  physical InputStream classes, 253-254
  PipedInputStream class, 254, 258-259
  read() method, 254-255
  reset() method, 255-256
  skip() method, 255
  SocketInputStream class, 254, 257-258
  StreamTokenizer class, 273-277, 347
  StreamTokenizer example, 277-280
  StringBufferInputStream class, 254, 259
OutputStream classes, 252-253, 270-272
  defined, 270
  methods, 270
  overview of, 252-253
  types of, 271-272
overview of, 251-252, 280
StreamTokenizer class, 273-280, 347
StringBufferInputStream class, 254, 259
String class in Java, 22-23
Stubs, 412-414
Super keyword in Java, 16-17
System class in Java, 347, 389-390, 392-394
  accessing environment variables, 393
  arraycopy() method, 393-394
  input, output, and error streams, 393
  overview of, 347, 389-390, 392-393
  See also Java language classes

T

TabbedPanel GUI example, 98-102
TableDef objects, 320-325
  fields of, 321-325
  overview of, 320
  See also Data Access Objects (DAO) API
TCP/IP protocol, 281-283
TextArea class, 116-117, 119
TextField class, 116-119
This variable in Java, 21-22
Three-dimensional graphics APIs, 420
Time-sequencing frames for animations, 173-176
Tip of the Day, 45
Tokens, parsing InputStream classes into, 272-280

Toolbars in Visual J++, 46-49
  Browse toolbar, 48
  creating, 49
  customizing, 49
  Debug toolbar, 48
  docking, 47
  Edit toolbar, 48
  InfoViewer toolbar, 46
  overview of, 46-47
  Project toolbar, 46
  Resource toolbar, 47-48
  Standard toolbar, 46
Transforming versus translating FilteredInputStream classes, 268
Trapping COM exceptions in Java, 229-230
Two-dimensional animation APIs, 419-420
Typefaces for Graphics objects, 159-160
Typelibs in Component Object Model, 223-224, 225, 226
Typical installation option, 42-43

U

Universally unique identifiers (UUIDs), 240-242
Updating records in DAO record sets, 329
URLs (uniform resource locators), 298-307
  content types, 301-303
  overview of, 300-301
  protocols and, 298-300
  resource content types, 305-307
  retrieving URL contents manually, 303-305
  URL class methods, 301-307
  See also Internet programming; World Wide Web
User interfaces. *See* Graphical user interfaces
Utility classes. *See* Java utility classes

V

Variables in Java, 7-12, 30-32, 393
  accessing environment variables for Java System class, 393
  access specifiers, 9-12
  built-in variable types, 8
  casting, 30-32

Index

casting between built-in types, 31-32
instance data and, 9
overview of, 7-9
references and, 9
static class data and, 9
this variable, 21-22
See also Fields
Variables window in Visual J++, 70
Vector class, 351-356
Viewing
   DAO record set values with fields, 328
   RDO result set field values, 342
Viruses, 208-209
Visual J++, 39-71
   adding object serialization APIs to, 400-409
   debugging, 48, 60-67
      breakpoints, 66-67
      Debug toolbar, 48
      overview of, 60-61
      starting debugging sessions, 62
      stepping through programs, 63-66
      stopping debugging sessions, 62
   dialog editor, 127-128
   InfoViewer window, 49-52
      docking, 51
      InfoViewer toolbar, 46
      navigating, 51-52
      overview of, 49-51
   installing, 41-44
      CD-ROM installation option, 43
      Custom installation option, 44
      Minimum installation option, 43
      overview of, 41-42
      Typical installation option, 42-43
   integrated development environment (IDE), 39-41
   projects, 52-60
      creating, 53-55, 59-60
      defined, 52-53
      Project toolbar, 46
   project window
      ClassView tab, 55-58
      FileView tab, 58-59
      overview of, 53
   QuickWatch feature, 67-71
      Call Stack window, 71
      overview of, 67-69
      Variables window, 70
      Watch window, 69-70
   toolbars, 46-49
      Browse toolbar, 48
      creating, 49
      customizing, 49
      Debug toolbar, 48
      docking, 47
      Edit toolbar, 48
      InfoViewer toolbar, 46
      overview of, 46-47
      Project toolbar, 46
      Resource toolbar, 47-48
      Standard toolbar, 46
Visual J++ CD, 41-45
   CD-ROM installation option, 43
   Custom installation option, 44
   Explore the CD option, 45
   Installing Internet Explorer 3.0 option, 45
   Introducing Visual J++ option, 45
   Minimum installation option, 43
   overview of, 41-42
   Typical installation option, 42-43
See also APIs; Data Access Objects (DAO) API; JDBC; Remote Data Objects (RDO) API

W

Watch window in Visual J++, 69-70
Workspace objects, 315-320
   collection properties and, 319-320
   creating, 316
   DBEngine object and, 315-316
   listing open databases, 319
   opening and creating databases, 316-319
   See also Data Access Objects (DAO) API
World Wide Web
   embedding applets in Web pages, 185-190
      applet archive files and, 188-190
      .CAB files and, 189-190, 217
      how applets are loaded by browsers, 186-188
      .JAR files and, 189-190
      overview of, 185-186
   Web browsers
      applet-aware browsers, 184-185

how applets are loaded by, 186-188
methods for browser/applet
 communications, 205-208
See also Internet programming; URLs

X

XOR painting mode for Graphics objects, 162-165